Advances in Web-Based Education:
Personalized Learning Environments

George D. Magoulas
Birkbeck College, University of London, UK

Sherry Y. Chen
Brunel University, UK

 **Information Science Publishing**

Hershey • London • Melbourne • Singapore

Acquisitions Editor:	Michelle Potter
Development Editor:	Kristin Roth
Senior Managing Editor:	Amanda Appicello
Managing Editor:	Jennifer Neidig
Copy Editor:	Jennifer Young
Typesetter:	Jennifer Neidig
Cover Design:	Lisa Tosheff
Printed at:	Yurchak Printing Inc.

Published in the United States of America by
Information Science Publishing (an imprint of Idea Group Inc.)
701 E. Chocolate Avenue
Hershey PA 17033
Tel: 717-533-8845
Fax: 717-533-8661
E-mail: cust@idea-group.com
Web site: http://www.idea-group.com

and in the United Kingdom by
Information Science Publishing (an imprint of Idea Group Inc.)
3 Henrietta Street
Covent Garden
London WC2E 8LU
Tel: 44 20 7240 0856
Fax: 44 20 7379 3313
Web site: http://www.eurospan.co.uk

Library of Congress Cataloging-in-Publication Data

Advances in web-based education : personalized learning environments / George D. Magoulas and Sherry Y. Chen, editors.
    p. cm.
  Summary: "This book provides coverage of a wide range of factors that influence the design, use and adoption of Personalized Learning Environments"--Provided by publisher.
  Includes bibliographical references and index.
  ISBN 1-59140-690-0 (hardcover) -- ISBN 1-59140-691-9 (softcover) -- ISBN 1-59140-692-7 (ebook)
  1. Web-based instruction. 2. Individualized instruction. I. Magoulas, George D. II. Chen, Sherry Y.
  LB1044.87.A38 2006
  371.33'44678--dc22
                            2005020193

British Cataloguing in Publication Data
A Cataloguing in Publication record for this book is available from the British Library.

All work contributed to this book is new, previously-unpublished material. The views expressed in this book are those of the authors, but not necessarily of the publisher.

Advances in Web-Based Education: Personalized Learning Environments

Table of Contents

Section III: Authoring and Exploring Content

Section IV: Approaches to Integration

Foreword

Let me begin by thanking the editor of this fascinating volume for inviting me to contribute a foreword. A risky enterprise for him—I am emphatically not an expert in this field. And risky for me too: what might I bring that is useful?

I will start with the notion of adaptive learning, a theme that permeates many of the papers. What does adaptation mean, exactly? Who or what is adapting ... and to whom? In scanning the contributions, it seems an unproblematic question: the computer is adapting to the learner, assessing what he or she requires, when to provide it, and adapting—changing, altering, adjusting—in order to accommodate to those needs.

I use the word "accommodate" deliberately. It was Piaget who pointed out that human learning can be thought of as adaptation, an ongoing process of organising experience. As is well known, the two major forms of adaptation are assimilation, in which new experiences are incorporated into existing cognitive structures, and accommodation, in which the elements of knowledge are restructured and reorganised to make sense of what is perceived and reflected upon. I guess that from the machine's point of view, both are involved, although I have the sense that—just like for humans—it is easier to assimilate information than to accommodate it.

I raise the Piagetian view of adaptation, because it is the clearest expression we have of the ways that learning actually occurs—at least on the individual level. The most important component of Piaget's theory is that learning involves equilibration, in which the learner strikes a balance between herself and her environment, between assimilation and accommodation. And it is this balance, a state of interaction between learner and environment in a constant state of flux to achieve dynamic equilibrium, that I think may be a useful metaphor for making sense of adaptation at the system level. The key point is that it may not always be helpful to think only of the organism adapting to the environment. On the contrary, it is important to try to understand how the environment is shaped by the learner's attempt to organise her experience of it.

This complexity of mutual interaction between learner and knowledge is one of the things that makes educational research so challenging. Educational researchers have learned the hard way that assessing the learning of "knowledge" in computational environments is difficult precisely because what is to be learned is itself changed by being computationally based. A graph on a computer screen is not the same graph that one draws on paper; it is not simply a way (or two ways) of "representing" knowledge, it is two different kinds of knowledge that point to two ways of viewing, say, a function and two sets of connections to (possibly) very different concepts. Given the infinite malleability of the computer—what Papert calls its "Protean" quality—this problem is very great indeed, and evaluating the efficacy of adaptation calls for novel and as yet untested methodological approaches.

This complexity is only compounded by the widespread acknowledgment that learning of all but the most elementary kinds of knowledge is best considered as a social, as well as a psychological phenomenon. What a person knows, how she comes to know it, and why are crucial aspects of the learning process, and certainly not adequately thought of—as was sometimes the case in the recent past—as a "social" context grafted on to an essentially individual development. Relatedly, and perhaps most importantly, it is activities and activity structures that are the most crucial element of formal learning, whether those activities are mediated by a teacher, by a computer, or by a computer-teacher. In this respect, finding the right grain size and focus of activities to address the required learning is at least as important as finding the right ways to adapt to what the learner knows (or does).

Before I leave the question of adaptation, I would like to point to one important, and relatively newly-established, strand of educational research that might be helpful. We know, I think, enough to state unequivocally that only certain types of learning (such as the acquisition of simple facts or the practice of routine procedures) can ever attempt to cast the computer invisibly, a tool whose functioning is transparent to the learner. On the contrary, uses of computational systems that involve construction—building models of systems, for example—necessitate a process of what French researchers have called "instrumentation": for any given individual, the computational artefact only becomes an "instrument"—a useful and expressive tool—through a process of transformation in two different directions. First, by endowing the tool with potential and actual uses; and second, by the tool "transforming" the individual, so that she can respond with the tool to tasks in hand. This is an unexpected complexity, in which tool and individual are reciprocally shaped, and it explains why the design of activities is so critical.

I cannot end without a word about "personalisation". It is, as every UK reader will know, the political theme of the moment. Quite what the politicians mean by personalisation is far from clear: sometimes "personalisation" and "choice" appear as synonyms as if rather difficult challenges (such as how choices are allocated) do not exist. Similarly, the Department for Education and Skills Web site informs us that personalised learning "has the potential to make every young person's learning experience stretching, creative, fun, and successful". It would, of course, be fine if that potential was realised, although it is far from clear what role, if any, is actually envisaged for digital technologies in this scheme. Nevertheless, whatever personalisation comes to mean, and whatever roles the computer is asked to play in the process, I simply want to strike a realistic note in favour of educational (not simply technical) research. As I hope I have made clear, there are real methodological challenges that have to be faced, and they are multi-disciplinary ones that will necessitate crossing boundaries between computer science and social science, as well as between sub-fields within this broad classification.

This is a timely book that will communicate a range of important ideas on the personalisation of Web-based learning environments to a wide international audience. It provides an introduction to some basic ideas for those who are curious about the field, as well as covering more advanced theoretical, method-ological, and practical issues. Congratulations to the contributors and editors of this volume for carrying this project forward.

Richard Noss
London Knowledge Lab
Institute of Education, University of London
14.10.04

Preface

Abstract

Web-based education has influenced educational practice, fostered initiatives to widen participation, increased learner autonomy, and facilitated informal and workplace learning. In this context, learning takes place progressively by making students actively participate in instructional decisions and supporting them individually to assess their personal learning goals. This book presents recent advances in Web-based education from various countries around the world that aim to accommodate the needs of individual learners. It includes 14 chapters that cover a variety of ways to integrate personalisation technologies in Web-based education and demonstrate their use and value in designing content, navigation, and interface adaptation to create the next generation of Web-based learning environments.

Introduction

The Web has changed the way we approach learning, the teaching practices we adopt, and how the curriculum is evolving. Web-based education has grown tremendously over the past few years, creating a variety of media-enhanced approaches to formal and informal learning, including innovative uses of ambient and mobile technologies. In this vein, a number of Web features have been exploited:

- **Communication mechanisms**, such as e-mail, newsgroups, Web conferencing, and chat rooms have been used to assist one-to-one instruction, facilitate exchange of ideas between learners and teachers, provide instructional feedback, and communicate with experts. They have been used extensively for enhancing learners' cognitive skills and increasing the amount of time available to each learner compared to traditional class hours.

- **Hypermedia** allowed an increased degree of interactivity compared to standard computer-based instruction by combining hypertext with multimedia. They have been used to accommodate learners' individual differences by allowing them to explore alternative navigation paths through educational content and linked resources according to their needs. They have been used to support a variety of educational uses, for example, information seeking, content presentation, exploration activities, and collaboration.

- **Accessibility** of structured and unstructured information resources, such as library catalogues, distributed databases, academic repositories, search engine results, course materials, and learning resources has widely facilitated information exchange and dissemination of educational activities and course materials to meet various educational objectives.

Nowadays, the majority of Web-based educational systems rely on learning environments and training programmes that support or supplement teaching and learning such as Oracle's Think.com, Learn Direct (www.learndirect.co.uk), Blackboard (www.blackboard.com), Xtensis (www.xtensis.co.uk), Knowledge Pool (www.knowledgepool.com), Mindleaders (mindleaders.com), COSE (www.staffs.ac.uk/COSE/), Colloquia (www.colloquia.net), Lotus Learning Space (www-136.ibm.com/developerworks/lotus/products/elearning/), RDN's Virtual Training Suite (www.vts.rdn.ac.uk), and WebCT (www.webct.com).

These systems have influenced practical Web-based education, and when used within a constructivist framework of learning, they can actively engage the learner in the interpretation of the content and the reflection on their interpretations. Nevertheless, the complexity of the learning experience poses a number of theoretical, methodological, and practical challenges with regards to accommodating learner's individual needs and maximising the effectiveness of Web-based education.

This book presents recent approaches to Web-based education that use personalisation technologies to adapt a learning environment in ways that accommodate learners' needs. The next section provides an introduction to the fundamentals of personalized learning environments and gives an overview of the book chapters.

Personalized Learning Environments

The ultimate goal of a constructivist approach is to allow learners to construct, transform, and extend their knowledge. Thus, learners take the responsibility of their learning by interacting with educational material that covers different knowledge levels and various learning objectives. However, learners have heterogeneous backgrounds and differ in traits such as skills, aptitudes, and preferences for processing information, constructing meaning from information, and applying it to real-world situations.

Personalisation technologies are defined as approaches to adapt educational content, presentation, navigation support, and educational services so that they match the unique and specific needs, characteristics, and preferences of each learner or a community of learners. Personalisation helps build a meaningful one-to-one relationship between the learner/teacher and the learning environment by understanding the needs of each individual and helps to reach a goal that efficiently and knowledgeably addresses each individual's need in a given context (Riecken, 2000).

Personalisation is usually applied by three different means: content level adaptation, presentation level adaptation, and navigation level adaptation. For example, content level adaptation in an educational system may be implemented by dynamically generating a lesson or assembling it from various pieces of educational material depending on the knowledge level of the learner. Thus, advanced learners may receive more detailed and in-depth information, while novices will be provided with additional explanations. Presentation level adaptation is typically implemented through a variety of techniques, such as adaptive text and adaptive layout. Adaptive text implies that the same Web page is assembled from different texts accommodating the learner's current need, such as removing some information from a piece of text or inserting extra information. Adaptive layout aims to differentiate levels of the subject content by changing the layout of the page, instead of the text, such as font type and size and background colour. Lastly, navigation level adaptation includes various techniques, such as direct guidance, adaptive ordering, link hiding, and link annotation.

Personalisation in a Web-based learning environment builds on a reasoning process or adaptation rational that is responsible for synthesising adaptive techniques and making decisions about the kind of adaptation needed to accommodate the needs of the current user in the given context. Obviously, this process of generating a hypermedia space that is dynamically adapted to the current needs of different learners requires understanding the individual. Understanding the learner in a typical classroom setting is achieved by observing what learners would say and do, their errors, and responses to tutors' queries. In personalized learning environments, learner modeling is the fundamental mechanism to personalise the interaction between the system and the learner. Learner model generation involves interpreting the information gathered during interaction in order to generate hypotheses about learner goals, plans, preferences, attitudes, knowledge, or beliefs. The generated learner models are stored in a database and used to identify current user needs, decide on the types of adaptation to be performed, and communicate them to a personalized interface.

First attempts in personalized, also called adaptive, learning environments appeared in the early 1990s. 1996 is considered as a turning point in the area of adaptive systems (Brusiolvsky, 2001). The timeline of Figure 1 gives a bird's eye view of the evolution of Web-based personalized learning environments. Although most of these educational systems released interim versions between major releases—one example is given here for the MetaLinks system (Murray, 2001; Murray, Condit, & Haugsjaa, 1998)—the timeline of Figure 1 includes only those releases that were considered to challenge further research in the area.

The Chapters of This Book

In order to develop an all-around understanding of the challenges in integrating personalisation technologies into Web-based education, this book is organized into four sections: (i) Modeling the Learner; (ii) Designing Instruction; (iii) Authoring and Exploring content, and (iv) Approaches to Integration.

Modeling the Learner

Recent approaches to Web-based education try to take into account various dimensions of individual differences, such as level of knowledge, gender, culture, cognitive styles, learning styles, and accessibility issues for the disabled and elderly, to create learner models. In Chapter I, Fan and Macredie examine published findings from experimental studies of interaction between gender differences and hypermedia learning and propose models to adapt the presentation of the content and the navigation on the basis of gender considerations, while in Chapter II, Souto, Verdin, and Palazzo M. de Oliveira describe a methodology to model the learner's cognitive ability level based on the observation and analysis of their behaviour in a Web-learning environment. The understanding obtained from this investigation will make possible to automate the diagnosis of learners' cognitive abilities and provide personalisation.

Razek, Frasson, and Kaltenbach in Chapter III model learners' context of interest and domain knowledge to establish the "dominant meaning" of a query and personalise the query and search results to the concepts being taught. Their

Figure 1. Evolution of Web-based personalized learning environments

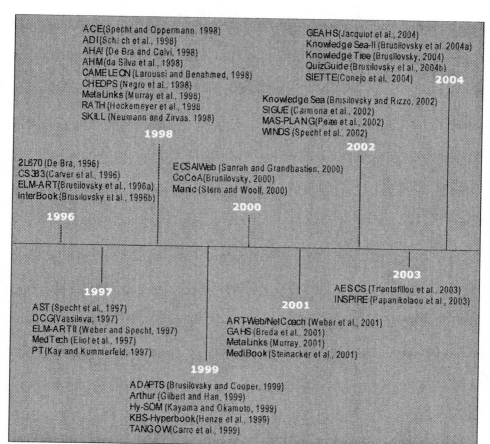

approach is incorporated into a cooperative intelligent distance learning environment for a community of learners to improve online discussions. Their experiments show that the dominant meanings approach greatly improves retrieval effectiveness in Web-based education.

In Chapter IV, Castillo, Gama, and Breda focus on the problem of tracking the changing learner needs and propose an adaptive predictive model that is used to determine what kind of learning resources are more appropriate to a particular learning style. Their approach is able to manage the uncertainty involved in detecting changes in the learner's behaviour and deviations from initial learning style preferences. The reported experiments show that the proposed probabilistic model is able to adapt quickly to changes in the learner's preferences and that it has potential to work in similar modeling tasks.

In Chapter V, the last chapter of this section, Czarkowski and Kay describe Tutor 3, the latest in a sequence of systems that they have created to provide adaptation of hypertext where the learner can maintain a real sense of control over their model and the personalized features of the environment. In their system, learners always have access to precise details of what has been adapted, how this adaptation is controlled and they are allowed to alter it. The chapter also includes a qualitative evaluation of Tutor 3, providing evidence that learners are able to understand both the adaptation and their power to control it.

Designing Instruction

The second section of the book covers instructional approaches to support adaptation in personalized learning environments. In Chapter VI, Papanikolaou and Grigoriadou present an approach to support learners in the accomplishment of their goals by enabling them to manipulate instructional approaches according to their own requirements and needs. The authors' instructional framework supports different instructional approaches, allowing learners to undertake control of the adaptation, and provides the basis for unifying several processes that formulate personalisation.

In Chapter VII, Armani and Botturi present MAID, a complete design method for adaptive courseware tailored to non-technical people. The MAID approach provides guidelines and tools that foster and enhance the communication between the technical staff in charge of managing the educational system and the tutors by adopting their instructional strategy as the pivotal point for the communication.

The next chapter by Gouli, Gogoulou, Papanikolaou, and Grigoriadou considers the assessment of student learning as an integral and essential part of the instruction and proposes personalized feedback to accommodate learners' individual characteristics and needs. Their approach attempts to model and analyse learner behaviour to evaluate their performance and support the development of metacognitive abilities through adaptive feedback. It is incorporated in a Web-based concept mapping tool which adapts the feedback in order to stimulate learners' reflection, as well as guide and tutor them towards the achievement of specific learning outcomes.

In the last chapter of this section, Gauss and Urbas explore the didactic value of adopting SCORM, a recently proposed technological standard for sharable content objects. They focus on pedagogical issues and the potential of adapting the navigation within this standard. Chapter IX also provides an empirical evaluation of a prototype learning environment and suggestions for future research in this promising area.

Authoring and Exploring Content

Issues of authoring, reusability, and interoperability are considered of vital importance in Web-based education. The third section of the book focuses on approaches to content development and exploration, as well as design of the adaptation.

In Chapter X, Cristea presents the various aspects of authoring and introduces a new flexible framework model named LAOS. To illustrate the applicability of this approach, the chapter describes an implementation of this framework in a Web-authoring environment, My Online Teacher, and reports on tests conducted in a classroom setting. The chapter discusses interfaces with existing standards and future trends. An alternative approach is proposed by Hoic-Bozic and Mornar in Chapter XI. Their system AHyCo enables teachers from areas other than IT to produce and interconnect complex hypermedia content by utilizing intuitive form-based user interfaces. They illustrate the use of AHyCo in a number of cases and present a small scale evaluation study. Lastly, in Chapter XII, Broberg follows a different approach to exploring and reading content by utilising the tool TEXT–COL. The author adopts a phenomenological approach to learning and investigates its applicability in the context of a system that supports readers to perform deep processing of texts, letting them change the appearance of text based on different strategies for categorizing words.

Approaches to Integration

Integration of adaptation techniques in existing educational systems as well as in new learning paradigms is considered the next challenging step in the evolution of personalized learning environments. Towards this direction, the last section of the book presents two chapters that approach this issue from different perspectives.

Jacobson in Chapter XIII argues that we should focus on principled design features for implementing adaptation in learning environments and on evaluations of the learning efficacy of particular design approaches. As an example of design and research in these two areas, the chapter discusses as a case study a program of educational hypermedia research related to the Knowledge Mediator Framework (KMF). First, a discussion of non-adaptive KMF hypermedia design elements and learning tasks is provided. Next, current efforts are discussed to create a KMF that supports personalisation using a Learning Agent module that employs semantic assessment and learner modeling in order to provide adaptive content and adaptive learner scaffolding.

Finally, in Chapter XIV, Specht integrates adaptation techniques, ubiquitous computing, and current research on mobile learning systems that enable support for contextualized learning. Several examples for new learning paradigms are analysed with respect to their potential for personalisation, mobile learning, and contextualization. The chapter also presents two examples of systems that integrate mobile learning solutions in existing educational systems for formal and workplace learning. The RAFT project is an application of computer based field trip support that demonstrates the integration of mobile learning tools in an established teaching method of school field trips, while the SMILES prototype shows how mobile learning technology can be integrated into existing e-learning services.

Concluding Remarks

Personalized learning environments adapt educational content, navigation support, assessment, and feedback in various ways to accommodate learners' needs. This book attempts to provide a comprehensive view of the state of the art in personalisation technologies for Web-based educational systems, describing systems and research projects from Europe, North and South America, and Australia. It covers several issues in generating adaptation, learner modeling, design considerations, and authoring tools, and presents several approaches to integrate personalisation technologies into practical educational systems. We are very grateful to the authors of the 14 chapters for contributing their excellent works and to the reviewers for providing constructive comments and helpful suggestions.

References

Breda, A. M., Castillo, G., & Bajuelos, A. L. (2001, September 13-15). A Web-based courseware in Plane Geometry. In J. C. Teixeira, F. M. Dionísio & B. Wegner (Eds.), *Proceedings of the International Workshop on Electronic Media in Mathematics*, Coimbra, Portugal. Retrieved from www.mat.ua.pt/gladys/Papers/EMM2001.pdf

Brusilovsky, P. (2000, June 19-23). Course sequencing for static courses? Applying ITS techniques in large scale Web-based education. In G. Gauthier, C. Frasson & K. VanLehn (Eds.), *Proceedings of 5th International Conference on Intelligent Tutoring Systems (ITS 2000)*, Intelligent tutoring systems, Lecture Notes in Computer Science, Vol. 1839, Montréal, Canada (pp. 625-634). Berlin: Springer Verlag.

Brusilovsky, P. (2001). Adaptive hypermedia. *User Modelling and User-adapted Interaction, 11*, 87-110.

Brusilovsky, P. (2004, May 17-22). KnowledgeTree: A distributed architecture for adaptive e-learning. *Proceedings of the 13ᵗʰ International World Wide Web Conference (WWW 2004)*, Alternate track papers and posters, New York (pp. 104-113). ACM Press.

Brusilovsky, P., & Cooper, D. W. (1999, May 11, Jun3 23-24). ADAPTS: Adaptive hypermedia for a Web-based performance support system. In P. Brusilovsky & P. De Bra (Eds.), *Proceedings of 2ⁿᵈ Workshop on Adaptive Systems and User Modeling on WWW, 8ᵗʰ International Word Wide Web Conference and 7ᵗʰ International Conference on User Modelling*, Toronto and Banff, Canada (pp. 41-47). Also Computer Science Report, No. 99-07, Eindhoven University of Technology, Eindhoven. Retrieved from http://wwwis.win.tue.nl/asum99/brusilovsky/brusilovsky.html

Brusilovsky, P., & Rizzo, R. (2002). Using maps and landmarks for navigation between closed and open corpus hyperspace in Web-based education. *The New Review of Hypermedia and Multimedia, 9*, 59-82.

Brusilovsky, P., Chavan, G., & Farzan, R. (2004a, August 23-26). Social adaptive navigation support for open corpus electronic textbooks. In P. De Bra, & W. Nejdl (Eds.), *Proceedings of 3ʳᵈ International Conference on Adaptive Hypermedia and Adaptive Web-Based Systems (AH2004)*, Lecture Notes in Computer Science, vol. 3137, Eindhoven, The Netherlands (pp. 24-33). Springer.

Brusilovsky, P., Schwarz, E., & Weber, G. (1996a, June 12-13). ELM-ART: An intelligent tutoring system on World Wide Web. In C. Frasson, G. Gauthier, & A. Lesgold (Eds.), *Proceedings of 3ʳᵈ International Conference on Intelligent Tutoring Systems (ITS-96)*, Intelligent Tutoring Systems, Lecture Notes in Computer Science, Vol. 1086, Montreal (pp. 261-269). Berlin: Springer Verlag. Retrieved from www.contrib.andrew.cmu.edu/~plb/ITS96.html

Brusilovsky, P., Schwarz, E., & Weber, G. (1996b, October 15-19). A tool for developing adaptive electronic textbooks on WWW. In H. Maurer (Ed.), *Proceedings of World Conference of the Web Society (WebNet'96)*, San Francisco (pp. 64-69). AACE. Retrieved from http://www.contrib.andrew.cmu.edu/~plb/WebNet96.html

Brusilovsky, P., Sosnovsky, S., & Shcherbinina, O. (2004b, November). QuizGuide: Increasing the educational value of individualized self-assessment quizzes with adaptive navigation support. *Proceedings of World Conference on E-Learning (E-Learn 2004)*, Washington, DC (pp. 1806-1813). AACE.

Carmona, C., Bueno, D., Guzman, E., & Conejo, R. (2002, May 29-31). SIGUE: Making Web courses adaptive. *Proceedings of 2ⁿᵈ International Conference on Adaptive Hypermedia and Adaptive Web-Based Systems (AH2002)*, Málaga, Spain (pp. 376-379).

Carro, R. M., Pulido, E., & Rodrígues, P. (1999, May 11, June 23-24). TANGOW: Task-based adaptive learner guidance on the WWW. In P. Brusilovsky & P. D. Bra (Eds.), *Proceedings of 2ⁿᵈ Workshop on Adaptive Systems and User Modeling on the World Wide Web*, Toronto and Banff, Canada (pp. 49-57). Also Computer Science Report, No. 99-07, Eindhoven University of Technology, Eindhoven.

Carver, C. A., Howard, R. A., & Lavelle, E. (1996). Enhancing learner learning by incorporating learner learning styles into adaptive hypermedia. *Proceedings of World Conference on Educational Multimedia and Hypermedia (ED-MEDIA96)*, Boston (pp. 118-123).

Conejo, R., Guzman, E., & Millán, E. (2004). SIETTE: A Web-based tool for adaptive teaching. *International Journal of Artificial Intelligence in Education, 14*(1), 29-61.

da Silva Pilar, D., Durm, R. V., Duval, E., & Olivié, H. (1998, June 20). Concepts and documents for adaptive educational hypermedia: A model and a prototype. In P. Brusilovsky & P. De Bra (Eds.), *Proceedings of 2ⁿᵈ Adaptive Hypertext and Hypermedia Workshop, 9ᵗʰ ACM International Hypertext Conference (Hypertext98)*, Pittsburgh, PA (pp. 35-43). Also Computing Science Reports, No. 98/12, Eindhoven University of Technology, Eindhoven.

De Bra, P. M. E. (1996). Teaching hypertext and hypermedia through the Web. *Journal of Universal Computer Science, 2*(12), 797-804. Retrieved from www.iicm.edu/jucs_2_12/teaching_hypertext_and_hypermedia

De Bra, P., & Calvi, L. (1998). AHA! An open Adaptive Hypermedia Architecture. *The New Review of Hypermedia and Multimedia, Special Issue on Adaptivity and User Modelling in Hypermedia Systems, 4*, 115-139.

Eliot, C., Neiman, D., & Lamar, M. (1997, November 1-5) Medtec: A Web-based intelligent tutor for basic anatomy. In S. Lobodzinski & I. Tomek (Eds.), *Proceedings of World Conference of the WWW, Internet and Intranet (WebNet97)*, Toronto, Canada (pp. 161-165). AACE.

Henze, N., Naceur, K., Nejdl, W. & Wolpers, M. (1999). Adaptive Hyperbooks for constructivist teaching. *Kunstliche Intelligenz*, 26-31.

Hockemeyer, C., Held, T., & Albert, D. (1998, June 15-17). RATH - A relational adaptive tutoring hypertext WWW-environment based on knowledge space theory. In C. Alvegård (Ed.), *Proceedings of 4th International conference on Computer Aided Learning and Instruction in*

Science and Engineering (CALISCE98), Göteborg, Sweden (pp. 417-423).

Jacquiot, C., Bourda, Y., & Popineau, F. (2004, June 21-26). GEAHS: A generic educational adaptive hypermedia system. In L. Cantoni & C. McLoughlin (Eds.), *Proceedings of World Conference on Educational Multimedia, Hypermedia and Telecommunications (ED-MEDIA2004)*, Lugano, Switzerland (pp. 571-578). AACE.

Kay, J., & Kummerfeld, B. (1997). User models for customized hypertext. Intelligent hypertext: Advanced techniques for the World Wide Web. In C. Nicholas & J. Mayfield (Eds.), *Lecture Notes in Computer Science, Vol. 1326*. Berlin: Springer-Verlag.

Kayama, M., & Okamoto, T. (1999, November 4-7). Hy-SOM: The semantic map framework applied on an example case of navigation. In G. Cumming, T. Okamoto, & L. Gomez (Eds.), *Proceedings of 7th International Conference on Computers in Education (ICCE99)*, Vol. 2, Chiba, Japan (pp. 252-259). Advanced Research in Computers and Communications in Education: Frontiers of Artificial Intelligence and Applications. IOS Press.

Laroussi, M., & Benahmed, M. (1998, June 15-17). Providing an adaptive learning through the Web case of CAMELEON: Computer Aided MEdium for LEarning on Networks. In C. Alvegård (Ed.), *Proceedings of 4th International conference on Computer Aided Learning and Instruction in Science and Engineering (CALISCE98)*, Göteborg, Sweden (pp. 411-416).

Murray, T. (2001, October 23-27). Characteristics and affordances of adaptive hyperbooks. In W. Fowler & J. Hasebrook (Eds.), *Proceedings of World Conference of the WWW and Internet (WebNet2001)*, Orlando, FL (pp. 899-904). AACE.

Murray, T., Condit, C., & Haugsjaa, E. (1998, August 16-19). MetaLinks: A preliminary framework for concept-based adaptive hypermedia. *Proceedings of Workshop WWW-Based Tutoring, 4th International Conference on Intelligent Tutoring Systems (ITS'98)*, San Antonio, TX. Retrieved from www-aml.cs.umass.edu/~stern/webits/itsworkshop/murray.html

Negro, A., Scarano, V., & Simari, R. (1998, June 20). User adaptivity on WWW through CHEOPS. In P. Brusilovsky & P. De Bra (Eds.), *Proceedings of 2nd Adaptive Hypertext and Hypermedia Workshop, 9th ACM International Hypertext Conference (Hypertext98)*, Pittsburgh, PA (pp. 57-62). Also Computing Science Reports, No. 98/12, Eindhoven University of Technology, Eindhoven.

Neumann, G., & Zirvas, J. (1998, November 7-12). SKILL – A scallable Internet-based teaching and learning system. In H. Maurer & R. G. Olson (Eds.), *Proceedings of World Conference of the WWW, Internet, and Intranet*

(WebNet98), Orlando, FL (pp. 688-693). AACE. Retrieved from http:// nestroy.wi-inf.uni-essen.de/Forschung/Publikationen/skill-webnet98.ps

Papanikolaou, K., Grigoriadou, M., Kornilakis, H., & Magoulas, G. D. (2003). Personalising the interaction in a Web-based educational hypermedia system: The case of INSPIRE. *User-Modeling and User-Adapted Interaction, 13*(3), 213-267.

Peña, C. I., Marzo, J. L., & de la Rosa, J. L. (2002, September 9-12). Intelligent sgents in a teaching and learning environment on the Web. In P. Kommers, V. Petrushin, Kinshuk, & I. Galeev (Eds.), *Proceedings of the 2nd International Conference on Advanced Learning Technologies (ICALT2002),* Kazan, Russia. IEEE Press.

Riecken D. (2000). Personalized views of personalization. *Communications of the ACM, 43*(8), 27-28.

Sanrach, C., & Grandbastien, M. (2000, August 28-30). ECSAIWeb: A Web-based authoring system to create adaptive learning systems. In P. Brusilovsky, O. Stock, & C. Strapparava (Eds.), *Proceedings of Adaptive Hypermedia and Adaptive Web-based Systems (AH2000),* Trento, Italy (pp. 214-226). Lecture Notes in Computer Science. Springer-Verlag.

Specht, M., & Oppermann, R. (1998). ACE- Adaptive courseware environment. *The New Review of Hypermedia and Multimedia, Special Issue on Adaptivity and User Modeling in Hypermedia Systems, 4,* 141-161.

Specht, M., Kravcik, M., Klemke, R., Pesin, L., & Hüttenhain, R. (2002, May 29-31). Adaptive learning environment (ALE) for teaching and learning in WINDS. *Proceedings of 2nd International Conference on Adaptive Hypermedia and Adaptive Web-Based Systems (AH'2002),* Málaga, Spain (pp. 572-581) . Lecture Notes in Computer Science, Vol. 2347. Springer-Verlag.

Specht, M., Weber, G., Heitmeyer, S., & Schöch, V. (1997, June 2). AST: Adaptive WWW-courseware for statistics. In P. Brusilovsky, J. Fink & J. Kay (Eds.), *Proceedings of Workshop Adaptive Systems and User Modeling on the World Wide Web, 6th International Conference on User Modeling, UM97,* Chia Laguna, Sardinia, Italy (pp. 91-95). Retrieved from www.contrib.andrew.cmu.edu/~plb/UM97_workshop/Specht.html

Steinacker, A., Faatz, A., Seeberg, C., Rimac, I., Hörmann, S., Saddik, A. E., & Steinmetz, R. (2001, June 25-30). MediBook: Combining semantic networks with metadata for learning resources to build a Web based learning system. *Proceedings of World Conference on Educational Multimedia, Hypermedia and Telecommunications (ED-MEDIA2001),* Tampere, Finland (pp. 1790-1795). AACE.

Stern, M. K., & Woolf, B. P. (2000, August 28-30). Adaptive content in an online lecture system. In P. Brusilovsky, O. Stock, & C. Strapparava (Eds.),

Proceedings of Adaptive Hypermedia and Adaptive Web-based Systems, Trento, Italy (pp. 225-238). Adaptive Hypermedia and Adaptive Web-based systems, Lecture Notes in Computer Science. Springer-Verlag.

Triantafillou, E., Pomportsis, A., & Demetriadis, S. (2003). The design and formative evaluation of an adaptive educational system based on cognitive styles. *Computers & Education, 41*(1), 87-103.

Vassileva, J. (1997). Dynamic course generation on the WWW. In B. D. Boulay & R. Mizoguchi (Eds.), *Artificial intelligence in education: Knowledge and media in learning systems* (pp. 498-505). Amsterdam: IOS Press.

Weber, G., & Specht, M. (1997, June 2-5). User modeling and adaptive navigation support in WWW-based tutoring systems. In A. Jameson, C. Paris, & C. Tasso (Eds.), *Proceedings of 6th International Conference on User Modeling*, Chia Laguna, Sardinia, Italy (pp. 289-300). Springer. Retrieved from www.psychologie.uni-trier.de:8000/projects/ELM/Papers/UM97-WEBER.html

Weber, G., Kuhl, H. C., & Weibelzahl, S. (2001, July 14). Developing adaptive Internet-based courses with the authoring system NetCoach. In P. D. Bra, P. Brusilovsky, & A. Kobsa (Eds.), *Proceedings of 3rd Workshop on Adaptive Hypertext and Hypermedia*, Sonthofen, Germany (pp. 35-48). Technical University Eindhoven. Retrieved from http://wwwis.win.tue.nl/ah2001/papers/GWeber-UM01.pdf

Section I

Modeling the Learner

Chapter I

Gender Differences and Hypermedia Navigation:
Principles for Adaptive Hypermedia Learning Systems

Jing Ping Fan, Brunel University, UK

Robert D. Macredie, Brunel University, UK

Abstract

Adaptive hypermedia learning systems can be developed to adapt to a diversity of individual differences. Many studies have been conducted to design systems to adapt to learners' individual characteristics, such as learning style and cognitive style to facilitate student learning. However, no research has been done specifically regarding the adaptation of hypermedia learning system to gender differences. This chapter therefore attempts to fill this gap by examining the published findings from experimental studies of interaction between gender differences and hypermedia learning. Analysis of findings of the empirical studies leads to a set of principles being proposed to guide adaptive hypermedia learning system design on the basis of gender differences in relation to (i) adaptive presentation and (ii) adaptive navigation support.

Introduction

Hypermedia systems have increasingly attracted the attention of educators and designers because of the adaptability that they afford individual learners (Large, 1996; Magoulas, Papanikolaou, & Grigoriadou, 2003). The potential of hypermedia learning systems rests in their ability not only to allow the retrieval and display of different media such as text, graphics, videos, and audio, but also to present information in a non-linear format and to accommodate learners with different characteristics (Jonassen & Grabinger, 1993; Nielsen, 1995). Such systems allow learners great navigation freedom and non-linear interaction with information. Learners are able to access and sequence information in accordance with their information needs (Lawless & Brown, 1997), which may enhance learning and "promote cognitive flexibility" (Triantafillou, Pomportsis, & Demetriadis, 2003, p. 89).

However, the great flexibility that hypermedia provides to learners also presents problems with regard to cognitive overload and disorientation (Conklin, 1987; Marchionini, 1988). Empirical evidence reveals that learners with individual differences benefit differently from hypermedia systems (Calisir & Gurel, 2003; Ford & Chen, 2000; Kim, 2001; Large, Beheshti, & Rahman, 2002; Last et al., 2002). One possible solution to cope with the problems is using adaptive hypermedia (Brusilovsky, 1996; Brusilovsky et al., 1998). Adaptive hypermedia systems possess the ability to adapt information to the specific needs of each individual learner by building a model of the user's goals, knowledge, and preferences (Brusilovsky, 2001). It is therefore the ideal way to accommodate the diversity of individual differences in hypermedia learning. Many studies have been conducted to develop systems that attempt to adapt to individual differences, including learning style (Carver et al., 1996; Gilber & Han, 1999; Specht & Oppermann, 1998) and cognitive style (Triantafillou et al., 2003; Magoulas et al., 2003). However, no research has been done regarding the adaptation of hypermedia learning systems to gender differences.

Gender differences have long been recognized as an important factor in student learning. Recent research reveals that gender differences also have a significant effect on student learning in hypermedia systems, with males and females demonstrating different navigation patterns and preferences toward hypermedia systems thus requiring different user interfaces and navigation support (Campbell, 2000; Large et al., 2002; Roy & Chi, 2003). This indicates that as the use of hypermedia learning systems has increased, so has the need to develop effective hypermedia systems that are adaptable to learners with gender differences.

In order to make hypermedia systems more efficient in catering for both genders, principles drawn from empirical evidence are urgently needed to guide the effective design of adaptive hypermedia learning systems. This chapter focuses on two core themes. Firstly, the chapter looks at how gender differences influence student learning in hypermedia systems by examining and analyzing gender differences using evidence from relevant experimental studies. Specifically, the analysis groups the research into four categories considered as important issues in the literature: attitude and perception; information seeking strategies; media choice; and learning performance. Secondly, building on the findings of the empirical studies, a set of principles is proposed to guide the design of adaptive hypermedia learning systems, addressing issues related to adaptive presentation and adaptive navigation support, and taking into account gender differences.

This chapter starts by examining and analyzing previous research on gender differences and hypermedia learning. Then it discusses the implications of gender differences for the design of adaptive hypermedia systems and presents principles and guidelines for designing adaptive hypermedia learning systems that accommodate individual differences through system adaptation on the basis of gender differences. Finally, conclusions are presented and future research areas are briefly discussed.

Research on Gender Differences and Hypermedia Learning

As hypermedia systems have become more widespread in educational settings, a growing body of research has been conducted to examine gender differences in hypermedia learning. Research suggests that gender differences have significant effects on students learning with regard to their information seeking strategy, navigation pattern, and preference toward the presentation of different media. However, no research has specifically looked at adaptation of hypermedia learning systems with respect to gender. This section will present a comprehensive review of previous research on the influence of gender differences in hypermedia learning generally, and seek to inform the discussion of adaptation in the next section. Specifically, the review will focus on four themes: (i) attitude and perception; (ii) information seeking strategy; (iii) media choice; and (iv) learning performance. These issues are considered paramount in system design (Ford et al., 2001; Liu, 2004; Riding & Grimley, 1999).

Attitude and Perception

Gender differences in attitude toward computers have long been considered as an important factor because they play a role in student success in computer-related tasks (Lim, 2002; Liu, 2004; Loyd & Gressard, 1984). Positive attitudes are associated with higher attainment while negative attitudes impose limitations on the extent to which computers can be used to enhance learning. There has been a great deal of research on the relationship between gender and attitude toward computers. However, the research on gender differences in attitude has yielded mixed results. This section will examine the existing research on attitude and perception of different genders toward educational technology in general and hypermedia learning systems in particular.

A great number of studies reveal that there are gender differences in attitude and perception towards the use of computers in learning. For example, in a longitudinal study investigating the relationship between gender and categories of computer use and attitudes toward computers, it was found that females were less positive about computers than males and used computers less frequently (Mitra, Steffensmeier, Lenzmeier, Avon, Qu, & Hazen, 2000). Liaw (2002) also examined gender differences in perceptions of computers and the Web and found significant differences, which showed male students had more positive attitudes towards computers and the Web compared to female students. Another longitudinal study conducted by Schumacher and Morahan-Martin (2001) examined gender differences in attitudes towards computers and the Internet and explored the relationship between computer and Internet attitudes, skills, and experiences. Participants were college students in 1989/90 and 1997. Compared with the incoming students in 1989/90, gender differences in many computer experiences and skill levels had diminished in the 1997 group, owing to the great exposure to computers and the Internet. However, gender differences in attitudes continued, with females reporting negative attitudes towards computers and the Internet, which in turn hampered computer and Internet experience. In addition, several other studies (Teasdale & Lupart, 2001; Whitley, 1996; Young, 2000) also suggest that females tend to have more negative attitudes towards computers than males. These studies suggested that females were more anxious, less confident, and had less ability of using computers than their male peers.

However, other studies indicate that there are no gender differences in attitudes toward computer. For example, Nelson and Cooper (1997) examined gender differences in computer use and attitudes. Subjects were 127 fifth graders (58 females and 69 males). They were asked to complete questionnaires assessing computer experience and attitudes toward computers. The finding showed that there were no gender differences in general attitudes toward computers. Both boys and girls were very positive about computers; there were also no gender differences in feeling comfortable with computers.

With regard to gender differences in attitudes and perceptions toward hypermedia learning systems, research has also yielded mixed results. For example, Leong and Hawamdeh (1999) conducted a study to examine gender differences in attitudes in using Web-based science lessons. Forty primary fifth grade pupils (17 boy and 23 girls) participated in the study. The results showed that girls found it easier to navigate the Web lesson pages, while the boys thought it was too confusing and the pages were too long. All of the girls liked using computers to learn; they liked learning new things with the use of computers. However, when using a computer to learn, the main dislike given by girls was that they got lost and did not know what to do next, whereas the boys did not like to read from the computer screen, owing to the fact that boys associate computers with games where little or no reading is involved (Leong & Hawamdeh, 1999).

Other studies have presented conflicting results. A recent study conducted by Liu (2004) examined the impact of a hypermedia learning system on the attitudes of students with different gender. One hundred forty five sixth graders partici-pated in the study (73 female and 72 male students). Attitude was assessed through questionnaires and interviews. The results suggested that there were no gender differences in the attitudes among the students in the study. Both boys and girls had positive attitudes towards the hypermedia learning system, and the results showed that male as well as female students enjoyed this learning system. This finding is consistent with other research (Dyck & Smither, 1994; Houle, 1996; Todman & Monaghan, 1994) on computer attitude and gender.

In addition, Koohang and Durante (2003) conducted a study to measure learners' perception of a Web-based distance learning program, which reveals similar results. One hundred six undergraduate students—50 males and 56 females—participated in the study. Gender was one of the variables investigated in the study to determine if difference in perception towards the Web-based learning program occurred between male and female participants. A 10-item Likert-type instrument was designed to collect information about the learners' perceptions of Web-based learning. Koohang and Durante (2003) found that there was no significant gender difference towards the Web-based distance learning program in their study. These findings seem to suggest that well-designed hypermedia learning systems can support student learning regardless of gender.

In summary, studies of gender differences in attitude and perception towards computers in general reveal mixed results, although research generally has found that males have more favorable attitudes toward computers than females. Research indicates that the negative attitudes of females towards computers are directly linked to the gender bias of many computer programs (Bhargava, 2002; Francis, 1994), and suggests that in order to address this, system design needs to be aimed to meet the needs of all learners, regardless of gender (Campbell, 2000; Passig & Levin, 2000). With regard to hypermedia learning systems, research also reveals mixed results. However, research does indicate that students' attitudes are of crucial importance to the success or failure of educational approaches because a negative reaction will inhibit learning, whereas a positive one will enhance learning (Leong & Hawamdeh, 1999). Since there is evidence that gender plays a part in determining attitude, it could be argued that more consideration should be given to gender differences when designing hypermedia learning systems.

Information Seeking Strategy

Information seeking is one of the learning processes that seems to be supported by hypermedia, because of its ability to integrate large volumes of information in alternative representations (Jonassen & Grabinger, 1990). Research evidence suggests that different individuals seek and process information using very different strategies. A significant number of studies has examined gender differences in information-seeking behaviors. Gender is considered as a major predictor of information-seeking approach on the Web (Ford et al., 2001; Moranhan-Martin, 1998). This section will present and analyze research results regarding gender differences in information-seeking strategies.

Various studies of information-seeking behavior have included gender differences as one of the variables. For example, Ford and Miller (1996) studied the influence of gender differences in information seeking on the Web. Seventy-five postgraduate students (40 males and 35 females) participated in the study, and significant differences were found according to gender. Compared with the male students, the female students seem relatively disoriented and disenchanted while seeking information on the Internet, and they generally felt themselves unable to find their way around effectively. In a recent study, Ford et al. (2001) investigated individual differences in Internet searching using a sample of 64 master's students with 20 male and 44 female participants. A 63-item questionnaire relating to Internet perceptions, levels of experience, and cognitive complexity was used; AltaVista was selected as the search engine. In line with previous findings, they found that female students had difficulties in finding their way effectively around the Internet and were more likely to get lost and feel not in control. These studies suggest that females tend to experience more difficulties in finding information on the Web and require support in terms of different user interfaces and navigation facilities.

Reed and Oughton (1997) conducted a study to determine whether student gender and other individual characteristics are factors in students' linear and nonlinear navigation of hypermedia. Eighteen graduate students participated in this study. The authors analyzed the navigation patterns at three different intervals to determine the relative temporal influence of these characteristics on linear and nonlinear navigation. The results showed that during the first interval, females took more linear steps than males. However, they did not take more linear steps during any other intervals, nor did they take more linear steps overall. Reed and Oughton (1997) concluded that gender was an early predictor of more linear navigation, with females positively relating to linear navigation during the early stage of system use.

In addition, Roy and Chi (2003) examined gender differences in searching the Web for information by analyzing student's patterns of search behavior. Fourteen eighth grade students, with equal numbers of boys and girls, participated in the study. A searching task was assessed through target-specific prompts and target-related questions. Searching behavior was measured by using field notes along with computer logs of all the Web pages accessed by students during their search. All search moves were categorized into one of the following four categories of search behavior: (i) submitting a search query in the Google search window; (ii) scanning the list of returned document excerpts which contain links to documents; (iii) selecting, opening, and browsing a particular document; and (iv) bookmarking a document location or taking notes. The findings showed that the overall pattern of search behavior was different for boys and girls. Boys tended to filter information at an earlier stage in the search cycle than girls, whereas girls were much more linear and thorough navigators than boys. Although boys and girls had similar background knowledge about the content domain and similar experience with Web searching, they found two distinct global patterns of search behavior: boys are horizontal searchers, and conversely, girls are vertical searchers.

The findings of Roy and Chi (2003) are in agreement with the results of Large et al. (2002), who investigated gender differences in collaborative Web searching. Fifty-three students, comprising 30 girls and 23 boys from two grade-six classes, were the subjects of the study. The results revealed that boys were using a different strategy to retrieve information from the Web than girls. In regards to gender effect on query formulation, they found that the group of boys used fewer words to formulate queries submitted to search engines, and often expected to find relevant information from just entering a single word. The group of girls, however, tended to use natural language queries (on keyword-based search engines) and open and closed quotations more often than boys. The findings indicate that boys preferred a broader search strategy than girls. With regard to gender effect on viewing Web pages, they found that boys spent less time viewing pages than girls. This finding is consistent with prior research indicating that boys found Web pages too lengthy to read (Leong & Haawamdeh, 1999) and were less interested in text than girls (Hancock et al., 1996). In regard to gender effect on browsing and information management, Large et al. (2002) found that the male group was more actively engaged in browsing than the female group, and the male group explored more hypertext links per minute. They also found that the boys tended to perform more page jumps per minute, entered more searches at search engines, and gathered and saved information more often than the girls.

These research findings suggest that gender is a major predictor of information seeking in hypermedia systems. Males and females possess different information-seeking strategies, with males preferring broader searching than females. Males and females also differ in their navigation styles, with females tending to navigate in a linear way. Empirical evidence also suggests that females tend to experience more difficulty finding information in hypermedia systems, implying that they might benefit from navigation support. As suggested by Ford et al. (2001), gender is a relatively fixed variable; thus it requires adaptability from the system perspective, suggesting that it is important that user interfaces to hypermedia systems should be developed to support adaptation to gender.

Media Choice

One of the distinct advantages of hypermedia is that it allows the integration of different media in hypermedia learning systems (Nielsen, 1993). Research indicates that males and females have different preferences regarding information presentation with different media. This section will look at the existing research on this issue to demonstrate gender differences in the preference of media and how different media benefit different genders.

A number of studies have examined gender differences in media choice in hypermedia learning systems. An early study by Braswell and Brown (1992) found that females reviewed videodisc segments more frequently and spent more time on tasks than males in an interactive video learning environment. Recent studies by Passig and Levin (1999, 2000) investigated gender differences amongst kindergarten students regarding their preferences to varying designs of multimedia learning interfaces. They attempted to find out the characteristics of multimedia interfaces that interest boys and girls. Ninety children (44 girls and 46 boys) were given a number of multimedia products with a range of interfaces to work through and then asked to fill in a simple questionnaire. The findings revealed that boys were more attracted to movement such as fast navigation, control, and choice, whereas girls were more attracted to visual aspects such as color, drawing, and writing.

In addition, Riding and Grimley (1999) explored the effects of gender differences along with cognitive style in student learning via multimedia and traditional materials. Two basic dimensions of cognitive style were examined: (i) the Wholist-Analytic dimension of whether an individual tends to process and organize information in whole or parts; and (ii) the Verbal-Imagery dimension of whether an individual is inclined to represent information during thinking verbally or in mental pictures. Eighty students (40 males and 40 females) from a primary school participated in the study. With regard to the mode of presentation of the multimedia materials, results indicated that girls who were Wholist-Imagers and Analytic-Verbalizers were better with presentations that had picture and sound than with those that had only picture and text. Girls who were Wholist-Verbalizers and Analytic-Imagers were better with presentations that had picture and text than those that had only picture and sound. The results were the opposite for boys. For both gender groups, performance was best with presentations that combined picture, text, and sound. The findings suggest that males and females process information in a different way, leading the authors to suggest that "gender differences may have important implications for the design and use of multimedia materials" (Riding and Grimley, 1999, p. 55).

In summary, hypermedia has great advantages in presenting information using different media. However, research indicates that males and females have different preferences in the presentation of different media, but it is not clear what kind of media benefit which gender. More research is needed in this respect. Nevertheless, it is claimed that cross-gender appealing products are most successful. Therefore, effective design of hypermedia learning systems should use different media to support different gender and explore adaptation as a way of delivery their variability.

Learning Performance

Gender-based differences in performance and interaction style in computer-supported learning environments are also recognized as an important focus for research (Gunn, 2003). A great deal of research has investigated gender differences in performance on learning and information seeking in hypermedia systems. Some research found that there were gender differences in the performance (Roy, Taylor, & Chi, 2003; Young & McSporran, 2001), whereas other studies revealed that no gender differences were found (Liu, 2004), highlighting that the results remain inconclusive. The section examines these studies in turn to provide a better appreciation of the issues in relation to the chapters focus.

A number of studies have examined gender differences in performance in hypermedia learning systems. There are, however, conflicting views about the nature and impact of these differences. Young and McSporran (2001) examined gender differences in student learning performance in a hypermedia learning system and found that females favored and performed better with online learning courses. The finding is consistent with previous research (McSporran, Young, & Dewstow, 2000; Young, Dewstow, & McSporran, 1999), which showed that older women scored better than younger men. Conflicting results arise from Roy et al. (2003) who conducted a study to investigate effect of gender difference on students' information-seeking performance and found that boys performed significantly better on gaining target-specific and target-related knowledge than girls.

The conflicting results are further complicated by a performance in a recent study by Liu (2004), which in part examined differences in a hypermedia learning system, and found no gender differences. Seventy-three female and 72 male sixth graders participated in the study. Learning performance was measured through a 25-item multiple-choice test, which was used to assess students' understanding of the various scientific concepts introduced in the system. The results showed that no gender difference was found, with male and female students performing equally well. This finding seems to suggest that well-designed hypermedia learning system might diminish, and even remove, gender differences.

In summary, research on gender differences in performance in hypermedia learning has yielded mixed results and presented conflicting views. Some research studies report that females perform better than males, whereas others revealed that males perform better than females. There also are studies demonstrating that there is no gender difference in performance. One explanation is that students' learning performance is related to the design of the system and the task type. Research found that boys performed better than girls on a male-stereotyped computer-based task, whereas on a gender-neutral, computer-based task it was found that there was no gender difference in performance (Joiner, 1998). Kelly (2000) suggests that a well-designed hypermedia learning system may assist in overcoming gender-related differences in confidence in both studying online and using the Internet in general.

Development of Principles and Guidelines for Adaptive Hypermedia Learning Systems

As discussed in the previous sections, males and females demonstrate great differences and preferences toward hypermedia learning systems in terms of information seeking, navigation styles, and media choices. With regard to information seeking, females tend to experience more difficulty finding information efficiently in hypermedia systems; with regard to navigation style, research suggests that boys are horizontal searchers whereas girls are vertical searchers in hypermedia systems. Additionally, females appear to navigate in a linear way while searching information in hypermedia systems. Conversely, males tended to navigate in a nonlinear way. With regard to media choices, males and females also show different preferences and benefit differently from different modes of multimedia presentation. Research has revealed that the results are opposite for boys and girls regarding the performance with presentations of picture and sound over those with picture and text. It was also found that boys did not like to read static screens consisting of text. In addition, empirical research on gender differences shows mixed results with respect to attitude and learning performance in hypermedia learning systems. Some found there were gender differences in attitude and learning performance, while others indicated no gender differences regarding learners' attitudes and learning performance in hypermedia learning systems. It can be argued that these mixed results arise from the design of the learning systems. Well-designed hypermedia learning systems could reduce the differences, making effective system design of crucial importance for the success of student learning in hypermedia systems. In order to facilitate student learning, it is essential that system should be designed to adapt to learners' individual characteristics, such as gender.

The results of the previous studies provide a basis for the design of adaptive hypermedia learning systems. Adaptive hypermedia systems can be developed to accommodate a variety of individual differences such as gender. According to Brusilovsky et al. (1998), adaptive presentation and adaptive navigation support are the two main adaptive hypermedia technologies used for providing adaptive hypermedia learning systems. The goal of adaptive presentation is to adapt the page content to knowledge, goals, and other characteristics of an individual user (Brusilovsky, 2003), and the goal of adaptive navigation support is to help users to find an appropriate path in a hypermedia learning system (Brusilovsky, 1996). Based on the findings of gender difference and hypermedia learning, along with the features of adaptive hypermedia systems, this section presents principles that to guide the design of adaptive hypermedia learning systems so that they accommodate both genders in relation to adaptive presentation and adaptive navigation support.

Principles Relating to Adaptive Presentation with Respect to User Interfaces and Media Presentation

Previous studies suggest that male and female students possess different attitudes and perceptions and show different preferences towards hypermedia learning systems. The following principles, which reflect the proceeding analysis of relevant research, suggest ways to design adaptive hypermedia learning systems to accommodate both genders in terms of user interfaces and media presentation.

- **Design gender-neutral hypermedia learning system.** Research indicates that females show less favorable attitudes towards computers. This is mainly due to the fact that many of today's computer software packages and games are aimed at male interests and preferences. Therefore, effective design needs to start with the basics—learning systems should be aimed to meet the needs of both male and female learners. Empirical evidence reveals that boys emphasize control, choice, and fast navigation, while girls emphasize writing, color, drawings, and help (Passig & Levin, 2000). Males and females also show different preferences in terms of the use of color, media presentation, and navigation facilities. The understanding of these preferences should be used to clearly inform design.

- **Use different background colors.** One way of providing adaptive presentation is through adaptive layout, which aims to differentiate levels of the subject content by changing the layout of the page such as font type and size and background color (Chen & Paul, 2003). Research reveals that females easily became lost and tended to experience more difficulty in finding information (Ford & Miller, 1996; Ford et al., 2001). Using different background colors may give learners an improved indication of where they are. For example, using a different background color at different levels such as topic level, subtopic level, and page level might enable the learner to jump to the different levels by identifying the colors. This, in turn, could help female learners to find their way around more effectively in the learning systems.

- **Provide a range of visual cue mechanisms to reduce disorientation.** Another way to support females who suffer disorientation problems in information seeking is to provide them with visual cues in the interfaces. Several different techniques can be applied to keep students informed about where they are, where they have been, and where they can go, such as:

1. Use different colors or fonts and sizes to highlight the place where the current page is located.
2. Use history-based mechanisms, such as check mark, to indicate accessed pages.
3. Provide "breadcrumbs" to track learner's navigation paths.

These mechanisms may, of course, also be helpful to male learners, but research highlights females as having heightened problems in this area.

- **Match different media to gender to improve content presentation.** As described earlier, research found that boys did not like to read static screens consisting of text on a computer screen (Hancock et al., 1996; Leong & Hawamdeh, 1999). This is probably due to the fact that boys associate computers with dynamic games animation. In addition, Riding and Grimley (1999) revealed that the results were opposite for boys and girls, in terms of performance with the presentations of picture and sound over those with picture and text, which indicates that boys and girls have different preferences of presentation mode for different media. Adaptive multimedia presentation (Brusilovsky, 2001) can be applied to accommodate the preferences of different genders. Adaptive hypermedia systems may provide a choice of different types of media (such as text, video, animation, picture, and sound), with which to present information to the learner. For example, different media or combinations of media can be used to present the same content, and the learner can then either choose the one that matches his/her preference, and/or adaptation mechanisms can be built in to provide a matched default setting based on gender.

Principles Relating to Adaptive Navigation Support

Research has shown that male and female learners demonstrated different information-seeking strategies and navigation styles in hypermedia systems. Below are principles drawn from the earlier analysis of relevant research that suggest ways to design adaptive hypermedia learning systems to accommodate both genders in terms of navigation support.

- **Provide direct guidance.** As indicated earlier, females experienced difficulty in finding their way around efficiently and did not know where to go next when seeking information in hypermedia systems. Providing adaptation to give direct guidance where appropriate may help females to avoid experiencing such disorientation problems. Adaptive hypermedia systems could provide direct guidance by using the "next" or "continue" (link) button, with the system effectively suggesting to the learner the next part of the material which should be visited.

- **Use link hiding.** Another way to help females decide which path to take to meet their information needs is by hiding links to pages not related to their current goal. Hiding links can help to support local orientation by limiting the number of navigation opportunities to reduce cognitive overload and enables the learner to focus on the most relevant links (De Bra et al., 2000).

- **Provide adaptive annotation.** Adaptive annotation is the most popular form of adaptive navigation support. Adaptive annotation of hyperlinks provides the user with additional information about the content behind a hyperlink. This could provide female learners with local orientation support as well. Also, annotation of links can function as a landmark to provide global orientation support.

- **Present different navigation tools.** Research suggests that males and females possess different information seeking strategies and navigation styles. To meet their needs, different navigation tools should be provided to facilitate learning. Concept maps are considered helpful to female learners to conceptualize and organize information in the learning system. With the concept map, learners can determine where they are in the learning systems and are able to jump to other areas of interests. In addition, to avoid disorientation, learning systems should also allow for guided searches for specific information by providing index lists of all available information.

Concluding Remarks

This chapter has examined and analyzed existing research on the interaction between gender differences and hypermedia learning. Research evidence reveals that there are gender differences in attitude and perception, information seeking strategy and navigation style, media preferences, and learning performance. In general, males show more favorable attitudes towards computers compared with females. With respect to information seeking, males demonstrate a broader search strategy than females. Females tend to experience more difficulty finding information efficiently in hypermedia systems, and they appear to navigate in a linear way while searching information in hypermedia systems. With regard to media choices, males and females also show difference preferences and benefit differently from different modes of multimedia presentation. These results indicate that it is essential that learning system should be designed to adapt to learners' gender differences as they are of crucial importance for the success of student learning in hypermedia systems.

Based on an analysis of the relevant empirical studies, the chapter has presented a set of principles to guide the effective design of adaptive hypermedia learning systems in relation to adaptive presentation and adaptive navigation support on the basis of gender differences. These principles and guidelines aim to help designers and educators to develop successful adaptive hypermedia learning systems that will cater for both genders so as to facilitate learning. However, the design principles described in this chapter focus on designing adaptive learning systems to target specific gender, so principles and guidelines on more generic issues are not covered. In addition, the adaptive design principles are only based on gender differences. Other individual variables, such as cognitive style, prior knowledge, computer experiences, and age are not included. Moreover, the research findings show that college age females have more negative attitude than males of the same age, but it is not true for middle school age girls. This seems to indicate that age difference might be the reason or the combination of gender and age that matters. Therefore future research is needed to investigate this further. As suggested by Brusilovsky (2003), in order to adapt to the needs of a diversity of learners, future research needs to continue to explore the interaction effects between hypermedia system features and individual differences so as to help adaptive hypermedia system designers in selecting the most relevant adaptation techniques. As more is learned about individual's cognition and learning, more effective principles can be developed to guide the design of successful adaptive hypermedia learning systems to cater for all learners.

References

Ayersman, D. (1996). Reviewing the research on hypermedia-based learning. *Journal of Research on Computing in Education, 28*(4), 500-525.

Bhargava, A. (2002). Gender bias in computer software programs: A checklist for teachers. *Information Technology in Childhood Education Annual, 2002*(1), 205-218.

Braswell, R., & Brown, J. (1992). *Use of interactive videodisc technology in a physical education methods class.* Paper presented at the Annual meeting of the American Educational Research Association, San Francisco (ERIC ED 348 936).

Brusilovsky, P. (1996). Methods and techniques of adaptive hypermedia. *User Modeling and User-adapted Interaction, 6*(2-3), 87-129.

Brusilovsky, P. (1999). Adaptive and intelligent technologies for Web-based education. In C. Rollinger & C. Peylo (Eds.), *Special issue on intelligent systems and teleteaching* (Vol. 4, pp. 19-25). Kunstliche Intelligenz.

Brusilovsky, P. (2001). Adaptive hypermedia. *User Modeling and User-adapted Interaction, 11*(1-2), 87-110.

Brusilovsky, P. (2003). Adaptive navigation support in educational hypermedia: The role of student knowledge level and the case for meta-adaptation. *British Journal of Educational Technology, 34*(4), 487-497.

Brusilovsky, P., Eklund, J., & Schwarz, E. (1998). Web-based education for all: A tool for developing adaptive courseware. *Computer Networks and ISDN Systems, 30*(1-7), 291-300.

Calisir, F., & Gurel, Z. (2003). Influence of text structure and prior knowledge of the learner on reading comprehension, browsing, and perceived control. *Computers in Human Behavior, 19*(2), 135-145.

Campbell, K. (2000). Gender and educational technologies: Relational frameworks for learning design. *Journal of Educational Multimedia and Hypermedia, 9*(2), 131-149.

Carver, C.A., Howard, R.A., & Lavelle, E. (1996). Enhancing student learning by incorporating student learning styles into adaptive hypermedia. *Proceedings of ED-MEDIA '96 – World Conference on Educational Multimedia and Hypermedia*, Boston (pp. 118-123).

Chen, S.Y., & Macredie, R.D. (2002). Cognitive styles and hypermedia navigation: Development of a learning model. *Journal of the American Society for Information Science and Technology, 53*(1), 3-15.

Chen, S.Y., & Paul, R.J. (2003). Editorial: Individual differences in Web-based instruction – an overview. *British Journal of Educational Technology, 34*(4), 385-392.

Conklin, J. (1987). Hypertext: An introduction and survey. *IEEE Computer, 9*(20), 17-41.

De Bra, P., Aerts, A. T. M., Houben, G., & Wu, H. (2000). Making general-purpose adaptive hypermedia work. *Proceedings of WebNet 2000 - World Conference on the WWW and Internet*, San Antonio, TX (pp. 117-123).

De Bra, P., Brusilovsky, P., & Houben, G. (1999). Adaptive hypermedia: From systems to framework. *ACM Computing Survey, 31*(4), 1-6.

Dyck, J. L., & Smither, J.A. (1994). Age differences in computer anxiety: The role of computer experience, gender, and education. *Journal of Educational Computing Research, 10*(3), 239-248.

Ford, N., & Chen, S. (2000). Individual differences, hypermedia navigation, and learning: An empirical study. *Journal of Educational Multimedia and Hypermedia, 9*(4), 281-311.

Ford, N., & Chen, S. (2001). Matching/mismatching revisited: An empirical study of learning and teaching styles. *British Journal of Educational Technology, 32*(1), 5-22

Ford, N., & Miller, D. (1996). Gender differences in Internet perceptions and use. *Aslib Proceedings, 48*, 183-192.

Ford, N., Miller, D., & Moss, N. (2001). The role of individual differences in Internet searching: An empirical study. *Journal of the American Society for Information Science and Technology, 52*(12), 1049-1066.

Francis, L.J. (1994). The relationship between computer-related attitudes and gender stereotyping of computer use. *Computers & Education, 22*(4), 283-289.

Gilbert, J., & Han, C.Y. (1999). Arthur: Adapting instruction to accommodate learning style. *Proceeding of WebNet '99, World conference of thee WWW and Internet,* Honolulu, HI (pp. 433-438).

Gunn, C. (2003). Dominant or different? Gender issues in computer supported learning. *JALD, 7*(1), 14-30.

Hancock, T. E., Stock, W. A., & Swindell, L. K. (1996). Gender and development differences in the academic study behaviors of elementary school children. *Journal of Experimental School Education, 65*(1), 18-39.

Houle, P. A. (1996). Toward understanding student differences in a computer skill course. *Journal of Educational Computing Research, 14*(1), 25-48.

Joiner, R. W. (1998). The effect of gender on children's software preferences. *Journal of Computer Assisted Learning, 14*(2), 195-198.

Jonassen, D. H., & Grabowski, B. L. (1993). *Individual differences and instruction.* New York: Allen & Bacon.

Jonassen, D., & Mandl, H. (1990). *Designing hypermedia for learning.* NATO, Serie.

Kadijevich, D. (2000). Gender differences in computer attitude among ninth-grade students. *Journal of Educational Computing Research, 22*(2), 145-154.

Kelly, K. (2000). The gender gap: Why do girls get turned off to technology? In D. T. Gordon (Ed.), *The digital classroom. The Harvard Education Letter*, Cambridge, MA (pp. 154-160).

Kim, K. S. (2001). Information seeing on the Web: Effects of user and task variables. *Library & Information Science Research, 23*, 233-255.

Koohang, A., & Durante, A. (2003). Learners' perceptions toward the Web-based distance learning activities/assignments portion of an undergraduate hybrid instruction model. *Journal of Information Technology Education, 2*, 105-113.

Large, A. (1996). Hypertext instructional programs and learner control: A research review. *Education for Information, 14*(2), 95-106.

Large, A., Beheshti, J., & Rahman, T. (2002). Design criteria for children's Web portals: The users speak out. *Journal of the American Society for Information Science and Technology, 53*(2), 79-94.

Last, D. A., O'Donnell, A. M., & Kelly, A. E. (2001). The effects of prior knowledge and goal strength on the use of hypermedia. *Journal of Educational Multimedia and Hypermedia, 10*(1), 3-25.

Lawless, K. A., & Brown, S. W. (1997). Multimedia learning environments: Issues of learner control and navigation. *Instructional Science, 25*(2), 117-31.

Leong, S., & Hawamdeh, S. (1999). Gender and learning attitudes in using Web-based science lessons. *Information Research, 5*(1). Retrieved from http://www.shef.ac.uk/is/publications/infres/paper66.html

Liaw, S. S. (2002). An Internet survey for perceptions of computers and the World Wide Web. *Computers in Human Behavior, 18*(1), 17-35.

Lim, K. (2002). Impacts of personal characteristics on computer attitude and academic users' information system satisfaction. *Journal of Educational Computing Research, 26*(4), 395-406.

Liu, M. (2004). Examining the performance and attitudes of sixth graders during their use of a problem-based hypermedia learning environment. *Computers in Human Behavior.*

Loyd, B. H., & Gressard, C. (1984). Reliability and factorial validity of computer attitude scales. *Educational and Psychological Measurement, 44*(3), 501-505.

Magoulas, G. D., Papanikolaou, K., & Grigoriadou, M. (2003). Adaptive Web-based learning: Accommodating individual differences through system's adaptation. *British Journal of Educational Technology, 34*(4), 511-527.

Marchionini, G. (1988). Hypermedia and learning: Freedom and chaos. *Educational Technology, 28*(11), 8-12.

McSporran, M., Young, S., & Dewstow, R. (2000). Does gender matter in online learning? *Proceedings of ALT- C*, Manchester (p. 45).

Mitra, A., Steffensmeier, T., Lenzmeier, S., Avon, R., Qu, N., & Hazen, M. (2000). Gender and computer use in an academic institution: Report from a longitudinal study. *Journal of Educational Computing Research, 23*(1), 67-84.

Morahan-Martin, J. (1998). Males, females, and the Internet. In J. Gackenbach (Ed.), *Psychology and the Internet: Intrapersonal, interpersonal, and transpersonal implications* (pp. 169-197). San Diego, CA: Academic Press.

Nelson, L. J., & Cooper, J. (1997). Gender differences in children's reactions to success and failure with computers. *Computers in Human Behavior, 13*(2), 247-267.

Nielsen, J. (1993). *Hypertext & hypermedia* (2nd Edition). Boston; London: Academic Press.

Nielsen, J. (1995). *Multimedia and hypermedia: The Internet and beyond.* London: Academic Press Limited.

Nielsen, J. (2000). *Designing Web usability: The practice of simplicity.* New Rider Publishing.

Passig, D., & Levin, H. (1999). Gender interest differences with multimedia learning interfaces. *Computers in Human Behavior, 15*(2), 173-183.

Passig, D., & Levin, H. (2000). Gender preferences for multimedia interfaces. *Journal of Computer Assisted Learning, 16*(1), 64-71.

Proost, K., Elen, J., & Lowyck, J. (1997). Effects of gender on perceptions of and preferences for telematic learning environments. *Journal of Research on Computing in Education, 29*(4), 370-384.

Reed, W.M., & Oughton, J.M. (1997). Computer experience and interval-based hypermedia navigation. *Journal of Research on Computing in Education, 30*(1), 38-52.

Riding, R., & Grimley, M. (1999). Cognitive style, gender, and learning from multi-media materials in 11 year old children. *British Journal of Educational Technology, 30*(1), 43-56.

Roy, M., & Chi, M. T. C. (2003). Gender differences in patterns of searching the Web. *Journal of Educational Computing Research, 29*(3), 335-348.

Roy, M., Taylor, R., & Chi, M. T. H. (2002). Searching for information on-line and offline: Gender differences among middle school students. *Journal of Educational Computing Research, 29*(2), 229-252.

Schumacher, P., & Morahan-Martin, J. (2001). Gender, Internet and computer attitudes and experiences. *Computers in Human Behavior, 17*(1), 95-110.

Specht, M., & Oppermann, R. (1998). ACE – Adaptive Courseware Environment. *The New Review of Hypermedia and Multimedia, 4*(1), 141-161.

Teasdale, S., & Lupart, J. (2001). Gender differences in computer attitudes, skills, and perceived ability. Presented at the *Canadian Society for Studies in Education*, Quebec, Canada.

Todman, J., & Monaghan, E. (1994). Qualitative differences in computer experiences, computer anxiety, and students' use of computers: A path model. *Computers in Human Behavior, 10*(4), 529-539.

Triantafillou, E., Pomportsis, A., & Demetriadis, S. (2003). The design and formative evaluation of an adaptive educational system based on cognitive styles. *Computers & Education, 41*(1), 87-103.

Whitley, B.E. (1996). Gender differences in computer-related attitudes: It depends on what you ask. *Computers in Human Behavior, 12*(2), 275-289.

Yates, S. J. (1997). Gender, identity, and CMC. *Journal of Computer Assisted Learning, 13*(4), 281-290.

Young, B. L. (2000). Gender differences in student attitudes towards computers. *Journal of Research on Computing in Education, 33*(2), 204-213.

Young, S., & McSporran, M. (2001). Confident men - Successful women: Gender differences in online learning. *Proceedings of National Advisory Committe on Computing Qualifications Conference,* Dunedin, New Zealand (pp. 433-436).

Young, S., Dewstow, R., & McSporran, M. (1999). Who wants to learn online? What types of students benefit from the new learning environment? *Proceedings of the National Advisory Committee on Computing Qualifications Conference*, Dunedin, New Zealand (pp. 293-300).

Chapter II

Modeling Learner's Cognitive Abilities in the Context of a Web-Based Learning Environment

Maria Aparecida M. Souto, Instituto de Informática, Brazil

Regina Verdin, PPGIE/UFRGS, Brazil

José Palazzo M. de Oliveira, Instituto de Informática, Brazil

Abstract

Our study is concerned with making the instruction suitable to the individual learner's characteristics. This chapter describes the methodology used to investigate how to model the learner's Cognitive Ability Level (CAL) based on the observation and analysis of his/her behaviour in a Web-learning environment. In our study, the CAL represents the learner's cognitive stage development according to Bloom's taxonomy. The methodology encompasses two phases: (i) the generation of the CAL classes for the target population and (ii) the study of learning trajectories of CAL classes in an experimental learning module. As a result, we have identified the CAL classes' parameters values that best discriminate these classes from the observation and analysis of their learning trajectory on the Web. The entire knowledge obtained from this investigation will make possible to automate the learners' CAL diagnostic. It will also give us the background to develop Web-learning environment contents.

Introduction

In the context of adaptive Web-based learning environments, there is a big challenge related to the development of a high quality pedagogical material and to intelligent and efficient online assistance to the remote learner. The adaptation of the course contents' presentation to the learner's individual characteristics is the major requirement of the Web-based learning environment. From psycho and pedagogical points of view, important questions must be carefully thought, such as:

- how to identify the aspects that positively influence a long distance learning process in a hypermedia environment;
- how to provide a psycho and pedagogical assistance to a broad variety of learners' cognitive profiles and how to manage their difficulties along the learning process; and
- how to deal with the absence of feedback to the teachers, who are not online or don't have information about the difficulties of the learners who, in turn, tend to feel isolated and potentially lost and discouraged.

Besides the psycho and pedagogical questions, several others arise under the computational point of view, such as:

- how to trace the learners' interactions with the pedagogical material over the Internet;
- how to computationally analyse and interpret the learner's behaviour along his/her learning process; and
- how to model the psycho and pedagogical characteristics of the learners.

A wide variety of studies are found in the literature stressing interest on these questions. They clearly demonstrated a trend towards taking into account individual learner's characteristics (e.g., learning style, cognitive style, emotions, personality, etc.) to adapt the instruction in a suitable manner.

Our study focuses on the computational modeling of the learner's CAL, aiming to customize the pedagogical strategies to this individual characteristic. Our main assumption relies on the idea that if the system could diagnose the learner's CAL characteristic by observing his/her interactions with it, it would guide the learner's learning process by stimulating the development of his/her cognitive abilities.

The development of the cognitive abilities certainly would increase learner's probability of success on a learning task. Consequently, the psycho and pedagogical advantages to the learner would be related to: (i) the smoothness on the progress of the learning task he/she performs; (ii) the increasing of the effectiveness of his/her contents apprenticeship; and (iii) the increasing of the learner's efficiency in the learning process.

Related Work

An important issue addressed in an adaptive system is related to the user model. According to Brusilovsky (1995), there are many features related to the current context of the users' work and to the user as an individual, which can be taken into account by an adaptive system. These features were identified as: user's goals, knowledge, background, hyperspace experience, and preferences.

Nowadays, there is a great trend of modeling the learner's individual characteristics in a complementary way compared to the learner's features mentioned by Brusilovsky. This tendency can be expressed by the cognitive science researchers concern in making the adaptation take into consideration the learner's individual characteristics such as: personality (Riding & Wigley apud Riding & Rayner, 2000), emotional factors (Soldato, 1995), gender (Reed & Oughton, 1997), learning orientations (Martinez & Bunderson, 2000), and cognitive and learning styles (Felder & Silverman, 1988; Ford & Chen, 2000; Riding & Cheema, 1998), among others.

The empirical researchers have been theorizing in different ways about and pursuing the relationship between some individual differences and learning environments trying to find out correlations between them. They have shown that some individual's characteristics were linked mainly to different learning strategies displayed in the environment. For example, Ford and Chen (2000) investigated the correlation between FD/FI cognitive style and different navigation strategies in a hypermedia environment. These authors observed that different cognitive styles displayed different learning strategies. However, this result has shown no significant interaction between strategies of different cognitive style and learning outcomes.

McManus (2000) investigated the correlation between the learner's self-regulation characteristic and the linearity level of the learning environment on the Web. The self-regulation characteristic is a complex mix of cognitive, metacognitive, motivational, and strategic psychological aspects that influence the learner's control during learning process, in the learning environment and interactions with it. The investigation results indicated that learners with high levels of self-regulation could benefit from their ability in organizing and structuring their instruction in non-linear environments.

Besides the empirical studies, several systems reviewed at the literature implemented individual characteristics such as cognitive and learning styles. Some of these systems have adopted an inductive framework to model these individual characteristics by using some sort of inferential technique such as machine learning. Other systems have adopted a deductive framework, based on an established psycho and pedagogical theory of learning. For example, in MANIC System (Stern & Woolf, 2000), the learner's characteristics considered in the adaptation are: level of difficulty and learning style preferences. The first one is determined by a pre-test. The other one is diagnosed by a Naïve Bayes classifier, a machine learning technique, which reasons (and learns) about the learner's preferences in terms of the content object features such as: media type, instructional type, level of abstractness of the content objects, as well as through his/her ordering preference of the different types of content objects.

The INSPIRE System (Papanikolaou et al., 2003) has adopted the learning style classification proposed by Honey and Munford (apud Papanikolaou et al., 2003). The learning style was classified through a questionnaire, according to the following categories: activist, reflector, theorist, and pragmatist. In the context of this system, the learner's learning style guides the presentation style of the instructional material. The main objective is to match the learning preferences of learners with an appropriate instructional material.

The AES-CS System (Triantafillou et al., 2003) is based on the FD/FI cognitive style. The FD/FI cognitive style is identified by the GEFT Test (Wittin et al. apud Triantafillou et al., 2003). This test is based on how the learner perceives and organizes the internal and external cues of a figure. The instructional strategies take into account learner's learning style preferences such as approach (global or analytical), control (learner or system), and structure (structured lessons or developed by learners), among others.

Our study differs from these works because it is based on high order thinking abilities according to Bloom's taxonomy (Bloom, 1972). This study is an attempt to define the navigational behaviour indicators that could better discriminate the

CAL groups. In order to accomplish our objective, we have adopted an exploratory empirical and inductive research framework. We expect that the main benefit of adjusting the instructional presentation to the learner's CAL characteristic is designing pedagogical strategies and didactic tactics to provide the learner with an in-depth learning and more complex thinking.

Purpose

Considering the CAL and the learning trajectories (LT) as the main constructs of our investigation, this study focuses on the search of the typical learning and cognitive behaviour of each CAL groups during the execution of an experimental learning module developed with this objective.

The purpose of this study is to model the learner's Cognitive Ability Level and integrate it within the learner model in the context of an adaptive learning environment via the Web. This means to investigate and generate a CAL classifier model by identifying the main attributes associated to each CAL classes and to establish an inference mechanism aiming to perform the online learner's CAL diagnostic based in the observation of the learner's LT.

To accomplish our investigation purpose, we have introduced two constructs: CAL and the LT as follows.

The Cognitive Ability Level

Bloom's taxonomy of educational objectives is composed of six categories of cognitive abilities: knowledge, comprehension, application, analysis, synthesis, and evaluation. An educational objective represents the changes that are expected to happen in the learner's behaviour during an educational process. In this taxonomy, the categories lay along a continuum, which goes from the concrete cognitive level (e.g., knowledge) to a more abstract one (e.g., evaluation) in a cumulative and ascendant way related to the abstract levels of thought.

In order to generate the CAL classes of the target population, the Ross Test (Ross & Ross, 1997) was selected. The Ross Test was conceived to measure the abilities pertinent to the upper cognitive abilities referred by Bloom (e.g., analysis, synthesis, and evaluation), in which eight cognitive processes are underlain: analytical reasoning, deductive reasoning, absent premises, abstract relations, sequential synthesis, questioning strategies, relevant and irrelevant analysis of information, and attributes analysis. The test requires the subject to perform a variety of tasks that reflect these abilities. The main emphasis of the

Figure 1. Observable navigational behaviour indicators used for the CAL classification

Learning Trajectory		
Preferences	Processing Velocity	Cognitive Actions

test is on the individuals' abilities to deal with abstractions from a verbal base. The ability to elaborate concepts from abstractions with verbal elements is a major component of the upper cognitive processes.

Therefore, in our study, the CAL represents the high order thinking abilities and the underlying cognitive processes typical of the individuals classified by the Ross Test. It is important to mention that the cognitive abilities refer to organized modes of operation in dealing with materials and problems and do not require specialized and technical information from the learner (Anderson et al., 2001).

The nomenclature and the conceptualization of the CAL classes will be described in the research method.

The Learning Trajectories

The LT construct was conceived aiming to capture and concretely represent the navigational behaviour of each CAL class that reflects the different level of cognitive abilities and processes. The LT is visible through a set of navigational behaviour indicators formed here by the didactic resources and presentation forms preferences, processing velocity, and cognitive actions (Figure 1).

Research Method

Our investigation has proceeded in two phases. The first phase has corresponded to the generation of the CAL classes (or stereotypes) that were used in our study. The second phase has corresponded to the search of the CAL classes' learning trajectories navigational behaviour indicators in an experimental learning module, specifically developed with this objective.

Research Questions

Considering our assumption that the CAL influences the use of different approaches of the new information in a learning process and that the learner's performance is related to how he/she learns, we pose three main research questions, focusing the investigation on the examination of the CAL classes' interactions with the experimental learning module.

1. How does one automate the online learner's cognitive ability level diagnostic, from the observation of his/her learning trajectory?
2. Which parameters better discriminate the CAL classes' learning trajectories?
3. How does one automate the acquisition of the necessary knowledge to diagnose (or classify) the online learner's cognitive ability level?

Design

This study was based in a quasi-experimental research, with quantitative and qualitative analysis and with post-test only (Figure 2).

The CAL was the independent variable. The measures corresponded to the dependent variables outcomes, that is, to the navigational behaviour indicators and the elapsed time as described in Phase 2. The treatment corresponded to the application of the experimental learning module, TDMA, specially developed with this objective.

Figure 2. Research design

Phase 1: The generation of the CAL classes		
Phase 2: The study of the CAL classes' learning trajectories		
Experimental CAL classes: • Analogue-Analytical • Concrete-Generic • Deductive-Evaluative • Analytical-Synthetic-Evaluative • Relational-Synthetic	**Dimensions Assessed**	
	Navigational Behaviour Indicators	Elapsed Time
	Measures	Measures
Phase 3: Analysis		

Phase 1: The Generation of the CAL Classes

In order to outline the learners' profiles, a psychological test, The Ross Test, was selected. The population tested was composed of a sample of 231 employees from the telecommunications company, selected from a target population of 1,121 subjects.

Data collection through Ross Test lasted six months, and collective sessions were composed of a maximum of 10 subjects in each meeting. Each meeting lasted an hour and a half, being divided in two successive sessions (of 45 minutes and 32 minutes, respectively), with a break of 15 minutes between sessions. The setting was accomplished in a room at the company, especially prepared for the application, with artificial illumination, good ventilation, and excellent control of external stimulus. The psychologists trained in the assessment procedure were responsible for the reading of the Ross Test instructions.

Instrument: The Ross Test

The Ross Test consists of 105 questions subdivided in two sections: the first with five parts and the second with three. The subjects are supposed to answer the questions on a separate answer sheet. The maximum time for completion varies from seven to 12 minutes, depending on the part. Figure 3 shows an example of a question that assesses the analogy cognitive process related to the analysis ability.

Figure 3. Example of a Ross Test question

First Session of The Test
Part I – Analogies
Time: 10 minutes
Read each sentence. Think about the relationship between the words and find a word that has the same relation with the underlined one:
Example: "wheat" is for "grow" such as "house" is for:
a.   Place
b.   Build
c.   Grain
d.   Hut
e.   Find
You should choose option (b) "build" because in order to obtain wheat you must make it grow and in order to have a house you must build it.

Analysing Data from the Ross Test

The data analysis was performed in three parts. In the first part, the Ross Test was assessed at three validity levels: (i) from the whole 105 test items (Alpha of Cronbach=0.923); (ii) from the eight cognitive processes (Alpha of Cronbach=0.8429); and (iii) from the three cognitive abilities (Alpha of Cronbach=0.8364). This means that the Ross Test was consistent and trustworthy. In order to validate the Ross Test for the target population, the main adaptation consisted in classifying the individuals according to their performance ranges at different test sections, instead of considering the item number at each section.

In the second part, we proceeded with factorial analysis. The factors analysed were related to the eight cognitive processes and the three abilities assessed by the Ross Test. The analogy cognitive process, which underlies the analysis ability, explained 72.61% of the total variance. The abstract relations and sequential synthesis processes, which underlie the synthesis ability, explained 39.41% and 33.87%, respectively. The deductive reasoning process, which underlies the evaluation, explained 62.97% of the total variance. The processes mentioned in this paragraph were the most predominant factors in each ability assessed. Table 1 shows the factorial analysis results.

Finally, the individuals were grouped in cluster analysis by their performance levels similarities in each cognitive processes and abilities assessed. The statistical analysis has generated five clusters in a range of [0, 5] in the dendrogram. Table 2 shows the analysis results and the CAL classes generated.

Table 1. Factorial analysis: Explaining the cognitive abilities and processes variance

Cognitive abilities	Cognitive Processes
Analysis: (Explains 75,37 % of total variance)	• Analogy (14 items) – 72.61 % • Absent premises (8 items) – 13.17 % • Relevant and irrelevant analysis of information • (15 items) – 14.22 %
Synthesis: (Explains 10,60 % of total variance)	• Abstract relations (14 items) – 39.41 % • Sequential synthesis (10 items) – 33.87 % • Attributes analysis (15 items) – 26.72 %
Evaluation: (Explains 14,03 % of total variance)	• Deductive reasoning (18 items) – 62.97 % • Questioning strategies (12 items) – 37.02 %

Table 2. CAL classes by performance (4-5 superior, 3 medium, 1-2 inferior)

CAL Classes	Subjects	Sample (%)	Psycho Pedagogical Abilities		
			Analysis (73.00%)	Synthesis (10.60%)	Evaluation (14.02%)
Analogue-Analytic	109	47.19	4 or 5	-	-
Concrete-Generic	60	25.97	1 or 2	-	-
Deductive-Evaluative	24	10.39	3	1, 2 or 3	4 or 5
Relational-Synthetic	07	3.03	3	4 or 5	
Analytic-Synthetic-Evaluative	31	13.42	3	1, 2, 3 and 4	1, 2 or 3

Table 2 shows the performance levels in the three cognitive abilities in each CAL. The subjects that were assessed as superior performance level (4 or 5) in analysis ability were classified as analogue-analytical level. The subjects that were assessed as inferior performance level (1 or 2) in analysis ability were classified as concrete-generic level. This could mean that the group tends to work with the whole information and uses less abstraction than the analogue-analytical group. The subjects that were assessed as superior in evaluation ability, medium-inferior in synthesis ability and medium analysis ability were classified as deductive-evaluative level and so on.

The fifth group was very heterogeneous and with no performance similarity in the abilities and cognitive processes assessed by the Ross Test. We hypothesized that the Ross Test was not refined enough to group some subjects according to their performance in the cognitive abilities and processes. Our solution for this problem could be to use another complementary test that would assess the same cognitive aspects. Even so, at that time, aware of this problem, we thought it worthy to investigate these CAL class trajectories in the Web learning session. The goal was to find a common set of learning behaviour indicators associated to this class.

Conceptualising CAL Classes

The CAL classes formed as a result of the statistical analysis represent the predominant cognitive process and correspondent ability in their performance in the Ross Test. Based on the statistical findings and the theoretical fundaments of the Ross Test, the cognitive psychologist has inferred the CAL classes cognitive functioning.

The analogue-analytical CAL class has shown predominance in analogy cognitive process and analysis ability. According to Bloom's taxonomy, this ability refers to the sub-set 4.20—relations analysis—which corresponds to the connections and interactions between elements and parts of the didactic resources. The information is hierarchically split in sub-parts and its relations are explained in order to facilitate the constructing of analogies between these parts by the learner.

The concrete-generic CAL class has shown almost no ability in analogy cognitive process and analysis ability. For that reason, the cognitive psychologist from the research team has supposed that subjects of this class tend to work with the whole information, use memorization strategies, and prefer to learn through linear and sequential browsing of the contents, in slots of concrete examples.

The deductive-evaluation CAL class has shown predominance in deductive reasoning process and evaluation ability. According to Bloom's taxonomy, this ability refers to the sub-set 6.10—judgements in terms of internal evidence— which corresponds to the evaluation of the accuracy of the didactic resources from such evidence as logical accuracy, consistency, and other internal criteria (Anderson et al., 2001, p. 277). Based on that, the cognitive psychologist has inferred that subjects of this class tend to identify the underlying logical patterns of the contents, making exhausting analyses of the coherence, validity and veracity of the data. Learners of this class are systematic and critic when searching new information.

The relational-synthetic CAL class has shown predominance in abstract relations process and synthesis ability. According to Bloom's taxonomy, this ability refers to the sub-set 5.30—derivation of a set of abstract relations—which corresponds to the development of a set of abstract relations either to classify or explain particular data or phenomena, or the deduction of propositions and relations from a set of basic propositions or symbolic representations (Anderson et al., p. 277). Based on this, the cognitive psychologist has inferred that subjects of this class tend to search learning of new information through the reorganization of the sub-parts of the information supplied in a conceptual and synthetic structure.

The analytical-synthetic-evaluative CAL class was grouped in a heterogeneous way and did not present any internal similarity related to the performance in the abilities and underlying cognitive processes, assessed by the Ross Test. But the ASE class's behaviour in the learning module indicated that this class's characteristics are similar to the ones of the AA and DE CAL classes.

Phase 2: The Study of the CAL Classes' Learning Trajectories

Aiming to identify the CAL's trajectories characteristics, we have carried out the investigation of learners while browsing a Web learning session. The CAL classes most representative subjects were measured, after the application of the experimental module, in two dimensions: navigational and temporal. The research has used a quantitative approach in a quasi-experimental post-test only design.

Treatment

The subjects were selected from the 231 classified by the Ross Test. Technicians and engineers, employees of the telecommunications company, and our research partners composed the sample. The selection criterion has corresponded to the more typical subjects of each CAL classes identified in the previous research phase.

Due to circumstantial issues of the company, the sample was formed with 35 subjects arranged in a non-equalitarian way within CAL classes. Predominantly, the mean age was over 40 years old, except for the subjects pertaining to AA CAL class who were around 30 years old. Approximately 50% of the subjects had a high school education level and the rest predominantly had a university degree level. Male subjects formed most of the sample.

The Experimental Learning Module

To investigate the cognitive functioning and pedagogical preferences of the CAL classes we developed the experimental learning module. According to training demands of the telecommunications company, the telecommunications course was chosen to be the first one. The telecommunications course is composed of topics and sub-topics, which present concepts and basic fundaments related to the telecommunications area.

The TDMA sub-topic (time division multiple access) was chosen as experimental instructional material considering that this was the mobile communication technology the company used. The TDMA is a sub-topic of the wireless topic. It was developed assuming that the learners had as pre-requisite a working knowledge on multiplex technology.

The interface of the TDMA sub-topic was developed to prevent the learner's inducement to a particular navigational behaviour. This approach makes possible the investigation about the learners' CAL class preferences and behaviour. Figure 4 shows the initial page of the TDMA, composed of two layers. In the top-left position, there are three buttons corresponding to the didactic resources, presentation forms and final evaluation options. On the other part of the page, there is a layer with didactic resources offered to the learner such as concepts, examples, exercises, and evaluation review. The learner would choose the didactic resources that best suited his/her CAL. After a learner's selection the

Figure 4. The TDMA initial page

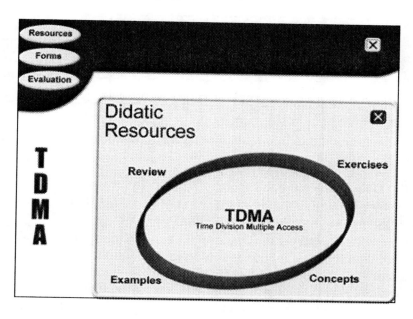

presentation forms are presented using the same graphical interface as the initial page.

The domain content was designed using traditional didactic practices such as: concepts (theoretical presentation), examples, exercises, evaluation review, and final evaluation. For each didactic resource, there is a presentation form set. These presentations include textual, graphical, and schematic forms or a mixture of all these (Figure 5). In a set, each presentation form refers to the same content being explained. The presentation forms varieties make possible for each learner to construct a customized trajectory that best fits the specific CAL.

Collecting Data

The research set was built in a laboratory with seven personal computers at the training centre in the telecommunications company. The purpose was to create a simulated and individualized learning environment on the Web. The psychologists and pedagogue's team supervised the execution of the TDMA by the learners. The learning sessions elapsed for a period of a month and a half. The researchers scheduled the sessions according to the employees' availability.

Figure 5. Didactic resources and presentation forms in the TDMA

Didactic Resources	Concepts	Exercises	Examples
Presentation forms	(101) - Textual only	(201) - True or False	(301) - Textual and figure
	(102) - Textual and figure	(202) - Related columns	(302) - Schematic and figure
	(103) - Schematic and figure	(203) - Simple choice	
		(204) - Fill the blanks	
		(205) - Simple choice and figure	

Before the TDMA execution, the learners were instructed about (i) the purpose of the investigation; (ii) the TDMA characteristics; and (iii) their flexibility to make choices while browsing the instructional material.

All learning environment information was recorded in the application database. The learner Web log was application-dedicated and the learners' interactions were sequentially recorded in a global log file. The log file recorded data/hour of the interaction, learner's identification, and visited Web pages. The learning environment used a client/server model. The client was developed using Web pages and Javascript/PHP tools and the Web server was implemented using Java servlets. The database access used JDBC connection.

A number of issues were considered in pre-processing logged data before the learner navigation patterns and preferences were analysed. These included: (i) cleaning/filtering the raw data to eliminate irrelevant items (i.e., learner menu accesses, connection faults records, and application information pages); (ii) grouping individual page accesses into semantic units (i.e., learner session accesses); (iii) integration of various data sources such as user CAL, age, instructional level, and gender; (iv) transforming alphanumeric codes into numeric; and (v) calculating time spent in each Web page the learner visited.

Variables and Their Measures

The navigational behaviour of the CAL classes was traced by a set of behaviour indicator variables (or dependent variables). These indicators have corre-sponded to the relative frequencies of the Web pages the learner accessed and to the relative elapsed time in those pages, during the execution of the TDMA.

The indicators were formed from the log file information, that is, learner identification, date and time of the access, and the Web page code (e.g., identifications of the didactic resource and presentation form accessed) as showed in Table 3.

Table 3. Indicator variables and their measures

Navigational behaviour indicators	Total of Web pages accessed	1.	Sum of the total pages accessed by the learner.
		2.	Sum of the total "concept" pages accessed by the learner.
		3.	Sum of the total "exercise" pages accessed by the learner.
		4.	Sum of the total "example" pages accessed by the learner.
	Relative frequency of didactic resources accessed	5.	Percentage of "concept" pages accessed related to the total pages accessed by the learner.
		6.	Percentage of "exercise" pages accessed related to the total pages accessed by the learner.
		7.	Percentage of "example" pages accessed related to the total pages accessed by the learner.
	Relative frequency of presentation forms accessed	8.	Percentage of each presentation form of "concept" pages related to the total "concept" pages accessed by the learner.
		9.	Percentage of each presentation form of "exercise" pages related to the total "exercise" pages accessed by the learner.
		10.	Percentage of each presentation form of "example" pages related to the total "example" pages accessed by the learner.
Elapsed time in Web pages indicators	Total elapsed time in web pages	11.	Sum of the total elapsed time in the TDMA.
		12.	Sum of the total elapsed time in the "concept" pages.
		13.	Sum of the total elapsed time in the "exercise" pages.
		14.	Sum of the total elapsed time in the "example" pages.
	Relative elapsed time in didactic resources web pages	15.	Percentage of the elapsed time in the "concept" pages accessed related to the total elapsed time in the TDMA.
		16.	Percentage of the elapsed time in the "exercise" pages accessed related to the total elapsed time in the TDMA.
		17.	Percentage of the elapsed time in the "example" pages accessed related to the total elapsed time in the TDMA.
	Relative elapsed time in presentation forms web pages	18.	Percentage of each presentation form of "concept" pages related to the total elapsed time in the "concept" pages accessed by learner.
		19.	Percentage of each presentation form of "exercise" pages related to the total elapsed time in the "exercise" pages accessed by learner.
		20.	Percentage of each presentation form of "example" pages related to the total elapsed time in the "example" pages accessed by learner.

The relative frequency indicators correspond to how much the learner has preferred a didactic resource and a presentation form available in the TDMA. The relative elapsed time indicators correspond to the processing velocity in a didactic resource and in a presentation form.

Results

Considering that we had no *a priori* assumptions about the typical CAL classes' LTs during a learning session over the Web, we have started our investigation with an exploratory analysis. All the analysis made in this study refers to the learners' interactions with the Web pages of the learning module up to the moment of the first evaluation. Our assumption is that until the first evaluation, the learner is likely more spontaneous and less concerned with his/her performance.

Navigational Preferences and Information Processing Velocity of the CAL Classes

To compare the measures of the CAL classes' behaviour indicators, we have proceeded with the indicators' values categorization. The indicators' values were categorized using two percentile points. The generated categories were labelled as low, medium, and high, corresponding to the intensity level in which the sample population accessed the didactic resources and presentation forms in the TDMA. Tables 4 and 5 summarize the indicators that best discriminate the behaviour patterns of the CAL classes.

The numeric values in Table 4 correspond to the mean relative frequency of didactic resources and presentation forms accessed by each CAL class. For example, considering that the mean of the total didactic resources accessed by the AA CAL class up to the first evaluation was 106, 50.34% of these accesses were of concept Web pages, 30.39% were of exercises Web pages, and 13.02%

Table 4. Summary of the intensity level patterns of didactic resources and presentation forms accessed by CAL classes

CAL classes			AA	CG	DE	ASE	RS
Mean of the total didactic resources up to the first evaluation			106	85	78	77	223
Relative frequencies of didactic resources accessed	Concepts		50.34	39.81	44.07	37.47	32.76
	Exercises		30.39	24.40	34.85	43.48	34.95
	Examples		13.02	28.28	13.16	12.99	28.40
Relative frequencies of presentation forms accessed	Concepts	101	7.49	3.67	6.06	3.84	7.27
		102	28.70	23.52	17.82	22.28	11.87
		103	14.15	12.62	20.18	11.36	13.62
	Exercises	201	2.92	5.59	7.88	7.77	4.27
		202	3.86	2.07	4.56	4.09	5.38
		203	8.55	9.05	5.34	3.23	12.19
		204	2.27	1.70	5.38	7.26	4.76
		205	12.80	6.00	11.68	21.12	8.35
	Examples	301	7.42	18.92	6.42	10.65	20.11
		302	5.59	9.35	6.74	2.34	8.29

☐ Low intensity   ▨ Medium intensity   ■ High intensity

Table 5. Summary of the intensity level patterns of the elapsed time in didactic resources and presentation forms accessed by CAL classes

CAL classes			AA	CG	DE	ASE	RS
Mean elapsed time in the didactic resource up to the first evaluation			1:36:35	1:13:36	1:35:19	1:42:09	2:37:37
Relative frequencies of didactic resources accessed	Concepts		36.37	28.13	31.24	29.34	24.19
	Exercises		27.45	21.12	25.07	34.20	44.42
	Examples		5.94	11.43	6.38	8.08	15.66
Relative frequencies of presentation forms accessed	Concepts	101	7.70	7.56	4.81	5.71	7.86
		102	21.41	13.14	15.75	17.17	9.59
		103	7.26	7.32	10.68	6.45	6.75
	Exercises	201	3.63	5.91	5.58	7.77	5.98
		202	9.20	3.81	7.01	4.09	19.72
		203	6.03	4.86	1.86	3.23	8.12
		204	2.67	3.08	6.11	7.26	6.42
		205	5.93	3.47	4.51	21.12	4.17
	Examples	301	7.42	8.57	3.78	6.83	11.96
		302	5.59	2.86	2.60	1.25	3.71

☐ Low intensity   ▨ Medium intensity   ■ High intensity

were of examples Web pages. This means that, related to the sample, the intensity level of didactic resources accesses by the AA CAL class was high[1] for the concept Web pages, and medium for the exercises and examples Web pages.

The numeric values in Table 5 correspond to the relative frequency of elapsed time in the didactic resources and presentation forms accessed by each CAL class. For example, considering that the mean elapsed time in didactic resources accessed by the AA CAL class up to the first evaluation was 1:36:35, 36.37% of this time was spent on concept Web pages, 27.45% was spent on exercises Web pages, and 5.94% was spent on examples Web pages. This means that, compared to the sample, the mean elapsed time in didactic resources accessed by the AA CAL class was medium[2] for the concept, exercises, and examples Web pages.

Cognitive Actions Patterns

The cognitive actions patterns correspond to the predominant didactic resources sequence chosen by the CAL classes. These patterns were extracted from the observation of the interaction sequences of the CAL classes' subjects. In order to accomplish this we have worked with the statistical mode by using a graphic view from the Excel tool (Figure 6). Figure 7 shows the cognitive action patterns found for each CAL class.

Figure 6. Example of the modal didactic resources in each interaction for the AA CAL Class

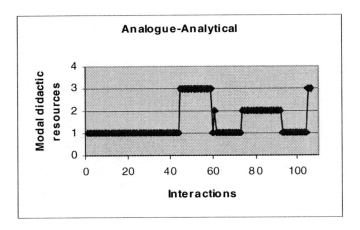

Figure 7. Cognitive actions patterns used by CAL classes

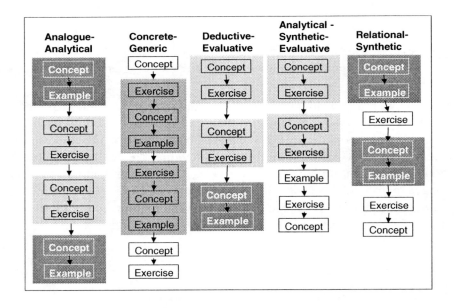

The mean access number (interactions) performed by the AA CAL class up to the first evaluation was 106. The predominant strategies used to approach the new information were the concept-example and concept-exercise sequences. The CG CAL class has performed a mean number of 84 accesses up to the first evaluation. The predominant strategy used was the exercise-concept-example sequence. The DE CAL class has performed a mean number of 77 accesses up to the first evaluation. Its preferable strategy was the concept-exercise sequence.

The ASE CAL class has performed a mean number of 76 accesses up to the first evaluation. As the DE class, the ASE CAL class used the sequence concept-exercise as the predominant strategy. Finally, the RS CAL class has used the sequence concept-example as the predominant strategy.

Research Questions Results

A discussion of the results appears in the context of the three research questions posed earlier. We started answering the research question 2, followed by the research questions 1 and 3.

Research Question 2: Which parameters better discriminate the CAL classes' learning trajectories?

The exploratory analysis allows us to infer a set of hypotheses about the typical CAL classes' learning trajectories as presented here. The hypotheses generated corresponds to the navigational behaviour indicator values that better discriminate the CAL classes.

Analogue-Analytical Class:

- Predominant cognitive actions patterns: concept-example and concept-exercise
- Use intensity of the concept didactic resource is high
- Use intensity of the textual presentation forms of concept is high

Concrete-Generic Class:

- Predominant cognitive actions pattern: exercise-concept-example
- Use intensity of the exercise didactic resource is low
- Use intensity of the example didactic resource is high
- Use intensity of the presentation forms of example is high

Deductive-Evaluative Class:

- Predominant cognitive actions pattern: concept-exercise
- Use intensity of the concept didactic resource is medium
- Use intensity of the schema and figure presentation form of concept is high
- Use intensity of the exercise didactic resource is medium
- Use intensity of the example didactic resource is medium
- Elapsed time intensity in the schema and figure presentation form of concept is high

Analytical-Synthetic-Evaluative Class:

- Predominant cognitive actions pattern: concept-exercise
- Use intensity of the exercise didactic resource is high
- Elapsed time intensity in the true or false and simple choice and figure presentation form of exercise pages is high

Relational-Synthetic Class:

- Predominant cognitive actions pattern: concept-example
- Use intensity of the concept didactic resource is low
- Use intensity of the exercise didactic resource is medium
- Use intensity of the example didactic resource is high

Research Question 1: How does one automate the online learner's cognitive ability level diagnostic?

As mentioned before, the task corresponding to the online learner's cognitive style diagnostic is a typical classification task. Schreiber et al. (2000, p. 125) describe a classification task as the "necessity to characterize an object (in our case the remote learner) in terms of the class to which it belongs (in our case CAL class). The underlying knowledge typically provides for each class constraints on the values of the object features (in our case learning trajectory's indicators variables or parameters)."

The typical CAL classes features stated when answering Research Question 2 enable us to identify the required knowledge components to be used in performing the classification task, that is, enable us to describe the corresponding knowledge model in an implementation-independent way.

However, our findings were not conclusive, and the hypothesis must be tested. Instead of presenting a learner CAL model, we propose a framework to test the hypothesis. The framework will take into consideration the instructional design aligned with the CAL and LT constructs. We will develop the instructional design based on Anderson et al.'s (2001) approach. The instructional design aligns educational objectives, instruction, and assessment. The alignment refers to the degree of correspondence among them in the taxonomy table. The taxonomy two-dimensional table represents the categories of knowledge (factual, conceptual, procedural, and metacognitive) and cognitive processes (remember, understand, apply, analyse, evaluate, and create).

Actually, Anderson et al. (2001) have reformulated the original Bloom's Taxonomy using cognitive process in place of behaviour and knowledge in the place of content. In our study, the LT is the concrete visualization of the CAL behaviour, what enable us to classify the learner's cognitive ability level based on the observation of his/her LT when interacting with the instructional material.

Research Question 3: How does one automate the acquisition of the necessary knowledge to diagnose (classify) the online learner's cognitive ability level, from the observation of his/her learning trajectory?

In knowledge systems, the knowledge required to implement some knowledge task (e.g., classification, diagnose, assessment, etc., as stated by Schreiber et al., 2000) can be obtained from the specialist or from an artificial agent that learns from the experience. Considering the former possibility, the specialist provides the necessary information to perform the task based on an established knowledge domain. About the latter one, Russell and Norvig (1995) state that: "whenever the knowledge system designer has incomplete knowledge of the environment, machine learning (ML) is the only way that an artificial agent can acquire what it needs to know ..." (p. 523).

Considering that we had no *a priori* knowledge about the CAL typical learning trajectories required to model the learner's CAL, we started the study through the manual exploratory analysis. This study enabled us to have a minimal knowledge required to carry on the learner's CAL modeling. Nevertheless, the manual analysis is very time consuming and limited to the current data available. In order to avoid these constraints, ML techniques have been used successfully in many applications, especially through the inductive learning paradigm (Batista, 2003).

Up to now, we have just glimpsed a solution to this third question using the supervised learning algorithms, as the ones presented by Michie, Spiegelhalter, and Taylor (1994).

From this point, our work must proceed by collecting more labelled examples, that is submit to the experimental learning module a more substantial number of subjects that had their CAL identified by the Ross Test aiming to make possible the successful application of these supervised learning algorithms.

Conclusions and Future Trends

In this chapter we have presented the methodology used to achieve the modeling of the learner's cognitive ability level. The methodology encompasses two main phases: (i) the generation of the CAL classes to the target population and (ii) the study of the CAL classes' learning trajectories. The experimental Web-learning environment was developed aiming to provide the learner with a set of varied didactic resources and presentation forms.

In our investigation, we had a specific goal: to model the learner's CAL characteristic for the target population from a telecommunications company (technicians and engineers) expecting to adapt the instruction to this characteristic. Our main interest was to investigate how he/she learns through his/her behavior, instead of investigating what the learner has learned.

Our major contribution is related to the knowledge acquired about how the CAL classes learn on the Web. As a result we have identified the CAL classes' parameters that better discriminate them from the observation and analysis of their learning trajectory. All the knowledge obtained from this investigation will make it possible to automate the learners' CAL diagnostic. It will also give us the background to develop Web-learning environment contents.

We do believe that the knowledge acquired will enable us to advance towards an adaptive Web-learning environment that supports the educators, in real time, on their hard and time consuming task of thoroughly track and assess all the activities performed by all learners. On the other hand, considering the benefits to the remote learner, the adaptation of the instruction to the learner CAL will encourage his/her cognitive development in in-depth learning.

The next stage of the research is the development of the instructional design as observed in the prior section (Research Questions Results) and the implementation of a full operational module over the web to confirm, or not, the hypothesis generated from our investigation. This development is under construction in the AdaptWeb[3] Project (Freitas, 2002).

References

Anderson, L. W., Krathwohl, D. R., Airasian, P. W., Cruikshand, K. A., Mayer, R. E., Pintrich, P. R., et al. (2001). *A taxonomy for learning, teaching, and assessing: A revision of Bloom's taxonomy of educational objectives*. New York: Longman.

Batista, G. E. A. P. (2003). *Data pre-processing in supervised learning machine*. [Pre processamento de dados em aprendizado de máquina supervisionado]. Unpublished Doctoral Dissertation, São Paulo University, São Paulo, Brazil: ICMC – USP.

Bloom, B. (1972). *Taxonomy of the educational objectives – cognitive domain* [Taxonomia dos Objetivos Educacionais]. Porto Alegre, Brazil: Editora Globo.

Brusilovsky, P. (1995). Methods and techniques of adaptive hypermedia. In P. Brusilovsky et al. (Eds.), *Adaptive hypertext and hypermedia* (pp. 1-43). The Netherlands: Kluwer Academic Publishers.

Felder, R.M., & Silverman, L.K. (1988). Learning and teaching styles in engineering education. *Journal of Engineering Education, 78*(7), 674-681.

Ford, N., & Chen, S.Y. (2000). Individual differences, hypermedia navigation, and learning: An empirical study. *Journal of Educational Multimedia and Hypermedia, 9*(4), 281-311.

Freitas, V., Marçal, V. P., Gasparini, I., Amaral, M. A., Proença Jr., L. M., Brunetto, M. A., et al. (2002, November). AdaptWeb: An adaptive Web-based courseware. In *Proceeding of ICTE - International Conference on Information and Communication Technologies in Education* (pp. 20-23). Badajoz.

Martinez, M., & Bunderson, V. (2000). Building interactive World Wide Web (Web) learning environments to match and support individual learning differences. *Journal of Interactive Learning Research, 11*(3), 163-195.

McManus, T.F. (2000). Individualizing instruction in a Web-based hypermedia-learning environment: No linearity, advance organizers, and self-regulated learners. *Journal of Interactive Learning Research, 11*(3), 219-251.

Michie, D., Spiegelhalter, D.J., & Taylor, C.C. (1994). *Machine learning, neural and statistical classification*. New York: Ellis Horwood.

Papanikolaou, K. A., Grigoriadou, M., Kornilakis, H., & Magoulas, G. D. (2003). Personalising the interaction in a Web-based Educational hypermedia system: The case of INSPIRE. *User-Modeling and User-Adapted Interaction, 13*(3), 213-267.

Reed, W. M., & Oughton, J. M. (1997). Computer experience and interval based hypermedia navigation. *Journal of Research on Computing in Education, 30*(1), 38-52.

Riding, R., & Cheema, I. (1991). Cognitive styles: An overview and integration. *Educational Psychology, 11*(3-4), 193-215.

Riding, R., & Rayner, S. (2000). *Cognitive styles and learning strategies – Understanding style differences in learning and behavior.* London: David Fulton Publishers.

Ross, J. D., & Ross, C. M. (1997). *Ross Test of cognitive processes* [Teste Ross dos Processos Cognitivos]. São Paulo, Brazil: Instituto Pieron de Psicologia Aplicada.

Russell, S., & Norvig, P. (1995). *Artificial intelligence: A modern approach.* NJ: Prentice-Hall.

Schreiber, A., Akkermans, H., Anjewierden, A., Hoog, R., Shadbolt, N., Van de Velde, W., et al. (2000). *Knowledge engineering and management: The common KADS methodology.* Massachusetts Institute of Technology.

Soldato, T., & Boulay, B. (1995) Implementation of motivational tactics in tutoring systems. *Journal of Artificial Intelligence in Education, 6*(4), 337-378.

Stern, M. K., & Woolf, B. P. (2000). Adaptive content in an online lecture system. In P. Brusilovsky, O. Stock, & C. Strapparava (Eds.), *Adaptive hypermedia and adaptive Web-based systems* (pp. 225-238). Berlin: Springer-Verlag.

Triantafillou, E., Pomportsis, A., & Demetriadis, S. (2003). The design and the formative evaluation of an adaptive educational system based on cognitive styles. *Computers & Education, 41*(1), 87-103.

Endnotes

[1]   To the sample, the intensity level of the mean didactic resources accesses range values corresponded to: (1) in using concept: *low:* up to 32 percent; *medium:* 32% to 50%; *high:* more than 50%; (2) in using exercise: *low:* up to 24%; *medium:* 24% to 40%; *high:* more than 40%; (3) in using example: *low:* up to 2%; *medium:* 2% to 25%; *high:* more than 25%.

[2]   To the sample, the intensity level of the mean elapsed time in didactic resources accesses range values corresponded to: (1) in using concept: *low:* up to 24%; *medium:* 24% to 39%; *high:* more than 39%; (2) in using

exercise: *low:* up to 21%; *medium:* 21% to 33%; *high:* more than 33%; (3) in using example: *low:* up to 2%; *medium:* 2% to 11%; *high:* more than 11%.

[3]   Homepage http://www.inf.ufrgs.br/~tapejara/adaptweb.

Chapter III

Dominant Meaning Approach Towards Individualized Web Search for Learning Environments

Mohammed A. Razek, El-Azhar University, Cairo, Egypt

Claude Frasson, University of Montreal, Canada

Marc Kaltenbach, University of Montreal, Canada

Abstract

This chapter describes how we can use dominant meaning to improve a Web-based learning environment. For sound adaptive hypermedia systems, we need updated knowledge bases from many kinds of resource (alternative explanations, examples, exercises, images, applets, etc.). The large amount of information available on the Web can play a prominent role in building these knowledge bases. Using the Internet without search engines to find specific information is like wandering aimlessly in the ocean and trying to catch a specific fish. It is obvious, however, that search engines are not intended to adapt to individual performance. Our new technique, based on dominant meaning, is used to individualize a query and search result. By dominant meaning, we refer to a set of keywords that best fits an intended meaning of the target word. Our experiments show that the dominant meanings approach greatly improves retrieval effectiveness.

Introduction

The main goal of Web-Based Adaptive Tutoring Systems (WBATS) is to adapt information to the particular needs of individual learners. To meet their needs, we must enrich their knowledge bases with information from many resources. We exploit the huge amount of Web information to build a system of this kind. Finding the right information at the right time, however, is a very time-consuming task; Web search engines present thousands of results, almost half of which are inappropriate (Pretschner & Gauch, 1999). Modern search engines attempt to take into consideration the structure of every document and set of words included within a Web document, but a semantic Web technique would find the meaning of each document (Berners-Lee, Hendler, & Lassila, 2001). Based on ontological terms, the content of each document would be meaningful. Note that the term user is often interchanged in this chapter with the term learner.

Individualization is one of the most powerful mechanisms for the semantic Web. Individualization and personalization are intimately related to each other. Researchers use them to customize the subject according to user interests. To be precise, they do so as a way of sharing information that satisfies the needs of individual users. Therefore, we can define Web individualization as "the process of adapting the topic and construction of a Web site to the individual needs of each user, taking advantage of the knowledge gained from his or her own behaviours and interests" (Eirinaki & Vazirgiannis, 2003). The goal of a Web individualization system is to "provide users with the information they want or need, without expecting them to ask for it explicitly" (Mulvenna, Anand, & Buchner, 2000).

In this sense, this chapter deals with a new technique, called dominant meanings (Razek, Frasson, & Kaltenbach, 2003d) and how it can be used to make individualized Web searches. How does it influence search results? The dominant meanings definition is known as "the set of keywords that best fit an intended meaning of a target word" (Razek, Frasson, & Kaltenbach, 2003a). This technique sees a query as a target meaning plus some words that fall within the range of that meaning. It freezes the target meaning, which is called a master word, and adds or removes some slave words, which clarify the target meaning.

For example, suppose that the query is "Java." The word "Java" has three well-known meanings: Java (computer program language), Java (coffee), and Java (Island). We use the learner's context of interest and domain knowledge to individualize the context of this target word. We do that by looking for keywords in the user profile (the learner's context of interest) to help in specifying the intending meaning. Because the target meaning is "computer program language", we look for slave words in the user profile that best fit this specific meaning—words such as "computer", "program", "awt", "application", and "swing".

In a major part of this chapter, we will try to solve answer the following problems: how to construct a method that allows us to find the dominant meanings from a document collection, how to select an intended meaning, and how select additional slave words. In short, we need to find a way of constructing this context and then using it to expand the query. We claim that individualizing the context of a search can significantly improve the results. Our idea is to represent the collection as a hierarchy of concepts. Each concept consists of some dominant meanings. And each dominant meaning is linked with a text fragment that defines it (Razek, Frasson, & Kaltenbach, 2003c). The more any query consists of dominant meaning, the more closely it is related to its search context.

For ranking documents, we have designed a semantic measure. This is what we call a "dominant meaning distance method." The measure estimates distance between the original query and the collection of retrieved documents based on existing sets of dominant meaning.

We have applied this technique to a learning environment. Our confidence intelligent tutoring system (CITS) (Razek et al., 2002c) has been developed to provide a cooperative intelligent distance learning environment for a community of learners to improve online discussions. To be adaptive and dynamic, this CITS searches the Web and collects documents related to every concept. The context-based information agent (CBIA) (Razek et al., 2003d) is presented as a case study. On the one hand, it takes advantage of discussions during a cooperative learning session to individualize a query. It can observe conversation, interpret inputs from learners, and then specify the current context. The agent would adapt its behavior accordingly, build a new query, and originate the search. On the other hand, this CBIA filters, organizes, and presents information that is immediately useful to the learners. We claim that making the context more specific can significantly improve search results. The agent specifies a context based on a learner's context of interest (Brown & Jones, 2002) and domain knowledge. Moreover, it helps establish what we call the "dominant meaning" of a query. Achieving this requires an accurate representation of the context of whatever domain knowledge is being taught. We will present the results of experiments conducted to compare the dominant-meaning approach with the approaches of existing search engines. However, a prototype application has been designed to help in building an intelligent distance learning environment; it can be used as domain-independent.

This chapter is organized as follows: the next section discusses several ways of improving Web search engines: query expansion, user profiling, and context query. Then, given a document collection and its concept, we present a method that allows constructing dominant meanings of each concept. That section also offers an answer the challenge of a dominant meaning representation. This representation enables us to specify queries that are best related to the search context. In a subsection, we present a way to extract the query's intended meaning and shed light on this measure and how to apply it. In the subsequent sections, we describe the CBIA as a real case study and present future trends and research issues. Finally, we present the conclusions.

Methods for Improving the Context of Search Results

Actually, we can retrieve relevant information if the search query takes into consideration individual user interests. A great deal of work has been done on improving the context of Web search results, query expansion, user profiling, and context queries.

Query Expansion

Before 1960, there were some attempts to expand initial requests based on statistical evidences (Spa, 1991). Afterwards, a great deal of work was done on expanding and modifying queries based on term co-occurrences data. Lesk (1969), Sparck-Jones and Barber (1971), and Minker, Wilson, and Zimmerman (1972) used the similarities between terms to expand queries by adding all the terms of those classes that contain query terms. More recently, some researchers have used automatic query expansion to enhance search results (Efthimiadis & Biron, 1994). As a result, Hang (Hang, Ji-Rong, Jian-Yun, & Wei-Ying, 2002) has proposed other methods, which depend on the analyses of learner logs. Hang's methods create probabilities of correlations between terms in queries and the retrieved documents that are mined from learner logs. This method has an obvious problem: if the clicked documents have words unrelated to the search context, the documents retrieved using the expanded query will be inadequate.

Suppose that the query is about the Java programming language, for instance, and the expanded query contains words such as "swing", "API", "applet", and so on. If a clicked document includes a high probability of correlation for the word "swing", it will be signed as relevant. But this document is irrelevant, in fact, because the document's main topic is the swing function and its properties in Java rather than the Java programming language.

As a result, we can say that query expansion cannot guarantee the delivery of information according to each user's interests. Moreover, it expands queries in the same way for every user. But user profiling can guarantee the intended meaning of a user's query and then help in retrieving prominent information.

User Profiling

Researchers use various ways to improve search results from Web queries. One way is to identify which information is available for improving the process of individualization. They do that by profiling user behaviour in order to predict user interests. We think that the better the user profiling, the better the personalized system. There are two types of profiling (Abramowicz, Kalazynski, & Wecel, 1999): subject-based profiling (SBP) and object-based profiling (OBP). SBP is the profile of a user with access to several objects. OBP is the profile of an object accessed by many users. The latter is equivalent to the idea of collaborative filtering (Pazzani, 1999).

Persona (Tanudjaja & Mui, 2002) depends on existing theory with regard to personalized searches and models user interest with an interactive query scheme, Web taxonomy provided by the open directory project. The open directory project provides one way to define the meaning of a query: building the taxonomy of words. Persona is based on user relevance feedback. Each positive and negative feedback has two functions. First, it refines the set of searches and re-ranks the results. Second, it builds the user's profile.

Scime and Kerschberg (2001) have developed the WebSift system. One mechanism allows a user to define the information needed as ontology of search keywords. This personal ontology is complemented with a standard thesaurus to accommodate possible differences between the user's terminology and the search engine's keywords.

Context Queries

For good primary retrieval, we need to specify queries that are closely related to search contexts. In fact, we need to find a way of constructing this context and then using it to expand the query. Using the context of interest (Brown & Jones, 2002) and the context surrounding a user-selected phrase (Finkelstein, Gabrilovich, Matias, Rivlin, Solan, Wolfman, & Ruppin, 2002); researchers have already studied several aspects of information interests.

IntelliZap (Finkelstein et al., 2002) is based on the client-server paradigm: a client application running on a user's computer extracts the context around text that has been highlighted by the user. Server-based algorithms analyze the context, selecting the most important words, and then prepare augmented queries for later searches. But a problem can occur when the content surrounding the marked query is not specific enough to specify any of the query's contexts.

SearchPad (Bharat, 2000) is an agent that explains the context as a set of previous information requests that have been produced by a user. This system works collaboratively with result documents and maintains relations between queries and links that are considered useful. SearchPad maintains these relations as its search context.

The similarity between two terms was measured by the Salton and McGill cosine formula (Salton & Mcgill, 1983). Using that measure, a term-by-term similarity matrix was produced, where each cell represented the similarity value between two terms.

The main difference between these systems and the CBIA is that only the latter analyzes the context of dominant meanings in text that has been typed by learners. Using the knowledge base of its domain knowledge, it can build a new Web searcher.

We suggest a measure called dominant meaning distance. This focuses on the query's main topic and dominant meaning. A query is supposed to look for its dominant meanings in a document (Gale, Kenneth, & Yarowsky, 1992) rather than for its keywords. We represent this in the form of a meaning vector.

The closeness of a query and a document is indicated by a value of the dominant meaning probability between them. In the next section, we discuss the dominant meaning technique.

Roles of the Dominant Meaning Technique

User profiling can help us to identify the intended meaning of a query, but it might not include enough slave words to formulate a precise query. Some researchers overcome this problem by using word taxonomies. Examples include the

Wordnet project at Princeton University, which is an online lexical reference system (one that organizes English words into synonym sets), the open directory project, and the Magellan hierarchy. These systems adopt user points of view to classify the contents of documents. Moreover, OBIWAN (Chaffee & Gauch, 2000) classifies the Web pages of a site by using a reference ontology based on that of Lycos (1999).

To specify the main concept of a current query, three questions must be answered: How can we construct a dominant meaning for each word? How can the system decide which intended meaning to choose? And how can it select words that must be added to the original query? The following subsections answer these questions in detail.

Constructing Dominant Meanings

In general, suppose that C is the fixed finite set of categories organized in a concept hierarchy and a given documents collection is pre-classified under the categories of C. The documents collection is a dynamic collection; therefore, we can add or delete some documents. However, if a new document enters the collection, we have to define its corresponding class in advance. To exemplify the classification problem, suppose that the collection consists of m concepts, that is, $C = \{C_k\}_{i=1}^m$. Given the finite set of documents for each concept, we try to represent the collection as a hierarchy of dominant meanings.

In this definition, each concept is represented by a finite set of documents $C_k = \{D_v^k \mid v = 1,...,r_k\}$. The question now is how can we use those documents to construct dominant meanings of the corresponding concept? In other words, those documents include some words that almost come with the corresponding concept. The challenge is how to determine those words. Actually, the more those documents are related to its domain knowledge, the more any concept consists of dominant meanings.

Each document is represented by a finite set of words $D_v^k = \{w_{jv}^k \mid j = 1,...,n_v\}$.

The w_{jv}^k's represent the frequency of word w_j occurs in document D_v^k which belongs to concept C_k. This frequency is computed as the number of times that the w_j occurs in the D_v^k. Stop words are those that occur commonly but are too general—such as "the", "an", "a", "to", and so on. Those words were developed as a list and removed from the collection. Sometimes, it is useful to search for words with similar stems, despite their specific endings. If your query is about the effects of cigarette smoking, for example, you might to find not only smoking but also smoke and smokers.

Our goal is to choose the top-T words which can represent the dominant meanings of concept C_k. To do that, we proceed as follows. Suppose that word w_c^k symbolizes concept C_k.

- Calculate the values of

$$w_{jv}^k \quad \forall j, v$$

- Suppose that C_{kv} is the frequency of concept C_k, which appears in document

$$D_v^k, \text{ where } v=1,\dots,r_k. \tag{1}$$

- Calculate the maximum value of $C_{kv} \ \forall v$,

$$F_c^k = \underset{v=1,\dots,r_k}{Max} \{C_{kv}\} \tag{2}$$

- Calculate the maximum value of $w_{jv}^k \ \forall j, v$,

$$F_{w_j}^k = \underset{v=1,\dots,r_k}{Max} \{w_{jv}^k\}, \text{ where } v=1,\dots,r_k \tag{3}$$

- Choose F_c^k, which satisfies $0 \le F_{w_j}^k \le F_c^k$
- Finally, consider the dominant meaning probability:

$$P_{kj} = P_{kj}(w_j \mid C_k) = \frac{1}{r_k} \left[\sum_{v=1}^{r_k} \frac{w_{jv}^k}{F_c^k} \right], \ j=1,\dots,n_v, \ k=1,\dots,m \tag{4}$$

So we divide w_{jv}^k by the maximum value F_c^k of the frequency of C_k, and then we normalize the results by dividing by the number of documents r_k in collection C_k. Based on formula (3), we clearly have $0 \le P_{kj}(w_j \mid C_k) \le 1$.

For each concept C_k, we rank the terms of collection $\{P_{k1}, P_{k2}, ..., P_{km}\}$ in decreasing order according to formula (4). As a result, the dominant meanings of the concept C_k can be represented by the set of words that corresponds to the set $\{P_{k1}, P_{k2}, ..., P_{kT}\}$; that is, $C_k = \{w_1^k, w_2^k, ..., w_T^k\}$, as shown in Figure 1.

For example, suppose that we are given a data structure collection containing six documents. Every two documents represent one of the following three concepts: *list*, *stack*, and *queue*. Therefore, to extract the most frequent words, we first remove all the non-significant words using an appropriate stop-words list such as Brown Corpus which uses 425 stop-words (Frakes & Baeza-Yates, 1992). Using formulas (1) to (4), we then compute the dominant meaning distance between a word in a query and its dominant meaning in a document. This enables us to evaluate dominant meaning probabilities for the master and slave words.

In this example, we can see that $k=1$, $m=3$, $r_1=2$, and $n_2=4$. The master word *list* appears 15 and 20 times in documents D_1^1 and D_2^1 respectively. Therefore, the second value (20) will be chosen as a maximum value. The slave words head, length, array-based, and linked weigh more than the others, because they have been chosen as the most frequent words.

The weight associated with each word in the list row indicates the dominant meaning probability of that word in the collection. It is evaluated as follows:

$$P_{11} = P_{11}(w_1 \mid C_1) = \frac{1}{2}\left[\sum_{v=1}^{2} \frac{w_{1v}^1}{F_c^1}\right] = \frac{1}{2}\left[\frac{w_{11}^1}{20} + \frac{w_{12}^1}{20}\right] = \frac{1}{2}\left[\frac{12}{20} + \frac{19}{20}\right] = \frac{31}{40},$$

$$P_{12} = P_{12}(w_2 \mid C_1) = \frac{1}{2}\left[\sum_{v=1}^{2} \frac{w_{2v}^1}{F_c^1}\right] = \frac{1}{2}\left[\frac{w_{21}^1}{20} + \frac{w_{22}^1}{20}\right] = \frac{1}{2}\left[\frac{14}{20} + \frac{15}{20}\right] = \frac{29}{40},$$

Table 1. An example for the master word list

	Master $C_{1v} =$ List, $k = 1$	Slave $w_{1v}^1 =$ Head	Slave $w_{2v}^1 =$ Length	Slave $w_{3v}^1 =$ Array-Based	Slave $w_{4v}^1 =$ Array-Based
Frequencies of D_1^1, $v = 1$	15	12	14	11	9
Frequencies of D_2^1, $v = 1$	20	19	15	17	11
Max. of C_{kv}	$F_c^1 = 20$	19	15	17	11
the dominant meaning probability	//	$P_{11} = \frac{31}{40}$	$P_{12} = \frac{29}{40}$	$P_{13} = \frac{28}{40}$	$P_{14} = \frac{20}{40}$

$$P_{13} = P_{13}(w_3 \mid C_1) = \frac{1}{2}\left[\sum_{v=1}^{2}\frac{w_{3v}^1}{F_c^1}\right] = \frac{1}{2}\left[\frac{w_{31}^1}{20} + \frac{w_{32}^1}{20}\right] = \frac{1}{2}\left[\frac{11}{20} + \frac{17}{20}\right] = \frac{28}{40},$$

$$P_{14} = P_{14}(w_4 \mid C_1) = \frac{1}{2}\left[\sum_{v=1}^{2}\frac{w_{4v}^1}{F_c^1}\right] = \frac{1}{2}\left[\frac{w_{41}}{20} + \frac{w_{42}}{20}\right] = \frac{1}{2}\left[\frac{9}{20} + \frac{11}{20}\right] = \frac{20}{40}.$$

We use the same method to compute the dominant meaning probabilities of both stack and queue.

Representing Dominant Meanings

The most important point of this chapter is that it shows how we can construct an efficient way to organize every C_k so that it can be stored and retrieved quickly. We have defined a graph, which performs the fundamental operations of storing words, finding them, and removing them from this graph. First, we need to describe the construction of a graph. To that end, we introduce a new notion: the dominant meaning graph (DMG). This represents the dominant meanings of all concepts. Our DMG is different from conceptual graphs (CGs) (Luger, 2002), which are labeled as graphs in which "concept" nodes are connected by "relation" nodes.

The proposed graph consists of a set of nodes and a set of edges. Nodes represent dominant meaning words for each concept C_k, as shown in Figure 1. To distinguish the words in each concept, we suppose that each concept is represented as follows: $C_k = \{w_1^k, w_2^k, ..., w_T^k\}$ $\forall k = 1, ..., m$. The main collection C is designed as the end node. Each edge has a non-negative weight P_{ij}, where P_{ij} represents the dominant meaning distance between words w_i and w_j according to the formulas (1) and (4) as follows: $P_{ij} = P_{kj}(w_i \mid w_j)$.

Dynamic changes in learner knowledge during a session lead to the DMG continually changing the graph's nodes and edges. This makes it very hard to find a specific node. Our new method gives us an advantage in exploring the problem. The DMG is not a free tree but a graph. Its shape is defined as follows:

- The root represents a target word (whole concept).
- The first children represent concepts, and each node is represented by only one word.

Figure 1. Dominant meaning graph (DMG) for representing the dominant meanings

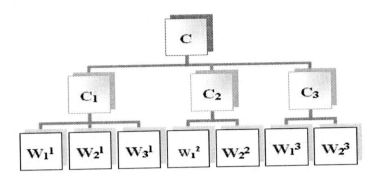

- Every internal node has one or more children.
- All edges of children connected to their parents are stored in decreasing order from left to right; the value of the left sibling's edge is greater than that of the right sibling, that is, $P_{j+1,k} > P_{j,k}$, $\forall j$, $k \geq 0$.
- The values of nodes and edges adapt dynamically because of a machine learning approach.
- All external nodes, except roots, are at the same level in the graph.

For example, Figure 2 shows the representation of the above example, using the dominant meaning approach. The hierarchy has three top-level categories list, stack, and queue. It has from four to five subcategories within each: list/head, list/length, list/array-based, list/linked, stack/array-based, stack/linked, and so on. In this model, the word list would be very discriminating at the first level. At the third level, more specialized dominant meanings could be used as features within the second list category. The same features could be used by more than one category. Array-based might be a useful feature (dominant meaning) for categories such as list/array-based, stack/array-based, and queue/array-based. But each feature might have one or more definitions. These definitions are associated with features by a link to one document in the knowledge base.

In the next subsection, we explain how to extract the main concept of any discussion through a learning session.

Figure 2. An example of a hierarchical representation for data structure collection example

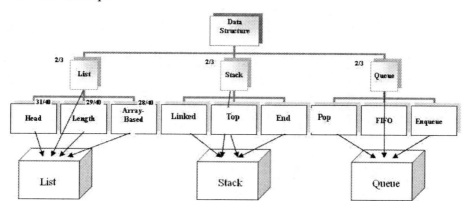

Extracting the Intended Meaning

We believe that the DMG can be used to extract the concept of any discussion. Suppose that two learners open a session about a specific concept.

The CBIA extracts some words through disscusion, say $E = \{w_2^2, w_3^1, w_2^3\}$. The problem is to find which concept properly represents these words. In other words, we need to find the best subset, C_k, one that belongs to whole concept c and contains most of the elements in E. It is obvious that traversing the DMG is an important problem and must therefore be taken into account.

Researchers have used many techniques to traverse the graph (Luger, 2002). For a large problem space, the graph's nodes must be searched in an organized way. Starting from a specific state (node) and moving toward a specific goal could solve the problem. We can use a depth-first search (DFS), a breadth-first search (BFS), and a best-first-search (Russel & Norvig, 2003).

To do so, we use the hill climbing search algorithm with some modifications. It uses search list to keep track of the current fringe and maintain states. It chooses node "C" as a starting point. We mark this node to show that it has been visited. The search list applies a heuristic evaluation to the edges. This is represented by the value of $P_{i,j}$, where P_{ij} represents the dominant meaning distance between words w_i and w_j.

Initially, the search list consists of the generated children that we intend to consider during the search. Suppose that we search for a child from the search list. After being opened, it can be expanded and removed. The proposed algorithm ends when a requested word is extracted from the search list (success), when we try to extract a child while it is empty (failure), or, in some cases, or when we generate a goal state (success). The input of our traverse algorithm is requested word w_r, and the output would be requested concept C_γ. The pseudocode for this algorithm search is as follows:

TRAVERS EDMG (Requested word w_r)

1.   *Put Search* List= [Starting point].
2.   *If* Starting point = w_r *then* C_r = Starting point,
         exit successfully and **return** C_r ;
3.   *While* Search List $\neq$ [ ] do begin
    1.   **Remove** the leftmost state from Search List, call it X.
    2.   *If* X = w_r *then* C_r = paraent (X), **exit** successfully and **return** C_r .
    3.   *If not* begin
        1.   **Generate** children and edges of X.
        2.   *For each* children of X
            1.   Calculate the edge heuristic value $H(E_i)=P_{i,j}$.
            2.   Sort children related to $H(E_i)$ as decreasing order.
            3.   Add sorted children to Front of Search List.
4.   If the goal has been found, announce success and return C_r .

Consider this algorithm of the directed graph in Figure 2. At each step, it removes the first element from the search list. If it meets the requested word, the algorithm returns to its parents (which led to the concept). If the first element is not a requested word, the algorithm generates its children and then applies heuristic evaluation $P_{i,j}$ to its edges. These states (children) are sorted in decreasing order according to heuristic values before being inserted at the top of the search list. This brings the best state to the front of the search list. For example, if we used this algorithm to look for the main concept of a set of words, $E = \{w_2^2, w_3^1, w_2^3\}$, we would get the set of corresponding concepts as $\{C_1, C_2, C_3, C_2\}$. We observe that concept C_2 is repeated twice; therefore, it will be considered the main concept. As a result, the dominant meaning vector of concept C_2 is represented as $V(C_2, w_1^2, w_2^2, ..., w_T^2)$.

Creating User Profiling

The main reasons for profiling in individualizing a Web search are to help identify user interests and to infer their intentions for new queries. We represent a user profile as a set of concepts (master words). A set of keywords (slave words) is joined with weights to each concept. These weights are computed according to the dominant meaning distance between the slave word and its master word as shown in formula (4). Therefore, the weight of a term in a concept reflects its significance in representing the user's interest in that concept.

This is currently done with the user concepts that represent their interests. Our approach allows learners to select their concepts. After that, it takes advantage of domain knowledge construction (as shown later in this section) to map these concepts along with their dominant meanings in relation to the user profile. This approach updates the user profile for every new query by mapping the dominant meaning of every new query's concept.

For example, as shown in Figure 3, suppose that the slave word array-based has a higher weight in the concept stack than the concept list. In the user's next query, therefore, the rate of the word array-based has a tendency to show that the master word stack is interesting.

Re-Ranking Results

Our proposed probability definition should improve retrieval effectiveness by imposing some constraints on submitted queries and retrieved documents. Following the example above, the query constructed by our proposed algorithm is represented as dominant-meaning vector $V(C_2, w_1^2, w_2^2, ..., w_T^2)$. In general, we suppose that the query is $V(C_h, w_1^h, w_2^h, ..., w_T^h)$, and the stream of Web documents is $\{D_s\}_{s=1}^{s=q}$. Based on the dominant meaning probability discussed later in this chapter, we compute the relevance of document D_s with respect to concept C_h, as follows:

$$P(C_h \mid D_s) = \frac{1}{T}\left[\frac{F(C_h \mid D_s)}{F_c^h} + \sum_{j=1}^{j=T}\frac{F(w_j^h \mid D_s)}{F_c^h}\right] \tag{5}$$

where, $\forall j=1,...,T \ \forall s=1,...,q$, and $F_c^h = \max_{s=1,...,q}\{F(C_h \mid D_s)\} > F(w_j^h \mid D_s)$

Figure 3. An example for a user profile construction

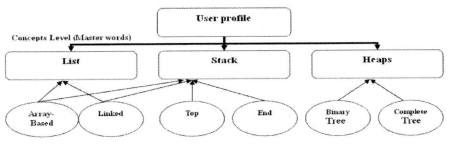

Function $F(C_h | D_s)$ represents the number of occurrence of concept C_h, which appears in document D_s and $F(w_j^h | D_s)$ represents the number of occurrence of the word w_j^h, which appears in document D_s. The purpose of this step is to measure the importance of each document in the stream. Formula (5) clarifies the restrictions that must apply to documents in order for them to be relevant. In the next section, we present the experiments and results.

Real Case Study

Current Web search engines allow users to enter queries. Users receive ranked documents. We suggest an approach that modifies construction of the search context by using the dominant meanings of the query as further inputs. Figure 4 shows a snapshot of two learners open a session using the CITS about a specific concept, say "queue", (Figure 4[1]). The CBIA deals with their session as follows. On the one hand, it observes discussions and captures some words. With these words, along with their dominant meanings, the CBIA constructs a query about the context of the main concept. On the other hand, it uses the constructed query to search the Web for related documents and present them to both learners. When it receives the results, the CBIA parses them and posts new recommended results to its user interface (Figure 4[2]). The CBIA supplies learners with a search results list, which shows the documents that rank highest and allows learners to retrieve its full content by clicking on them (Figure 4[3]).

Here is a summary of the functions of the CBIA user interface. It allows learners to interact with their profiles by adding, deleting, and modifying the context of interest. It provides them with several documents related to the current learning session's concept, and it allows them to browse on the Web.

For effective primary retrieval, we need to specify queries that are closely related to the search context. In fact, we must define a way by which to construct this context and then use it for expanding the query. Figure 5 shows a diagram of the CBIA. The framework of the CBIA consists of the following operations:

1. extracting some words from the current learning session;
2. using user profiles to specify the session's current concept;
3. extracting the current concept's corresponding dominant meanings;
4. updating user profiles with new meanings;
5. construct a query related to the context of session; and
6. re-ranking results that come from the Web.

Figure 4. CITS user interface

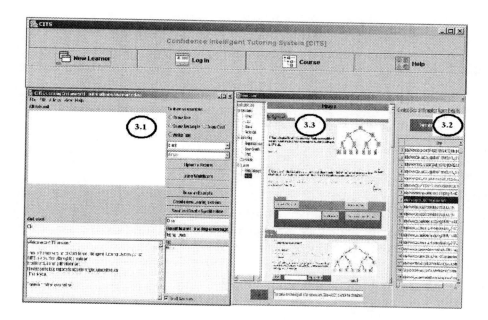

Figure 5. Information and processing flow of the context-based information agent

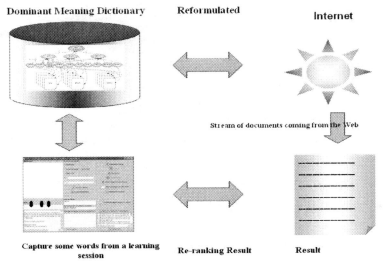

Dominant Meaning Dictionary   **Reformulated**   **Internet**

Stream of documents coming from the Web

Capture some words from a learning session   **Re-ranking Result**   **Result**

Experiments and Results

In this section, we describe a series of experiments conducted to reveal practical gains from the proposed approach of dominant meanings.

Dominant Meanings vs. Keywords

The goal of this experiment was to demonstrate the effectiveness of the dominant meanings approach in retrieval. It was conducted on two collections: MED, and CACM (Gale et al., 1992). These tests are often used to evaluate the effectiveness of information retrieval systems. Table 1 presents their main features and the number of documents. In addition, it indicates the number of queries with relevant information, the number of terms, the average number of terms per document and query, and the average number of relevant documents per query.

The experiment was conducted in two stages: training and retrieval. During the training stage, we built a dominant meaning graph of each collection, using the method proposed elsewhere in this chapter. For the comparative experiments, we computed the threshold of dominant meaning distance for relating one word with its dominant meanings. We used 20% of the documents in each collection as a training set for fitting this threshold parameter.

Table 1. Collection used for experiment

Collection	MED	CACM
Number of Documents	1033	3204
Number of Queries	30	52
Number of Terms	8663	7121
Average Terms in Query	271	356
Average relevance Documents	23.2	15.31

During the retrieval stage, we indexed documents and queries as usual. We then computed the dominant meaning distance between a word in a query and its dominant meanings in a document, using formulas (1-4).

Therefore, if the dominant meaning vector of a word in the query were either greater than or equal to the threshold parameter, the document would be considered relevant; otherwise, it would be considered irrelevant. The algorithm is summed up as follows:

Training Stage:
1. Build dominant meanings graph of the MED collection.
2. Compute dominant meanings vectors for each query.

Retrieval Stage:
1. Index the collection.
2. For each query and each document:
   - Compute the average dominant meaning distance between the dominant meaning vector of a word in the query and those of its dominant meaning in the document
   - If (the average dominant meaning distance > the dominant meaning threshold)
     Then consider the document is relevant
     else   consider it irrelevant.

Table 2 shows performance improvement when the query is expanded by using the dominant meanings constructed by our approach. The normal evaluation measures, precision and recall, were used. Precision is the ratio between the number of relevant documents retrieved and the total number retrieved. The average precision of a query is the average of precisions calculated when a relevant document is found in the rank list. We evaluated results by applying the average precision of a set of queries for 11 points of recall. Table 2 indicates that our dominant meaning approach produced a considerable improvement: 14.8% in retrieval effectiveness.

Table 2. Improvement using dominant meaning approach

Collection	MED	CACM
Average Precision of Original queries	0.534	0.562
Average Precision of dominant meanings queries	0.682	0.741
Improvement	14.8%	17.9%

This experiment showed that a significant improvement in retrieval effectiveness can be achieved by creating a dominant meaning query and using a dominant meaning graph. The latter is an appropriate model, therefore, for encoding the distribution of terms in a document collection. And dominant meanings give a more accurate distance between words in the query and dominant meanings in the document.

In the next subsection, we will present another experiment for validating the performance of the CBIA. We compared its performance with those of three major search engines: Google, AltaVista, and Excite.

Context-Based Information Agent vs. Other Search Engines

As we have just shown, dominant meaning probability performed well. The main goal of this evaluation was to assess the effectiveness of the CBIA in the accuracy of a search engine's results. To clarify this goal, we compared the dominant meaning probability's values of the CBIA results against those of Google and AltaVista, and Excite. We used original queries only.

The whole point of the CBIA is to use dominant meaning vectors as queries instead of using the original queries. Using formulas from (1) to (4), we analyzed the concepts of domain knowledge, say "data structure", in order to extract the preliminary dominant meanings for each concept.

As a result, the concept "queue" included all related words—such as V (queue, reer, front, fifo), and so on—that can be added to the dominant-meanings vector. The algorithm is summarized as follows:

> **Training Stage:**
> 1. Build dominant meanings graph of the domain knowledge (data structure course).
> 2. Build original queries (concepts without dominant meanings).
> 3. Compute dominant-meaning vectors of original queries.
> 4. Compute threshold for each query.
>
> **Retrieval Stage:**
> 1. For each original query
>   - Send it to the two proposed search engines.
>   - For each query and each document.
>   i) Compute the average dominant meaning distance between the dominant meaning vector of a word in the query and those of its dominant meaning in the document.
>   ii) If (the average dominant meaning distance > the dominant meaning threshold) then consider the document relevant else consider it irrelevant
> 2. Send it to the two proposed search engines via the CBIA
>   - For each query and each document.
>   - Compute the average dominant meaning distance between the dominant meaning vector of a word in the query and that of its dominant meaning in the document.
>   - If (the average dominant meaning distance > the dominant meaning threshold) then Consider the document relevant else Consider it irrelevant.

Since learners tutoring systems are normally interested in the top-ranked documents, this experiment will compute the average dominant meaning probability of the top-20-ranked documents. The level of improvement changes from one search engine to another. Our experiment shows that the degree of relevance is much higher at the CBIA working with Google than with AltaVista.

Figure 6 shows that the retrieval effectiveness of the standard retrieval method with Google, AltaVista, and Excite varied randomly between 0 and 0.19. This must be why learners wasted most of their time looking for information that might be found only after many efforts at browsing through the results. The figure shows that our dominant meaning method yields more performance improvement with all three search engines: Google, AltaVista, and Excite. Meanwhile, results for the CBIA were consistently better than others; they recommended the top-ranked documents.

Future Trends and Research Issues

The future of information available on the Web cannot yet be envisioned. The amount of information that can be transferred over the Internet has doubled every year since 1984 (Legon, 2003). Consequently, there should be many information resources to help in building individualized adaptive systems. New

Figure 6. Improvement using the CBIA with Google, AltaVista, and Excite search engines

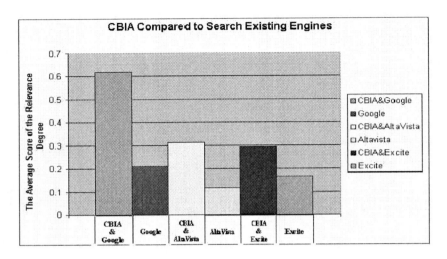

techniques would be needed to get these resources. There are many distinct challenges for search engines, and each opens up new research problems.

We focused in this chapter on how to individualize Web search engines by means of context queries that use the dominant meaning technique. This technique was very effective, but it dealt only with textual documents. Searching for non-textual ones will gain importance in the near future (Byer, 1998).

An important problem that remains to be solved is how to formulate the presentation of results related to each user. To do that, we might use a socio-psychological technique. This would identify situations in which people need information, what information they need, and how it might be used. It would enable individualized services for several users, each of whom requires different types of information (Abramowicz et al., 1999).

Until now, the dominant meanings approach has dealt with documents written in English, but many Web documents are written in other languages. We could enrich the theory and practice of the dominant meanings approach by tackling multilingual documents.

In our future work, we plan to use an important issue, such as user satisfaction, to enhance the evaluation of the dominant meaning approach.

Conclusion

This chapter presented a dominant meanings technique to be used for individualizing Web search engines. This technique treats the original query as a master word and its dominant meaning as a slave word. To be effective, it requires an accurate representation of the context of the domain knowledge being taught. We suggested a new graph, the dominant meaning graph, to represent domain knowledge.

This model is intended to develop a new probabilistic measure, the dominant meaning probability, one that would measure the closeness between the master word and its slave words rather than the similarity between a query term and the terms of documents.

To individualize a query, we developed the context-based information agent, which takes advantage of discussions during a cooperative learning session to individualize search queries. It can observe conversation, interpret the inputs from learners, and then specify the current context. On the other hand, the CBIA would filter, organize, and present information that is immediately useful to learners.

Experimental results indicate that the accuracy of queries generated by our technique is consistently better than that of those using the original query alone.

References

Abramowicz, W., Kalazynski, P., & Wecel, K. (2002). *Filtering the Web to feed data warehouses*. London; Heidelberg, UK: Springer-Verlag.

Berners-Lee, T., Hendler, J., & Lassila, O. (2001). *The Semantic Web*. Scientific American.

Bharat, K. (2000). SearchPad: Explicit capture of search context to support Web search. *The International Journal of Computer and Telecommunications Networking, 33*(1-6), 493-501.

Brown, P. J., & Jones, G. J. F. (2002). Exploiting contextual change in context-aware retrieval. *Proceedings of the 17th ACM Symposium on Applied Computing,* Madrid (pp. 650-656).

Byer, D. (1998). Full-text indexing of non-textual resources. *Journal of Computer Networks and ISDN Systems, 30,* 141-148.

Chaffee, J., & Gauch, S. (2000). Personal ontologies for Web navigation. *Proceedings of CIKM 2000*, Kansas City, Missouri (pp. 188-194). ACM.

Efthimiadis, E. & Biron, P. (1994). UCLA-Okapi at TREC-2: Query Expansion Experiments. *Proceedings of the Second Text Retrieval Conference (TREC-2)* (pp. 500-515).

Eirinaki, M., & Vazirgiannis, M. (2003). Web mining for Web personalization. *ACM Transactions on Internet Technology, 3*(1), 1-27.

Finkelstein, L., Gabrilovich, E., Matias, Y., Rivlin, E., Solan, Z., Wolfman, G., & Ruppin, E. (2002). Placing search in context: The concept revisited. *ACM Transactions on Information Systems, 20*(1), 116-131.

Frakes, W. B., & Baeza-Yates, R. (1992). *Information retrieval: Data structures and algorithms.* NJ: Prentice Hall.

Gale, A. W., Kenneth, W. C., & Yarowsky, D. (1992). One sense per discourse. *Proceedings of the Fourth DARPA Speech and Natural Language Workshop* (pp. 233-237).

Hang, C., Ji-Rong, W., Jian-Yun, N., & Wei-Ying M. (2002). Probabilistic query expansion using query logs. *Proceedings of the WWW8,* Honolulu, HI (pp. 325-332). ACM.

Legon, J. (2003). *Scientists: Internet speed record smashed.* Retrieved from http://www.cnn.com/2003/TECH/internet/03/07/speed.record/

Lesk, M. E. (1969). Word-word association in document retrieval systems. *American Documentation, 20*(1), 27-38.

Luger, G.F. (2002). *Artificial intelligence: Structures and strategies for complex problem solving.* Addison Wesley.

Lycos (1999). *Lycos: Your personal Internet guide.* Retrieved from http://www.lycos.com

Minker, J., Wilson, G. A., & Zimmerman, B. H. (1972). An evaluation of query expansion by the addition of clustered terms for a document retrieval system. *Information Storage and Retrieval, 8*(6), 329-348.

Mulvenna, M. D., Anand, S. S., & Buchner, A. G. (2000). Personalization on the net using Web mining. *Communication ACM, 43*(8), 123-125.

Pazzani, M. J. (1999). A framework for collaborative, content-based and demographic filtering. *Artificial Intelligence Review, 13*(5-6), 393-408.

Pretschner, A., & Gauch, S. (1999). Ontology based personalized search. *Proceedings of the 11th IEEE International Conference on Tools with Artificial Intelligence* (pp. 391-398).

Razek, M. A., Frasson, C., & Kaltenbach, M. (2003a). Granularity degree towards adaptive course presentation online. *Proceedings of the International Conference on Computers in Education, ICCE2003,* Hong Kong (pp. 504-508).

Razek, M. A., Frasson, C., & Kaltenbach, M. (2003b). Web course self-adaptation. *IEEE/WIC International Conference on Intelligent Agent Technology (IAT 2003)*, Halifax, Canada (pp. 614-617).

Razek, M. A., Frasson, C., & Kaltenbach, M. (2003c). Re-using Web information for building flexible domain knowledge. *The 16th Canadian Conference on Artificial Intelligence*, Halifax, Nova Scotia, Canada, Lecture Notes in Artificial Intelligence (pp. 563-567).

Razek, M. A., Frasson, C., & Kaltenbach, M. (2003d). Context-based information agent for supporting intelligent distance learning environment. *Proceedings of the 12th International World Wide Web Conference*, Budapest, Hungary, Mta Sztaki.

Razek, M., Frasson, C., & Kaltenbach, M. (2002). A confidence agent: Toward more effective intelligent distance learning environments. *Proceedings of the International Conference on Machine Learning and Applications (ICMLA'02)*, Los Anglos, CA (pp. 187-193).

Russel, S. J., & Norvig, P. (2003). *Artificial intelligence: A modern approach* (2nd edition). Upper Saddle River, NJ: Prentice Hall.

Salton, G., & McGill, M. (1983). *Introduction to modern information retrieval*. New York: McGraw Hill.

Scime, A., & Kerschberg, L. (2001). WebSifter: An ontological Web-mining agent for e-business. *IEEE/DS-9*, 187-201.

Sparck-Jones, K. (1991). Notes and references on early classification work. *SIGIR Forum, 25*(1), 10-17.

Sparck-Jones, K., & Barber, E. B. (1971). What makes an automatic keyword classification effective? *Journal of the ASIS, 18*, 166-175.

Tanudjaja, F., & Mui, L. (2002). Persona: A contextualized and personalized Web system sciences. *Proceedings of the 35th Annual Hawaii International Conference* (pp. 843-852).

Chapter IV

An Adaptive Predictive Model for Student Modeling

Gladys Castillo, University of Aveiro, Portugal

João Gama, University of Porto, Portugal

Ana M. Breda, University of Aveiro, Portugal

Abstract

This chapter presents an adaptive predictive model for a student modeling prediction task in the context of an adaptive educational hypermedia system (AEHS). The task, that consists in determining what kind of learning resources are more appropriate to a particular learning style, presents two issues that are critical. The first is related to the uncertainty of the information about the student's learning style acquired by psychometric instruments. The second is related to the changes over time of the student's preferences (concept drift). To approach this task, we propose a probabilistic adaptive predictive model that includes a method to handle concept drift based on statistical quality control. We claim that our approach is able to adapt quickly to changes in the student's preferences and that it should be successfully used in similar user modeling prediction tasks, where uncertainty and concept drift are presented.

Introduction

In the last decade we have attended to an increased development of adaptive educational hypermedia and Web-based systems (AEHS). An AEHS is able to adapt its contents and presentations to specific characteristics of students. The keys for adaptation are the domain model and the student model. The former represents the knowledge about the subjects to be learned and serves as the base for structuring the hypermedia contents. The latter stores different assumptions about the student (e.g., knowledge, preferences, goals, etc.). An AHES uses the information stored in both models to implement adaptive algorithms and techniques. An extended discussion of adaptive hypermedia, and in particular, AEHSs can be found in Brusilovsky (2001).

Student modeling involves the construction and updating of the student model. Traditionally, most of student modeling systems have been limited to maintain assumptions related with the student's knowledge, which can be acquired during evaluation activities. However, over the last years there has been an augmented interest in modeling other kind of assumptions about the student, such as the learning style and preferences. An AEHS can make use of this kind of information to decide more effectively how to adapt itself to each student individually.

Usually the students' learning style is acquired using one of existing psychometric instruments. By matching a learning style with some relevant characteristics of the learning resources, these systems can determine which resources are most appropriate for a particular student. As a rule, the acquired assumptions about the students' learning style are no longer updated during their interactions with the system. Moreover, the deterministic rules included in their decision models also never change.

There are some typical issues that are critical concerning a successful implementation of the prediction task, that consists in determining what kind of learning resources are more appropriate to a particular learning style in a real student modeling scenario:

(i)   Although multiple models to categorize the students according to their learning styles have been developed it is difficult to determine how exactly a person learns. Therefore, the information about the student's learning style acquired by psychometric instruments encloses some grade of uncertainty.

(ii) During the interactions with the system, the student can change his/her preferences for another kind of learning resource that no longer matches with his/her determined learning style. It is because either the acquired learning style information needs to be adjusted or the student simply changes his/her preferences motivated by other unknown reasons (some hidden contexts). This kind of problem is known as concept drift in the machine learning community.

This chapter aims at presenting a new adaptive machine learning approach for the described prediction task. Our approach is based on an adaptive predictive model capable of fine-tuning its parameters to reflect more accurately the student's preferences. Moreover, this also includes a method to handle concept drift (Castillo, Gama, & Medas, 2003). This method uses a P-Chart (Montgomery, 1997), an attribute Shewhart control chart, to monitor the learner's performance over time. Although this drift-detection method is broadly applicable to a range of domains and learning algorithms, we choose Naïve Bayes classifier (Mitchell, 1997), one of the most used learning algorithms in user modelling, as our predictive model. Furthermore, we propose the use of Adaptive Bayes (Gama & Castillo, 2002), an incremental adaptive version of the Naïve Bayes classifier. This algorithm includes an updating scheme that allows better fitting of the current model to new observations. We argue that the proposed adaptive predictive model can be implemented in any AEHS where we need to adapt the presentation based on the student's learning style and preferences. Finally, we claim that our approach should be successfully used in similar user modeling prediction tasks, where uncertainty and concept drift are presented.

The next section reviews some student modeling approaches based on learning styles. We then cover the use of machine learning in user modeling. This section focuses the concept drift problem in concept learning. We present some adaptive learning approaches to deal with concept drift developed in the area of information filtering. Finally, we briefly introduce the concept drift detection method using P-Chart. The following section describes GIAS, an AEHS that we are actually developing to illustrate our approach. The subsequent sections describe the adaptive predictive model for the prediction task based on learning styles and present some experiments to evaluate our approach using simulated students. Finally, we present the conclusions and future work.

Learning Style in Student Modeling

Learning style can be defined as the different ways a person collects, processes, and organizes information. As was argued in several works, we also claim that to effectively adapt interaction a student model must include information about the student's learning style. This assertion is based on the fact that different people learn differently (Felder, 1996): some people tend to learn by doing, whereas others tend to learn concepts; some of them like better written text and/ or spoken explanations, whereas others prefer learning by visual formats of information (pictures, diagrams, etc.). Consequently, the student's learning style can influence the student's preferences that usually guide the system's adaptation. Moreover, the learning style information is not subject-specific, and can be used across many AEHSs.

A pioneer work incorporating learning styles in AEHSs was proposed by Carver, Howard, and Lane (1999) to support a computer science hypermedia course. The authors developed an adaptive hypermedia interface to tailor the presentation of course material based on the determination of what types of media are appropriate for different learning styles. For each course tool they compute a rate (on a scale from 0 to 100) to determine the amount of support for each learning style. The obtained rate is combined with the student's profile to produce a unique ranking of each media type from each learning style.

USD (teaching support units) is an intelligent tutoring system to support distance learning in the WEB (Peña, Marzo, & de la Rosa, 2002). The adaptation technique is approached by a multi-agent system named MAS-PLANG. The student agent implements case-based reasoning for student modeling with the aim to retrieve the relevant didactic contents (taking into account media formats and instructional strategies), navigation tools and navigation strategies based on the student's learning style. The learning style is acquired, as usually, by a psychometric instrument. Next, they assign some distributions to different materials considering which learning styles are more appropriate for different instructional strategies, media formats, and navigation tools. Although the authors refer that the initial student's profile is fine-tuned to reflect more faithfully the student's learning style here it is not clear how this updating is carried out.

INSPIRE (Papanikolaou, Grigoriadou, Magoulas, & Kornilakis, 2002) is an AHES that integrates theories of instructional design with learning styles. The student's learning style can be acquired using a psychometric instrument or defined by the own student. The domain model is structured in three hierarchical levels: learning goals, concepts, and educational materials. Lessons are based on combinations of educational materials. The adaptation is based on the students' knowledge level and learning style. The former is used to adapt the lesson contents and the navigation support. The latter is used to determine the appropriate instructional strategy for presenting the content, that is, lessons are tailored to learners according to his/her learning styles.

In MANIC (Stern & Woolf, 2000) the student's learning style is not directly used, but it is approached by the student's preferences concerning the type of media, the instructional type and the level of abstraction of the content objects, as well as the place where these objects must be presented to the students. The tutor learns the student's preferences via machine learning by observing which objects he/she shows or hides (a stretch-text technique is used to adapt the presentation). A Naïve Bayes classifier predicts whether a student will want certain content objects. Those objects predicted as "wanted" will be shown to the user, while the others will not be shown. For each student, an example space is created based on the information about the content objects that, in the past, were either wanted or not wanted by the student. Population data is used to improve the accuracy of predictions.

Finally, a good survey of other works related with the use of learning styles in AEHS can be found in Papanikolaou et al. (2002).

Machine Learning for User Modeling

User modeling systems are basically concerned with making inferences about the user's assumptions from observations of their behavior during his/her interaction with the system. On the other hand, machine learning is concerned with the formation of models from observations. Hence, in the last years, the use of machine learning techniques in user modeling has become increasingly popular. Observations of the user's behavior can provide training examples that a machine learning system can use to induce a model designed to predict future actions (Webb, Pazzani, & Billsus, 2001).

Concept Drift in Supervised Learning

The prediction task based on learning styles is related to the task of concept learning, a particular case of supervised learning (Mitchell, 1997).

Suppose that f: $X \rightarrow C$ maps from a feature space $X \subset \Re^N$ to a fixed set C of k classes $C = \{c_1, ..., c_k\}$. The goal of supervised learning is therefore: given a set of labeled examples $(x, f(x))$ to induce a learner (hypothesis) h_L: $X \rightarrow C$ that approximates f as closely as possible. The function f is called the target concept. In the case of concept learning the outputs are Boolean (e.g., $C = \{yes, no\}$). A positive (negative) example is an example labeled "yes"("no").

As a rule, supervised learning assumes the stability of the target concept. Nevertheless in many real-world problems, when the data is collected over an extended period of time, the learning task can be complicated by changes in the distribution underlying the data or changes in the own target concept. This problem is known as concept drift. Concept drift scenarios require incremental learning algorithms, able to adjust quickly to drifting concepts (Webb et al., 2001). Depending on the rate of the changes we can distinguish concept drift (gradual changes) of concept shift (abrupt changes). For instance, in the context of our predictive task the student preferences of learning resources can change with time.

In machine learning drifting concepts are often handled by time windows or weighted examples according to their age or utility (see Klinkenberg & Renz, 1998, for a brief review). In general, approaches to cope with concept drift can be classified into two categories: (i) approaches that adapt a learner at regular intervals without considering whether changes have really occurred; (ii) approaches that first detect concept changes, and next, adapt the learner to these changes accordingly.

Examples of the former approaches are weighted examples and time windows of fixed size. Weighted examples are based on the fact that the importance of an example should decrease with time. When a time window is used, at each time step the learner is induced only from the examples that are included in the window. Here, the key difficulty is how to select the appropriate window size: a small window can assure a fast adaptability in phases with concept changes but in more stable phases it can affect the learner performance, while a large window would produce good and stable learning results in stable phases but can not react quickly to concept changes.

To detect concept changes, the second group of approaches monitor the value of some performance indicators over time. If during the monitoring process a concept drift is detected, the learner is adapted accordingly. For instance, such an approach was proposed by Klinkenberg and Renz (1998) and by Lanquillon (2001). A deeper discussion about these and other similar approaches can be found in Castillo et al. (2003).

The Concept Drift Detection Method Based on P-Chart

Similar to Lanquillon, the underlying theory we use is the Statistical Quality Control (SQC) theory (Montgomery, 1997). The main idea behind SQC is to monitor the value of some quality characteristic in the production processes. Shewhart controls chart, the basic tool of SQC, is a useful monitoring technique that helps distinguish trends and out-of-control conditions in a process. This allows process correction thus reducing its variability.

The values of the quality characteristic are plotted on the chart in time order and connected by a line. The chart has a center line and upper and lower control limits. If a value falls outside the control limits, we assume that the process is out-of-control, that is, some "special causes" have shifted the process off target. In addition to control limits we can also use upper and lower warning limits, which are usually set a bit closer to the center line than the control limits.

If the distribution of the quality characteristic is (approximately) normal with mean μ and standard deviation σ, it is well known, that approximately 99.7% of the observations will fall within three standard deviations of the mean of the statistics. Therefore, if μ and σ are known we can use them to set the parameters of the control chart, as follows:

$$\mathbf{CL} = = \mu - \text{ the center line is set to the \textit{mean} value}$$

$$\mathbf{LCL} = \mu\text{-}3\sigma \text{ and } \mathbf{UCL} = \mu\text{+}3\sigma \quad \text{- the \textit{lower} and \textit{upper control limits}}$$

$$\mathbf{LWL} = \mu\text{-}k\sigma \text{ and } \mathbf{UWL} = \mu + k\ \sigma, 0{<}k{<}3 \text{ - the \textit{lower} and \textit{upper warning limits}}$$

(3.1)

However, in most cases μ and σ are unknown and they must be estimated from previously observed values.

The control charts are classified according to the type of quality characteristic that they monitor: variables or attributes. P-Chart is an attribute control chart for the proportion of a dichotomous "count" attribute. The quality characteristic represents the sample proportion of one of the two outcomes. For large sample size n the sample proportion is approximately normal with parameters:

$$\mu = p \quad \text{and} \quad \sigma = \sqrt{\frac{p(1-p)}{n}}$$

(3.2)

where p is the population proportion. Suppose that we obtain the estimate $\hat{p}$ of the parameter p from previous data by some estimator. Then, from equations (3.1) and (3.2), the parameters of the P-Chart for each individual t-th sample with size n_t would be:

$$\text{UCL} = \hat{p} + 3\sqrt{\frac{\hat{p}(1-\hat{p})}{n_t}}; \ \text{CL} = \hat{p}; \ \text{LCL} = \max\left\{0, \hat{p} - 3\sqrt{\frac{\hat{p}(1-\hat{p})}{n_t}}\right\}$$

$$\text{UWL} = \hat{p} + k\sqrt{\frac{\hat{p}(1-\hat{p})}{n_t}}; \text{LWL} = \max\left\{0, \hat{p} - k\sqrt{\frac{\hat{p}(1-\hat{p})}{n_t}}\right\}, 0 < k < 3$$

(3.3)

A usual procedure to obtain $\hat{p}$ is by the weighted average of m preliminary sample proportions. Further we call the estimate $\hat{p}$ the target value.

We explore the use of the P-Chart for detecting concept drift in the following online framework for supervised learning: without loss of generality we assume that data arrives to the learner in batches over time. In real application this means that the incoming examples can be grouped by days, weeks, and so on. For each batch, we use the current learner to classify the examples. The quality characteristic to be monitored is the sample error rate, a sample proportion of the misclassified examples (to evaluate it user feedback about the correct class is required). If the monitoring process detects concept drift, the learner is adapted accordingly. Next, the adapted learner is used to predict the class labels of the examples of the next batch.

In summary, the problem of handling drifting concepts can be viewed as the problem of the detection of the last moment when a concept drift occurred. The data stream can be analyzed as a sequence of different contexts: a set of examples with stationary distribution. Therefore, the monitoring process aims to detect and extract these contexts between drifts.

Suppose that at time t a new context begins to be processed. All the time when a lower error rate is achieved, the learner will try to improve, or at least, to maintain its performance level. For this reason, we propose to estimate the target value using the minimum value for the error rate in the current context instead of using some average of previous observed values. Suppose that $\text{Errs}^{(t)}$ is the error rate for the context $s^{(t)}$ at time t and $\text{SErrs}^{(t)}$ its standard deviation. Let Err_{min} denote the minimum-error rate. Err_{min} is initialized to some big number. Next, at each time step, if $\text{Errs}^{(t)} + \text{SErrs}^{(t)} < \text{Err}_{min}$ then Err_{min} is set to $\text{Errs}^{(t)}$.

Figure 1 presents the incremental adaptive method for handling concept drift based on P-Chart (Castillo et al., 2003). In each time step, the algorithm begins by determining the sample error rate for the current batch. Next, the target value is estimated by the minimum value Err_{min}. All the chart parameters are computed by the equations 3.3 (because a low sample error rate is desirable, we don't need to use the low limits here). If the current sample error Err_t is above the upper control limit, a concept shift is suspected. We assume that a new context is beginning and only the examples from this new context are used to re-learn the learner. If the last alert occurred at the previous time step (LastAlert=t-1) a new context began at the time indicated in FirstAlert. If the current sample error is above the upper warning limit and it occurred at two or more consecutive times a concept drift is suspected and the examples of this batch are not used to update the learner. If neither a concept shift nor concept drift is suspected the learner is updated to combine the current learner with the examples of the current batch.

Figure 1. General algorithm for handling concept drift using P-Chart

```
Procedure HandleConceptDriftWithPChart
                 (data,learner,k,mean_estimator())
 for t=1 to N  //for each batch with size n_t at time t
   Err_t:=Err(Batch_t,Learner);
   CL:= mean_estimator();
   Sigma:=sqrt(CL*(1-CL)/n_t);
   UCL:=CL+3.Sigma; UWL:=CL+k.Sigma;
   If Err_t > UCL then          /* concept shift suspected
   {If LastAlert=t-1 then t_ini:=FirstAlert else t_ini:=t;
       learner:=ReLearnFrom(learner,Batch_t_ini)}
   else
     If Err_t > UWL then        /* concept drift suspected
       If LastAlert=t-1 then    /* consecutive alerts
         LastAlert:=t
         else                   /* it can be a false alarm
           {learner:= UpdateWith(learner , Bacth_t)
            FirstAlert:=t, LastAlert:=t}
       else                     /* no changes was detected
         learner ←UpdateWith(learner , Batch_t);
 Next t;
 return: learner
 End
```

The precise way in which a learner can be updated in order to include new data depends basically on the learning algorithm employed. There are two main approaches: (i) re-build the learner from scratch; (ii) update the learner combining the current model with the new data. For instance, updating a Naïve Bayes classifier is simple: the counters required for calculating the prior probabilities can be increased as new examples arrive.

GIAS: An Adaptive Hypermedia Educational System

GIAS is a prototype WWW-based adaptive authoring-tool to support learning and teaching. The authors can organize all the available online learning resources associated to each topic of the course to support the learning processes of their students. On the other hand, the students can make use of this repository of learning resources for consulting and studying.

The main function of GIAS's adaptation is to help the students to explore a repository of learning resources associated to a set of educational goals. The ideal situation is when the student has too many options to choose from and the system can recommend him/her to explore those resources which are more appropriate to his/her learning style and preferences. Therefore, the adaptation techniques are focused on the appropriate selection of the course's topics and learning resources based on the student's goals, knowledge level, learning style, and preferences.

The main difference between our approach and other similar approaches is that we try to adapt and fine-tune the initial acquired information about the student's learning style and preferences by observing the student's interactions with the system. We represent the matches between the student's learning style and the characteristics of learning resources into a predictive model (a learner). Moreover, we propose an adaptive predictive model capable of adapting quickly to any change of the student's preferences.

Similar to most of AEHSs, the main components of GIAS are the domain model and the student model. The domain model is composed by the cognitive model (for knowledge representation) and the course model (for course representation). The student model represents, collects, and predicts assumptions about the student's characteristics. Moreover, GIAS includes an author module to manage the information of the domain model and an instructional module to make decisions about how and what to adapt based on the information stored in the domain and student models. This includes three main processes: course generation, topic generation, and test generation. Here, we focus on the course model, the student model, and the topic generation process.

Course Model

The course model (see Figure 2) is organized into three-layers: the goal layer (the course's goals), the topic layer (the course's topics), and the resource layer (a set of learning resources). Each goal is associated to a set of topics and each course topic is associated to a set of learning resources. Between the topics we can define aggregation relationships. A learning resource is an implementation of a learning activity in a multimedia support. Table 1 shows the resource features and their possible values.

Figure 2. GIAS course model

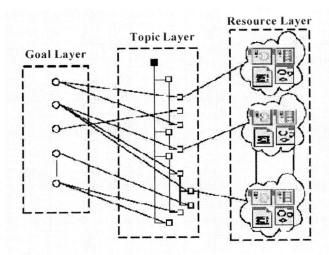

Table 1. Establishing resource features and their possible values

Attribute	Value
ResourceID	
Description	
Author	
Language	Portuguese/ Spanish/ English
Creation Data	
Learning Activity (LA)	*Lesson objectives/Explanation/Example/Conceptual Map/Synthesis Diagram/ Glossary / Summary /Bibliography /HistoricalReview /Inter.Activity*
Activity Type	*to explain the new concepts/ to exemplify the new concepts/ to support the cognitive process/ to help or to coach the student*
Resource Type (RT)	*Text/HTML Text/Picture/Animated Picture/ Animated Picture with Voice/ Audio /Video /Software*
Difficulty Level	*Low/Medium/High*
Concept/skill List	

Different learning resources may support a learning activity in different multimedia formats. For example, suppose we have a theorem proof supported by two different media formats: a static text that describes this proof, or an animated image with voice that explains this proof step by step. We should suggest to a visual student the study of this proof using the animated image with voice, and to a verbal student the study of the proof using the static text.

The Student Model

A student model can represent individual students (individual approach) or group of users with similar characteristics (stereotype approach). In GIAS we use both of these approaches to model the student.

For each student his/her individual student model is composed of:

- **Profile Model:** Stores personal information about the student (name, age, learning style)

- **Cognitive Overlay:** Records the system beliefs of the student's knowledge about the domain cognitive model. Consequently, the student is classified as novice, intermediate or expert.

- **Predictive Model:** Represents the student preferences about the learning resources.

- **Course Overlay:** Stores the information gathered by the system about the student's interactions with the course (e.g., how many times he/she has visited a topic or learning resource, performance in evaluation activities, etc.).

The learning style model that we adopted is the Felder-Sylverman model (Felder, 1996). This classifies students in five dimensions: input (visual vs. verbal), perception (sensing vs. intuitive), organization (inductive vs. deductive), processing (active vs. reflective), understanding (sequential vs. global). We use the Index of Learning Styles questionnaire (ILSQ) of Felder and Soloman to assess preferences on input, perception, and understanding. For each dimension a person is classified as having a mild, moderate, or strong preference for one category.

The acquisition of student's learning style is done explicitly or implicitly. When a new student logs into the system, he/she is given the option of exploring the course according to his/her learning style or without it. If a student chooses to use learning style, the student must answer to the ILSQ and the obtained scores are recorded in his/her profile model. On the contrary, the student's learning style should be inferred by observing the student's interactions with the system. In this chapter we assume that the acquisition of the student's learning style is done explicitly.

The Topic Generation Process

The topic generation process (see Figure 3) is executed whenever a student requests the contents of a topic. The student's predictive model is used to classify the available resources.

The choice of the suitable learning resources for a topic depends on the resource's characteristics and on the student's cognitive state, learning style and preferences.

Figure 3. The topic generation process

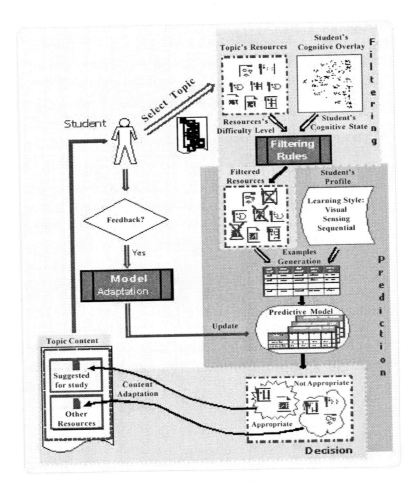

This process is performed according to the following steps:

1. **Filtering:** Using some deterministic rules, the learning resources are filtered according to the matching between the resource's difficulty level and the student's knowledge level.

2. **Prediction:** Using the actual predictive model, each filtered resource is classified as "appropriate" or "not appropriate" for the student. With this purpose, examples including the learning style features (stored in the student model) and the resource's characteristics (stored in the domain model) are automatically generated and classified by the actual predictive model. As a result the set of available resources is partitioned into these two classes.

3. **Decision:** An HTML page is sent to the student including two separated ranked lists: "resources suggested for study" list with the links for those resources classified as "appropriate" and "other resources for study" list with the links for those resources classified as "not appropriate".

4. **Adaptation:** Whenever a new example is observed and evaluated, the predictive model is adapted accordingly.

The User Modeling Prediction Task

Figure 4 shows the prediction task that consists of determining whether a given resource is or not appropriate for a specific learning style by using the information about the resource and the student's learning style as input, and having the output category representing how strongly the resource is appropriate for this student.

The Example Features and Its Values

The examples are described through five attributes: the first three characterizing the student's learning style and the last two characterizing the learning resource. The possible values for each attribute are presented in Table 2.

For instance, suppose the following example: VisualVerbal:**Verbalmoderate**; SensingConceptual:**Sensingmild**; SequentialGlobal:**Globalmild**; Learning Activity: **explanation**; Resource Type: **audio**. The predictive model must determine if a learning resource that implements a learning activity such as "explanation" in a multimedia support of type "audio" would be appropriate for a student

Figure 4. The prediction task

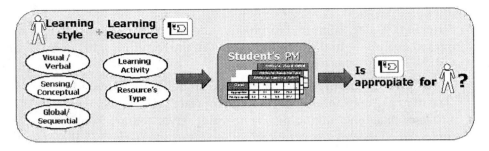

Table 2. Establishing attributes and their possible values

Attributes	Values
Characterizing the student's learning style	
VisualVerbal	VV*i*, VV ∈ {Visual, Verbal}, *i* ∈ {*mild, moderate, strong*}
SensingConceptual	SC*i*, SC ∈ {Sensing, Conceptual}, *i* ∈ {*mild, moderate, strong*}
GlobalSequential	GS*i*, GS ∈ {Global, Sequential}, *i* ∈ {*mild, moderate, strong*}
Characterizing the learning resource	
Learning Activity (LA)	*Lesson objectives/Explanation/Example/Conceptual Map/Synthesis Diagram/ Glossary / Summary /Bibliography /HistoricalReview /Inter.Activity*
Resource Type (RT)	*Text/HTML Text/Picture/Animated Picture/ Animated Picture with Voice/ Audio /Video /Software*

with a moderate preference for verbal category, a mild preference for sensing category, and a mild preference for a global category.

Further, to simplify the prediction task we will not discriminate the preferences for a category as mild, moderate or strong. For example, in the previous example, the student is simply classified as verbal, sensing, and global. Consequently we only have eight different learning styles.

The Predictive Model

Naïve Bayes (NB) classifiers (Mitchell, 1997) are probabilistic classifiers that are suitable for problems where there is uncertainty as to the correct answer. They use Bayes theorem with the assumption that the attributes are independent given the class (hence the term Naïve) to compute class probability distributions in term of their prior probabilities and the conditional probabilities of the attributes. All the required probabilities are computed from the training data: a frequency counter is required for each class, and a frequency counter for each attribute-value in combination with each class.

Although it is well known that most real world problems do not meet independence assumptions on which the NB classifier is based, because of its simplicity, easy use, and incremental nature, it is one of the most implemented classifiers in real-world applications. NB classifier, in particular, has been successfully applied in many user modeling system (e.g., information filtering) for acquiring interest profiles. For instance, in Pazzani and Billsus (1997) an intelligent agent called Syskill&Webert uses a NB classifier to determine whether a page would be interesting to a user. Billsus and Pazzani (1999) developed an intelligent agent named New Dudes, which learns about users' interests to compile daily news stories. This agent uses a short-term model that learns from the most recent observations and a long-term model (a NB classifier) that computes the predictions for stories not classified by the short model. The personalized WebMatcher proposed by Mladenic (1996) also implements a NB classifier to recommend links on other Web pages. Schwab, Wolfgang, and Koychev (2000) implement NB classifiers to learn interest profiles from positive evidence only.

We use Adaptive Bayes (Gama & Castillo, 2002), an adaptive version of the NB classifier, to induce the predictive model. Adaptive Bayes includes an updating scheme to better fit the current model to new data: after seeing each example, first, we increment the counters, and then we adjust them in order to increase the confidence on the correct class. The amount of adjustment is proportional to the discrepancy between the predicted class and the observed class.

Implementation Details

We implement a stereotyping approach to initialize each student's predictive model. For this purpose, we also maintain a stereotype predictive model for each learning style. Firstly, we define some matching rules between a learning style and the resource's characteristics to determine which resources are more appropriate to a particular learning style. After that, we use the predefined matching rules to randomly generate some training examples, and then we use these generated examples to initialize the counters for each stereotype predictive model. Therefore, the acquired information about the student's learning style helps us to initialize the student's predictive model from its related stereotype model.

During the further interactions with the system, the student's predictive model will adapt to better fit the current student's preferences by observing the student's behavior. The most recent observations gathered trough relevant feedbacks represent the user's current preferences better than older ones. A critical task at this point is how to obtain relevant feedback, that is, a relevant set of positive and negative examples for the learning task. We propose obtaining positive examples implicitly by observing visited links. However, obtaining a relevant set of negative examples is more difficult. With this aim, we propose the user to rate the resources explicitly. In future works we plan to investigate other methods to obtain more relevant feedback. The set of obtained examples are used to adapt the student's predictive model in the way it is explained in the previous chapter.

Evaluation of the Predictive Model

Our evaluation measures the accuracy of the model's predictions on a set of artificial datasets that were specially generated to simulate concept drift scenarios for the described prediction task. Namely, we employed simulated students (Vanlehn, Ohlsson, & Nason, 1994), a technique commonly used in student modeling, to evaluate the predictive model's performance. Therefore, each generated artificial dataset represents a simulated student.

Dataset Generation and Experimental Setup

Note that students' predictive models enclose different underlying target concepts for different learning styles, and that, each individual predictive model is initialized from its associated stereotype model according to the student's learning style.

The basic idea enclosed in the generation of simulated students is based on the following facts that really exist in this context: for instance, suppose a verbal student. Learning resources that match with a verbal student should be appropriate for him/her. Hence, the underlying target concept can be represented by the following logical rule:

IF LearningStyle Is Verbal AND

    (ResourceLearningActivity OR ResourceType) matches Verbal

  THEN Resource is Appropriate

Nevertheless, during the further interaction with the system, the student can change his/her preferences for another kind of learning resource that no longer matches with his/her predefined learning style. This means that the initial concept no longer matches the student's behaviour (a concept change happened), and thus, the predictive model must learn another concept ("rule"), like this:

IF LearningStyle Is Verbal AND
    (ResourceLearningActivity OR ResourceType) matches Visual
THEN Resource is Appropriate

Moreover, these changes in the student's preferences can lead to further adjustments in the student learning style.

Therefore, we generated simulated students for the eight possible learning styles. For each learning style, we generated datasets with 1600 examples: first, we randomly generated each feature value (see Table 2), and then, we classified each example according to the current concept. After every 400 examples the concept was changed. We grouped the examples into 32 batches of equal size (50 examples each). We also generated training datasets with 200 examples (according to the first concept) to initialize the stereotype predictive models.

We conducted the experiments in the online framework for supervised learning described in the previous chapter section. We evaluated the predictive accuracy of two learning algorithms: Naïve Bayes (NB) and Adaptive Bayes (AB) in combination with each of the following approaches: a non-adaptive approach (the baseline approach), fixed size window with a size of six batches (FSW) and our approach (Figure 1) using the min value as mean estimator and k=1. We denote our approach PMin.

For each learning style, we estimated the predictive accuracy over 10 runs (in each run we used a different generated dataset). The final estimator of the predictive accuracy of each combination "algorithm-approach" is the average of the eight accuracy estimations (one for each learning style).

Experimental Results and Analysis

In Figure 5 you can see an illustration of one P-chart for monitoring the sample error rate in one of the generated datasets.

The sample error rates are plotted on the chart and connected by a line. In each time step, the center line is adjusted according to the minimum value of the error rate in the current context. This P-Chart detected the three concept shifts that really exist in the data: the two first concept shifts (after t=8 and t=16) were

Figure 5. A P-Chart for monitoring the sample error rate

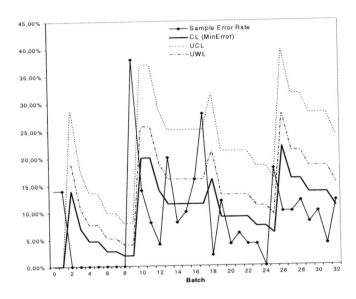

detected immediately (those points that fall above the current control limit) and the third concept shift (after t=24) was detected with slight delay. However, beginning at t=25, the P-Chart starts detecting an upward trend of the sample error, that is, a concept drift (those points that fall outside the warning limits). When further, at t=27 the concept shift is signaled, all the examples beginning at t=25 are considered to belong to the same context and they all are used to re-learn the model.

Figure 6 shows the averaged accuracy of all the combinations "algorithm-approach" after each batch, respectively. At first, the performance of all approaches is good enough; however, those combined with Adaptive Bayes show a better performance. After the first change has occurred, the performance of non-adaptive approaches decreases significantly (they can not identify concept changes), and the performance of the FSW approach can recover a little because it re-learns regularly from the last six batches. In contrast, Pmin can quickly recover its performance decrease as the learning progresses. Moreover, PMin, instead of the FSW, whose performance depends on the window size, doesn't depend on any parameter.

Table 3 compares, for all the learning styles and combinations "algorithm-approach", the average predictive accuracy over all the batches, and Table 4 shows some comparative studies of the performance for a pair of approaches using paired t-tests with a confidence level of 95 percent. A + (-) sign in the

Figure 6. Comparison of the averaged accuracy of each combination "algorithm-approach"

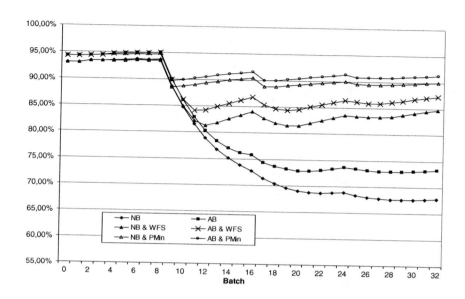

Table 3. Predictive accuracy of the two learning algorithms (NB and AB) combined with three approaches (baseline, FSW, PMin) for the eight different learning styles

Approaches	LS 1	LS 2	LS 3	LS 4	LS 5	LS 6	LS 7	LS 8	Avg Acc.
(1) NB	70.50	64.42	69.59	64.71	77.33	77.27	57.83	60.51	**67.77**
(2) NB & FSW	86.86	85.11	83.06	78.81	87.48	85.98	86.66	84.48	**84.80**
(3) NB & PMin	91.41	90.96	91.24	89.15	90.27	90.03	90.25	89.30	**90.04**
(4) AB	75.73	70.79	73.42	67.01	80.61	80.09	70.38	68.24	**73.28**
(5) AB & FSW	89.04	87.39	86.69	82.01	89.33	88.43	89.06	87.12	**87.38**
(6) AB & PMin	91.90	91.61	92.62	90.87	91.77	90.60	91.84	89.30	**91.31**

column "mean" means that the first approach obtains a better (worse) result with statistic significance. Note that the mean of the accuracy is significantly different with high probability as given by the p-value.

Studies I and II compare adaptive approaches that deal with concept drift against the baseline non-adaptive approach in combination with Naïve Bayes and Adaptive Bayes, respectively. The results show that a significant improvement is achieved by using any adaptive method instead of the non-adaptive one for both the learning algorithms. Study III compares the two adaptive approaches

Table 4. Summary of results comparing the predictive accuracy of a pair of approaches

			Results for the differences between the averaged accuracies					Paired t-test
			Mean	Std Err	Median	Min	Max	Two sided, α=0.05 p-value
I	(2) vs. (1)	+	17.03	6.96	15.23	8.71	28.83	0.00023
	(3) vs. (1)	+	22.27	6.80	23.05	12.76	32.42	0.00004
II	(5) vs (4)	+	14.01	4.04	14.16	8.34	18.88	0.00002
	(6) vs (4)	+	18.03	4.95	20.01	10.51	23.86	0.00002
III	(3) vs. (2)	+	5.24	2.75	4.30	2.56	10.34	0.00101
	(6) vs (5)	+	3.93	2.37	2.82	2.17	8.86	0.00222
IV	(4) vs. (1)	+	5.51	3.39	4.53	2.30	12.55	0.00250
	(5) vs. (2)	+	2.58	0.58	2.42	1.85	3.63	0.00000
	(6) vs. (3)	+	1.27	0.64	1.44	0.49	2.26	0.00078

FSW and PMin in combination with the two learning algorithms, respectively. The results shows that the performance of P-Chart is significantly superior to the performance of FSW, where the learner is adapted regularly without considering whether a concept change really occurs. The last study (IV) compares the two learning algorithms. The results show that Adaptive Bayes significantly outperforms Naïve Bayes for all the approaches. In general, a more significant improvement is achieved when adaptive methods are combined with Adaptive Bayes.

Conclusions and Future Work

In this chapter, we presented an adaptive predictive model for a student modeling prediction task based on learning styles. The main difference between our approach and other similar approaches is that we try to adapt and fine-tune the initial acquired information about the student's learning style and preferences from the student's interactions with the system using machine learning techniques. We represent the matches between the learning resources and the student's learning style into an adaptive predictive model that is able to quickly adapt to any change of the student's preferences. We also present a general method to handle concept drift using P-Charts, which is broadly applicable to a range of domains and learning algorithms.

Although we have not performed an evaluation yet with real users, the obtained results using artificial students show that our adaptive approach consistently recognizes concept changes and that, the learner can adapt quickly to these changes in order to maintain its performance level. This means that our predictive model is able to adapt quickly to the changes in the user behavior in order to reflect more accurately the current student's preferences. In the near future, we plan to evaluate our approach with real students and with other Bayesian Network classifiers.

Acknowledgments

This work was developed in the context of project ALESII (POSI/EIA/55340/2004).

References

Billsus, D., & Pazzani, M. J. (1999). A hybrid user model for news stories classifications. In J. Kay (Ed.), *Proceedings of the Seventh International Conference on User Modeling,* Canada (pp. 99-108). Springer-Verlag.

Brusilovsky, P. (2001). Adaptive hypermedia. *User Modeling and User-Adapted Interaction, 11,* 87-110.

Carver, C. A., Howard, R. A., & Lane, W. D. (1999). Enhancing student learning trough hypermedia courseware and incorporation of student learning styles. *IEEE Transactions on Education, 42*(1), 33-38.

Castillo, G., Gama, J., & Medas, P. (2003). Adaptation to drifting concepts. In F. M. Pires & S. Abreu (Eds.), *Progress in Artificial Intelligence, Lecture Notes in Artificial Intelligence, 2902* (pp. 279-293). Springer-Verlag.

Felder, R. M. (1996). Matters of style. *ASEE Prism, 6*(4), 18-23.

Felder, R. M., & Soloman, B. A. (n.d.). *Index of learning style questionnaire.* Retrieved from http://www2.ncsu.edu/unity/lockers/users/f/felder/public/ILSdir/ilsweb.html

Gama, J., & Castillo, G. (2002). Adaptive Bayes. In F. Garijo, J. Riquelme, & M. Toro (Eds.), *Advances in Artificial Intelligence - IBERAMIA 2002,*

Lecture Notes in artificial intelligence (Vol. 2527, pp. 765-774). Springer-Verlag.

Klinkenberg, R., & Renz, I. (1998) Adaptive information filtering: Learning in the presence of concept drifts. *Proceedings of the ICML-98 workshop Learning for Text Categorization* (pp. 33-40). AAAI Press.

Lanquillon, C. (2001). *Enhancing test classification to improve information filtering.* Ph.D. Dissertation, University of Madgbeburg, Germany. Retrieved from http://diglib.uni-magdeburg.de/Dissertationen/2001/carlanquillon.pdf

Mitchell, T. (1997). *Machine learning.* McGraw Hill.

Mladenic, D. (1996). *Personal WebWatcher: Implementation and design.* Technical Report, IJS-DP-7472.

Montgomery, D. C. (1997). *Introduction to statistical quality control* (3rd ed.). New York: John Wiley & Sons.

Papanikolaou, K. A., Grigoriadou, M., Magoulas, G. D., & Kornilakis, H. (2002). Towards new forms of knowledge communication: The adaptive dimension of a Web-based learning environment. *Computers and Education, 39*(4), 333-360.

Pazzani, M. J., & Billsus, D. (1997). Learning and revising user profiles: The identification of interesting Web sites. *Maching Learning, 27,* 313-331.

Peña, C. I., Marzo, J. L., & de la Rosa, J. L. (2002). Intelligent agents in a teaching and learning environment on the Web. *Proceedings of the Second International Conference on Advanced Learning Technologies (ICALT2002),* Russia.

Schwab, I., Wolfgang, P., & Koychev, I. (2000). Learning to recommend from positive evidence. *Proceedings of intelligent user interfaces* (pp. 241-247). ACM Press.

Stern, M. K., & Woolf, B. P. (2000). Adaptive content in an online lecture system. In P. Brusilovsky, O. Stock, & C. Strapparava (Eds.), *Adaptive hypermedia and adaptive Web-based systems.* Lecture notes in computer science, Vol. 1982 (pp. 227-238). Berlin: Springer-Verlag.

Vanlehn, K., Ohlsson, S., & Nason, R. (1994). Applications of simulated students: An exploration. *Journal of Artificial Intelligence in Education, 5*(2), 135-175.

Webb, G., Pazzani, M., & Billsus, D. (2001). Maching learning for user modeling. *User Modelling and User-Adapted Interaction, 11,* 19-29.

Chapter V

Giving Learners a Real Sense of Control Over Adaptivity, Even If They Are Not Quite Ready For It Yet

Marek Czarkowski, University of Sydney, Australia

Judy Kay, University of Sydney, Australia

Abstract

This chapter describes Tutor3, the latest in a sequence of systems that we have created to provide adaptation of hypertext where the user can maintain a real sense of control over the adaptivity. In Tutor3, the user always has access to precise details of what has been adapted to them, how this adaptation is controlled, and they can alter it. We describe both the user's and the hypertext author's view of the system. We then report a qualitative evaluation of the system in terms of the ways that users were able to understand both the adaptation and their power to control it. We conclude that while users do expect adaptivity, they do not expect to be able to control it. We discuss the challenges this creates for building adaptive systems that users can control effectively.

Introduction

Adaptive hypertext, at its best, offers the promise of a personalised document and interaction that meets the individual's particular preferences, knowledge, and goals. There are many situations where this could be of immense value. For example, consider the case of hypertext learning environments. These offer potential improvements in learning outcomes if they deliver some of the benefits that appear to be achievable in one to one tutoring (Bloom, 1984). Equally importantly, users who have sensitive information needs may appreciate it if this is personalised. For example, in an evaluation of adaptive presentation of information for patients with cancer (Cawsey, Jones, & Pearson, 2000), there was a strong preference for the adapted version of the information.

While personalisation has the potential to offer considerable benefits, it also has some serious problems. In this chapter, we are particular concerned with one class of these. They are associated with the potential for adaptive systems to be unpredictable and irritating because the user is unable to determine what is adapted, how that adaptation is controlled and how they can manage the personalisation processes. Users may be surprised or irritated by systems that are "too smart". Users may be subject to the hunting problem, where the system and the user simultaneously attempt to adapt to each other (Browne, Totterdell, & Norman, 1990). It is also quite possible that the author of the adaptive hypertext system has made a mistake, such as providing copious detail when the user has asked for minimal information. This could be due to a simple coding error where a single "not" was omitted or incorrectly included.

To delve into this issue, we first need to identify the core elements of an adaptive hypertext. While these will vary across systems, they would generally include the following four elements.

- A user model is an essential part of an adaptive hypertext system since it is the system's knowledge of the user and is the driving force determining exactly what is adapted and how. The user model may be very simple, perhaps a set of Boolean flags or an arbitrarily complex representation.

- The adaptable content. This might be as simple as text snippets, each of which is either selected or not for a particular user. At the other extreme, it may be a complex knowledge representation.

- The adaptation process which combines the above two elements to produce the adaptive presentation.

- The user modelling process which determines the user model and its evolution over time. Like all the other elements, this can range from a very simple form, such as the user always setting the values of some flags in what is often called customisation. At the more complex end of the spectrum, it may involve machine learning, based on information collected about the user or it may involve information and knowledge about other users such as stereotypic users (Rich, 1979) and deep knowledge of the domain.

Each of these constitutes one part of the process of producing an adaptive hypertext. Each could be responsible for presenting a different hypertext to different users. If the user is surprised at what they see in such a hypertext environment, it might be due to an error in any of these elements. Even if there is no error, a user might wonder why the system presented the information that it did. They may also wonder what other people would see that they did not. If they watch over the shoulder of another user of the same adaptive hypertext system, they may well be surprised at differences in the way the system treated that user compared with the way it treated them. If the user model was defined some time ago, the user may have completely forgotten the details of the set up. In that case, if the user has changed over time and the system does not model that change, its adaptation could be wrong and increasingly so. If users choose to share login accounts, they may not realise the impact this has on adaptation. We have been working to explore ways to address these problems by making adaptive hypertext that is scrutable, by which we mean that the user can delve into each of the elements of the adaptation to see what it is doing and we would like to support the user in controlling at least some of these elements.

Consider, for example, the two pages shown in Figures 1 and 2. These are two of the possible adapted forms of a single Web page in our adaptive hypertext system called Tutor. In a typical adaptive hypertext system, the user who is presented with the page shown in Figure 1 has no way of knowing that another user would see the form in Figure 2. Further, the user would not be easily able to determine why the system chose to adapt in the way that it did. A critical difference between Tutor and more conventional hypertext systems is indicated by the link at the bottom left. This "How was this page adapted to you?" link enables the user to scrutinise the processes underlying the adaptation.

The adaptation performed by Tutor can be coarse-grained or fine-grained. In the above example, a whole paragraph has been adapted. However, adaptive content can range in size, be it a whole page, paragraph, word, or even a single HTML element. This gives the author flexibility as they can write adaptive words

Figure 1. Example of a page adapted to a student who wants to learn as much as possible

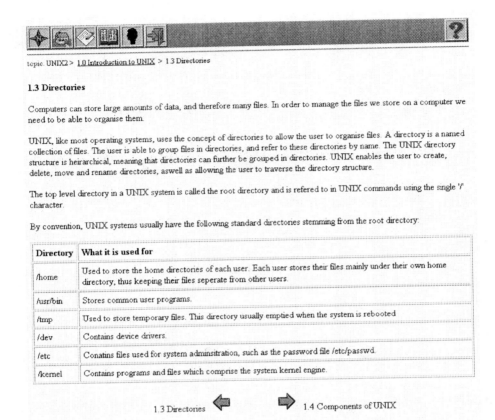

mid-sentence rather than providing two versions of the paragraph which would otherwise be the same. Since HTML browsers support different forms of media (text, sound, image), it is possible to adaptively include or exclude these forms of media based on the user's profile.

Tutor is a generic framework for the presentation of adaptive Web based course material. Tutor can host multiple courses, each with its own set of adaptive lesson pages. To define a new course, the author writes the learning material as a set of documents in the adaptive tutorial mark-up language (ATML). An ATML document is essentially an HTML 4.0 document with additional mark-up that is used to describe adaptive content. Next the ATML documents are uploaded to

Figure 2. Same page as in Figure 1 but this time adapted to a student who wants to learn just enough to pass

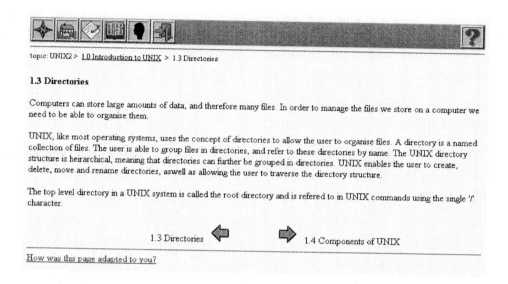

the Web server where the Tutor Web site is hosted and the course is ready to be accessed by students. All this makes Tutor quite unexceptional as an adaptive hypertext system as we use well-known techniques for adaptive content presentation and adaptive navigation. The distinctive aspect of our series of Tutor systems, and the focus of this paper, is that Tutor represents an exploration of how to build scrutability into adaptive hypertext.

The next section of this chapter provides some background to our motivations for building a scrutably adaptive hypertext and some of the work that has influenced the design of Tutor3. Next is a brief overview of some of the user's view of Tutor3 and the next section describes the adaptive hypertext author's view. Then we describe the evaluation of Tutor's support for user control with the results in the following section. We conclude with a discussion of lessons learnt from the current series of experiments with Tutor.

Background

There is a growing debate within the field of adaptive systems over how much control should be given to the user as well as how much transparency there should be to the inner workings of the system. A debate on direct manipulation interfaces vs. interfaces driven by software agents highlighted understanding and control as key usability issues with adaptive systems (Maes & Schneiderman, 1997). An agreed outcome of that discussion was that users need to understand the adaptive operation of an adaptive system in order to trust it to perform tasks on their behalf. In addition, users must feel as though they have ultimate control over the system if and when they choose to exercise it. We believe that understandability of an adaptive system's response and empowerment of the user to control this response are key usability issues that are yet to be fully addressed by designers of adaptive systems. This is vital if we are to trust adaptive systems to perform critical tasks on our behalf. We extrapolate this to non-critical tasks.

Another motivation for helping the user understand the adaptive operation is that increased privacy laws in many countries stipulate that where a system stores personal information about a user, the user has a right to view and to modify that information and understand how it is used (Kobsa, 2002). Ultimately, this requires that the user not only has access to their user model but also understands, to some degree, how the adaptive system processes their user model to produce an adaptive response.

Another possible reason for scrutability relates to the possibility that the adaptive hypertext could have errors in the adaptation. The more complicated the hypertext, the less efficient the authoring (Calvi & Cristea, 2002) and the more opportunities exist for authoring errors. One approach to this problem is to improve authoring tools. This is undoubtedly an important field of research. For example, tools have been developed for AHA! (Calvi & Cristea, 2002; Cristea & Aroyo, 2002).

While AHA! has a similar architecture and adaptivity features to Tutor, its authoring tools include a specialised editor to define concepts and adaptation rules and a graph editor which allows the author to visually link concept nodes (Calvi & Cristea, 2002; Cristea & Aroyo 2002; De Bra, Aqerts, Berden, de Lange, Rousseau Santic, Smits, & Stash, 2003). Such authoring tools will help reduce the difficulty in authoring adaptive hypertext and also reduce the number of errors. However, it is not possible to completely eliminate mistakes. In fact, a scrutable interface could be used as a debugging tool by the adaptive hypertext author as it should clearly explain how a page was adapted to the user.

A closely related problem can occur where there is mismatch between the user's understanding and the author's intention. For example, an adaptive maths course may offer the user the choice of an easy or hard version of the course. A user might request the easy version, only to find it is too easy and that they would have actually preferred more challenging material.

There is a substantial and growing body of work that makes the user model available to the user (Bull, Brna, & Pain, 1995). In particular, in educational contexts, there has been considerable interest in the potential of supporting reflective learning by creating suitable interfaces to the user model as reported, for example, in two workshops (Bull, Brna, & Dimitrova, 2003; Morales, Pain, Bull, & Kay, 1999). Even in systems where the work is not explicitly concerned with supporting student reflection, there are many cases where the learner is given some insight into the system's model of the learner. For example, Corbett and Anderson (1995) describe a teaching system that provides a set of "skillometers" which show a summary of the learner model in terms of the degree to which a set of skills has been learnt. Of course, displaying the user model provides the user with access to some understanding of just one of the core elements of the personalisation.

There has also been some work on providing greater user control in adaptive hypertext. For example, a Web site for a conference was used for an empirical study to explore user's reactions to controllability of the adaptive system (Jameson & Schwarzkopf, 2002). The system was intended to help attendees compile a program of events they would attend at the conference and made personalised recommendations of events that might interest the user, based on their interaction with the system. Usage and subjective feedback was compared for different configurations of the system: (i) the system made recommendations only when the user requested them, or (ii) the system made recommendations automatically. Users played with the system in all configurations and provided subjective feedback. The study found that both configurations had their advantages in certain situations and based on the user's personal preferences. However, the type of user control we are exploring is quite different to that of this study. In the first system configuration, the user could basically invoke the adaptive function when desired. However, the user could not, for example, control the outcome of this function. Nor could the user delve into their user model and update it to directly change the type of recommendations provided by the system. What if, for example, the system believed the user was interested in attending presentations about intelligent agents when the user was actually interested in direct manipulation interfaces? It is this type of control that we are exploring with Tutor.

POP (Höök, Karlgren, Waern, Dahlbäck, Jansson, Karlgren, & Lemaire, 1996) represents another important piece of work in this it area. It was an adaptive hypertext help system which aimed to achieve transparency and user control. It did this by allowing users to drive the user modeling by specifying their task, expressed in terms they were familiar with. It supported exploration of the adaptive hypertext with specially marked hotwords, which the user could select to see a set of questions they could ask about unfamiliar concepts. The adaptive content could be opened or closed. This represents an interface with support for user control of the user model and the ability to see the full hypertext. It did not enable the user to see why a particular part of the text was made directly visible, or not, because of the details of the user model. Notably, however, POP had a quite complex internal structure which was hidden in its internal black box. This meant it was then impossible for the user to go beyond viewing the user model.

An important aspect of our work on Tutor has been a focus on simplicity. To place our work in context, the adaptivity features and architecture of Tutor are similar to the early versions of AHA! (De Bra et al., 2003). However, we have focused on building a user interface to facilitate scrutability rather than extending the adaptive hypertext capabilities.

In summary, several researchers have indicated the importance of user control, especially in learning environments. Then, in addition, several researchers have explored ways to make the user model open to learners and to use this to support learning. However, Tutor represents the first system to go beyond open or even scrutable user models; it makes the adaptivity and associated processes open to the learner and controllable. The systems mentioned above have enabled the user to access, view, and perhaps modify the user model, but not the process driving the adaptation; it is this process which has been highlighted as equally as important by Maes and Schneiderman (1997).

Essentially, our goal of building a scrutably adaptive hypertext creates two quite different classes of challenge. On the one hand, we need to design an architecture for an adaptive hypertext system and to do this in a way that makes it possible for the user to scrutinise the adaptation processes. This poses considerable technical challenges. The other, quite different class of challenge is the creation of a suitable interface that supports users in scrutinising the adaptivity. Clearly, there is a real interaction between these two aspects: we would expect that it is far more difficult to build effective interfaces to more complex systems, with highly sophisticated representations for the user model as well as complex mechanisms for representing and generating the hypertext. For example, if the generation is based upon deep natural language generation with complex planning processes and the user model is an executable representation, it is not at all obvious how to make all these aspects and their interactions accessible and understandable to a user. Accordingly, we decided to begin with a very modest form of adaptation and to evaluate that before proceeding to more sophisticated forms. We were also encouraged in this decision since it seems that quite modest levels of adaptation, with correspondingly simple user models, may be quite useful. For example, Strachan, Andserson, Sneesby, and Evans (2000) observed that users liked customisations based on a simple user model.

The design of the Tutor interface has been strongly influenced by the ELM-ART system (Brusilovsky, Schwarz, & Weber, 1996; Brusilovsky & Weber, 2001), which teaches the LISP computer language. As indicated in the following description, the elements of the interface, including the course map and uses of colour, follow what appears to have been a successful interface for that system.

Increasing user control over adaptivity raises a new set of challenges. Given full control of their user model and the adaptivity, the user could sabotage the function of system by changing their user model beliefs such that the model no longer reflects them accurately (Kay, 2001). The user could quite easily undo all the hard work the adaptive system has done to form its assessment of the user. One remedy for this is to restrict access to parts the user model. A different approach, used in Mr. Collins (Bull & Pain, 1995), is to force the user to negotiate changes to their user model. Mr. Collins allows the user to inspect their user model to see beliefs the system holds about them, offer their own self assessment and then negotiate with the system to change its beliefs about the user. The user has to correctly answer test questions to convince the system.

Another problem of added user control and transparency is the additional cognitive load that it places on the student. The user of an adaptive system is busy using that system for its intended purpose, whether it is learning, searching, entertainment, or something else. We envisage that typically the user's interactions with the scrutability component will be brief and infrequent. Some likely scenarios are:

- the user may become curious about the adaptivity;
- the user might wonder what content they are missing out on;
- a page presented to the user seems to contain irrelevant content;
- the user believes their preferences, interests, or knowledge have changed or are not being catered to by the system; and
- the user is simply experimenting with the interface.

Despite our argument for the importance of use control and transparency, we do not expect user to frequently exercise their control. This contrasts with the case studied by Jameson and Schwarzkopf (2002). Indeed, we observed that users only scrutinised the adaptation infrequently in out field trials of Tutor (Czarkowski & Kay, 2000).

However, when the user chooses to take control, this should be possible. In fact, this highlights the difficulty in developing an interface to support scrutability. Not only are adaptivity and scrutability relatively new concepts for many users, the interface must be simple enough for a casual user to understand yet powerful enough to support the expert user.

It is possible that scrutability may need to become a more frequently used feature of an adaptive system, if humans are to trust adaptive systems to perform more critical tasks on their behalf. Naturally, in cases where users employ adaptive systems or software agents to carry out important work or make decisions on their behalf, they would expect to have the ability to understand, and as needed to change, the systems behaviour and the process with which it makes decisions.

Tutor has gone through several versions. The first version was evaluated in a field trial (Czarkowski & Kay, 2000). This appeared to be quite successful, with a total of 113 students registering with the system, 29 percent exploring the adaptivity and, of these, 27% checking what had been included as part of the adaptation and where content had been excluded. This evaluation identified limitations, too. While it did show material that had been adaptively included, it showed only the location of material excluded. Also, some users failed to appreciate that they could affect the adaptation, at any time, by altering their answers to the profile questions. In essence, the Tutor evaluation showed promise but also identified ways that the scrutability support was incomplete. These concerns were addressed in Tutor2. We performed a qualitative evaluation to assess whether users could scrutinise its adaptation effectively (Czarkowski & Kay, 2002, 2003). This evaluation indicated that users could *not* do the basic scrutability tasks we had defined as essential. So, in light of these findings, we completely redesigned the adaptation explanation to the form it has in Tutor3, the version described in this paper.

Overview of Tutor from the Student Perspective

To use Tutor, the student must first register for a username and password. Once registered, they log in and select from the list of available courses. On entering a course, Tutor requires the user to complete a questionnaire form (see Figure 3). The student's answers define their user model for the course. Students entering the course for the first time will have a blank profile and must fill in answers on the questionnaire. Those who have previously accessed the course have the option of updating their previous answers. When the student saves their profile, Tutor navigates to the teacher's instructions page.

The teacher's instructions page, like all lesson pages, has the icons that can be seen in Figures 1 and 2. Each has its text description as a mouse over. These icons are, in the order that they appear on the screenshots:

- **Course map:** gives an overview of the whole course and the student's progress through the course.
- **Teacher's instructions page:** this is the first page the student sees after the login and profile validation process, so this is the place for the teacher's

announcements and bulletin board. It is used as the course home page but has all the features of a regular lesson page.

- **Notes editor:** a free-form set of arbitrary entries by the student, supporting the student in actively recording information as they work through the course.

- **Glossary:** essentially another adaptable page, but generally would have many links to it through the course.

- **Profile page:** shows the questionnaire used to establish the user model and can be used at any time to update it.

- **Exit:** to leave the course.

- **Online help page:** at the far right; this describes the interface and system features, including adaptation and scrutability support.

As we have already mentioned, Figure 1 and Figure 2 show how a typical lesson page is adapted differently for students who have different user models. The page in Figure 1 has been adapted to a student who is revising the course and wants to gain a mastery of all the course material. In contrast, the page in Figure 2 has been adapted to a student who is hoping to learn just enough to pass. Note that the page in Figure 1 has an additional (fourth) paragraph of text and a table that lists conventionally used UNIX directory names. The hypertext author considered this material was not needed to gain a bare pass. So, when the user model indicates that this is all the user wants to do, it is not shown. However, where the user model indicates the user wants a broader understanding, it is included. Note also that in Figure 1 an additional right arrow labelled *6.0 Review Questions* has been included in the page. This is a hyperlink to another lesson page that contains additional review questions. It appears only where the user model indicates the user wants to revise the course material.

Profile Page

The profile page presents a set of questions and uses their answers to establish the user model. An example of a typical profile page is shown in Figure 3.

The student must complete every question on the profile page before they are shown course material. Every time a student enters the course, Tutor displays the profile page pre-populated with the student's current data. This gives the student an opportunity to reflect on their learning strategy, immediate goals, and interests and to update their profile should they wish to do so.

Tutor provides the possibility of links to examples of the effect of a question. This is intended for cases where it is hard to formulate the question clearly and where

Figure 3. Example of a profile page

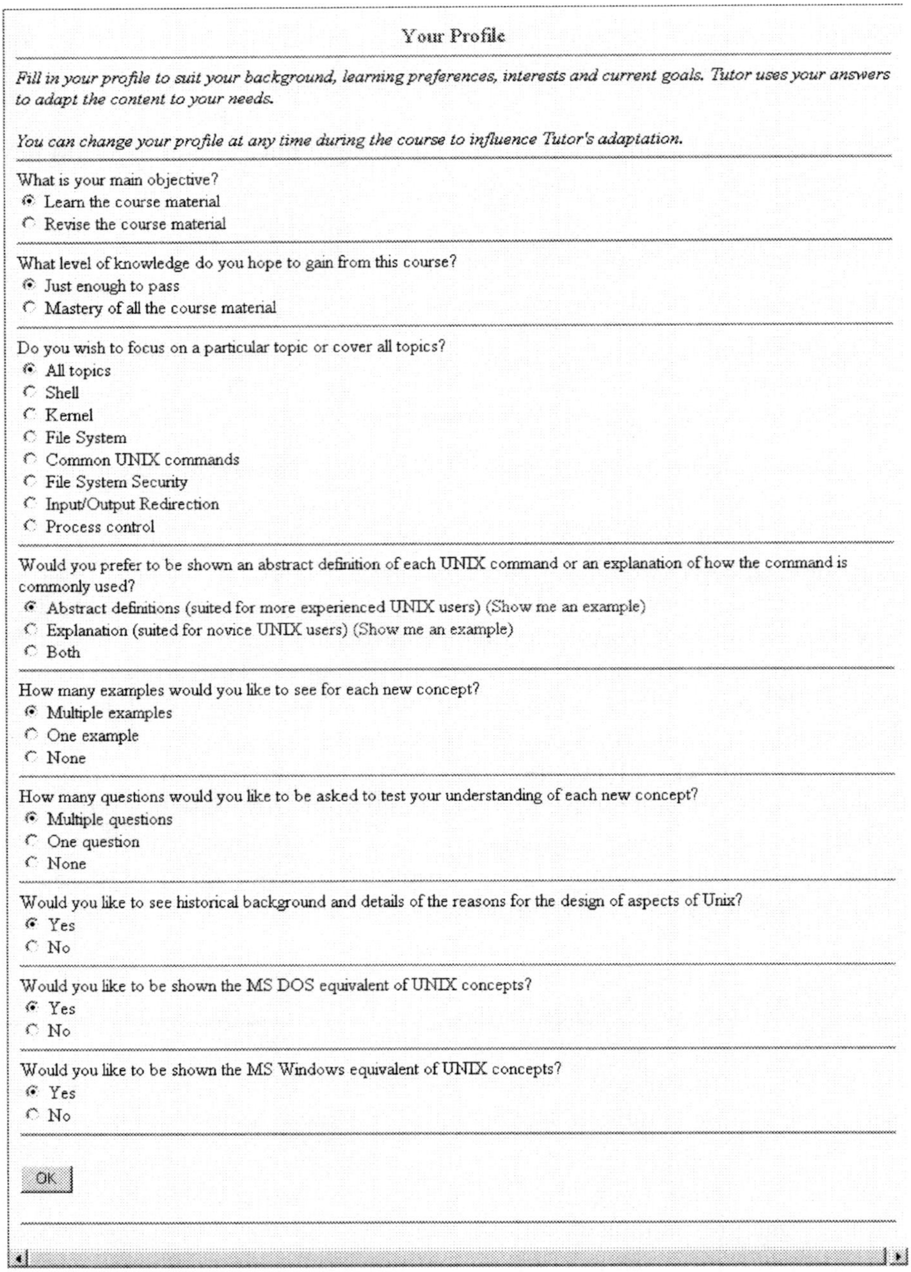

Your Profile

Fill in your profile to suit your background, learning preferences, interests and current goals. Tutor uses your answers to adapt the content to your needs.

You can change your profile at any time during the course to influence Tutor's adaptation.

What is your main objective?
- ⦿ Learn the course material
- ○ Revise the course material

What level of knowledge do you hope to gain from this course?
- ⦿ Just enough to pass
- ○ Mastery of all the course material

Do you wish to focus on a particular topic or cover all topics?
- ⦿ All topics
- ○ Shell
- ○ Kernel
- ○ File System
- ○ Common UNIX commands
- ○ File System Security
- ○ Input/Output Redirection
- ○ Process control

Would you prefer to be shown an abstract definition of each UNIX command or an explanation of how the command is commonly used?
- ⦿ Abstract definitions (suited for more experienced UNIX users) (Show me an example)
- ○ Explanation (suited for novice UNIX users) (Show me an example)
- ○ Both

How many examples would you like to see for each new concept?
- ⦿ Multiple examples
- ○ One example
- ○ None

How many questions would you like to be asked to test your understanding of each new concept?
- ⦿ Multiple questions
- ○ One question
- ○ None

Would you like to see historical background and details of the reasons for the design of aspects of Unix?
- ⦿ Yes
- ○ No

Would you like to be shown the MS DOS equivalent of UNIX concepts?
- ⦿ Yes
- ○ No

Would you like to be shown the MS Windows equivalent of UNIX concepts?
- ⦿ Yes
- ○ No

[OK]

---

an example of its effect should be clearer. The sample page can be accessed by the student via a hyperlink labelled *Show me an example* positioned next to the profile option. For example, for the fourth profile question in Figure 3, the user can view a sample of a typical lesson page that has abstract definitions of concepts, and another version of the same page showing what the author has called explanations.

The profile page is important as it is central to the scrutability component of Tutor. The student must understand how to read and edit their profile in order to change the personalisation to achieve the desired effect. Note that there is explanatory information at the top of on the profile.

Scrutinising the Adaptation

On pages where content has been adaptively included or excluded, Tutor dynamically includes the hyperlink *How was this page adapted to you?* at the bottom of the page. On pages with no adaptation (as in Figure 9), the text "There was no adaptation on this page" appears instead of the link.

Clicking this link displays an adaptation summary, just below the link. For example, the adaptation summary that would be displayed for Figure 2 is shown in Figure 4. This summary is the starting point for scrutinising the adaptation of the current page. It tells the student which elements from their profile caused the adaptation and allows the student to probe even deeper, to see specifically what has been included or excluded because of their profile.

The adaptation summary has several elements. It begins with information describing how to scrutinise the adaptation. Also, the text at the bottom of the adaptation summary reminds the user that they can change their profile settings by clicking the user profile icon in the top menu.

The core of this page is the list of each user model attribute that caused adaptation of the page. This is expressed in terms of the profile questions so that it should be familiar. Against each question is the user's current answer. The third column displays a hyperlink labelled *show me*. For example, the last row in Figure 4 indicates that there has been adaptation because the student answered *Just enough to pass* for the profile question *What level of knowledge do you hope to gain from this course?*

Clicking this hyperlink opens a separate browser window to display the adaptation explanation page in Figure 5 and this indicates adapted content by the background colour. It shows adaptation associated with the single profile question that the user selected with the *show me* link. It is in a separate window so that the user can compare this annotated version of the page to the original version.

Figure 4. Example of an adaptation summary on a page that has been adapted to a student

How was this page adapted to you?

Some of the content on this page was included or excluded based on your answers to the following profile questions. For example, if some content was not seen as useful to you then it was excluded.

Click the "show me" link to see the included/removed content. This will open another window highlighting in green content that was included, highlighting in red content that was excluded.

Profile Question	Your Answer	Highlight Included/Excluded content
What is your main objective?	Learn	show me
What level of knowledge do you hope to gain from this course?	Just enough to pass	show me

Remember you can change your profile settings by selecting the following icon in the top menu

[hide explanation]

The colour choices follow a traffic light metaphor, an idea inspired by ELM-ART (Brusilovsky et al., 1996; Brusilovsky & Weber, 2001): content that was included is highlighted with a green background (which is the light grey in the figure). Content that was excluded is highlighted in red (which appears as a darker grey in the picture). This is explained to the user in the key at the top of the adaptation explanation page. The key shows the selected profile question, the student's current answer and explains the colour coding.

For example, from Figure 4, if the user clicks the *show me* hyperlink next to the profile question *What level of knowledge do you hope to gain from this course?*, the adaptation explanation page will be displayed as in Figure 5. On this page, the fourth paragraph under the section titled *1.3 Directories* and the table below it are highlighted in red, indicating the content was adaptively excluded from the page. In our test environment with Netscape 4.7 browsers, moving the mouse over the *i* icon (just above the red paragraph) pops up the following text informing the user why the context was excluded, and how to change this adaptation:

This content was excluded since your answer to the above profile question was "Just enough to pass". To make this content included, change your

Figure 5. Example of an adaptation explanation page (as seen in Internet Explorer) — accessed by clicking the "show me" link in Figure 4 for the profile question "What level of knowledge do you hope to gain from this course?"

Adaptation Explanation		
Profile Question: What level of knowledge do you hope to gain from this course? **Your Answer:** Just enough to pass	**Key:**	content that was included
		content that was excluded

Instructions: Move your mouse over each info icon ⓘ for further explanation.

topic: UNIX2 > 1.0 Introduction to UNIX > 1.3 Directories

1.3 Directories

Computers can store large amounts of data, and therefore many files. In order to manage the files we store on a computer we need to be able to organise them.

UNIX, like most operating systems, uses the concept of directories to allow the user to organise files. A directory is a named collection of files. The user is able to group files in directories, and refer to these directories by name. The UNIX directory structure is heirarchical, meaning that directories can further be grouped in directories. UNIX enables the user to create, delete, move and rename directories, aswell as allowing the user to traverse the directory structure.

The top level directory in a UNIX system is called the root directory and is refered to in UNIX commands using the single '/' character.
ⓘ

By convention, UNIX systems usually have the following standard directories stemming from the root directory:

Directory	What it is used for
/home	Used to store the home directories of each user. Each user stores their files mainly under their own home directory, thus keeping their files seperate from other users
/usr/bin	Stores common user programs.
/tmp	Used to store temporary files. This directory usually emptied when the system is rebooted
/dev	Contains device drivers.
/etc	Contains files used for system administration, such as the password file /etc/passwd.
/kernel	Contains programs and files which compose the system kernel engine

This content was excluded since your answer to the above profile question was **'Just enough to pass'**. To make this content included, change your answer to **'Mastery of all the course material'** in the profile editor by clicking the head icon in the main window.

1.3 Directories 1.4 Components of UNIX

Please close this window and return to the main window.

answer to "Mastery of all the course material" in the profile editor by clicking the head icon in the main window.

In Internet Explorer 5+ browsers the text is displayed by default underneath the adaptive content, as it appears in Figure 5.

From the adaptation summary table on the main page (Figure 4), the student can open a separate adaptation explanation page for each profile attribute that affected adaptation and thus compare how different profile questions affected the adaptation of the page.

Course Map Page

The course map, such as the one shown in Figure 6, provides an additional navigation option that allows students to randomly access course pages. This complements the links that authors will typically create on each page of the course. The course map displays a list of hyperlinks to all lesson pages in a course. Hyperlinks are cascaded to indicate the hierarchical relationship between pages. For example, the first page of a new chapter is left justified, with pages within that chapter being offset to the right.

Whilst the list of hyperlinks to pages is the same for each user, the hyperlinks are colour coded to provide adaptive navigational guidance. As in ELM-ART (Brusilovsky et al., 1996; Brusilovsky & Weber, 2001), colour coding of hyperlinks in Tutor (both in the course map and on a lesson page) is based on a traffic light metaphor. For any hyperlink, the author may specify zero or more pre-requisite pages. If the student has visited all the pre-requisite pages, the hyperlink will appears in green, indicating the student is ready to learn the material. If the student has not visited all the pre-requisite pages, the hyperlink appears in red. If the student has already visited a page, its hyperlink will appear in black, but still underlined to distinguish it from normal text. Hyperlink colour coding indicates which pages the hypertext author considers the student should read or not, based on the current state of the user's user model. At the same time, the student is free to access any page.

Once opened, the course map stays open until closed. One way to use Tutor is to keep the course map open while working through the course. Clicking a hyperlink in the course map loads the lesson page in the main browser window. If the course map is left opened, its display is updated as the user accesses a lesson page, updating the effect of pre-requisites that become satisfied. For example, Figure 6 shows a course map where the student has accessed the first page of the course. The hyperlink to the first page, *1.0 Introduction to UNIX,*

Figure 6. Example of the course map

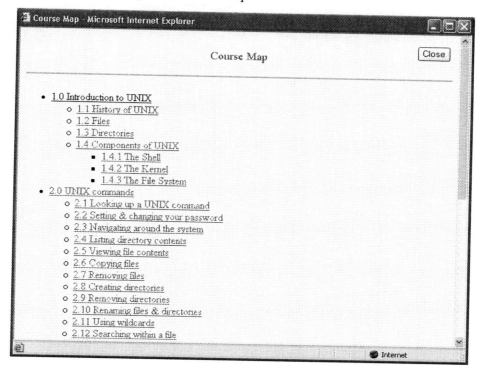

appears in black. Since the first page was a pre-requisite for the second and third pages, their hyperlinks are green (in Figure 6 *History of UNIX* and *1.2 Files* are green). All other pages in the course map have the second and third pages as pre-requisites, hence they are all displayed in red.

Notes Editor

The notes editor enables the student to make their own notes while they are working through a course. Each time the notes editor is accessed, the course name and current timestamp are appended to the current notes (see Figure 7). The student's notes are stored by Tutor and displayed when the notes editor is accessed.

Clicking the *Save and Print* button parses the notes (which can be marked-up in HTML as shown in the figure) and renders this as a printable page that the student can print or save to their local machine.

Figure 7. Notes editor showing notes in raw form as entered by the student

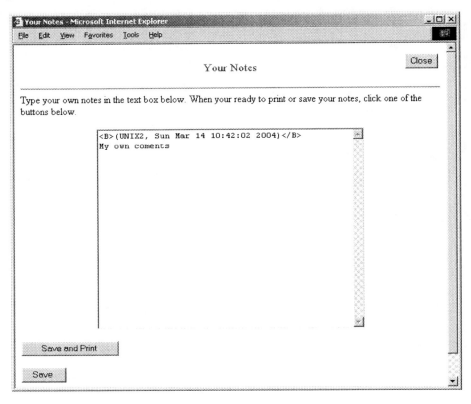

Glossary Page

This is intended for the usually glossary role, with descriptions of terms used in the course. An example is shown in Figure 9. The glossary page can be adapted and that adaptivity scrutinised as for other pages, however, Figure 9 shows a non-adaptive page to raise the point Tutor3 also inform the user when there was no adaptation on the page. Glossary pages that are adaptive include the scrutability interface as in Figure 4. Figure 8 shows the annotation of a hyperlink to the glossary entry for the word *group*. The glossary word is displayed in bold face and the hyperlink is annotated with the text *see glossary*, displayed in green font. Hyperlinks to glossary entries are annotated in this way, that is, differently from regular hyperlinks, since they operate differently. Clicking the glossary hyperlink in Figure 8 opens the glossary page in a separate browser window and jumps to the selected word as shown in Figure 9 whereas clicking a regular hyperlink

Figure 8. Annotation of hyperlinks to glossary entries

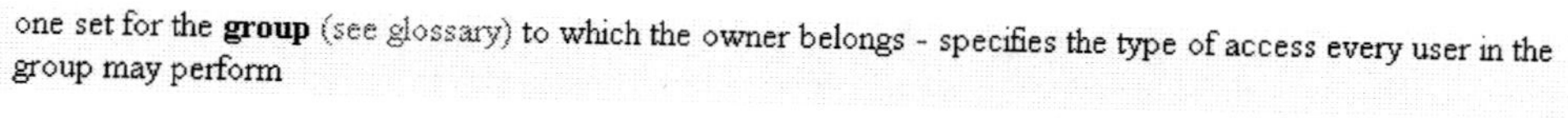

one set for the **group** (see glossary) to which the owner belongs - specifies the type of access every user in the group may perform

Figure 9. Typical Glossary page. Lesson and glossary pages that do not have adaptive content display the text There was no adaptation on this page at the bottom of the page. In a previous version of Tutor we displayed the link How was this page adapted to you? whether there was adaptation or not and we found if students clicked on the link to reveal no adaptation, they were very unlikely to try the link on another page.

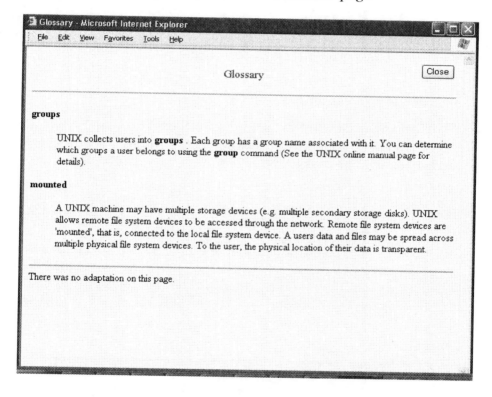

navigates to the anchored page, losing the information on the current page. The glossary hyperlink allows the student to continue with the main task in the lesson window, whilst consulting the glossary. Once the user understands this operation, the intention is that they will feel comfortable that they can click this link and view the glossary definition without loosing their current place in the main lesson page.

Overview of Tutor for the
Adaptive Hypertext Author

Tutor's adaptivity is driven by the markup of any HTML document with its ATML language. We have designed ATML to make it easier for an author to create adaptive hypertext. ATML has mark-up elements for interactive multiple choice questions, chapter and topic headings, glossary hyperlinks and page hyperlinks. If the author includes these tags in the lesson, Tutor dynamically translates this into HTML and generates the JavaScript code for the interactive features. This means that the author can ignore style and presentation of the course material and is free to concentrate on the teaching content.

ATML conforms to the XML 1.0 specification, and allows the user to include HTML 4.0 elements which are XML compliant. To create a new course in Tutor, the author first creates a set of ATML documents:

- um.xml – to generate the profile page
- coursemap.xml – to generate the course map page
- teacher.xml – to generate the teacher's instructions page, which the teacher can use as a bulletin board
- glossary.xml – to generate the glossary page
- <pagename>.xml – adaptive lesson pages of teaching material

The author can also add elements to a style sheet (CSS1 compliant) definition document. The styles can then be used in the course material. Once these documents are uploaded to the server Web site, the new course is ready to be accessed by students. The following sections will describe ATML more detail.

ATML: Profile Page

An extract of the profile page ATML used to generate the page in Figure 3 is shown. The *course* element defines a globally unique course identifier, in this case *UNIX2*. This tells Tutor that the following user model attributes relate to the UNIX2 course. Next the document contains definitions for peach user model attribute (*pref* element), the questionnaire text that is displayed on the profile page (*desc* element) and the possible answers (*answer* elements).

Figure 10. Excerpt of ATML used to generate profile page in Figure 3

```xml
<?xml version="1.0"?>
<um>
<course id="UNIX2" />

<pref id="MainGoal">
    <desc text="What is your main objective?" />
    <answer value="Learn">Learn the course material</answer>
    <answer value="Revise">Revise the course material</answer>
</pref>

<pref id="Level">
    <desc text="What level of knowledge do you hope to gain from this
course?" />
    <answer value="Just enough to pass">Just enough to pass</answer>
    <answer value="Mastery of all the course material">Mastery of all the
course material</answer>
</pref>

...

</um>
```

ATML: Adaptive Lesson Page

An ATML lesson page may contain adaptive and non-adaptive teaching material written in HTML or sourced from external HTML documents, or ATML tags to include interactive multiple-choice questions and various ATML link types. An excerpt of the ATML used to generate the lesson page in Figure 1 is shown in Figure 11.

Of particular importance is the *adapt* tag since it controls adaptation. In Figure 11, the paragraph starting with "By Convention ..." will only be displayed to users whose user model shows a value of *Mastery of all the course material* for the attribute *Level*. Referring to the profile page ATML, Figure 3, it can be seen that this attribute is the profile question *What level of knowledge do you hope to gain from this course?*. The low level attribute name *Level* is used internally and is not displayed to the user. This approach was chosen to avoid verbose ATML. Figure 11 also shows how ATML can be used to generate adaptive page links. In this example, a link to the page titled *6.0 Review Questions* is included to users who have indicated revision as their main objective. The rendered page link can be seen in Figure 1. A similar approach is used by the AHA system (De Bra et al., 2001). It also uses mark-up to describe adaptive fragments that are conditionally displayed to the user if the user model satisfies the inclusion criteria. The mark-up used by AHA is more expressive than Tutor, but hence more complicated.

Figure 11. Excerpt of ATML used to generate lesson page in Figure 1

```
<?xml version="1.0"?>
<lesson>
<page>

<topic><link src="Courses/UNIX2/p1.xml" text="1.0 Introduction to UNIX"/>
</topic>
<title>1.3 Directories</title>

<P/>Computers can store large amounts of data, and therefore many files. In
order to
manage the files we store on a computer we need to be able to organise
them.

...

<adapt cond="Level" value="Mastery of all the course material">
By convention, UNIX systems usually have the following standard directories
stemming from the root directory:
</adapt>

...

<adapt cond="MainGoal" value="Revise">
<pagelink>
<prev auto="true" />
<next src="Courses/UNIX2/p6.xml" title="6.0 Review Questions"/>
</pagelink>
</adapt>

</page>

</lesson>
```

Evaluation of Tutor Support for Scrutability

At a high level, the aim of our experiment was to gain insight to whether our tool for scruatability was effective. For it to be effective meant the users

- could understand the purpose of profile questions was to establish their user model;
- were able to determine what was adapted; and
- could demonstrate control over adaptation by changing answers to profile questions.

Our evaluation of Tutor3 was qualitative, based on a think-aloud (Neilsen, 1994). This has the merit of being relatively low cost and giving insights into the causes of difficulties.

Selection of Participants

Following Neilsen, we selected five participants for the evaluation. They have different backgrounds and varying degrees of computer literacy: one was a secondary school student, two were third year computer science degree students and there were two adult participants with basic computer literacy skills. Table 1 shows a summary of each participant's age group, education level and computer literacy.

Overall, they represent a quite computer literate group; all had previously used the Internet. Due to the small number of participants we can not make claims about the implications for all World Wide Web users and we have to interpret findings with some caution.

The Participant's Task

We designed a scenario around a fictitious person, Fred. This meant that all participants were dealing with the same student profile and we could predict the exact adaptation each should see. This, in turn, meant that all participants did exactly the same task and should have seen exactly the same screens.

Each participant was provided with a worksheet. This described Fred's learning goals, interests and background. Participants were asked to assume the role and background of Fred and use Tutor3 to start working through the beginning of the Introductory UNIX course. Participants were presented with one page of the worksheet at a time so they could not jump ahead. Participants we allowed to spend as much time as required. We observed the participants as they completed the task to record their comments. In addition, the system logged all their interactions with the interface. The participants were not given any training or a demonstration of the system.

Table 1. Summary of participant backgrounds

		Participant ID			
	1	**2**	**3**	**4**	**5**
Age group	21-25	21-25	18-21	18-21	14-18
Education Level	Post Secondary school study	Post Tertiary study	Computing undergrad	Computing undergrad	Secondary school
Computer literacy	Basic	Basic	High	High	Moderate

Table 2. A sample of questions in a worksheet completed by participants in the evaluation of Tutor3

Part	Concept	Questions presented in worksheet
1	Understanding the purpose of profile questions	• Will Tutor use Fred's profile settings? If so, what will it use Fred's profile settings for? • Where does Tutor get information about Fred to use to perform adaptation of the content to suit him? • Will Fred be able to influence or control the way Tutor adapts content to him? If so how?
2	Ability to determine what was adapted	• What would you do in the system to find out whether Tutor adapted any material on the Teacher's Instructions page to you? • Did your answer to the profile question *What is your main objective?* have any effect on the contents of the Teacher's Instructions page? How do you know this? • Was any content specifically excluded because of your answer to the profile question *What is your main objective?* If so, what was the content?
3	Demonstrating control over adaptation by changing answers to profile questions	• Now consider what the first sentence on the page would read had you answered the profile question *What is your main objective* with *Revise the material.* Without changing your answer just yet, write out how you think the sentence would read. *By the end of this course you will have ...* • Explain what actions you would have to perform in the system to change your answer to the profile question *What is your main objective?* • Change your answer for the profile question *What is your main objective* to *Revise the material.*

The tasks of the worksheet were designed so that each basic issue was explored in three subtasks. This provided internal consistency checks, an important concern since there are degrees of understanding and we wanted insight into just how well each participant was able to scrutinise the adaptation. Extracted questions from the worksheet are shown in Table 2. These reflect our core evaluation goals as described at the beginning of this section.

The first part of the worksheet instructed the user to register with the system, log on and select the Introductory UNIX course. The first task was to complete the profile of Fred by answering questions on the profile page (as in Figure 3). The worksheet did not specify the answers for each question but did describe Fred's learning goals, interests and background. Each participant was then asked questions from the first block in Table 2.

The second part of the worksheet asked each participant to navigate to a specific page. Then, participants were asked to determine whether any of the content on that page was adapted to Fred, based on the answer to the profile question: *What is your main objective?* The participants had to indicate any adapted content and whether it was included or excluded. To perform this task, the user had to notice and click the hyperlink: *How was this page adapted to you?*

The third part of the worksheet involved what-if experiments. The participant was asked to guess the content of a specific paragraph, assuming Fred were to change his answer for the profile question *What is your main objective?* to *Revise the material.* Answering this question should not have required any guesswork. The answer is on Adaptation Explanation as in Figure 5.

Results

Understanding the Purpose of Profile Questions

The participants first had to answer the eight profile questions, as Fred would have. These appeared as in Figure 3, with additional questions about preferences for abstract explanations, numbers of examples and self-test questions, interest in historical background and understanding of other operating systems. For this experiment, the critical aspects about Fred's background were that he wanted to learn (not revise) and he was not interested in historical background information. All participants answered these profiles questions consistently with the information we provided about Fred which meant that the pages displayed to them in the experiment had the same adaptations.

The participants completed the profile and answered the first set of questions from Table 2. At this stage, they have not been shown any adapted content and have not had any opportunity to play with the scrutable interface. Their answers to the worksheet were based purely on the information shown in the profile page and any prior experience with adaptive systems. Note that text on the profile page, included below, already gives away the answers.

"Fill in your profile to suit your background, learning preferences, interests and current goals. Tutor uses your answers to adapt the content to your needs.

You can change your profile at any time during the course to influence Tutor's adaptation."

In their answers to the first two questions, all participants stated their profile answers would influence the way material would be presented to them. However, participants had difficulty with the question *Will Fred be able to influence or control the way Tutor adapts content to him? If so how?* Participants 1 and 2 correctly stated that by answering the profile questions in a way that suits Fred, they had control over the adaptation. Participants 4 and 5, on the other had, answered "No". Participant 3 answered "Yes, but I don't know how." Through questioning participants about their answers after the experiment, we know that what participants 1, 2, 4, and 5 meant was that although they believed they could initially influence the system through their profile answers, they expected that once they started working through the course they would no longer be able to influence the system or change their profile. All believed there were factors influencing adaptation other than the profile they would not be able to control. Note that this is despite the help text on the profile page, as in Figure 3. Participant 5 is an interesting case because later on in the experiment when he realised he could change his profile answers, he returned to change his answer to state *"Yes, by changing the way he responds to things."*

Ability to Determine What Was Adapted

The next part of the worksheet asked participants to navigate to a specific page, explain how it was adapted and explain whether the profile questions had any impact on this adaptation. Recognising the link between the profile questions and the adapted content was central to being able to understand and control the adaptation. We expected participants would find this exercise straightforward. However, this was quite challenging for most participants.

Participants 1 and 2 could not work out how to determine what was adapted and needed help in accessing the explanation in order to continue the worksheet. To perform this task, the user had to notice and click the hyperlink *How was this page adapted to you?* at the bottom of the page (as in Figure 1). Participant 1 answered the worksheet correctly but without looking at the adaptation explanation. This participant's answer to the profile question *What is your main objective?* was *Learn*. Thus, when they saw the word *Learn* was highlighted on the screen, they assumed it was adapted because of that profile question without really analysing the adaptation explanation. Participant 2 could not understand the adaptation explanation, believing the highlighted content was content Tutor wanted to annotate as important rather than annotate as adapted content.

Participant 3 also could not work out how to access the adaptation explanation. However, their work-around method for determining adapted content was to go back to the profile page, change the profile answers, navigate back to the lesson page and study the content for changes. This participant correctly identified the included content but struggled to identify excluded content visually.

In contrast, Participants 4 and 5 quite easily found the link to access the adaptation explanation, found the correlation between the highlighted adapted content and their profile answers. We observed that Participant 5, in particular, very carefully examined all the text on the screen. Other users looked at the pages but seemed to ignore any help text offered by the system.

Demonstating Control Over Adaptation by Changing Answers to Profile Questions

The final part of the worksheet tested whether the participant was able to demonstrate control over adaptation. In fact, this is really re-testing the previous concepts since if a participant truly understood how to determine what content was adapted and that the adaptation was due to their profile, they would already understand they can control adaptation by changing their profile answers.

The worksheet asked participants to alter the adaptation on a particular page. The first question asked the participant to guess what the content of the page would be, assuming a specific profile setting, without actually changing the profile. To answer this question, we expected the participant would examine the adaptation explanation which shows how the content would be affected based on a change to the profile.

Participant 1 examined the adaptation explanation carefully and learnt how to read it. They correctly guessed the adapted content and were able to change their profile to prove they were correct. Participant 2, was still confused and could not work out how to access the profile page. Participant 3, who had not yet discovered the adaptation explanation, was not able to guess the expected page content. Participant 4 had previously demonstrated an understanding of the adaptation explanation but did not realise that the facility could be used to predict the content of the page in this case. Participant 5 had no problems correctly answering and testing their answers to the worksheet.

There was no time limit imposed on completing the worksheet. Participant 2, who performed the worst, took about twice as long as most of the other participants, who took between 20 and 31 minutes. Since this included the time to complete the worksheet and to think aloud, it is not indicative of the time needed to explore the way material is adapted.

Overall, only Participants 1 and 5 seemed to fully understand how to interpret the adaptation explanations and were able to use the explanations to control the inclusion/exclusion of content to a desired effect. Participant 2 understood the profile played a role in the adaptation but could not understand the adaptation explanation or work out how to change the adaptation. Participant 3 did not discover the adaptation explanation until late in the evaluation but then demonstrated understanding of it.

Discussion and Conclusions

There are a number of key findings and concerns raised through this experiment. With the small sample size in the qualitative experiment, we need to be cautious about any strong claims. However, we can identify some important and interesting outcomes that are important for our goal of supporting scrutability and control over adaptation.

The participants in our study were comfortable our simple user models used to capture information to achieve personalisation.

Our users did understand the concept of a user model. They appreciated that the system would store information about them and in return provide personalised material.

The participants in our study understood that they had input to the personalisation process, but needed convincing that they could control it as well.

Having filled in their initial profile, all participants could appreciate that their user model would influence the personalisation of material. However, some of our users needed time to work out that they could control the personalisation. They appeared to believe that once they filled in their profile, that would be the end of their input. It seems that our users, perhaps due to previous experiences, assumed they did not have any control over the adaptation. One user expressed surprise at the extent to which they could control the adaptation. Notably, users learnt they could control adaptation and they achieved this by reading the instructional text presented by the system; no intervention was required.

Although users need convincing they have control over the Tutor's adaptation, it deserves mention that we have had feedback from users requesting tractability and control. Participants in evaluations of earlier Tutor versions (Czarkowski & Kay, 2000, 2001), stated they want to see all the information available for a page, that is, to see the content that was excluded by adaptation. It seems that there is a group of users who do not always trust the adaptation and do want to see what they have missed out on.

Building an interface for scrutability support is difficult.

A key concern, highlighted by the experiment, was that users had difficulty finding the scrutability tools when needed. Participants 1, 2, and 3 required help to find the link *How was this page adapted to you?* Participant 4 found this link without help. Due to a browser anomaly, Participant 5 was presented with the adaptation explanation without having to click the link. This last serendipitous case suggests that it might be helpful if the user is presented with this information at critical times such as the first page viewing. This reduces the need for the user to discover, ab initio, where to look for the information.

Although we had provided some instructional text explaining how to access the adaptation explanation and profile page, users who skimmed over the interface tended to ignore this. They then had difficulty completing the evaluation. Also, Tutor has online help, accessed via the large question mark icon on each lesson page as well as on a hyperlink near the link *How was this page adapted to you?* None of our users accessed the online help.

One of the challenges of supporting scrutability is that we would expect users to only want to explore this facility very irregularly. This is not an element for which users would be trained as part of the normal use of the interface. Typically, users would have no need for it over long periods of time and use of the interface. However, when there is a suitable trigger, such as unexpected behaviour, we want the user to be able to work out how to delve into the adaptation. So, for example, the learner who has asked for the broader view of the course may have a busy week and decide that they need to focus on the core needed to pass in that week. At that point, they need to be able to work out how to effect that change. Similarly, if the user is surprised to see quiz questions when they indicated that they did not want them, they should be able to check to see how those questions were put there, be that because the hypertext author made a mistake in the adaptation tag or simply decided to present them to all users, regardless of their user model.

At the beginning of this chapter, we identified four core parts of an adaptive hypertext. At this stage, Tutor has the simplest form for each of these that we could devise for a practical adaptive hypertext. It operates on the basis of a very simple user model and a single source of user modelling information, namely the user's answers to profile questions. This makes the interpretation of the user model very simple. Tutor has a very simple adaptation mechanism, based on the limited power of the ATML adaptation language. However, we have found that this basic level of personalisation still poses substantial interface challenges.

Overall, it seems that the notion of adaptivity was familiar to our users. This is consistent with the growing use of adaptivity. However, the idea that they had could control the adaptation was new. We have made progress in building a more effective interface for scrutability in the three versions of Tutor. On the basis of the current evaluations, if we imagine that these users had been using Tutor in an authentic learning context and they had cause to wonder about the adaptivity, it is unclear whether they would have thought to try to scrutinise the adaptivity. Even if they had found the relevant links, it is seems that some would not have been able to work out, unaided, exactly what was adapted and how. Our next step is to further refine the interface and to evaluate it in a more authentic environment where the users are actively trying to learn the information presented. We propose to introduce a small number of errors in the adaptation in the hope that these will create the motivation to scrutinise the adaptivity. In terms of refining our interface, we will explore ways of informing the user they can scrutinise the interface without requiring them to search for a seemingly invisible link at the bottom of the page. One idea so far is to introduce the scrutable interface on the profile page by providing a demonstration. This would also help to present the connection between the profile answers and the user's control over adaptation.

There are many situations in which a user might wish to understand and control the adaptivity of an adaptive hypertext system. Supporting this is proving quite difficult. Providing the user with the ability to understand or at least trace an adaptive system's response and provide input to the system to alter its adaptivity function are key usability issues that are yet to be fully explored by adaptive systems. However, these are key features adaptive system must have if users are to trust the adaptivity on critical tasks performed on their behalf.

The evaluations we have reported for the current version of Tutor confirm our previous observations of the interface challenges of supporting scrutability of adaptation based on simple user models and modelling processes and simple adaptivity processes. We have much work ahead in further refining the interface support for scrutability of hypertext adaptation as well as extending it to more complex hypertext adaptations.

References

Bloom, B. S. (1984). The 2 sigma problem: The search for methods of group instruction as effective as one on one tutoring. *Educational Researcher, 13*, 4-16.

Browne, D., Totterdell, P., & Norman, M. (1990). *Adaptive user interfaces.* San Diego, CA: Academic Press.

Bull, S., & Pain, H. (1995). Did I say what I think I said, and do you agree with me? Inspecting and questioning the Student Model. *Proceedings of World Conference on Artificial Intelligence in Education,* Washington DC (pp. 501-508). AACE.

Bull, S., Brna, P., & Dimitrova, V. (Eds.). (2003). *Proceedings of Learner Modelling for Reflection Workshop, Volume V of the AIED2003 Supplementary Proceedings* (pp. 209-218).

Bull, S., Brna, P., & Pain, H. (1995). Extending the scope of the student model. *User Modeling and User-Adapted Interaction, 5*(1), 45-65.

Brusilovsky, P., Schwarz, O., & Weber, G. (1996). ELM-ART: An intelligent tutoring system on the World Wide Web. In C. Frasson, G. Gauthier, & A. Lesgold (Eds.), *Proceedings of the Third International Conference on Intelligent Tutoring Systems, ITS-96* (pp. 261-269). Berlin: Springer.

Calvi, L., & Cristea, A. (2002, May). Towards generic adaptive systems: Analysis of a case study. In P. De Bra, P. Brusilovsky, & R. Conejo (Eds.), *Proceedings of the Second International Conference on Adaptive Hypermedia and Adaptive Web-Based Systems,* Malaga, Spain (pp. 79-89). Springer.

Cawsey, A. J., Jones, R. B., & Pearson, J. (2000). The evaluation of a personalised health information system for patients with cancer. *User Modeling and User-Adapted Interaction: The Journal of Personalization Research, 10*(1), 47-72.

Corbett, A. T., & Anderson, J. R. (1995). Knowledge tracing: Modeling the acquisition of procedural knowledge. *User Modeling and User-Adapted Interaction, 4,* 253-278.

Cristea, A., & Aroyo, L. (2002, May). Adaptive authoring of adaptive educational hypermedia. In P. De Bra, P. Brusilovsky, & R. Conejo (Eds.), *Proceedings of the Second International Conference on Adaptive Hypermedia and Adaptive Web-Based Systems,* Malaga, Spain (pp. 122-132). Springer.

Czarkowski, M., & Kay, J. (2000). Bringing scrutability to adaptive hypertext teaching. In G. Gauthier, C. Frasson, & K. VanLehn (Eds.), *ITS 2000, Intelligent Tutoring Systems* (pp. 423-432). Springer.

Czarkowski, M., & Kay, J. (2001). Tutor: Support for scrutably personalised documents. *Proceedings of ADCS 2001, Australian Document Computing Symposium* (pp. 29-36). Retrieved from http://www.ted.cmis.csiro.au/adcs01/

Czarkowski, M., & Kay, J. (2002). A scrutable adaptive hypertext. In P. De Bra, P. Brusilovsky, & R. Conejo (Eds.), *Proceedings of AH 2002, Adaptive Hypertext 2002* (pp. 384-387). Springer.

Czarkowski, M., & Kay, J. (2003). How to give the user a sense of control over the personalization of adaptive hypertext? *Workshop on Adaptive Hypermedia and Adaptive Web-Based Systems, User Modeling 2003 Session* (pp. 121-132). Retrieved from http://wwwis.win.tue.nl/ah2003/proceedings/

De Bra, P., & Ruiter, J. P. (2001, October). AHA! Adaptive hypermedia for all. *Proceedings of the WebNet Conference* (pp. 262-268).

De Bra, P., Aqerts, A., Berden, B., de Lange, B., Rousseau B., Santic, T., Smits, D., & Stash, N. (2003). AHA! The Adaptive Hypermedia Architecture. *Proceedings of the International Conference on Hypertext and Hypermedia 2003*, Nottingham, UK (pp. 81-84).

Höök, K., Karlgren, J., Waern, A., Dahlbäck, N., Jansson, C. G., Karlgren, K., & Lemaire, B. (1996). A glass box approach to adaptive hypermedia. *Journal of User Modeling and User Adapted Interaction, Special Issue on Adaptive Hypermedia, 6*(2-3), 157-184.

Jameson, A., & Schwarzkopf, E. (2002). Pros and cons of controllability: An empirical study. P. De Bra, P. Brusilovsky, & R. Conejo (eds), *Proceedings of AH'2002, Adaptive Hypermedia and Adaptive Web-Based Systems* (pp. 193-202). Springer.

Kay, J. (2001). Learner control. *User Modeling and User-Adapted Interaction, Tenth Anniversary Special Issue, 11*(1-2), 111-127. Retrieved from http://umuai.informatik.uni-essen.de/anniversary.html

Kobsa, A. (2002). Personalized hypermedia and international privacy. *Communications of the ACM Archive, Special Issue: The Adaptive Web, 45*(5), 64-67.

Maes, P., & Schneiderman, B. (1997). Direct manipulation vs. interface agents: A debate. *Interactions, IV*(6), 42-61.

Morales, R., Pain, H., Bull, S., & Kay, J. (Eds.). (1999). Open, interactive, and other overt approaches to learner modeling. *Proceedings of the workshop at AIED 99. International Journal of Artificial Intelligence in Education, 10,* 1070-1079.

Nielsen, J. (1994). Estimating the number of subjects needed for a thinking aloud test. *International Journal of Human-Computer Studies, 41*(1-6), 385-397.

Rich, E. (1979). User modeling via stereotypes. *Cognitive Science, 3,* 355-66.

Weber, G., & Brusilovsky, P. (2001). ELM-ART: An adaptive versatile system for Web-based instruction. *International Journal of Artificial Intelligence in Education, Special Issue on Special Issue on Adaptive and Intelligent Web-based Educational Systems, 12*(4).

Section II

Designing Instruction

Chapter VI

Building an Instructional Framework to Support Learner Control in Adaptive Educational Systems

Kyparisia A. Papanikolaou, University of Athens, Greece*

Maria Grigoriadou, University of Athens, Greece

Abstract

Recently there has been a growing appreciation concerning learner control over the learning/instructional process, leading to the development of mixed-initiative systems where learners are allowed to take varying levels of control. The design of Adaptive Educational Systems (AES) that provide such learner control opportunities through their adaptive and adaptable dimensions, is a challenging research goal that requires a certain understanding of the learning and instructional processes. To this aim, in this chapter we focus on the educational background that should underlie the design of adaptation and learner-system interaction in the context of AES used for Web-based education. We propose an instructional framework that supports a variety of instructional approaches and provides guidelines that unify several processes underlying adaptation such as structuring the domain knowledge, developing the content, and planning individualised support—assessment—learner control opportunities. This framework incorporates a variety of approaches over instruction and assessment, in order to accommodate the diversity of learners' needs and preferences, and enable them to choose when, what, and how to learn. The theoretical background underlying the design of the framework and the implications for Web-based AES design are also discussed.

Introduction

In Web-based education, centrally available systems are used to deliver instruction, allowing a user to learn transcending typical time and space barriers. In this context, the challenge posed for both the education and the computer science research communities is the exploitation of the innovative characteristics of the Internet for the development of educational systems, flexible enough to accommodate learners' individual differences and promote learners to take control over the instructional process. Instruction for learning is, and has always been, a complex and multifaceted challenge. Especially in Web-based education where tutors are mainly facilitators rather than the main agents, the instructional approach adopted to guide the interactions taking place among the educational system, the learners and the educational content should aim to: (i) provide learners with the appropriate resources and guidance towards the accomplishment of their goals accommodating their individual approach to learning, and (ii) stimulate and actively engage learners in learning providing them opportunities to take control over the instructional process. However, the sharing of control between the learner and the system is a critical issue as there is always the possibility that unrestricted control and lack of learning goals can dampen the power of learning (Lawless & Brown, 1997). Thus, issues of learning and didactics become more prominent for the development of Web-based learning environments, and several critical questions are emerging, such as: (i) which instructional approaches are appropriate for incorporation in a Web-based environment where learners are usually adults and where the variety of learners taking the same course is large, and (ii) how to design learner control opportunities that allow learners to decide when and how to take control over instruction, in a way that enhances learning, builds positive attitudes and heightens self-efficacy.

In the context of Web-based education, Adaptive Educational Systems (AES) (Brusilovsky, 1996, 1999, 2001; Brusilovsky & Peylo, 2003) emerged as an alternative to the traditional "one-size-fits-all" approach in the delivery of instruction. AES possess the ability to make intelligent decisions about the interactions that take place during learning and aim to support learners without being directive. Taking into account that, learners will be able to achieve their learning goals more efficiently when pedagogical procedures accommodate their individual differences (Federico, 1991), and that learners appear to benefit from learner control opportunities (Federico, 1999; Jonassen, Mayes, & McAleese, 1993), research in the area of AES has been focused on methods and techniques that integrate such functionalities in real systems.

Critical issues that affect the educational perspective of AES are the instructional approach guiding system-learner interaction, and the type of adaptation, which depends on the amount of control a learner has over the adaptation (for a taxonomy of different types of adaptation see Kobsa, Koenemann, & Pohl, 2001). As far as the latter is concerned, lately there is a growing appreciation concerning the learner control over the learning process (Kay, 2001), leading to systems where learners are allowed to take varying levels of initiative. The development of Web-based AES in which learners are individually supported in accomplishing their personal learning goals (adaptive dimension of AES) and at the same time they are allowed to control when, what, and how to learn (adaptable dimension of AES), requires a certain understanding of the learning and instructional processes. In this direction, the design of a coherent instructional framework, which integrates instructional decisions that lead to the adaptation, is a challenging research goal motivated by the expected learning benefits.

In this chapter we focus on the educational background that should underlie the development of AES used for Web-based education. We propose an instructional framework that supports a variety of instructional approaches, allows learners to take control over the system and provides guidelines that unify several processes underlying adaptation such as structuring the domain knowledge, developing the content, and planning individualised support—assessment—learner control opportunities.

Instructional Approaches and Learner Control in Adaptive Educational Systems

Different instructional approaches have been used in AES providing the central concept of the interactions that take place between the learner and the system and/or the basis for designing their building elements, such as learner model, domain knowledge, instructional model, and adaptive engine. In several cases, these approaches build on teaching expertise or built on a theoretical background that reflects specific learning/instructional theories.

For example, AST (Specht, Weber, Heitmeyer, & Schöch, 1997) adopts a variety of instructional strategies, which simulate strategies used by teachers when teaching different types of concepts in statistics: learning by example, learning by reading texts, or learning by doing. These strategies are responsible for deciding how to sequence the educational material in relation with specific learning outcomes, and thus they imply the type of educational material to be developed. In the Dynamic Course Generation (DCG) system (Vassileva, 1997), courses are generated dynamically depending on the learning goal that learners select. These courses can be dynamically changed, following specified teaching rules and strategies of the Generic Task Model (GTE) (Van Marke, 1998), to suit better to learner's individual goals, progress, and preferences. GTE provides an instructional model that reflects the instructional knowledge and expertise underlying human teaching. In Arthur (Gilbert & Han, 1999), alternative styles of instruction are used, which differ in the type of media they utilize. The implementation of these alternative styles of instruction requires the development of multiple types of educational material that use different types of media for each particular section of the course. In AES-CS (Triantafillou, Pomportsis, & Demetriadis, 2003) adaptation is based on the Field Dependent—Field Independent cognitive style model. Several instructional strategies have been incorporated in the system that accommodate learners' cognitive style in relation to: the approaches (global versus analytical), the control options (program versus learner control), the contextual organizers (advance organizer, post organizer), the study instructions (provide minimum or maximum instructions), the feedback, and the lesson structure. The domain in which these functions build is a set of concepts designed by the expert-instructor. Lastly, in INSPIRE (Papanikolaou, Grigoriadou, Kornilakis, & Magoulas, 2003), adaptation is based on a comprehensive instructional framework which builds on a combination of instructional design theories about planning the content and delivery of instruction, with the learning style theory, providing the basis for delivering individualized content that accommodates learners' knowledge level and learning style. This framework guided the development of the domain model and the educational material, the representation of learner's knowledge and learning style, and the design of pedagogical rules guiding the system's adaptive behaviour. In the KBS Hyperbook system (Henze, Naceur, Nejdl, & Wolpers, 1999), learners work with projects and the system adapts the project resources to their knowledge level and/or learning goals. Thus, learner-system interaction is based on activities, which have been developed according to the project-based learning theory.

Lately there is a growing appreciation of sociocognitive practices in which learners take control over the learning process and construct their knowledge through collaboration with peers and/or teachers. For example, Ecolab (Luckin & du Boulay, 1999) is an interactive learning environment, which assists children (aged 10 and 11 years) to learn about food webs and chains. Ecolab provides appropriately challenging activities to children to cope with, as well as the right quantity and quality of assistance. The theoretical framework on which Ecolab is based was inspired by Vygotsky's theory about ZPD (Zone of Proximal Development), which is an appealing idea about how to support learners to learn. Another interesting approach, which is based on sound theoretical principles, has been adopted in SCI-WISE (White, Shimoda, & Frederiksen, 1999). SCI-WISE supports learners to develop lifelong learning skills, that is, to learn how to learn via inquiry and understand the sociocognitive and metacognitive processes that are involved. It houses a community of software agents, which give strategic advice and guide learners as they undertake collaborative research projects and as they reflect on and revise their inquiry process.

As far as learner control issues are concerned, in several AES different levels of adaptation have been adopted, depending on who takes the initiative, the learner or the system, ranging from system driven to learner driven adaptation. In particular, learner control can take several forms such as learner controlling (Kay, 2001): choice of learning tools/teacher/learning peers, choice of time of learning (on-demand learning), their learner model, system's domain and teaching beliefs, or the amount of control.

The I-Help (Bull & McCalla, 2002) system fits the model of on-demand learning. I-Help assists learners as they try to solve problems while learning a subject. To this end, I-Help supports a network of peers that help each other out, that is, selects appropriate peers to assist a learner and then sets up a one-on-one peer help session between the helper and the helpee based on a number of factors. User-adapted online documentation systems, which aim to assist users in learning what they want, are also closely related to the on-demand learning approach. For example, PUSH (Höök, Karlgren, Waern, Dahlbäck, Jansson, Karlgren, & Lemaire, 1996) aims at developing and testing intelligent help solutions to information seeking tasks. Höök et al. (1996) suggest that in order to give users a sense of control, the systems' internal workings should be transparent and their actions should be predictable to users.

Different approaches have been adopted in AES for introducing adaptability and providing learner control opportunities. ELM-ART (Weber & Brusilovsky, 2001) provides learners with the option to access their model and modify the assumptions of the system about their knowledge level on the different pages of the educational content, their preferences concerning the screen design and the adaptation technologies used. ELM-ART uses multiple sources of information about the learning status of each page of the course, such as the learners' estimation of their knowledge level and the knowledge of the system about learners' assessment results in solving exercises, tests, or programming problems. In AST as well as in Hypadapter (Hohl, Bocker, & Gunzenhauser, 1996) when learners first log on the system they submit an introductory questionnaire to initialise their own learner model. Questionnaires provide learners with a means of controlling and customizing various aspects of these systems at the beginning of the interaction as well as during the learners' interaction with the system (Hypadapter). In DCG, learners take control over the system depending on their aptitudes. For example, if the learner is considered as "motivated" and "success-driven" then s/he is allowed to select what to study next, and how (i.e., the task and method of instruction); in case s/he is considered as "unsure" and "not confident" then the system takes on the initiative to decide what s/he should do next. In AES-CS learners are allowed to intervene in the instructional process by modifying the status of the corresponding instructional strategies through their model and/or appropriate interactive features of the system. Lastly, INSPIRE supports several levels of adaptation, allowing the learners to decide on the level of control they wish to exercise. It offers opportunities to learners to deactivate adaptation and undertake full control over the system, or to let the system generate individualised lessons, or to intervene in the lesson generation process reflecting on their own perspective. As far as the latter is concerned, learners have always the option to access their learner model, reflect upon its contents (learner's knowledge level on the concepts of the domain and learning style), and change them in order to guide system's instructional decisions.

The adaptable dimension of many AES is based on providing learners the option to check and update their characteristics stored in their learner model. This approach enables learners to see how the system models their individual characteristics relative to standards set by the system and update them. As system adaptation is mainly based on the learner model, an open learner model is a fundamental part of learner control (Kay, 2001). Open learner modelling is a broad issue in the learner modelling area focusing on the use of open leaner models (OLM) as a learning resource. To this aim, a variety of approaches have been proposed concerning the contents, interaction and form of OLM in AES (Bull, Brna, & Pain, 1995; Dimitrova, 2001; Kay, 1995; Mitrovic & Martin, 2002; Dimitrova, 2003). At this point we should mention the LeMoRe group, which has members from all around the world and one of its main aims is to advance the theoretical study and the application of approaches to opening the learner model to learners and others involved in the learning process, such as teachers and peers (visit http://www.eee.bham.ac.uk/bull/lemore/ for more information).

Theoretical Foundations

The theoretical foundations for the proposed instructional framework come primarily from the instructional science and cognitive science, drawing on the view of learning as an active process of knowledge construction and of instruction as anything that is done to facilitate purposeful learning.

The purpose of designed instructional interventions is to activate and support learning. Towards this direction, alternative instructional/learning theories and approaches have been proposed as to how it should be done (Jeroen, Merriënboer, & Kirschner, 2001). Jonassen et al. (1993) propose that the initial acquisition phase is better served by classical instructional design techniques while complex and constructivist environments serve advanced knowledge learners better. Along this line, Ertmer and Newby (1993) argue that the instructional approach adopted for novices may not be efficiently stimulating for a learner who is familiar with the content. Moreover, recently there is an increased interest on collaborative learning which is supposed to lead to deeper level learning, critical thinking, shared understanding, and long term retention of the learned material, providing opportunities for developing social and communication skills, and developing positive attitudes towards co-members and learning material. In this context instructional interventions should aim to enhance social interaction among the group members in ways that encourage elaboration, questioning, rehearsal, and elicitation (Kreijns, Kirschner, & Jochems, 2003).

Following this line of research, a learning-focused instruction paradigm should better exploit the diversity of perspectives and methods proposed (Reigeluth, 1999a; Jeroen, Jeroen, Merriënboer, & Kirschner, 2001). In this direction, an important issue that should also be considered is learner control, which is assumed as an alternative procedure for accommodating instruction to the dynamic characteristics of learners (Federico, 1999). In the context of a Web-based educational system, learner control can cause problems as well as offer benefits. Learner control is intuitively appearing because it is assumed that learners will be more motivated if allowed to control their own learning (Lin & Hsieh, 2001; Steinberg, 1989). Along this line Kay (2001, p. 122) suggests that "given the importance of cooperation by the learner if learning is to be achieved, we have no choice but to trust the learner with control." However, it is also argued that the effectiveness of learner control depends to a large extend on how well each learner can decide which instructional/learning strategy is optimal for him/her at any one moment (Federico, 1999). This raises the important issue for Web-based education as to whether all types of learners appreciate being given control over instruction. Thus, a challenge posed for adaptive instruction and personalisation in order to succeed to their educational potential, is to provide alternative approaches to learners enabling them to: (i) adapt instruction to their learning needs and individual differences, which as several studies reveal have significant effects on learning (Chen & Paul, 2003; Papanikolaou & Grigoriadou, 2004), and (ii) take control over instruction when they wish to.

The proposed instructional framework builds on the above-mentioned ideas adopting a variety of approaches over instruction and assessment, aiming to enable learners to choose when, what, and how to learn. To this end, the instructional design and the constructivist perspectives are used to design alternative opportunities for learning in a Web-based educational context. The instructional approaches proposed differ in the amount of structure, control, and support provided to learners including highly *constructivist* approaches that build on the on-demand learning theory, as well as more *prescriptive* approaches. In the former approaches, learners are basically on their own to figure out where and how to acquire the knowledge, skills, and attitudes, and the system provides them with individualised support when they ask to. In the latter approaches, structured educational material and guidance are provided to help learners acquire the knowledge, skills, and attitudes, accommodating their individual differences with the aim to advice but not directing them.

A Framework for Designing Instruction

The proposed instructional framework provides guidelines for the design of aligned learning opportunities. It draws a picture of how the content, assessment and instruction work together to build purposeful lessons that provide learner control opportunities. The main aim is to provide researchers with an educational background, comprehensive enough to support a variety of instructional decisions that underlie the design of adaptation and learner-system interaction in the context of an AES. To this end, we propose a set of guidelines, accompanied by representative examples and alternative theories which could be adopted for the implementation of a real system (see Table 1).

Table 1. The main elements of the instructional framework. Each element is accompanied by a set of guidelines, and by representative examples and alternative theories proposed for the implementation of a real system.

Framework elements	Design guidelines	Examples
Learning goals *The main topics of the curriculum are presented as learning goals enabling learners to select the one they prefer or need to study*	Define a set of *learning goals* from the fundamental topics of the curriculum in a way that can be recognized and selected even by a novice learner independently of his/her previous selections. Provide learners with the option to select a learning goal to study according to their needs and preferences. For each goal provide relevant learning outcomes, information about its fundamental concepts, and a brief overview, in order to support learners in selecting the one to study.	In DCG and INSPIRE a set of learning goals are proposed to learners. In KBS-Hyperbook learners can define their own learning goals or can request new goals from the hyperbook.
Instructional approaches *Different instructional approaches are provided to learners enabling them to select the one most appropriate to their knowledge and preferences*	Define a set of instructional approaches, which differ in the amount of structure, learner control and support provided to learners. Provide learners with the option to select an instructional approach. For each one provide a brief overview of the main idea and its functionality, in order to support learners in selecting the most appropriate. Design each instructional approach so as to provide: – individualised content following learner's profile – individualised support following learner's profile – multiple assessment opportunities – meaningful tasks and activities in which learners take an active role – collaboration opportunities	Samples of representative instructional approaches / approaches adopted by different systems are presented below. INSPIRE generates a sequence of individualized lessons following learner's learning goals, progress and learning style. The lesson contents, the sequencing and the presentation of multiple types of educational material (e.g., theory, examples, exercises, activities) are adapted to learners' profile. In KBS-Hyperbook learners work on projects and the system supports them by providing appropriate material and guidance. Project results are used to represent and to assess learners' knowledge. In SCI-WISE learners undertake collaborative research projects and a community of software agents, such as a planner, a collaborator, and an assessor, supports them providing strategic advice and guidance.
Assessment *Multiple assessment opportunities are provided aiming to (i) stimulate learners to assess the quality, quantity and retention of their learning, and (ii) support the system's adaptation by providing data for the learners' progress*	– Provide *self-assessment opportunities* in the educational content through a plurality of assessment tasks that actively engage learners and stimulate them to assess and record their own progress and study accordingly (*formative assessment*). – Provide formal assessment aligned with the content in order to assess retention of learning following specific criteria given in terms of objectives and competences which state what learners must achieve (*summative assessment - criterion-referenced assessment*). – Provide feedback to learners' answers in order to support the learning process, provoke reflection on and articulation of what was learned. *Feedback* to learners' answers might include different types of information such as comments on the correctness, precision, and timeliness of the answers, learning guidance, motivational messages, lesson sequence advisement, critical comparisons, learning focus (Sales, 1993; see also the chapter "An Adaptive Feedback Framework to Support Reflection, Guiding and Tutoring" in this book).	Self-assessment opportunities can be provided through a variety of tasks included in the content such as, questions, exercises, activities (INSPIRE), and projects (KBS Hyperbook). ELM-ART and INSPIRE use automatically corrected assessment tests for the main topics of the domain in order to get the necessary information about learners' knowledge and adapt accordingly. In KBS-Hyperbook, project results are used to represent and to assess what topics / concepts a learner has successfully applied or learned. Different types of feedback that can be provided are (Chi, 1996; Mory, 1996): *suggestive feedback* which follows learners' wrong answers aiming to alert the learner that there is a problem (e.g., INSPIRE provides feedback that refers to the consequences of learners' answers aiming to redirect their thinking), and *reinforcing feedback* which follows learners' right answer so as to justify the correctness of the particular answer (INSPIRE).

Table 1. (continued)

Framework elements	Design guidelines	Examples
Content *The educational content includes all the concepts important to the curriculum and comprise of multiple independent modules which can be re-used by different instructional approaches*	– Define a set of *learning goals* derived from the fundamental topics of the domain (see above for a more detailed description). – For each learning goal build a *conceptual structure* based on design principles extrapolated from instructional theory. This structure should include all the necessary concepts comprising the goal and their interrelations. – Develop *educational material* for each domain concept to support learning / achievement of specific skills / performance levels. Develop multiple knowledge modules of different types of educational resources as well as authentic and meaningful tasks that may support multiple instructional approaches. – Organise and present the content in hypermedia form	All the concepts comprising a learning goal may be organised in a *conceptual structure* following a specific sequencing such as the elaboration sequencing (Reigeluth, 1999b) used in INSPIRE, hierarchical sequencing, procedural sequencing, simple-to-complex sequencing (learning-prerequisite, topical, spiral, subsumptive, Web sequence). The *educational material* may be organised in different levels that correspond to specific skills or performance levels which learners are expected to develop/succeed following a specific taxonomy such as those proposed in (Merrill, 1983) used in INSPIRE, (Jonassen et al., 1993; Mayer, 2002; Reigeluth & Moore, 1999). At each level, the educational material may include multiple types of resources/activities such as questions, exercises, examples, activities and projects aiming to cover a range of learning styles (knowledge modules in INSPIRE, AST). The above modularity of the content allows the use of its different components - concepts, knowledge modules - by different instructional strategies. AST adopts a variety of instructional strategies, such as learning by example, learning by reading texts, learning by doing. The educational material is reused by these strategies, which are responsible for deciding how to sequence the educational material in relation with specific learning outcomes.
Individualized support *Individualized support is provided following learners' individual differences and needs, aiming to advice instead of directing learners*	Support learners in taking control over the instructional process and the adaptation. Provide learners with information about the different functionalities of the system that lead to the adaptation and about the influence of their actions on the system's functions. Support learners in accomplishing their tasks by providing individualized content, guidance, and navigation advice. Learners should be allowed to decide on their next steps and not be restricted to follow system suggestions.	The externalisation of the learner model can be used to provide learners with information about the system's adaptation and the opportunities they are offered to control it (ELM-ART, INSPIRE). Different adaptation technologies such as adaptive presentation, adaptive navigation support, curriculum sequencing, problem-solving support, adaptive collaboration can be used for providing individualized content, guidance and navigation advice following learners' individual differences (ELM-ART, DCG, AST, INSPIRE, AES-CS) In SCI-WISE, a community of software agents give strategic advice and guide learners as they undertake research projects, reflect on and revise their inquiry processes.

The proposed framework comprise of the following elements (see Table 1):

(a) **Learning goals.** Learners select what to study. Learning goals focus on the topics that are important to the curriculum, defined in a way that can be recognised and selected by learners.

(b) **Instructional approaches.** Learners select among alternative instructional approaches that reflect different pedagogical perspectives.

(c) **Assessment.** Multiple assessment opportunities are provided. Assessment aims to support learners in identifying their own progress (self-assessment) and provide the system with the necessary information about the learners' level of performance.

Table 1. (continued)

Framework elements	Design guidelines	Examples
Learner control opportunities *Learners undertake an active role in the learning process and they are allowed to take varying levels of initiative*	Provide learners with the options to: – decide what to learn; – decide how to learn; – decide when to learn; – control the adaptation; – control the amount of control;	*What to learn*: Learners select a learning goal to study (DCG, INSPIRE) and the content is presented in a hypermedia form enabling learners to follow their own paths (ELM-ART, INSPIRE) *How to learn*: Learners select their learning peer / teacher / companion (SCI-WISE), the type of content to study (INSPIRE). *When to learn*: In Ecolab and I-Help, learners ask for support when they need to. In Ecolab, a more able learning partner assists a learner as s/he attempts to complete an activity. I-Help supports a network of peers that help each other out. *Control over adaptation*: In ELM-ART and INSPIRE learners have the option to intervene in the adaptation process by modifying their model. Oppermann (1994) suggested the usage of adaptive tips that the system provides to learners in order to lead them through the adaptation and explain its use. Höök et al. (1996) suggest that adaptation should be inspectable, controllable and predictable by users and propose the glass box approach. *Control the amount of control*: The expertise and behavior of the different types of advisors that SCI-WISE provides to learners are easily modifiable by learner designers. Moreover learners have the option to switch roles from time to time, so that each gets an opportunity to be in charge of the different components of cognitive and social expertise. In INSPIRE learners may follow system's suggestions, or intervene and guide the instructional process, or deactivate adaptation and take full control over the system.

(d) **Content.** Learners are provided with structured content comprised of independent modules. It includes critical objectives, declarative and procedural knowledge on all the concepts that learners need to know.

(e) **Individualized support.** It aims to help learners accomplish their goals and take more responsibility for their own learning.

(f) **Learner control opportunities.** Learners are informed about the internal workings of the system and they are provided with opportunities to control the instructional process.

Example of Implementation

Researchers and teachers that have embraced the idea of building lessons based on an instructional framework recognize the depth of decision making that exists with each framework space. In this section, aiming to improve the understand-ability of the proposed framework and facilitate its application, we provide an example for implementing the aforementioned guidelines.

Learners are provided with a set of *learning goals* and two *instructional approaches*, a prescriptive and a constructivist one, from which they may actively and continuously (during the interaction) select the one most appropriate to their needs and preferences. In particular, the prescriptive approach provides structured content in a specific sequence matching learners' knowledge level and/or learning style, as well as individualised study guidelines. The constructivist approach provides learners with a project to accomplish, accompanied by supportive content & resources (Web and human resources). In both approches, projects are used as a building element in organizing learners' study: learners select a learning goal from a set of meaningful ones, independently of their previous selections, and then they have the option to start working on a project (constructivist approach) or start studying the provided content and then continue with a project (prescriptive approach). Moreover, learners may work on a project alone or by collaboratively participating in a group. In such groups learners undertake specific roles, they conduct research and share knowledge in the pursuit of a meaningful, consequential task using different communication tools provided by the system such as discussion lists, e-mail, and chat.

The *content* is comprised of units, such as concepts and educational material modules that can be reused by the different instructional strategies. The notion of learning goals is used in order to build a hypermedia structure that provides learners with an overview of how all the relevant information fits together. To this end, each goal is associated with a project and a conceptual structure that includes all the necessary concepts and their relationships—outcomes, prereq-uisites, and related concepts. The conceptual structure of a learning goal is organized following the elaboration sequence (Reigeluth, 1999b) which starts with the broadest, most inclusive and general concepts and proceeds to nar-rower, less inclusive, and more detailed concepts, until the necessary level of detail has been reached. The educational material of each outcome concept consists of a variety of knowledge modules which aim to support learners in achieving three levels of performance (Merrill, 1983): (i) the Remember level includes theory presentation of the concept, introductory or self-assessment questions/tasks, and instances of the concept, (ii) the Use level includes hints from the theory, application examples, exercises, activities, self-assessment questions/tasks, and (iii) the Find level includes specific cases in the form of small projects (see in Figure 1 the structure of the educational material of an outcome and in Figure 2 the different knowledge modules comprising an educational material page of the Use level). *Assessment* tests are provided for each concept including different types of questions that correspond to the three levels of performance (Remember, Use, and Find). *Self-assessment opportunities* are provided through automatically corrected assessment tests, and different tasks, such as exercises, activities, and projects, included in the educational material as described above.

In case learners select a learning goal to study and the *prescriptive approach*, then the system generates a sequence of individualised lessons. These lessons are organized around specific outcome concepts that learners should study in order to successfully accomplish their goal. In particular, the system provides *individualised support* to learners by:

- generating a sequence of lessons which gradually reveal the conceptual structure of the learning goal following learners' progress (as the learner progresses, more detailed concepts appear following the conceptual structure of the goal—see above how the content is organised);
- providing individualised navigation advice by annotating the lesson contents (use of visual cues) reflecting learners' competence on the different concepts (see Figure 1); and
- providing individualised presentation of the educational material following learners' learning style, for example, Activist, Reflector, Theorist, and Pragmatist proposed by Honey and Mumford (1992) (see Figure 2).

After learners have reached a level of competence, the system proposes to them a project to work with. Note that the provided content includes cases (see above the educational material modules developed to support the Find level of performance) that lead learners to deal with different perspectives of the project, aiming to support them to gradually acquire the necessary level of competence.

Even in the prescriptive approach, learners are provided with *opportunities to take control* over the system. They are provided with the option to change their individual characteristics, that is, knowledge level on the concepts of the goal and learning style, and in this way to intervene in different stages of the lesson generation process reflecting on their own perspective. In this process the system supports learners by providing appropriate information about its functionalities and the options provided. In any case, learners are allowed to follow the system's advice or deactivate adaptation and work on their own.

In case learners select a goal to study and the *constructivist approach*, then the system proposes to them a project to work with. Project presentation includes three integrated components (Jonassen, 1999): project context (the project statement presents all the contextual factors that surround the problem as well as the role of the learner[s] in this context), project representation (engage learners in activities which present the same type of cognitive challenges as those in the real world), and problem manipulation space (where learners

Figure 1. The contents of the first lesson generated for a novice who selected the learning goal "Cache Memory" include two outcome concepts "The role of cache memory" and "Mapping techniques". The educational material of prerequisite concepts accompanies each outcome. The educational material of the outcomes is organized in three levels (Remember, Use, and Find). The structure of the lesson contents is denoted by means of different icons. The colored icons (marked with a bullet) accompany pages that are proposed to the learner for study (navigation advice) following his/her knowledge level.

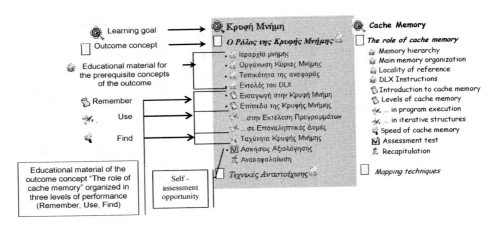

generate a hypothesis and search for appropriate information in order to argue for it). Also, an assessment pre-test is provided with each project, so as to assess learner's prior knowledge on the different concepts involved in the project. Based on this information the system will be able to provide *individualised support* in the problem manipulation space, that is, provide the appropriate concepts (those on which the learner has insufficient knowledge), suggest Web resources, peers to ask for support (peer selection process is also based on learners' knowledge level and learning style). In more detail, in the project manipulation space, the content includes all the available educational material (corresponding to the Remember, Use, and Find levels) for the proposed concepts graphically annotated. Thus, individualised navigation advice is provided through annotation of the proposed content based on learner's learning style, for example, Activists, who are motivated by experimentation and attracted to challenging tasks, are advised to start studying the small projects

Figure 2. Learners with different learning styles view different presentations of the educational material: for Reflectors the presentation at the Use level of performance is "Example-oriented" proposing the learner to start with an experimentation activity, and use the provided example, hints from the theory, and the solved-exercise in case s/he needs help.

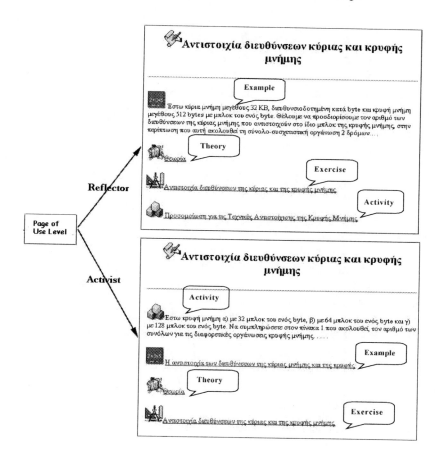

included in the Find level of each concept, whilst Reflectors, whil perfer to collect and analyse data before acting, the material included in the Remember level. Lastly, apart from the support provided in the project manipulation space, learners have always the option to go back to the structured content and study following system's suggestions (prescriptive approach) or search within the content for the information they need.

Conclusions

The design of AES that allow learners to take varying levels of initiative is a challenging research goal focusing on the adaptable dimension of these systems. Research in this direction has a lot to benefit from the educational literature. Otherwise, adaptation design may become technology driven rather than allowing technology to serve as a resource that supports learners' needs.

The instructional framework described in this chapter unifies several processes that formulate the adaptation of an AES, focusing on its educational perspective. Learner control is a critical issue in the proposed framework: the aim of adaptation is to suggest and advice learners on their study, navigation, and so on, providing them with the option to decide on their steps. Learners select the learning goal they would like to study and they have the option to select the instructional approach to follow. Additionally, learners are provided with the option to decide on the level of guidance provided by the system and in any case, either to follow system advice or work on their own.

From the technological perspective, the proposed framework provides an educational basis for modelling the building elements of adaptive Web-based educational systems: the domain knowledge, the learner model (although in this chapter this issue has not been covered) and the adaptive engine (adaptivity and adaptability). In particular, modelling the domain is a critical issue in the area of adaptive instruction, as it should support content reusability. One of the major goals of content re-use is to support the generation of personalized courses enabling the production of several versions of the same course targeted to different audiences, from the same rich set of learning objects (IULO, 2000). Thus, the decomposition of the content based on instructional/learning theory aims to enhance the educational perspective of its re-use under a variety of instructional situations and learner profiles.

References

Brusilovsky, P. (1996). Methods and techniques of adaptive hypermedia. *User Modeling and User-Adapted Interaction, 6*(2/3), 87-129.

Brusilovsky, P. (1999). Adaptive and intelligent technologies for Web-based education. In C. Rollinger & C. Peylo (Eds.), *Kunstliche Intelligenz, Special Issue on Intelligent Systems and Teleteaching,* 19-25.

Brusilovsky, P. (2001). Adaptive hypermedia. *User Modeling and User-Adapted Interaction, 11*(1/2), 111-127.

Brusilovsky, P., & Peylo, C. (2003). Adaptive and intelligent Web-based educational systems. *International Journal of Artificial Intelligence in Education, 13,* 156-169.

Bull, S., & McCalla, G. (2002). Modelling cognitive style in a peer help network. *Instructional Science, 30,* 497-528.

Bull, S., Brna, P., & Pain, H. (1995). Extending the scope of the student model. *User Modeling and User-Adapted Interaction, 5*(1), 44-65.

Chen, S. Y., & Paul, R. J. (Eds.). (2003). Special issue on individual differences in Web-based instruction. *British Journal of Educational Technology, 34*(4), 385.

Chi, M. T. H. (1996). Constructing self-explanations and scaffolded explanations in tutoring. *Applied Cognitive Psychology, 10,* 33-49.

Dimitrova, V. (2003). StyLE-OLM: Interactive open learner modelling. *International Journal of AI in Education, 13*(1), 35-78.

Ertmer, P. A., & Newby, T. J. (1993). Behaviorism, cognitivism, constructivism: Comparing critical features from an instructional design perspective. *Performance Improvement Quarterly, 6*(4), 50-72.

Federico, P.-A. (1991). Student cognitive attributes and performance in a computer-managed instructional setting. In R. Dillon & J. Pellegrino (Eds.), *Instruction: Theoretical and applied perspectives.* New York: Praeger.

Federico, P.-A. (1999). Hypermedia environments and adaptive instruction. *Computers in Human Behavior, 15,* 653-692.

Gilbert, J. E., & Han, C. Y. (1999). Adapting instruction in search of "a significant difference". *Journal of Network and Computer Applications, 22,* 149-160. Retrieved from http://www.idealibrary.com

Henze, N., Naceur, K., Nejdl, W., & Wolpers, M. (1999). Adaptive Hyperbooks for constructivist teaching. *Kunstliche Intelligenz,* 26-31.

Hohl, H., Bocker, H. D., & Gunzenhauser, R. (1996). Hypadapter: An adaptive hypertext system for exploratory learning and programming. *User Modeling and User-Adapted Interaction, 6*(2-3), 131-156.

Honey, P., & Mumford, A. (1992). *The manual of learning styles.* Peter Honey, Maidenhead, Published and Distributed by Peter Honey.

Höök, K., Karlgren, J., Waern, A., Dahlbäck, N., Jansson, C-G., Karlgren, K., & Lemaire, B. (1996). A glass box approach to adaptive hypermedia. *User Modeling and User-Adapted Interaction, 6*(2-3), 157-184.

IULO: The instructional use of learning objects. (n.d.). Online edition. Retrieved from http://reusability.org/read/

Jeroen, J. G., Merriënboer, V., & Kirschner, P. A. (2001). Three worlds of instructional design. *Instructional Science, 29*, 429-441.

Jonassen, D. (1999). Designing constructivist environments. In C. M. Reigeluth (Ed.), *Instructional-design theories and models: A new paradigm of instructional theory, Volume II*. Mahwah, NJ; London: Lawrence Erlbaum Associates.

Jonassen, D., Mayes, T., & McAleese, R. (1993). A manifesto for a constructivist approach to uses of technology in higher education. In T. Duffy, J. Lowyck & D. Jonassen (Eds.), *Designing environments for constructive learning. NATO ASI Series F, Vol.105*. Berlin: Springer-Verlag.

Kay, J. (1995). The um toolkit for cooperative user modeling. *User Modeling and User-Adapted Interaction, 4*(3), 149-196.

Kay, J. (2001). Learner control. *User Modeling and User-Adapted Interaction, 11*(1/2), 111-127.

Kobsa, A., Koenemann, J., & Pohl, W. (2001). Personalized hypermedia presentation techniques for improving online customer relationships. *The Knowledge Engineering Review, 16*(2), 111-155.

Kreijns, K., Kirschner, P. A., & Jochems, W. (2003). Identifying the pitfalls for social interaction in computer-supported collaborative learning environments: A review of the research. *Computers in Human Behavior, 19*, 335-353.

Lawless, K., & Brown, S. (1997). Multimedia learning environments: Issues of learner control and navigation. *Instructional Science, 25*, 117-131.

Lin, B., & Hsieh, C. (2001). Web-based teaching and learner control: A research review. *Computers and Education, 37*, 377-386.

Luckin, R., & Du Boulay, B. (1999). Ecolab: The development and evaluation of a Vygotskian design framework. *International Journal of Artificial Intelligence in Education, 10*, 198-220.

Mayer, R. E. (2002). A taxonomy for computer-based assessment of problem solving. *Computers in Human Behavior, 18*(6), 623-632.

Merrill, M. D. (1983). Component display theory. In C. M. Reigeluth (Ed.), *Instructional design theories and models: An overview of their current status*. Hillsdale: Lawrence Erlbaum Associates.

Mitrovic, A., & Martin, B. (2002). Evaluating the effects of open student models on learning. In P. De Bra, P. Brusilovsky, & R. Conejo (Eds.), *Proceedings of the Second International Conference on Adaptive Hypermedia and Adaptive Web-Based Systems* (pp. 296-305). Berlin, Heidelberg: Springer-Verlag.

Mory, E. H. (1996). Feedback research. In D. H. Jonassen (Ed.), *Handbook of research for educational communications and technology* (pp. 919-956). New York: Simon and Schuster Macmillan. Retrieved from http://www.aect.org/intranet/publications/edtech/32/index.html

Oppermann, R. (1994). Adaptively supported adaptability. *International Journal of Human-Computer Studies, 40*, 455-472.

Papanikolaou, K. A., & Grigoriadou, M. (2004). Accommodating learning style characteristics in adaptive educational hypermedia. In G. Magoulas & S. Chen (Eds.), *Proceedings of the Workshop on Individual Differences in Adaptive Hypermedia in AH2004, Part I,* Eidhoven, The Netherlands (pp. 77-86).

Papanikolaou, K. A., Grigoriadou, M., Kornilakis, H., & Magoulas, G. D. (2003). Personalizing the interaction in a Web-based educational hypermedia system: The case of INSPIRE. *User-Modeling and User-Adapted Interaction, 13*(3), 213-267.

Reigeluth, C. M. (1999a). What is instructional-design theory and how is it changing? In C. M. Reigeluth (Ed.), *Instructional-design theories and models: A new paradigm of instructional theory, Volume II.* Mahwah, NJ; London: Lawrence Erlbaum Associates.

Reigeluth, C. M. (1999b). The elaboration theory: Guidance for scope and sequencing decisions. In C. M. Reigeluth (Ed.), *Instructional-design theories and models: A new paradigm of instructional theory, Volume II.* Mahwah, NJ; London: Lawrence Erlbaum Associates.

Reigeluth, C. M., & Moore, J. (1999). Cognitive education and the cognitive domain. In C. M. Reigeluth (Ed.), *Instructional-design theories and models: A new paradigm of instructional theory, Volume II.* Mahwah, NJ; London: Lawrence Erlbaum Associates.

Sales, G. C. (1993). Adapted and adaptive feedback in technology-based instruction. In J. V. Dempsey & G. C. Sales (Eds.), *Interactive instruction and feedback* (pp. 159-175). Englewood Cliffs, NJ: Educational Technology.

Specht, M., Weber, G., Heitmeyer, S., & Schöch, V. (1997). AST: Adaptive WWW-content for statistics. In P. Brusilovsky, J. Fink, & J. Kay (Eds.), *Proceedings of Workshop "Adaptive Systems and User Modeling on the World Wide Web", Sixth International Conference on User Modeling, UM97,* Italy (pp. 91-95). Retrieved from http://www.contrib.andrew.cmu.edu/~plb/UM97_workshop/Specht.html

Steinberg, E. R. (1989). Cognition and learner control: A literature review, 1977-1988. *Journal of Computer-Based Instruction, 6*(4), 117-121.

Triantafillou, E., Pomportsis, A., & Demetriadis, S. (2003). The design and the formative evaluation of an adaptive educational system based on cognitive styles. *Computers & Education, 41*, 87-103.

Van Marcke, K. (1998). GTE: An epistemological approach to instructional modeling. *Instructional Science, 26*(3/4), 147-191.

Vassileva, J. (1997). Dynamic course generation on the WWW. In B. D. Boulay & R. Mizoguchi (Eds.), *Artificial intelligence in education: Knowledge and media in learning systems* (pp. 498-505). Amsterdam: IOS Press.

Weber, G., & Brusilovsky, P. (2001). ELM-ART: An adaptive versatile system for Web-based instruction. *International Journal of Artificial Intelligence in Education, 12*(4), 351-384.

White, B. Y., Shimoda, T. A., & Frederiksen, J. R. (1999). Enabling students to construct theories of collaborative inquiry and reflective learning: Computer support for metacognitive development. *International Journal of Artificial Intelligence in Education, 10*, 151-182.

Endnote

*   Kyparisia A. Papanikolaou is also affiliated with the Department of Technology Education and Digital Systems, University of Piraeus, Greece.

Chapter VII

Bridging the Gap with MAID:
A Method for Adaptive Instructional Design

Jacopo Armani, Università della Svizzera italiana, Switzerland

Luca Botturi, Università della Svizzera italiana, Switzerland

Abstract

This chapter presents MAID, a complete design method for adaptive courseware tailored for non-technical people. Adaptive hypermedia systems represent a great potential for e-learning. Nevertheless, instructors and designers find it difficult to develop adaptive applications in real educational environments, mainly because no structured design method is available. The main principle upon which the method relies is that the basis for the exploitation of adaptive features in education is the definition and implementation of an instructional strategy. The MAID approach provides guidelines and tools that foster and enhance the communication between the technical staff in charge of managing the hypermedia system and the instructor by adopting her/his instructional strategy as the pivotal point for the communication.

Introduction

The creation of adaptive courseware started with expert systems and CAI (computer assisted instruction) and produced milestone applications as ISIS-TUTOR (Brusilovsky & Pesin, 1994) or SKILL (Neumann & Zirvas, 1998) and TANGOW (Carro, Pulido, & Rodríguez, 2001). These projects developed self-learning courses with adaptive tutoring, and traced a route by which, some years later, adaptive platforms could be developed, such as AHA! (De Bra & Calvi, 1998; De Bra, Aerts, Smits, & Stash, 2002a) or KBS Hyperbook (Henze & Nejdl, 1999). Adaptive platforms are general-purpose systems that allow the production of courseware for any content. It can be surely stated that the last decades of research in the field of adaptive hypermedia systems (AHS) produced a wide leap forward in terms of technical solutions and systems. Nevertheless, "just a handful of these systems are used for teaching real courses, typically in a class lead by one of the authors of the adaptive system" (Brusilovsky, 2004, p. 1), and also few institutions or companies systematically exploit adaptive components in their e-learning programs.

We claim that this gap between the maturity of technical developments and their use in the educational practice is also due to a lack of methodological support in the design of adaptive courseware, that is, of expertise in using adaptive components and systems in order to implement and enhance a course as conceived by a non-technical instructor.

The major concern of this chapter is MAID, a method for the design of adaptive educational application, suitable to a situation in which an instructional designer, familiar with some adaptive platform, is producing a course with an instructor or a subject matter expert (SME). A second concern of this chapter is a call to all AHS developers for defining not only tools, but also methods that may make the tools actually usable to educators.

This chapter first presents an overview of the literature, with particular emphasis on the instructional strategies, claiming that the definition of a specific strategy is the basis for the sound development of adaptive applications. The MAID method is then presented in detail by a case study. The following section recaps the method, and provides generalization insights and guidelines for designers. Finally, the results of the work are discussed and some outlook is provided.

Literature Review

About Instructional Strategies

When an instructor or SME thinks of a course, s/he thinks about it in a unitary way, and conceives an instructional strategy, that is, a method for having the students achieve the course goals. The design of instructional events indeed, supported by any kind of technology, from WebCT to virtual reality, requires a strategy (Bates, 1999; Bates & Poole, 2003). Smith and Ragan (1999), building on the foundations by Reigeluth (1983), define a strategy as a plan for action including three main dimensions:

1. **Organization:** the structure and clustering of content;
2. **Delivery:** the media involved in the delivery; and
3. **Management:** the organization of the learning activity into a unitary schedule.

To our concerns, the definition of organizational strategy is the most relevant. Smith and Ragan (1999) write that "organizational strategy characteristics refer to how instruction will be sequenced, what particular content will be presented, and how this content will be presented" (p. 113). In particular, they name a set of activities that should be considered as part of the definition of an organizational strategy, namely:

1. Content selection
2. Content clustering
3. Content sequencing
4. Definition of generative (active) or supplantive (passive) approach
5. Definition of instructional events

When talking of instructional strategy, we will refer to this definition; a clear assessment of these issues paves the road for an integrated and effective exploitation of adaptive hypermedia techniques into a course.

A strategy could be synthetically expressed with a statement such as "this course is problem-driven and learners work in groups" or "this course follows constructivist principles and provides learners with resources they are free to use as they like, provided that they reach the negotiated goals". The definition or selection of a strategy requires a complete instructional analysis (Dick & Carey, 1996) and should move from the definition of learning goals (Anderson & Krathwohl, 2001; Gagné, Briggs, & Wager, 1992).

Educational literature has defined a number of different instructional strategies suitable for different learning goals and drawing from different learning theories, but this is not the place for a thorough discussion or for an exhaustive review. The point is that the definition of an instructional strategy is the basis for the development of an instructional event; more precisely, and this is more relevant for the current analysis, it is the basis for the definition of the role of technologies in the instructional event. This means that:

1.   The decision to use a certain technology such as AHS should be derived from the instructional strategy.
2.   The decision about how to use technologies should also be strategy-driven.

The question "How can AHS be profitably exploited in real educational environment?" should be operatively translated into "How can AHS support the implementation of this instructional strategy?" MAID was conceived as a communication support for finding a sound answer in course design.

Design of AEHS: An Open Issue

The AHS field has been for years a boiling pot throwing out newer and newer tools and techniques to support learners, and indirectly teachers as well. Yet, the issue is: now that we have plenty of tools, how shall we use them?

In order to tackle the issue, some researchers (Aroyo, Dicheva, & Cristea, 2002) use task ontology to support instructors and content provider of adaptive educational hypermedia systems (AEHS) in their authoring effort. Their goal is creating an ontology of the most common tasks (adding/removing/editing) and objects (pages, hyperlinks, etc.) authors have to deal with while producing courseware. Based on such an ontology, they aim at the development of an intelligent authoring tool that can provide an intelligent support to the design of adaptive courseware. Other researchers (Brusilovsky, 2004) aim at design straightforward authoring tools for developing adaptive courseware starting from the analysis of the state of the art of the current learning management systems (LMS).

Yet in order to use tools (or authoring tools) to build complex applications such as AEHS, we need a method. This change in the way of considering design issues was indirectly addressed by Brusilovsky (2003): his work is the first attempt to raise the issue of AEHS design. The paper presents a review of the design principles embedded in the most relevant AEHS, trying to distil a common design process. According to him, "the design of an adaptive hypermedia system involves three key sub-steps: structuring the knowledge, structuring the hyperspace, and connecting the knowledge space and the hyperspace" (p. 380).

1.   **Structuring the knowledge** refers to representing the information we have about the domain, the student, and the educational goals in terms of the internal language of the system.

2.   **Structuring the hyperspace** deals with the issue of connecting the pool of pages with each other. The review shows clearly that several strategies (e.g., hierarchical, rhetorical, and object oriented structures) have been applied so far to achieve different goals.

3.   **Connecting the knowledge space and the hyperspace** refers, in a few words, to the issue of mapping the knowledge level into the level of pages, content fragments, and links.

Brusilovsky concludes that the field of AHS "is probably too young to produce a good number of design authoring tools ... that can be used by non-programming authors to develop an educational AHS ... The reason for that is reasonably clear: Before producing a real authoring tool, a research group has to develop an explicit design approach that usually requires developing one or more educational AHS" (*Ibidem,* p. 342). As Brusilovsky suggests, the problem of the lack of authoring toolkits stems from the lack of design methods.

On a parallel track, other researchers (Koch, 2001; Papasalouros & Retalis, 2002) are focusing on design models: high-level representations of how an AEHS should be. These approaches come from software engineering, but unfortunately, the results are usually UML-based schemas which require special training to read, and technical expertise to draw.

Instructional Design and Adaptive Systems

Although many research prototypes of AEHSs refer to results from Instructional Design, for instance the emphasis on constructivist approaches (Henze & Nejdl, 1999), and on learning styles (Grigoriadou, Papanikolaou, Kornilakis, & Magoulas, 2001), very little space has been devoted to bridge the existing gap between the communities of instructional design (ID) and AEHS.

A contribution in this direction comes from Park and Lee (2004). Their work presents the state of the art of the adaptive instructional systems, starting from the pre-technologic era (adapting classroom-based instruction), to Web-based systems. They point out that, although the tradition of adaptive instruction precedes the AEHS, nevertheless, the two fields seem never to meet each other: "Unfortunately, this technical development has not contributed significantly to an intellectual breakthrough in the field of learning and instruction" (p. 677). Among the reasons for the limited success of AEHS, the authors see a lack of theoretical foundations.

The AHAM Meta-Model

In order to create a framework model, we relied on the work done by De Bra_, Houben, and Wu (1999) with AHAM—adaptive hypermedia application model (Figure 1). AHAM is an attempt to generally describe the main features of the majority of AHS and to provide a sound basis for the development of new AHS. From our point of view, AHAM provides a high-level description that fits the structure of all the major AEHS available—thus describing the elements that we can use for translating and implementing an instructional strategy.

Figure 1. The AHAM reference model

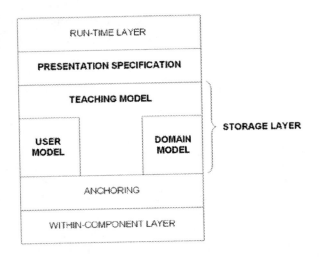

The main elements of AHAM are:

1. The **Run-time layer**, which comprises the functions for rendering the pages and tracking the user's responses.

2. The **Presentation Specification**, that is, the definition of the possible behaviours of the application interface to the actions of the user (adaptive areas and elements, active elements, link annotation, etc.). We will call it **Interface Model**.

3. The **Teaching Model**, that is, the set of rules or principles that define the behaviours of the application. We will call it *Interaction Model*.

4. The **User Model**, that is, the system representation of the user and of her/his current status.

5. The **Domain Model**, that is, the system representation of the content of the hypermedia application, in terms of structure, concepts, pages, or nodes.

6. The **Anchoring** and **Within-component layer**, that is, the primitives for building the adaptive system.

The idea is that any educational AHS defines, explicitly or implicitly, all of these elements. For any of them, several choices are possible. For example, the domain model can consider pages or nodes as its main elements, or abstract concepts with semantic connections (Botturi, 2001). The user model can be a simple copy of the domain model (De Bra & Calvi, 1998) or can contain other static or dynamic information, or can be implemented by a Bayesian network (Armani, 2001, 2003; Henze & Nejdl, 1999).

MAID: A Method for the Adaptive Instructional Design

Going through the presentation of the MAID model, imagine a small design team, where a SME or an instructor, works with an instructional designer and with a media producer or Web programmer.

The pivotal point for understanding MAID is the idea that in order to create an adaptive application that actually supports and enhances the educational experience from an adaptive platform, the instructional strategy should be translated into the "language" of the adaptive platform. For achieving this, first it should be understood and shared by all team members. The existence and availability of a method for creating this shared understanding is the key for actualizing the potential of AEHS.

The MAID Meta-Model

According to AHAM, in order to build from scratch an AEHS, a designer should consider all its elements. Yet considering existing general purposes AEHSs (that is to say adaptive platforms), some parts of the AHAM are not at stake. Namely, the storage layer and the presentation specifications are the only parts susceptible to modification by the instructional team; in fact, the run-time layer (which comprises the functions for rendering the pages and tracking the user's responses) and the within-component layer, with all the primitives for building an adaptive system, are usually part of the system logic.

Before focusing on our model, let's depict the key elements that constitute an adaptive hypermedia system in what we may call a meta-model (Figure 2): the domain model, the user model, the interaction model and finally the interface model.

Notice that elements influence each other. For example, the user model is usually built on the domain model, as in the case of overlay models (De Bra, Aerts, Houben, & Wu, 2000). Moreover, the interface model is created on the basis of the interactions that should be achieved. The interaction model is the real pivotal element, as it defines the rationale for the behavior of the application, and, as it will become clear further on, strictly depends on the instructional strategies.

Figure 2. MAID meta-model

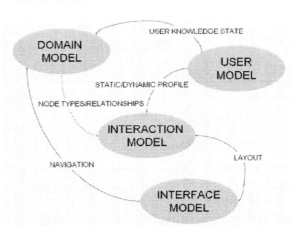

All the elements are affected by the instructional requirements and the technical possibilities and constraints that define the broad boundaries of the application.

The Method

The MAID design method starts at a point in which the designers have performed a complete instructional analysis, have defined with the instructor or SME an instructional strategy, and have decided to consider AEHS as a viable support for the course. For example, one may decide to give the students a problem-driven task that must be accomplished autonomously using the resources available on the adaptive system, or it is possible to decide to adopt a more traditional approach, where the class must attend an online (adaptive) lesson.

MAID is composed by five steps that define the process, each with a set of output documents, and by a lifecycle of the process.

MAID Steps

The MAID steps cover all the elements of AHAM, and they are:

1. **Interaction model:** define the application behavior;
2. **Domain model:** define the content structure;
3. **User model:** define the relevant information about the user;
4. **Interface model:** map the behavior in user interface elements; and
5. **Implement and testing:** implement and test the system.

MAID Lifecycle

As usual with design methods, MAID as well has to cope with creativity and with a set of complex interrelated issues. The meta-model presented in Figure 2 clearly indicates the set of relationship existing between the adaptive application models. The definition of each of them influences all the others, so that a spiral-like lifecycle is unavoidable. For instance, the results of the testing phase also will probably provide indications about the re-design of some parts of the application. The only way to reduce as much as possible the number of iterations between the tasks is to "start with the end in mind", meaning that a careful instructional analysis of the learning scenario that is going to be designed with MAID can dramatically cut down the cycles in the following design phase. The discussion section will provide additional insights.

A Case Study: Effective E-Mail for Managers

In order to show MAID in a real scenario, in this section we present a complete case study developed at the University of Lugano in May 2003, reporting the production of an adaptive unit about the effective use of e-mail for young managers. The idea was to provide a one-hour self-instruction module about the basic and advanced functions of e-mail (namely of Microsoft Outlook) and about effective e-mail communication.

The learners are therefore young managers who use e-mail a lot. They might be considered able to use a computer and browse the Web. They are likely to use the application during their office time, in a set of short sessions (15-20 minutes). The topics they are interested in are basic and advanced e-mail functions, and the effective communicative use of e-mail.

The goals for the unit are defined as follows:

1.   Learners master basic e-mail functions (create a message, use formatting, insert automatic signature, etc.);
2.   Learners know how to use advanced e-mail functions (out-of-office reply, reception confirmation, rules for automatic archiving, etc.);
3.   Learners are aware of the communicative implications in the use of e-mail;
4.   Learners improve their use of e-mail according to their communicative goals.

The strategy selected considers the following elements:

1.   Learners will study individually, without any support;
2.   The unit will take one-hour average time for completion;
3.   The application will consider each learner's learning styles and offer accordingly specific media types (images, audio, text) and content types (explanations or examples);
4.   The application will consider each learner's expertise level (beginner, expert, advanced) and propose topics consequently.

Technical Solution

The adaptive platform selected for the implementation was AHA 1.0, at the time the only adaptive system easily downloadable and installable. AHA! supports two kinds of adaptation:

1. **Link annotation:** a link may change color for a specific learner according to the pre-requirements the learner has achieved. A link can be recommended, to-be-avoided, visited, or neutral.

2. **Selective release (of fragments):** pages may contain conditional blocks that are visualized to a single user according to her/his level of knowledge, for example, if s/he visited a particular page, or got at least 50 for concept X.

AHA! offers great flexibility, in terms of content structuring and navigation behavior design, as well as interface design. The issue was therefore to exploit AHA! as a low-level adaptive engine, on the top of which a more complex model can be built, implementing the specific instructional strategy.

STEP 1: Interaction Model

During this step the designer has to decide how the application will behave in response to the user's interaction. The interaction model specification produced by the designers is presented below, along with notes clarifying the decision making process:

---

1. The application should consider users individually
   This comes automatically with AHA! that, as the greatest part of current AHS only considers single users, with no grouping, but of course other adaptive platforms may behave differently.
2. The application should consider the learners' learning styles for selecting media and content types.
3. Learners directly express their preferences via a specific interface device
   This clearly constitutes an requirement for the Interface Model, as it will be clearer later on.
4. The application should track the expertise level of the learners, and show recommended topics according to learner's progress.
5. The learners' starting expertise is tested at the beginning of their first session, then the system tracks their progress in the background.
6. The user model is closed
   Meaning that the learner has no control over it.
7. The selection of content should happen through an adaptive navigation menu, which expands with the increase of expertise
   `This is another requirement for the interface model.`

With this specification document, the designers could move to the definition of the domain, user and interface models.

STEP 2: Domain Model

The MAID domain model represents the designer's knowledge about the content and structure of the learning content, in a form translatable to system internal data structures.

Since traditional knowledge-based adaptive systems use a network of nodes for describing the domain model, the MAID domain model specification document takes the form of a network of nodes, or node map. The nodes within the network may represent concepts, pages, or whatever atomic element of the hypermedia. Their interconnections may convey both structural (e.g., part-of, specialisation, etc.) and rhetoric/pedagogic relations (is prerequisite, is analogous to, etc.).

First of all, the team draws the node map that represents the domain. The nodes may be clustered in islands for readability concerns, where each island gathers nodes about the same sub-topic (Botturi 2001). For this case, the designers defined three node types (Figure 3):

Figure 3. "Effective e-mail" : domain model (node map)

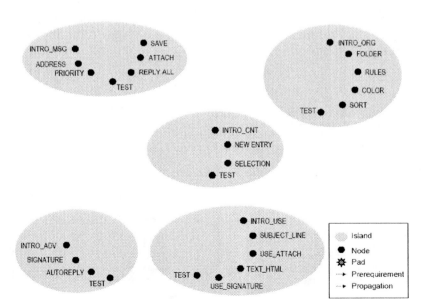

1.   Explanations with examples;
2.   General introductions to topics (tagged with the prefix 'INTRO_'); and
3.   Tests (called 'TEST').

Moreover, in order to provide some more structure to the design, the designers used islands, organizing the content in topics (in the figure the labelling of the topics is omitted to improve readability).

Notice that each island contains a 'TEST' page: these node are a sort of self-test where the user could get a synthetic self-evaluation of her/his own learning, and are *not* used for updating the user model (in fact, this was not specified in the strategy).

On the node map, the design team has to draw the structural relations that occur between nodes. AHA! allows the definition of two kinds of relationships between pages[1]:

1.   **Prerequisites**, that is, the relationship existing between a concepts A and B when the learner must know B prior to visiting A in order to get a complete understanding of A; and

Figure 4. "Effective e-mail": domain model (prerequisite network)

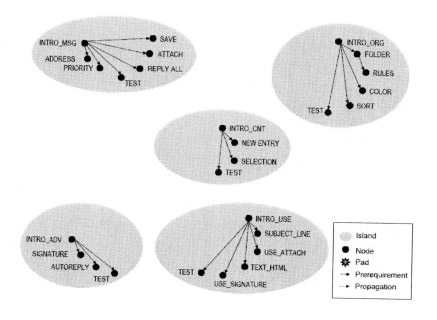

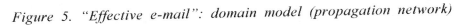

Figure 5. "Effective e-mail": domain model (propagation network)

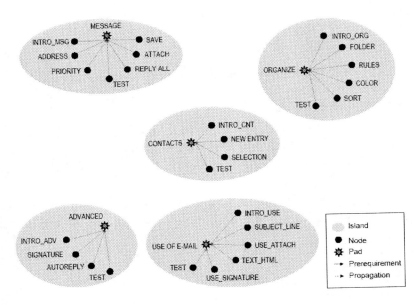

2.   **Propagation**, that is, the relationship existing between concepts A and B meaning that, when the learner understands A, he also understands "something" of B.

The result is shown in Figure 4 and Figure 5.

The basic idea for tracing prerequisites is that learners can visit any page for any island (i.e., topic) only when they first got the introduction to that topic. The only exception, due to nature of content, is between the FOLDER and RULES nodes (in the top right island).

Propagations from each node in an island are collected into that island's pad (Figure 5). Pads are nodes that are not linked to any physical HTML page, that is, they are abstract nodes. In this example, they enable the designer to enhance the system's tracking of the learners' knowledge state, by representing an indication of the average value of the learner's knowledge about the topic of the corresponding island in which the pad is located.

Thus in this case study, the domain model specification document is composed by the three sub schemas presented above, namely: the node map (Figure 3), the prerequisite map (Figure 4), and the propagation map (Figure 5).

STEP 3: User Model

The user model is the source of the personalisation features of the applications. The data of a user model may be categorized in:

1. **Static data:** information about the user such as name, date of birth, and so on;
2. **Dynamic data:** may contain preferences, knowledge status, and interests;
3. **Contextual information:** usually session or task states (e.g. current client's browser, screen resolution, last unfinished topic, etc.).

AHA! user model is composed only by some static data (username and password, university) and by a replication of the domain model for each learner (an overlay model) tagged with further information recording the learner's interactions and representing her/his knowledge status. The overlay model is kept up-to-date indicating:

1. If the learner visited a concept (i.e. the page coupled with that concept);
2. A number quantifying the learner's knowledge of the concept. Generally speaking, if a learner has all the necessary prerequisites for a concept and s/he visits it, he will get a score of 100; else a lower score, for example, 35.

Since AHA! user model does not explicitly provide ways for adding dynamic user's traits, the designers defined two non-content islands (Figure 6) recording the learners' media preference and expertise levels, exploiting the same page/pad notation used in the domain model.

According to the interaction model specification, the learner is asked to express her/his media preferences by clicking on particular application pages (therefore they will be included in the interface model), that will store the information in the corresponding preference node.

Analogously, the expertise level will be tested during the first session (the FIRST_TEST page). The test leads to a result page ("BEGINNER", "AD-VANCED", or "EXPERT") that record the initial level in the "LEVEL" pad. During other sessions, the interface is in charge of offering new topics according to the progress of each learner, as specified in the interface model later on.

At the end of this step the team has developed the user model specification document composed by: user's traits model (Figure 6) and the overlay model (omitted here, because it is a copy of Figure 3).

Figure 6. "Effective e-mail": user model (user's traits model)

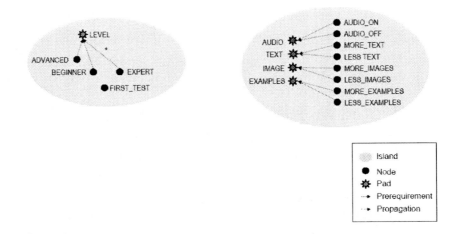

STEP 4: Interface Model

The interface is the shallow part of the application, the place where the user-machine interaction occurs—hence it should embody the essence of the interaction model as it has been envisaged in STEP 1.

The aim of this phase is to define the adaptation features at the user interface level. In particular some issues are extremely relevant, such as: What is the layout of the pages (content/navigation)? What elements of the layout are adaptive and what are static? How does the user control navigation? If it is the case, how does the user update the user model?

The interface model is defined through two representations:

1. One or more layout templates, each of them specifying what interface elements are used for controlling the navigation (i.e., adaptive access to the topics according to the learner's expertise level) and the media preference.

2. An access and navigation map: it is an annotated copy of node map of the domain model specification document specifying what pages are accessible given a specific user model status.

In our case study, the designers defined only one layout template (Figure 7). At this stage still some interface specifications are missing, as they are strictly dependent on the low level engine which is used to implement the pages.

Figure 7. "Effective e-mail" interface model layout

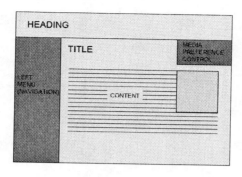

Figure 8. "Effective e-mail": interface model (access and navigation map)

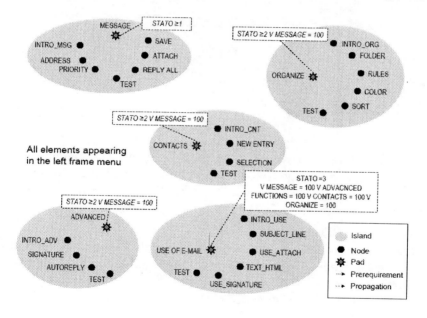

The access and navigation map is a copy of the node map integrated with information about the navigation dynamic. The navigation behaviour may be expressed both by adding notes to existing nodes in natural language and by drawing paths between nodes. In this example, the design team used only notes (Figure 8). The annotations indicate the conditions that should be verified in the user model for showing the corresponding link to the island introduction in the left frame menu.

Figure 9. Screenshot taken from "Effective E-mail" adaptive course

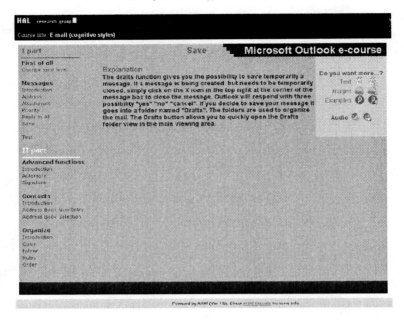

STEP 5: Implementation and Testing

The implementation of the application from the MAID documentation, in the case study, was a straightforward process: the domain model was translated into three lists (nodes, prerequisites and propagations) to which the additional user model islands were added. The interface was then implemented in HTML, inserting the adaptive code, and then parsed to XML. Figure 9 shows a screenshot from the application.

The correct behaviour of the student's preferred media selection was tested selecting different kinds of media on a page. This task was repeated for a sample of pages that belong to different islands and it was repeated for each kind of user type (beginner, expert, and advanced). The navigation consistency for each user's level was also tested, verifying that at each level a user may access only the corresponding topics.

This case study showed the whole MAID method in practice. In order to foster its understanding by the reader, the following section will recap the method, and will discuss its generalization with respect to both the application domain, and the adaptive platform.

MAID: Summary and Generalization

The five steps that the design team should undergo for the development of an educational adaptive application from an existing adaptive platform according to MAID are shown in Table 1.

Table 1. MAID: The five steps of the process

#	STEP	GOAL	ISSUES	OUTPUT DOC
1	INTERACTION MODEL	Define the application behavior	▪ What can the user do? ▪ How does the system get information from the user's behaviour? ▪ How does the system adapt to user?	Interaction Model Specification Document (list of all the features of the systems)
2	DOMAIN MODEL	Represent to the system the designer's knowledge about content	▪ What types of node ▪ What do they mean with respect to the strategy? ▪ What kind of relation types are there? ▪ What are the relations between nodes?	Domain Model Specification Document: ▪ Node map (list of all the nodes of the network, grouping in islands) ▪ Relation networks (a network map for each relation type)
3	USER MODEL	Represent to the system the relevant user's information	▪ What static data are needed? ▪ What dynamic data are needed? ▪ What session data are needed?	User Model Specification Document: User: ▪ Trait's model (list of the user's preferences, interests, etc.) ▪ Overlay model (knowledge, interests, etc, related to the Domain Model)
4	INTERFACE MODEL	Define adaptive layout	▪ How is the layout arranged? ▪ What are its elements? ▪ How can the user navigate the hypertext? ▪ How is the application made understandable?	▪ Layout template(s) (one or more template showing the layout of the elements in a page) ▪ Access map (annotated node map showing the access conditions of the pages, and the available paths between them)
5	IMPLEMENTING & TESTING	Implement and proof-check the application	▪ Is the user model gathering information according to specification? ▪ Is the Interface presenting elements according to interaction specification? ▪ Are there any un-reachable pages? Why?	*none*

STEP 1: Interaction Model

During this step the designer should express how the application will behave in a way that allows the technical staff to understand how the system changes state and how the state modifications are reflected in the user interface. This means figuring out how the adaptive application will support the selected instructional strategy. This phase is crucial because it influences the following steps (Figure 2): starting from the interaction model, the designer will design the user model, the domain model, and the interface model so that they implement the expected interaction.

Notice that the interaction model usually is strongly application-dependent. Each adaptive platform comes with a set of adaptive features and with specific user tracking features. Thus, depending on the degree of modularity of the target application, this phase could be more or less time-consuming. In the case of general-purpose adaptive systems, like AHA! v.1.0, Interbook (Brusilovsky, Eklund, & Schwarz, 1998), or KBS Hyperbook, that come with a predefined interaction model that can not be customized at all, the designer, instead of listing the desired interactions, should be aware of the permitted ones. However, recently some new systems allow the designer to define her/his own interaction model (De Bra, Aerts, Smits, & Stash, 2002b; Stash & De Bra, 2003); in this case the task is harder, but also with a higher degree of freedom.

The issue at stake here might be phrased as "What are the features that will be used to accomplish a specific goal?" For example, "the system link hiding feature is used to hide the links to not-ready documents until the student passes a test on the topic".

The output of this step is a common list of statements in natural language describing the application behaviour; alternatively, some UML diagrams may be coupled with the document in order to better describe the key interactions.

STEP 2: Domain Model

Although each platform uses specific definition of nodes, pages, or concepts, the designer has to decide what do the nodes represent in this very application: they can be concepts, content pages, lessons, exercises, tasks, scenarios, problems, and so on, or a combination of them. The type of a node depends on the instructional strategy. If the strategy is problem solving, then nodes can straightforwardly represent problem statements and supporting contents for scaffolding. In a traditional lesson-oriented course, nodes may represent content pages and exercises. Finally, in a scenario-based course they are likely to be mainly tasks and steps.

It is important to notice that the same adaptive features acquire a different meaning according to the types of nodes, and therefore according to the instructional strategy. For example, link hiding might simply mean "the student is not ready for this content" in a content-based application, while is could mean "the student does not need this particular scaffolding for this task" in a problem-based environment.

This diversification of node functions is a high-level abstraction that does not need to be necessarily translated as-is to the system logic, but it supports the design team in reflecting on and manipulating the functional elements that set up the domain, thus keeping them focused on the instructional strategy they have adopted.

The documentation produced in this step includes:

1. **The node map:** As shown in the case study, for creating the domain model, the team essentially draws a map node map that represents the domain. The nodes may be clustered in islands for readability concerns, where each island gathers nodes about the same semantic or functional meaning.

2. **Relation networks:** On the node map the design team will have to draw the structural, pedagogical/rhetoric relations that occur between nodes. We suggest drawing a diagram for each relation type, in order to improve readability of such networks.

STEP 3: User Model

The user model is the source of the different personalisation features the application supports.

Generally speaking, the user's data can be classified in:

1. User's traits (data which is not related to domain knowledge)
2. Knowledge-related data

The former set includes the user's name, date of birth, learning style, and so on.

The latter is the set of user's knowledge/interests/preference level for each specific node of the domain model. This second kind of data is usually represented by an overlay model superimposed to the domain network—this is common in many systems like AHA!, and KBS Hyperbook. In this case, MAID suggests simply copying the node map from the domain model.

Figure 10. Example of user model: traits and overlay models

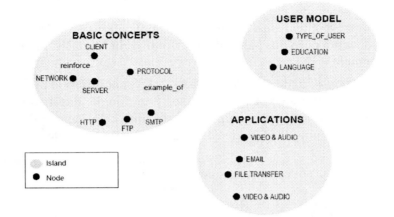

Moreover, according to the instructional strategy, the designer might need to store in the user profile information that the platform does not consider. MAID proposes to add this additional information directly into this copy of the node map. In this way the domain data and user/session data are kept together, so that it is possible to think about their interaction with ease[2].

Figure 10 shows the user model from an hypothetic course on "Introduction to the Internet", where we record the knowledge level of each page taken from the overlay node map (cf. basic concepts and applications islands), and three new variables for each learner (cf. user model island): the type_of_user indicating the learner's degree of use of the Internet, the learner's language (language) and prior education (education). Notice that user nodes may also be grouped in islands.

STEP 4: Interface Model

The aim of this phase is to define the adaptation features at the user interface level. In particular some issues are extremely relevant, such as:

1. What is the layout of the pages (content/navigation)?
2. What elements of the layout are adaptive and what are static?
3. What are the opportunities for navigation for the user?

Figure 11. Example: Interface model

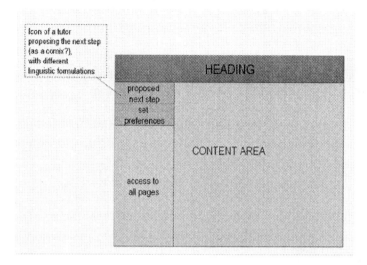

Given the complexity of AEHS, the general usability of the application is the major concern here.

During this step, the designer will produce a layout template for each significant page of the application, which defines the main parts of the screen and their functions. Comments may be added in order to specify which adaptive features of the platform will be exploited. It might be necessary to annotate the diagram with a definition of the dynamics of the adaptive menus/maps, for example, stating the conditions for showing/hiding the different parts of the menu on the screen. The example for the "Introduction to the Internet" course is presented in Figure 11. Notice the menu that provides access to all the application pages, plus the slot for the "proposed next step" (i.e., the application proposal for the next page). The annotation points out that the next step is proposed by a tutor-icon. The layout should then be developed as a complete graphical mock-up.

Access Map

Optionally, an access map can be provided to depict access condition or conditional paths that should be enabled/disabled by the user interface. The access map can be an annotated copy of the familiar node map taken from the domain model documentation, stating paths and conditions among page-nodes.

STEP 5: Implementation and Testing Phase

If all the steps have been properly accomplished, the implementation step should be a straightforward process of translation from the MAID documents to the configuration files needed to set up the course on the adaptive platform. The real issue at this stage is the implementation of the single application pages or files that contain embedded adaptive code, as this might require additional technical expertise from the Web programmers. The resources required and the degree of difficulty strictly depend on the selected adaptive platform, but the idea is that at this stage, the designer, SME and technical staff have developed a sound shared understanding of their goal.

During and after the implementation, it is important to check if the application actually behaves as envisaged at design time. MAID suggests conducting a sequence of tests checking the consistent update of the user model (Wu & De Bra, 2001), the effects on the user interface, navigation consistency and eventually code bugs.

Discussion

Why Using MAID?

MAID is a domain-independent design method to create high level representations of an AEHS. Although the method is general, it fits well the implementation stage of virtually every knowledge-based adaptive system. One of its advantages is the graphic notation, integrated within a rational design process of AEH, which allows conveying the basic design objects and principles to non-experts, making MAID a communication catalyst. MAID's step-by-step process also provides guidance for the designers, leading them to think systematically to all the necessary ingredients that constitute a (hopefully) successful AEHS, before even starting to implement it.

Moreover, the way the steps are arranged helps to add system requirements incrementally, without forcing to anticipate design solutions before the time. For instance, design opportunities at the interface model step are only influenced by the statements of the previous steps, in terms of boundaries/requirements: the same interaction requirement may be achieved with different interface design solutions; the same node at the level of the domain model may be accessed in different ways at the level of the interface/navigation model.

A "Hectic" Process

We anticipated that the several relations that occur between the different phases of the method may lead to frequent cycles on already taken steps. This is especially the case of the triangle domain model—user model—interface model. The reason is that all of them rely on the interaction model. For example, sometimes we must foresee some hypothesis on the interface model (e.g., defining a first layout diagram with indications of the adaptive parts), in order to define the user model variables and the domain concepts which will be exploited for the adaptation. Moreover, to ensure that the user model and the domain model in concert work as we expect, we have to take them in consideration cyclically. Finally, the testing phase usually shows some inconsistent behaviour that is imputable to mistakes in one of the models.

Limits of the Method

MAID was developed through the experience that the authors matured during the design of adaptive courseware with AHA! 1.0. Some of the steps could be more difficult to perform with other adaptive platforms. For example with the KBS Hyperbook system, which adopts a Bayesian Network (BN) as user model, the designer has little to nothing control on the user model update rules, because the BN formalism makes all the inferences. This increases the importance of domain modelling that must take into account the way the BN works. The domain model of some adaptive platform could have a more complex structure which requires more specific diagrams.

The method should be adapted to the design team, for example, it may be useful to write more or less detailed documentation, or use UML diagrams instead of simple text descriptions for the interaction model.

Finally, while MAID is certainly useful for structuring small-scale adaptive courses, with a handcrafted nature, it becomes rapidly unmanageable when representing large, data-intensive Web sites; in this scenario, different methods and modelling primitives are being researched.

An Additional (Critical) Step: Achieving the Student's "Awareness"

We have chosen to clearly separate the design phase from the release, because of the different issues that come at stake. Nevertheless, we want to stress the importance of a critical step for the success of the courseware: the first presentation to the end-users. Every Web site usually has a learning curve before the user may use it efficiently; an adaptive course, which has potentially unstable interfaces, with conditional fragments that appear and disappear, needs "aware" users.

This student's awareness can be achieved in different ways, for example, through self-explicative interfaces, or giving the user the possibility to inspect and modify her/his user model, or scheduling a kick-off lesson where the system is presented to the class.

Future Trends

A complete design model for implementing adaptive applications is one of the key elements for making AHS accessible to a large number of potential users. Testing done with MAID indicated that also non-technical instructors and designers, if supported by skilled designers, may exploit the potential of adaptivity in real educational environments.

An obvious improvement for MAID would be a refinement of its steps and its accurate testing with different adaptive platforms. The development of a MAID CASE tool would also be an interesting development.

Finally, widening the scope of observation, three main elements deserve a particular notice for the evolution of this research track:

1.   Within the AHS field, it is remarkable that some adaptive platforms, like AHA! v. 2.0 are being developed as open systems, supported by a complete authoring tool. We believe that the development of such a tool can be enhanced by the existence of a sound design methodology.

2.   In the broader field of educational technologies, the AHS community can look with interest to the development of learning object standards, such as IMS (IMS, 2003) or SCORM (SCORM, 2003). The object oriented modelling of educational applications in fact provides a sound basis for a common definition of AHS; on the other hand, object-oriented e-learning platforms may gain from adaptive features. What is required for creating a real synergy between the two of them is a method for adapting learning unit structures and selecting learner-tailored learning objects. From this point of view, an integration of MAID or of a similar method with a learning-object compliant and adaptive platform would be a promising achievement.

3. Finally, we recall that instructional strategies—that are specific for each instructional unit—belong to broader categories, such as constructivist strategies, problem-based strategies, and so on. An open research track is the definition of adaptive patterns for types of strategies, under two respects:

(a) Defining types of adaptive application behaviours suitable to support particular instructional strategies.

(b) Defining types of interaction models, domain models (namely types of nodes), and user models that designers can use as starting point for the implementation of particular instructional strategies.

Conclusions

This chapter started with the observation that, despite the great technical advances achieved by AHS in the last decade, adaptive applications are not a commonly used tool in real educational environments. We claimed that this is due to the lack of a sound design method for the development of adaptive application supported by available adaptive platforms. The core of the chapter provided a complete presentation of MAID (Method for Adaptive Instructional Design). The method is focused on the idea of implementing a particular instructional strategy through its translation into a formal description, understandable by the adaptive platform. The description is based on AHAM, and includes the interaction model, the domain model, the user model, and the interface model. The complete MAID method is structured in five phases. Each of them was introduced and illustrated by examples. The lifecycle of MAID was also discussed. A complete case study proposed a picture of the method in practice. Finally, the method was discussed and some outlooks in the field of AHS and in other fields were presented.

The major claim of this chapter is the necessity of offering a design method for supporting the actual exploitation of AHS in real educational environments. From a practical point of view, this means training designers to help instructors and educators to translate their ideas and strategies into adaptive applications. In this direction, MAID is a communication tool that enables technical staff, designers, and instructors to share with each other. With MAID, the content of this communication process focuses on the instructional strategy, keeping technical details in the background.

References

Anderson, L. W., & Krathwohl, D. R. (2001). *A taxonomy for learning, teaching and assessing. A revision of bloom's taxonomy of educational objectives.* New York: Addison Wesley Longman.

Armani, J. (2001). *Progettazione e sviluppo di un'applicazione ipermediale adattativa per uso didattico.* Master thesis. Biblioteca centrale del Politecnico di Milano.

Armani, J. (2003). The AdLearn framework: Automatic planning and tutoring system for self studying. *International Studies in Communication Sciences* (in print).

Aroyo, L., Dicheva, D., & Cristea, A. (2002). Ontological support for Web courseware authoring. *ICALT'02*, Las Vegas, NV.

Bates, T. W. (1999). *Managing technological change.* San Francisco: Jossey-Bass.

Bates, T. W., & Poole, G. (2003). *Effective teaching with technologies in higher education.* San Francisco: Jossey-Bass.

Botturi, L. (2001). *Seaway tracker. An adaptive navigational engine for educational applications.* Master thesis. Lugano: BUL.

Brusilovsky, P. (2003). Developing adaptive educational hypermedia systems: From design models to authoring tools. In T. Murray, S. Blessing, & S. Ainsworth (Eds.), *Authoring tools for advanced technology learning environment* (pp. 377-410). Dordrecht: Kluwer Academic Publishers.

Brusilovsky, P. (2004). KnowledgeTree: A distributed architecture for adaptive e-learning. *WWW 2004*, New York.

Brusilovsky, P., & Pesin, L. (1994). ISIS-Tutor: An adaptive hypertext learning environment. *Japanese-CIS Workshop on Knowledge-Based Software Engineering*, Tokyo, Japan.

Brusilovsky, P., Eklund, J., & Schwarz, E. (1998). Web-based education for all: A tool for developing adaptive courseware. *Computer Networks and ISDN Systems [Proceedings of 7th International World Wide Web Conference]*, 30(1-7), 291-300.

Carro, R. M., Pulido, E., & Rodríguez, P. (2001). TANGOW: A model for Internet based learning. *IJCEELL - International Journal of Continuing Engineering Education and Life-Long Learning*, 11(1-2). Retrieved March 2004, from http://www.inderscience.com/ejournal/c/ijceell/ijceell2001/ijceell2001v11n12.html

Cristea, A., & Aroyo, L. (2002). Adaptive authoring of adaptive educational hypermedia. *AH 2002*, Malaga, Spain.

Czarkowski, M., & Kay, J. (2002). Scrutable adaptive hypertext. *AH 2002*, Malaga, Spain.

De Bra, P., & Calvi, L. (1998). AHA! An open adaptive hypermedia architecture. *The New Review of Hypermedia and Multimedia, 4*, 115-139.

De Bra, P., Aerts, A., Houben, G. J., & Wu, H. (2000). Making general-purpose adaptive hypermedia work. *AACE WebNet Conference,* San Antonio, TX.

De Bra, P., Aerts, A., Smits, D., & Stash, N. (2002a). AHA! meets AHAM. *AH 2002*, Malaga, Spain.

De Bra, P., Aerts, A., Smits, D., & Stash, N. (2002b). AHA! Version 2.0, More adaptation flexibility for authors. *ELEARN 2002*, Montreal, Canada.

De Bra, P., Houben, G. J., & Wu, H. (1999). AHAM: A dexter-based reference model for adaptive hypermedia. *ACM Conference on Hypertext and Hypermedia*, Darmstadt, Germany.

Dick, W., Carey, W., & Carey, L. (2001). *The systematic design of instruction* (6th edition). New York: Harper Collins College Publishers.

Gagné, R. M., Briggs, R., & Wager, W. (1992). *Principles of instructional design* (4th edition). TX: HBJ College Publishers.

Grigoriadou, M., Papanikolaou, K., Kornilakis, H., & Magoulas, G. (2001). *INSPIRE: An INtelligent System for Personalized Instruction in a Remote Environment*. Revised Papers from the International Workshops OHS-7, SC-3, and AH-3 on Hypermedia: Openness, Structural Awareness, and Adaptivity, Lecture Notes in Computer Sciences (pp. 215-225). ACM Press.

Henze, N., & Nejdl, W. (1999). Adaptivity in the KBS hyperbook system. *Second Workshop on Adaptive Systems and User Modeling on the WWW*, Banff, Canada.

Henze, N., Naceur, K., Nejdl, W., & Wolpers, M. (1999). Adaptive hyperbooks for constructivist teaching. *Kunstliche Intelligenz, 4*.

IMS (2003). *IMS Specification*. Retrieved September 25, 2003, from http://www.imsproject.org

Koch, N. (2001). *Software engineering for adaptive hypermedia systems*. PhD thesis, Verlag Uni-Druck, Munich.

Merrill, M. D. (2003). *Does your instruction rate 5 star?* Retrieved August 2003, from http://www.id2.usu.edu/5Star/Index.htm

Neumann, G., & Zirvas, J. (1998). SKILL – A scalable Internet-based teaching and learning system. *WebNet 98*, Orlando, FL.

Papasalouros, A., & Retalis, S. (2002). Ob-AHEM: A UML-enabled model for adaptive educational hypermedia Applications. *Interactive Educational Multimedia, 4.*

Park, O., & Lee, J. (2004). Adaptive instructional systems. In D. H. Jonassen (Ed.), *Handbook of Research on Educational Communications and Technology* (2nd ed). AECT. Retrieved from http://www.aect.org (members only)

Quatrani, T. (2001). *Introduction to the unified modeling language.* Retrieved September 25, 2003, from http://www.rational.com/media/uml/intro_rdn.pdf

Reigeluth, C. M. (1983). *Instructional-design theories and models: An overview of their current status.* NJ: Lawrence Erlbaum Associates.

SCORM (2003). *SCORM specification.* Retrieved September 25, 2003, from http://www.adlnet.org/index.cfm?fuseaction=scormabt

Smith, P. L., & Ragan, T. J. (1999). *Instructional design.* New York: John Wiley & Sons.

Stash, N., & De Bra, P. (2003). Building adaptive presentations with AHA! 2.0. *PEG Conference*, St. Petersburg, Russia.

UML (2003). *Resource center.* Retrieved September 25, 2003, from http://www.rational.com/uml

Wu, H., & De Bra, P. (2001). Sufficient conditions for well-behaved adaptive hypermedia systems. *Lecture Notes in AI [Proceedings of the WI Conference], 2198* (pp. 148-152).

Wu, H., Houben, G. J., & De Bra, P. (1999). Authoring support for adaptive hypermedia applications. *ED-MEDIA 1999*, Seattle, WA.

Endnotes

[1]   Both for prerequisites and propagation, AHA! requires the specification of absolute or relative (percentage) values for each relationship. These were omitted from the maps in order to improve legibility.

[2]   Another issue we should mention is whether the user profile (or part of it) should be opened to the user (Czarkowski & Kay, 2002) so that s/he can change some particular values (for example, the student may set her/his knowledge levels on some topics), or not. It is important that this decision is made in the perspective of the instructional strategy. It is in fact possible that the activities supported by the adaptive application are just a part of the

whole course or instructional unit, and it may happen that a learner gets a particular insight in some topic during a classroom session, that the adaptive system clearly cannot record. According to the responsibility and learning independence of the learners, the designer may choose to let them directly update values in their profile. In the User Model documentation, the designer may annotate the corresponding variables that can be inspected/ modified by the learner.

Chapter VIII

An Adaptive Feedback Framework to Support Reflection, Guiding and Tutoring

Evangelia Gouli, University of Athens, Greece

Agoritsa Gogoulou, University of Athens, Greece

Kyparisia A. Papanikolaou, University of Athens, Greece

Maria Grigoriadou, University of Athens, Greece

Abstract

In this chapter, an adaptive feedback framework (AFF) is proposed for the provision of personalized feedback accommodating learners' individual characteristics and needs in the context of computer-based learning environments. Multiple informative, tutoring, and reflective feedback components (ITRFC) are incorporated into the framework, aiming to stimulate learners to reflect on their beliefs, to guide and tutor them towards the achievement of specific learning outcomes and to inform them about their performance. The proposed framework adopts a scheme for the categorization of learners' answer, introduces a multi-layer structure and a stepwise presentation of the ITRFC and supports adaptation of the provided feedback both in the dimensions of adaptivity and adaptability. The adaptivity of the AFF is based on the gradual provision of the ITRFC and on the adaptive presentation of the ITRFC according to the learner's knowledge level, preferences and interaction behaviour. The adaptability of the AFF enables learners to have control over the feedback presentation in order to guide the adaptive dimension of the framework. In the context of the Web-based concept map assessment tool referred to as COMPASS, the proposed framework has been adopted for the provision of personalized feedback in concept mapping tasks. A preliminary evaluation of the framework in the context of COMPASS showed that the AFF led the majority of the learners in reviewing their maps, reconsidering their beliefs and accomplishing successfully the underlying concept mapping task.

Introduction

Feedback is considered as a key aspect of learning and instruction (Mory, 1996). Bangert-Drowns, Kulik, Kulik, and Morgan (1991) emphasize that "... any theory that depicts learning as a process of mutual influence between learners and their environments must involve feedback implicitly or explicitly because without feedback, mutual influence is by definition impossible. Hence, the feedback construct appears often as an essential element of theories of learning and instruction". Effective feedback aims to (i) assist learners in identifying their false beliefs, becoming aware of their misconceptions and inadequacies, and reconstructing their knowledge, (ii) help learners to determine performance expectations, identify what they have already learned and what they are able to do, and judge their personal learning progress, and (iii) support learners towards the achievement of the underlying learning goals (Mason & Bruning, 2001; Mory, 1996). Thus, feedback should guide and tutor learners as well as stimulate and cultivate processes like self-explanation, self-regulation, and self-evaluation, which require reflection (Chi, de Leeuw, Chiu, & Lavancher, 1994; Vosniadou, 2001). Moreover, feedback should be aligned, as much as possible, to each individual learner's characteristics, since individuals differ in their general skills, aptitudes, and preferences for processing information, constructing meaning from it and/or applying it to new situations (Jonassen & Grabowski, 1993).

Characteristics that influence the effectiveness of feedback concern the type of feedback, the amount of the provided information as well as the adaptation to learners' individual differences. Various types of feedback have been proposed and investigated in literature (see reviews by Bangert-Drowns et al., 1991;

Mason & Bruning, 2001; Mory, 1996), providing different levels of verification and elaboration. The level of verification and elaboration determines the amount of the provided information. Moreover, many researchers introduce the notions of adaptive feedback (i.e., different learners receive different information) and adaptable feedback (i.e., learners have the possibility to choose the feedback that suits their needs or preferences) (Jackson, Krajcik, & Soloway, 1998; Sales, 1993) in an attempt to compensate for the weakness of generic feedback to "communicate" with learners and to provide personalized information.

Empirical studies, investigating whether the type and the amount of feedback are related to learners' individual differences, draw implications for the degree of success or failure experienced by learners. Hedberg and McNamara (1985) found that field dependent (FD) learners had fewer errors when their errors were explained and they were given strategies for correcting them, whereas field independent (FI) learners had fewer errors when only the correctness/incorrectness of their answer was provided. In the study of Arroyo, Beck, Beal, Wing, and Woolf (2001), it was revealed that boys benefit more from explanations that are fast to check and go through, while girls devote their time to go through any kind of explanation and do better with hints that are highly structured and interactive.

As far as the adaptation of feedback to learners' individual differences is concerned, little systematic research is available. The studies reported in the feedback literature discuss either theoretical frameworks for adapting feedback mainly to learners' knowledge level or research efforts in the context of computer-based learning environments. In the latter case, the adaptation of feedback is usually based either on the structured form of the feedback (i.e., the amount of the provided feedback is gradually increasing or different types of feedback are provided gradually) or on one or more learners' individual characteristics such as knowledge level and gender. As far as the adaptable dimension of feedback is concerned, the research reported in literature is minimal; the proposed approaches allow learners to intervene in the feedback presentation process at a limited degree, by enabling them to select the type of feedback they prefer at a specific stage of the feedback process.

The research work presented in this chapter takes previous work on feedback one step further by proposing an adaptive feedback framework (AFF) that integrates adaptivity and adaptability, supports processes of tutoring, guiding and reflection and provides as much as possible a general-domain independent form of feedback in order to serve various domains. Multiple informative, tutoring and reflective feedback components (ITRFC) are incorporated into the framework in an attempt to stimulate learners to reflect on their beliefs, to guide and tutor them towards the achievement of the learning outcomes addressed by an activity/task, and to serve learner's individual preferences and needs. The adaptivity of the AFF is based on the gradual provision of the ITRFC, which are structured in different layers and on the adaptive presentation of the ITRFC, which accommodates learner's knowledge level, preferences and interaction behaviour. The adaptability of the AFF enables learners to have control over the feedback presentation in order to guide the adaptive dimension of the framework. The AFF was realized and preliminary evaluated in the context of the Web-based concept map assessment tool referred to as COMPASS.

The chapter is organized as follows. In the next section, research on the feedback area and especially on adaptive feedback is reviewed, as well as the discriminative characteristics of the AFF are introduced. Following, the AFF is presented in detail, in terms of the proposed scheme for the categorization of the learner's answer, the different ITRFC incorporated into the framework, the multi-layer structure of the ITRFC and their stepwise presentation, as well as the adaptive and adaptable dimensions of the framework. In the next section, our effort to use the proposed AFF in the context of COMPASS is presented. The chapter ends with concluding remarks and further research directions.

Literature Review on Feedback and Rationale for the AFF

In most computer-based learning environments, feedback is provided to learners at the end or during the elaboration of an activity/task/assignment, either (i) automatically by the system (computer-generated feedback) such as in IN-SPIRE (Papanikolaou, Grigoriadou, Kornilakis, & Magoulas, 2003), where information about the correctness of the answer is provided in conjunction with explanations, hints and examples, or (ii) by the tutor (human-generated feedback) such as in FFS (Wang, Wang, Wang, & Huang, 2004), where the tutor can assign scores and make comments/suggestions to learners based on the learners' answer to the provided reflective questions, or (iii) by peers (human-generated feedback) (in case of peer and/or collaborative assessment) such as in NetPeas (Lin, Liu, & Yuan, 2001), where the peers provide feedback to learners as answers to specific evaluation criteria. Regarding the first case, usually, different types of feedback are exploited and immediate feedback is provided; however, most of these environments do not focus on the provision of personalized feedback and the appropriateness of the provided feedback depends on the capabilities of the system in analysing and evaluating the learner's answer. In the second case, the analysis and the evaluation of the learner's answer is carried out by the tutor without being restricted to the capabilities of the system and the feedback can be characterized potentially as personal as the tutor knows the learners on an individual basis; however, delayed feedback is provided and the frequency and the quality of feedback may be limited in cases where a large number of learners are supported/guided by the tutor (Ross & Morrison, 1993). Since, we are interested in computer-generated feedback, which is adapted on learners' needs and preferences, in the following, research approaches falling under this area are presented.

A literature review regarding the provision of adaptive feedback, showed that there are several research efforts which can be grouped in the following categories: (i) adaptive feedback schemes proposed at a theoretical level (e.g., Mason & Bruning, 2001), (ii) research efforts, especially in computer-based tutoring environments; these efforts are based on the idea that the gradual provision of the appropriate feedback information represents a way of adapting the feedback to learners' needs (e.g., Arroyo, Beck, Woolf, Beal, & Schultz, 2000; Fiedler & Tsovaltzi, 2003; Mathan & Koedinger, 2003; Mitrovic & Martin, 2000; Narciss & Huth, 2004), and (iii) research efforts investigating the provision of feedback based on learners' individual differences, which mainly concern learner's knowledge level and/or gender (e.g., Arroyo et al., 2001; Stern, Beck, & Woolf, 1996).

In Table 1, a presentation of various adaptive feedback approaches is attempted in terms of (i) their context (theoretical level or computer-based learning environments), (ii) the underlying domain, (iii) the goals/processes served (guiding, tutoring, reflection), (iv) the types of feedback supported, (v) the adaptation process (adaptivity and adaptability) followed and (vi) the adaptive mechanism supported (gradual provision of the same type of feedback or different types of feedback and/or adaptation of feedback according to one or more learner's individual characteristics).

The adaptive feedback mechanisms presented in Table 1, accommodate mainly the learners' knowledge level while a limited degree of flexibility is provided to learners to adjust and intervene in the feedback presentation process. In case of the gradual provision of feedback, usually the same type of feedback is provided in different steps, while the amount of feedback is differentiated. Also, these approaches mainly focus on guiding and tutoring processes and they usually restrict the provided help in a domain-specific context. Thus, open issues in the area are (i) the design of a framework which supports the provision of adaptive as well adaptable feedback in a way that enhances learning and serves processes such as reflection, and (ii) the design of a general domain-independent form of feedback able to be incorporated in different learning environments and to serve a variety of domains.

In an attempt to elaborate on the above issues and contribute to the adaptive feedback area, we propose the adaptive feedback framework (AFF) (see Table 1), which exploits different types of feedback, takes into account several learners' individual differences, and supports learner control in order to integrate adaptivity and adaptability in the feedback process. The proposed AFF builds on and expands the abovementioned research efforts in the provision of personalized feedback in computer-based learning environments. It interweaves the gradual presentation of help with the adaptive presentation of feedback accommodating not only the learners' knowledge level but also their preferences and interaction behaviour and enables learners to intervene in the feedback provision process at various levels.

The AFF incorporates various informative, tutoring and reflective feedback components (ITRFC), aiming to serve processes of assessment and learning by (i) informing learners about their performance, (ii) guiding and tutoring learners in order to identify their false beliefs, focus on specific errors, reconstruct their knowledge and achieve specific learning outcomes addressed by an activity/task, and (iii) supporting reflection in terms of encouraging learners to "stop and think" and giving them hints on what to think about. The ITRFC follow as much as possible a general domain-independent form in order to serve various domains. Also, the ITRFC are structured in different layers in order to support the gradual provision of the right amount of feedback information. The stepwise presentation of the ITRFC follows their layered structure and enables learners to elaborate on the feedback information and try again. Moreover, the presentation of the appropriate feedback components on each layer is adapted to the learners' knowledge level, preferences and interaction behaviour. As far as the adaptable dimension is concerned, learners have the possibility to intervene in the feedback presentation process by selecting the preferred layer of feedback and the preferred feedback component, in accordance with their own perceived needs and preferences.

The Adaptive Feedback Framework

In the following, we present the AFF in terms of (i) the answer categorization scheme adopted, (ii) the multiple ITRFC included, (iii) the layered structure of the ITRFC and the way these are presented to the learner, and (iv) both the adaptive and adaptable dimensions of the framework.

An Answer Categorization Scheme

The generation of effective feedback depends heavily on evaluating the learners' answers during the interaction. In the AFF, learner's answer on an activity/task is evaluated according to specific criteria with respect to the expected

Table 1. Presentation of various research efforts, including the proposed adaptive feedback framework, which provide personalized feedback

Research Efforts	Context	Domain	Goal/Processes	Types of Feedback supported	Adaptation Process	Adaptive Mechanism
Mason and Bruning (2001)	Theoretical Framework	Domain Independent	Assist developers and instructors in developing effective feedback in computer-based educational settings	(i) Knowledge-of-correct-response with response-contingent (ii) Knowledge-of-correct-response with topic-contingent (iii) Knowledge-of-response with topic-contingent (iv) Knowledge-of-response with delayed knowledge-of-correct-response plus response-contingent (v) Answer-until-correct with delayed topic-contingent	Adaptivity	Based on the learners' knowledge level and prior knowledge. Variables such as task complexity and timing of feedback are taken into consideration for the adaptation of feedback
Narciss and Huth (2004)	An adaptive tutoring feedback algorithm is proposed and implemented in the context of a multimedia learning environment	Mathematics	Tutoring/Guiding	(i) Knowledge of response (ii) Bug-related feedback	Adaptivity	Gradual provision of different types of feedback following a three-step feedback procedure
Excel Tutor (Mathan & Koedinger, 2003)	Computer-based learning environment	Computer Science	Tutoring/Guiding	(i) Questions having the form of multiple choice (ii) Succinct explanations of errors	Adaptivity	Gradual provision following a three-step feedback procedure
SQL Tutor (Mitrovic & Martin, 2000)	Computer-based learning environment	Computer Science	Tutoring/Guiding	(i) Positive/negative feedback (ii) Error flag (iii) Hint (iv) All errors (v) Partial solution (vi) Complete solution	Adaptivity. Adaptability supported only for the last three types of feedback	Gradual provision of the first three types of feedback

Table 1. (continued)

Research Efforts	Context	Domain	Goal/Processes	Types of Feedback supported	Adaptation Process	Adaptive Mechanism
Animalwatch (Arroyo et al., 2000)	Computer-based learning environment	Mathematics	Tutoring/Guiding	Hints	Adaptivity	Gradual increase of the level of information
(Arroyo et al., 2001)				Hints: a classification of the hints is supported according to their degree of symbolism and their degree of interactivity	Adaptivity	Adaptation based on learners' cognitive development and gender
Fiedler and Tsovaltzi (2003)	An algorithm proposed in the context of the DIALOG project	Mathematics	Tutoring/Guiding	Hints (A taxonomy of hints is supported)	Adaptivity	Gradual provision from less to more informative hints based on the number and kind of hints produced so far, the number of wrong answers and the category of the learner's answers
Stern et al. (1996)	Computer-based learning environment	Mathematics	Tutoring/Guiding	Hints	Adaptivity	Gradual presentation from simple to more specific hints Adaptation based on learners' knowledge level
Adaptive Feedback Framework (AFF)	Theoretical Adaptive Feedback Framework realized in the web-based learning environment COMPASS	Domain Independent	Reflection/ Tutoring/ Guiding	(i) Correctness-Incorrectness of Response (ii) Correct Response (iii) Performance Feedback (iv) Tutoring Feedback Units associated with various modes of knowledge modules such as a definition, example, similar problem and solution of others (v) Explanation of the Response (vi) Belief Prompt-Rethink Write (vii) Error-Task Related Questions	Adaptivity Adaptability supported for all layers of feedback and feedback components	Gradual provision of the different types of feedback (feedback components) following their layered structure (four layers are supported) and based on the category of the learner's answer Adaptation based on learners' knowledge level, preferences and interaction behaviour

answer defined by the tutor (expert's answer). The evaluation process aims not only at the determination of the correctness/incorrectness of the answer but also at the localization of the errors, if any, and at a meaningful characterization of the answer conveying the learner's error(s). To this end, an answer categorization scheme is proposed. The characterization of the learner's answer feeds the process of the stepwise presentation of the feedback components (see the next section and Figure 1).

In order to formulate the scheme for the categorization of the learner's answer, we define as (i) *part of the answer*: one or more elements constituting the learner's answer (e.g., in a fill-in-the-blank question, the learner's answer is consisted of the different parts required to be filled), (ii) *complete answer*: the answer in which all the required parts are present, independently of the correctness of the given values, (iii) *accurate answer*: the answer in which the values of all the given parts are correct.

The answer categorization scheme and the evaluation criteria proposed in the AFF build on the scheme proposed by Fiedler and Tsovaltzi (2003), that is, completeness, accuracy, and missing out, which is further enriched with the criteria of superfluity and non-applicability. According to our scheme, the learner's answer is characterised as:

- **InComplete:** when at least one part of the answer is missing and the rest given parts are accurate.

- **InAccurate:** when the answer is complete, but at least one part of the answer is inaccurate.

- **InAccurate-Superfluous:** when the answer is complete, but at least one part of the answer is inaccurate, in particular, this part is characterized as superfluous, that is, it contains the required elements plus one or more elements. Although the learner's answer could also be characterized as inaccurate, these two characterizations are discriminated as they locate different types of errors that could be individually treated by concretising the feedback components provided.

- **Missing:** when all the expected parts of the answer are missing.

- **InComplete-InAccurate:** when at least one part of the answer is missing and at least one of the rest parts is characterised as inaccurate.

- **Complete-Accurate:** when the answer is the expected one.

- **Not Applicable:** when it is not possible to evaluate the learner's answer and infer a safe conclusion.

The Informative, Tutoring and Reflective Feedback Components

The term ITRFC refers to the different components of feedback, which aim to stimulate learners to reflect on their beliefs and guide and tutor them towards the enrichment/reconstruction of their knowledge and the successful completion of an activity/task. The proposed ITRFC exploit various feedback types reported in literature and offer different levels of verification and elaboration in order to serve learners' individual preferences and needs. The ITRFC are classified in the following three categories (see Figure 3 for indicative examples):

- **Informative Feedback:** aims to inform the learner about the correctness of his/her answer and his/her performance. It includes the following components:

  (a) **Correctness-Incorrectness of Response (CIR):** informs learners whether their answer is correct/incorrect (usually mentioned in literature as knowledge-of-response or knowledge-of-result).

  (b) **Correct Response (CR):** supplies learners with the correct response (usually mentioned as knowledge-of-correct-response).

  (c) **Performance Feedback (PF):** informs learners about their current state; this information is included in the learner model, which is maintained by the system during the interaction, that is, performance on the activity (before the provision of feedback), the concepts/topics that learners know, the number and the type of errors corrected, the number of attempts before each error correction, the number of errors for which the CR was provided, the total time spent for the accomplishment of the activity/task, the learner's preferences on the feedback components before and after the accomplishment of the activity/task (as they are recorded in the course of the elaboration of the activity based on the learner's interaction behaviour).

- **Tutoring Feedback:** aims to tutor learners by enabling them to review learning material relevant to the attributes of the correct response. It includes the following components:

  (a) **Tutoring Feedback Units (TFU):** supply learners with additional learning material. The TFU are structured in two levels, TFU1 (compulsory defined) and TFU2 (optionally defined), differing on the level of information detail they provide. In particular, TFU1 present the corresponding topic/concept in general and may be independent of the activity, while TFU2 present the corresponding topic/concept in more detail in the context of the activity/task under consideration. TFU2 are provided only if learner insists on his/her belief after providing TFU1. The TFU1 are associated with various modes of knowledge modules, which constitute multiple representations of the topic/concept under consideration. The knowledge modules are structured in two levels, explanatory level and exploratory level. The explanatory level includes the following modes of knowledge modules: (i) a description illustrating attributes relevant to the topic/concept under consideration and/or presenting the topic/concept in the context of related topics/concepts and (ii) a definition of the topic/concept under consideration. The exploratory level includes the modes: (i) an image, (ii) an example, (iii) a similar problem followed by its solution, and (iv) any solutions of others given to the specific problem. It is considered necessary to provide, at least, one knowledge module from each level for every topic/concept. The multiple levels (i.e., explanatory and exploratory) and the different modes of knowledge modules aim to serve learners' individual preferences and to cultivate skills such as critical and analytical thinking, ability to compare and combine alternative solutions, ability to make generalizations, and so on. In any case, the tutor is responsible to design and develop the appropriate knowledge modules of each level, taking into account several factors such as the content of the topic/concept under consideration, the difficulty level of the specific topic/concept, and the addressed learning outcomes.

(b) **Explanation of the Response (ER):** informs learners about the correctness or incorrectness of their answer and explains why the incorrect response is wrong or why the correct response is correct.

- **Reflective Feedback:** aims to promote reflection and guide learners' thinking about their response, explore situational cues and underlying meanings relevant to the error identified. Two types of reflection prompts are included: generic and directed prompts. Generic prompts simply ask learners to "stop and think" without providing instruction in what to think about, while directed prompts give learners hints about what to think, attempting to point learners towards a particular direction (Davis, 2003). In this context, reflective feedback includes the following components:

(a) **Belief Prompt-Rethink Write (BP-RW) (generic prompt):** consists of (i) the *learner's belief* in order to bring the learner "in front" of his/her belief and encourage him/her to rethink his/her belief, and (ii) a *prompt* to write any keywords and/or explanations concerning his/her belief.

(b) **Error-Task Related Questions (E-TRQ) (directed prompts):** gives learners a hint, in the form of question, to rethink and correct the identified false belief.

Most of the ITRFC follow a general form (template), which is mainly domain-independent (see Table 2). However, specific parts of the general form depend on the domain under consideration, and the activity/task itself, aiming to provide meaningful help and guide learners to the appropriate directions. Moreover, the form of the E-TRQ depends on the proposed categorization scheme of the learner's answer (see previous section), while the TFU are domain-dependent feedback components.

Structuring and Presenting the Feedback Components

The ITRFC are structured in different layers and a stepwise presentation of the ITRFC, following their layered structure, is realized. The stepwise presentation offers the opportunity to (i) provide gradually the appropriate feedback information to each learner and (ii) enable learners at each step to exploit the feedback information and try again. To this end, the stepwise presentation of the ITRFC represents a way of adapting the feedback to learners needs. The following layers are supported:

- **First Layer:** The Belief Prompt-Rethink Write (BP-RW) feedback component and a combination of the Correctness-Incorrectness of Response (CIR) component with the BP-RW (CIR+BP-RW) are included. In case the learner's answer is characterized as complete-accurate, the BP-RW is provided in order to confirm the learner's confidence and enable him/her to rethink his/her belief (without informing him/her if it is correct or not) and explain the answer. In case the learner's answer is characterized as missing, the feedback components of the first layer are ignored. In all other cases, the CIR+BP-RW are provided. The provision of the feedback components of the first layer aims to enable learners to rethink their beliefs and to get into a self-explanation process in order to identify any errors made mainly by accident.

Table 2. The categories of feedback supported by the AFF, the feedback components included, and their general form (template). The general form of feedback (i.e., the sentence-starter and the questions) is denoted in italics, while the learner's or the expert's belief as well as alternative statements that depend on the context are included in [].

Categories of Feedback	Feedback Components	The General Form of the ITRFC	
Informative Feedback	Correctness-Incorrectness of Response (CIR)	*Your answer is* [correct/incorrect]	
	Correct Response (CR)	*The correct answer is*	
	Performance Feedback (PF)	*Your initial performance level on the activity is characterized as* .... *You have learned the concepts*	
Tutoring Feedback	Tutoring Feedback Units (TFU)	A general form is not supported.	
	Explanation of the Response (ER)	*The answer is* [correct/incorrect] *because* ...	
Reflective Feedback	Belief Prompt-Rethink Write (BP-RW)	*You believe that* .... *Try to* .... • [mention any keywords associated with your answer] • [explain in a paragraph why you believe this] • [execute the pseudocode statement by statement]. *Do you insist on your belief?*	
	Error-Task Related Questions (E-TRQ)	The form of the E-TRQ depends on the categorization scheme for the learner's answer (see "An Answer Categorization Scheme")	
		In case of a learner's InComplete Answer	*Do you really believe that the answer contains only the parts* ....?
		In case of a learner's Missing Answer	*Do you consider that you could add* ....?
		In case of a learner's InAccurate Answer	*Do you really believe that* [Learner's belief]? Or *I believe that* [Expert's belief]. *Do you agree with this?*
		In case of a learner's InAccurate-Superfluous Answer	*Do you want to reconsider the part* .... *in your answer* [Learner's Belief]?

- **Second Layer:** The Error-Task Related Questions (E-TRQ) or the Tutoring Feedback Units (TFU) in conjunction with the E-TRQ (TFU+E-TRQ) are included. The provision of the specific feedback components aims to (i) guide learners and redirect their thinking by giving them a hint, and (ii) tutor learners by enabling them to review learning material relevant to the attributes of the expected answer. The specific components are provided according to the learners' individual characteristics (see the next section).

- **Third Layer:** In the third layer, components that inform learners about the correct response and any accompanied explanations, if available, are included. The feedback components of the Correct Response (CR) or the CR in conjunction with the Explanation of the Response (CR+ER) are provided, according to the learners' individual characteristics (see the next section). Also, the ER is provided in case the learner's answer is characterized as complete-accurate.

- **Fourth Layer:** Finally, in the fourth layer, learners are informed about their performance. The Performance Feedback (PF) component is provided after the completion of the activity/task and enables learners to have access on their learner model as it is constructed in the course of the activity (see the adaptable dimension of the AFF in the next section).

The proposed stepwise presentation is carried out as follows (also see Figure 1). At the beginning, the learner submits his/her answer, which is evaluated and characterized according to the proposed answer categorization scheme, presented earlier in the chapter. The feedback components of the first layer are provided (first step) in all cases except from the case of a "missing" answer. Then, the learner elaborates on the provided feedback information and gives a new answer or insists on his/her belief. The former case (new answer) triggers the evaluation process and the presentation of feedback starts from the beginning (first step). The latter case triggers the provision of the feedback components of the second layer (second step) (or the third layer in case the learner's answer is complete and accurate), giving learner one more opportunity to exploit the feedback information. In case the learner does not insist on his/her previous answer and provides a new answer, the process starts from the beginning (evaluation and first step), while in case the learner insists on his/her belief, feedback components of the third layer (third step) are provided. The feedback component of the fourth layer is provided after the completion of the activity/task.

An indicative example, in the context of an introductory programming course, which demonstrates the proposed ITRFC and the transition from one layer to the next, is given in Figure 3. The activity under consideration (Figure 2) focuses on the "While Loop" and asks learners to make the required changes to the given pseudocode in order to have a correct solution to the given problem. The changes that learners should perform include (i) the change of the control condition (statement no. 2; the correct answer is "While (count <= 12) do"), and (ii) the

Figure 1. The stepwise presentation of the ITRFC based on their layered structure

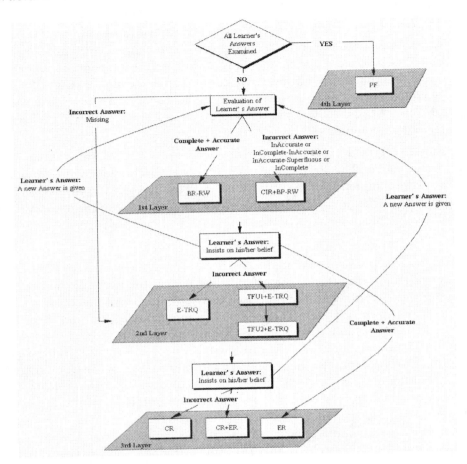

addition of the update statement of the control variable (after the [4] statement, the learner should insert the statement [5]: count <- + 1). In Figure 3, indicative answers that may be given by a learner, illustrating and clarifying the answer categories, are presented. Regarding TFU1, indicative knowledge modules of exploratory and explanatory level are also given. In order to avoid complexity, some arrows from the feedback components of the first and the second layer to the ER feedback component of the third layer are omitted.

Figure 2. An activity in the context of an introductory programming course

Consider the following problem: The computer lab of a high school consists of 12 computers. The teacher wants to write a program in order to keep a record of the serial numbers of the computers. Write a program, in the form of pseudocode, which reads the serial numbers of the computers. The following is a given solution in the form of pseudocode. You have to make all the required modifications in order to have a correct solution according to the context of the given problem.

Solution:
```
[1]    count <- 1
[2]    While (count = 12) do
[3]        Write 'give the serial number of the computer'
[4]          Read s_n
[5]    end_while
```

The Adaptive and Adaptable Dimensions of the Feedback Framework

In the context of the AFF, adaptation is considered as the concept of making adjustments in the presentation of the available feedback components (see the previous section) in order to accommodate a diversity of learners' needs and preferences. The adaptive and adaptable dimensions of the AFF are based on the learner's individual characteristics, which are maintained in his/her learner model. Thus, the learner model needs to keep information on learner's knowledge level, preferences on different feedback components and different levels of TFU1 (i.e., explanatory and exploratory), number and types of errors identified, and learner's interaction behaviour (e.g., the times that specific feedback components have been selected by the learner). Initially, the learner denotes his/her preferences and initiates the learner model, which is continuously updated during the interaction in order to keep always the "current state" of the learner.

With regard to the adaptive dimension of the framework, the learner's knowledge level, preferences and interaction behaviour are used as the main sources of adaptation during the feedback provision process. In particular,

- The *knowledge level* determines which feedback components of the second (E-TRQ or TFU+E-TRQ) and the third layer (CR or CR+ER) are going to be provided. For example, for learners with low knowledge level, the TFU+E-TRQ component is provided at the second layer, while for

Figure 3. An example demonstrating the stepwise presentation of the ITRFC for a specific error on the control condition in the context of the activity of Figure 2. In the boxes, the generated feedback messages are presented: the general form is denoted in bold, the part of the general form which is concretized in the context of the specific domain/answer is denoted in underline, the feedback content defined by the tutor is denoted in plain text, and the learner's belief (answer) or the expert's belief or the part of the learner's answer are denoted in " ".

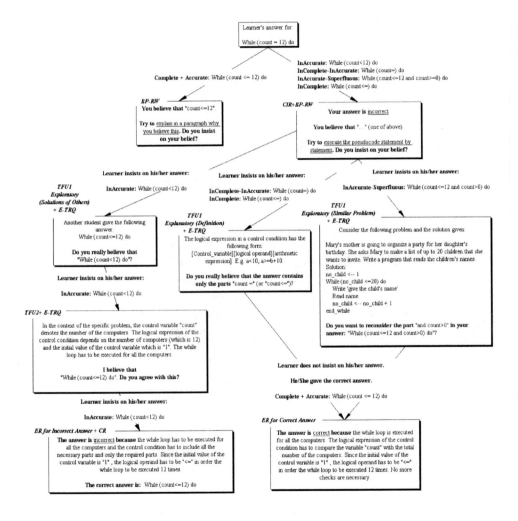

learners with high knowledge level, the CR component is provided at the third layer.

- The learner's *preferences* determine (i) the feedback components that will be available in case the learner's knowledge level is characterized as mediocre and (ii) the levels of the TFU1 (i.e., explanatory or exploratory) that will be available in case that the TFU+E-TRQ is provided. For example, if the TFU+E-TRQ is to be provided and the learner prefers the explanatory (exploratory) level of TFU1, then one of the knowledge modules belonging to the explanatory (exploratory) level is provided (knowledge modules are selected randomly if all of them are available).

- The learner's *interaction behaviour* influences the presentation of the feedback components in the course of the second and the third layer. The attributes that are taken into account concern the number of times that the learner accessed specific (i) feedback components, (ii) levels of TFU1, and (iii) knowledge modules of TFU1. For example, if the exploratory level of TFU1 is to be provided and the favourite knowledge module of the learner is the example (as it is recorded from his/her interaction behaviour) and it is available for the specific concept/topic under consideration, then the example is provided, ignoring the random selection of the available knowledge modules. As the interaction behaviour of the learner may supersede the rules for the provision of feedback according to learner's knowledge level and preferences, it is necessary to define a threshold, denoting the importance of the different types of rules. If the learner's observable behaviour exceeds the particular threshold, then the interaction behaviour is taken into account.

The adaptable dimension of the AFF provides learners the option to (i) control the feedback presentation process by selecting the feedback component they prefer, the levels of the TFU1 (i.e., explanatory or exploratory) and the knowledge modules of the TFU1, ignoring the ones proposed by the framework, and (ii) check their learner model and update their initial preferences as well as their preferences inferred by the system during the interaction. This flexibility allows learners to play an active role in their own learning and make their own decisions to meet their own needs and preferences.

Providing Personalized Feedback in COMPASS on the Basis of the AFF

The AFF was exploited and preliminary evaluated in the design of the feedback process of the web-based concept map assessment tool referred to as COMPASS (COncept MaP ASSessment). In COMPASS, learners undertake assessment activities, which are based on concept maps. A concept map is comprised of nodes (concepts) and links (relationships between concepts) (Novak & Gowin, 1984). Concept mapping is the process of organizing concepts in a hierarchical manner and forming meaningful relationships between them. As concept maps provide a means to capture, elicit and represent qualitative aspects of the learner's knowledge and promote meaningful learning (Mintzes, Wandersee, & Novak, 2000; Novak & Gowin, 1984), they have been successfully used in many disciplines, particularly in science, as an instructional tool, as a tool to promote meaningful learning, as an assessment tool, and as a curriculum organization guide in teaching (Jonassen, Reeves, Hong, Harvey, & Peters, 1997; Mintzes et al., 2000). In concept mapping environments, feedback is usually tailored to specific common errors identified on the learners' concept maps, without taking into account the learners' individual characteristics or needs (Chang, Sung, & Chen, 2001; Cimolino, Kay, & Miller, 2003).

Having as an objective to interweave assessment and instruction and exploit the value of concept maps as assessment and learning tools, we have developed COMPASS (Gouli, Gogoulou, Papanikolaou, & Grigoriadou, 2004b), which serves (i) *the assessment process* by employing a variety of activities and applying a scheme for the qualitative and quantitative estimation of the learner's knowledge and (ii) *the learning process* through the "Knowledge Reconstruction + Refinement" (KR+R) process. The "KR+R" process aims to provide feedback, tailored to each individual learner in order to support reflection, to guide and tutor learners and subsequently to enable them enrich/reconstruct their knowledge. To this end, the proposed AFF has been exploited in the design of the "KR+R" process. Following, we briefly present how each feature of the AFF has been used and "adapted" in the context of COMPASS. More specifically:

- The *learner's answer categorization scheme* supported by the AFF has been concretized and realized according to the proposed error categorization scheme for concept mapping tasks, presented in Gouli, Gogoulou, Papanikolaou, and Grigoriadou (2004a), and has been incorporated and implemented in the diagnosis process of the tool. More specifically, the characterizations used are: incomplete when an "incomplete relationship" or an "incomplete proposition" error is identified, missing for a "missing concept and its relationship" or a "missing relationship" error, inaccurate for an "incorrect concept" or an "incorrect relationship" error, and inaccurate-superfluous for a "superfluous concept" or a "superfluous relationship" error.

- The structure of the feedback components follows the four layers of the AFF.

    (a) The feedback components regarding the first, the third and the fourth layer, have been developed on the basis of the proposed general form of the ITRFC (Table 2).

    (b) *The form of the error-task related questions (E-TRQ)* (feedback component of the second layer) has been differentiated according to the specific error categories identified for concept mapping tasks (Gouli et al., 2004a).

    (c) *The tutoring feedback units (TFU)* (feedback component of the second layer) concern (i) the concepts represented on the expert's concept map and/or the concepts included in the provided list of concepts (in case a list of concepts is supported) (TFUC) and (ii) specific propositions that the tutor anticipates errors/false beliefs (TFUP). Both the TFUC and the TFUP follow the structure described in the AFF for TFU.

The incorporation of the AFF in the "KR+R" process of COMPASS was based on two pilot empirical studies conducted in a real classroom environment of secondary education; the teacher simulated the function of the AFF, while the learners elaborated on concept mapping tasks addressing issues of the "Introductory Informatics" course (see Gouli et al., 2004a, for a detailed description of the studies).

The aim of the first study was to investigate whether the stepwise presentation of the feedback components and the design of the E-TRQ, as the only source of feedback for the second layer, can help learners towards the direction of identifying their errors, reconsidering and correcting them appropriately. The results indicated that (i) all the learners after the provision of feedback improved their performance, (ii) the provision of the feedback components of the first layer was proved to be adequate and helped learners to check for accidental constructions, (iii) the form of the E-TRQ helped learners, especially those with knowledge level above average, in revising their beliefs and refining their knowledge, and (iv) in cases of learners with low knowledge level, a form of tutoring feedback was required in order to help them identify and revise their beliefs.

The aim of the second study was to investigate whether the design of the adaptive dimension of the framework can stimulate learners to revise their maps. As the study was carried out in a simulation mode, the learner's interaction behaviour was not considered as a source of adaptation. Although, the results were primitive, they have been encouraging, indicating that the proposed feedback framework led the majority of the learners in reviewing their maps, reconsidering their beliefs and accomplishing successfully the concept mapping task. However, data gathered from a larger sample, using COMPASS as a concept map assessment tool, under longer periods of time, are considered necessary for the evaluation of the AFF.

Concluding Remarks

The research work presented in this chapter contributes to the field of adaptive feedback in computer-based learning environments by proposing an adaptive feedback framework. The discriminative characteristics of the AFF, compared to other approaches in the area, are: (i) the use of multiple informative, tutoring and reflective feedback components, which follow, as much as possible, a general domain-independent form and serve processes of guiding, tutoring and reflection; (ii) the adoption of reflective feedback components that encourage learners to "stop and think" and give them hints indicating potentially productive directions for reflection; (iii) the structure and the variety of the tutoring feedback components (i.e., explanatory and exploratory levels and different modes of knowledge modules) that support learners with different preferences and cultivate various skills; (iv) the structure of the ITRFC in multiple layers and their stepwise presentation that supports the gradual provision of feedback and enables learners to elaborate on the feedback information and try again; (v) the adaptive dimension of the framework that interweaves the gradual provision of the ITRFC with the adaptive presentation of the feedback, accommodating learners' knowledge level, preferences, and interaction behaviour; and (vi) the adaptable dimension of the framework that enables learners to undertake control over the feedback presentation in order to guide the adaptive dimension of the framework.

The preliminary evaluation of the AFF during the implementation phase of the COMPASS tool revealed that the incorporation of multiple ITRFC and their structuring/presentation enabled the majority of the learners in reviewing their maps, reconsidering their beliefs and accomplishing successfully the concept mapping task. However, a comprehensive evaluation study is considered necessary in order to investigate several issues such as the effectiveness of the AFF in learner's learning achievement, in supporting processes of guiding, tutoring and reflection, in accommodating learner's individual differences as well as in supporting learner control over the feedback presentation. This evaluation study will be conducted in the context of a real computer-based learning environment, in the near future.

Furthermore, although the AFF may serve various domains, the extent to which a computer-based learning environment can incorporate AFF depends on the ability of the environment to automatically analyse the learner's answer in its constituent's parts in order to be assessed on the basis of the proposed answer categorization scheme. Moreover, in the AFF, the learner's answer is assessed with respect to the expected answer defined by the tutor/expert. Further research should investigate the way that the AFF can be incorporated in learning environments where alternative approaches of analyzing/assessing learners' answers (e.g., latent semantic analysis approach) are supported.

Finally, open issues in designing and developing computer-generated adaptive feedback that could direct future research are (i) the adaptable dimension of a feedback mechanism, that is, how can the learner contribute to the feedback process and under which conditions s/he should undertake control over the system; (ii) how a feedback mechanism can stimulate and engage learners in the processes of self-regulation and self-explanation by enabling them to judge their answers in relation to those of peers, or judge their peers; (iii) how learners' cognitive and learning styles influence the effectiveness of particular components/modes of feedback and how these characteristics can be accommodated in the feedback process; and (iv) the use of natural language techniques for analysing/assessing learners' answers and generating adaptive feedback.

References

Arroyo, I., Beck, J., Beal, C., Wing, R., & Woolf, B. (2001). Analyzing students' response to help provision in an elementary mathematics Intelligent Tutoring System. In R. Luckin (Ed.), *Papers of the AIED-2001 Workshop on Help Provision and Help Seeking in Interactive Learning Environments* (pp. 34-46).

Arroyo, I., Beck, J., Woolf, B., Beal, C., & Schultz, K. (2000). Macroadapting Animalwatch to gender and cognitive differences with respect to hint interactivity and symbolism. *Proceedings of the Fifth International Conference on Intelligent Tutoring Systems* (pp. 574-583).

Bangert-Drowns, R., Kulik, C., Kulik, J., & Morgan, M. (1991). The instructional effect of feedback in test-like events. *Review of Educational Research, 61*, 213-238.

Chang, K., Sung, T., & Chen, S-F. (2001). Learning through computer-based concept mapping with scaffolding aid. *Journal of Computer Assisted Learning, 17*(1), 21-33.

Chi, M., de Leeuw, N., Chiu, M-H., & Lavancher, C. (1994). Eliciting self-explanation improves understanding. *Cognitive Science, 18*, 439-477.

Cimolino, L., Kay, J., & Miller, A. (2003). Incremental student modelling and reflection by verified concept-mapping. *Supplementary Proceedings of the AIED2003: Learner Modelling for Reflection Workshop* (pp. 219-227).

Davis, E. (2003). Prompting middle school science students for productive reflection: Generic and directed prompts. *The Journal of the Learning Sciences, 12*(1), 91-142.

Fiedler, A., & Tsovaltzi, D. (2003). Automating hinting in an intelligent tutorial dialog system for mathematics. *Proceedings of the IJCAI 2003 Workshop on Knowledge Representation and Automated Reasoning for E-Learning Systems*, Acapulco, Mexico. Retrieved 2004 from http://www.uni-koblenz.de/~peter/ijcai-03-elearning/

Gouli, E., Gogoulou, A., Papanikolaou, K., & Grigoriadou, M. (2004a, August). Designing an adaptive feedback scheme to support reflection in concept mapping. *Proceedings of the Adaptive Hypermedia Conference 2004: Workshop on Individual Differences in Adaptive Hypermedia*, Eindhoven, The Netherlands (pp. 126-135).

Gouli, E., Gogoulou, A., Papanikolaou, K., & Grigoriadou, M. (2004b, September). COMPASS: An adaptive Web-based concept map assessment tool. *Proceedings of the First International Conference on Concept Mapping*, Pamplona, Spain.

Hedberg, J., & McNamara, S. (1985). Matching feedback and cognitive style in a visual CAI task. Paper presented at the *Annual Meeting of the American Educational Research Association*, Chicago. (ERIC Document Reproduction Service NO. ED 26015).

Jackson, S., Krajcik, J., & Soloway, E. (1998). The design of guided learner-adaptable scaffolding in interactive learning environments. *Proceedings of ACM, CHI'98 Human Factors in Computing Systems* (pp. 187-194).

Jonassen, D., & Grabowski, B. (1993). *Handbook of individual differences, learning and instruction.* Hillsdale, NJ: Lawrence Erlbaum Associates.

Jonassen, D., Reeves, T., Hong, N., Harvey, D., & Peters, K. (1997). Concept mapping as cognitive learning and assessment tools. *Journal of Interactive Learning Research, 8*(3/4), 289-308.

Lin, S., Liu, E., & Yuan, S. (2001). Web-based peer assessment: Feedback for students with various thinking styles. *Journal of Computer Assisted Learning, 17*, 420-432.

Mason, B., & Bruning, R. (2001). *Providing feedback in computer-based instruction: What the research tells us.* Retrieved 2004 from http://dwb.unl.edu/Edit/MB/MasonBruning.html

Mathan, S., & Koedinger, K. (2003). Recasting the feedback debate: Benefits of tutoring error detection and correction skills. In U. Hoppe, F. Verdejo, & J. Kay (Eds.), *Artificial intelligence in education, shaping the future of learning through intelligent technologies, Proceedings of AIED 2003* (pp. 13-20). Amsterdam: IOS Press.

Mintzes, J., Wandersee, J., & Novak, J. (2000). *Assessing science understanding: A human constructivist view.* Educational Psychology Series, Academic Press.

Mitrovic, A., & Martin, B. (2000). Evaluating the effectiveness of feedback in SQL-Tutor. In Kinshuk, C. Jesshope, & T. Okamoto (Eds.), *Proceedings of International Workshop on Advanced Learning Technologies, IWALT2000,* Palmerston North, New Zealand (pp. 143-144).

Mory, E. (1996). Feedback research. In D. H. Jonassen (Ed.), *Handbook of research for educational communications and technology* (pp. 919-956). New York: Simon & Schuster Maxmillan.

Narciss, S., & Huth, K. (2004). How to design informative tutoring feedback for multimedia learning. In H. M. Niegemann, R. Brünken, & D. Leutner (Eds.), *Instructional design for multimedia learning* (pp. 181-195). Münster, Germany: Waxmann.

Novak, J., & Gowin, D. (1984). *Learning how to learn.* UK: Cambridge University Press.

Papanikolaou, K., Grigoriadou, M., Kornilakis, H., & Magoulas, G. (2003). Personalizing the interaction in a Web-based educational hypermedia system: the case of INSPIRE. *User-Modeling and User-Adapted Interaction, 13*(3), 213-267.

Ross, S., & Morrison, G. (1993). Using feedback to adapt instruction for individuals. In J. Dempsey & G. Sales (Eds.), *Interactive instruction and feedback* (pp. 177-195). Englewood Cliffs, NJ: Educational Technology Publications.

Sales, G. (1993). Adapted and adaptive feedback in technology-based instruction. In J. Dempsey & G. Sales (Eds.), *Interactive instruction and feedback* (pp. 159-176). Englewood Cliffs, NJ: Educational Technology Publications.

Stern, M., Beck, J., & Woolf, B. (1996). Adaptation of problem presentation and feedback in an intelligent mathematics tutor. In C. Frasson, G. Gauthier, & A. Lesgold (Eds.) *Proceedings of the Third International Conference on Intelligent Tutoring Systems* (pp. 605-615). New York: Springer-Verlag.

Vosniadou, S. (2001). *How children learn.* International Academy of Education. Educational Practices Series, 7. Retrieved 2002 from http://www.ibe.unesco.org/International/Publications/EducationalPractices/prachome.htm

Wang, T. H., Wang, W. L., Wang, K. H., & Huang, H. C. (2004). A case study of Web-based instruction (WBI): The effectiveness of using frontpage feedback system (FFS) as metacognition strategy for freshmen biology teaching. *International Journal on E-Learning, 3*(2), 18-27.

Chapter IX

Adaptable Navigation in a SCORM Compliant Learning Module

Boris Gauss,
Center of Human-Machine-Systems, Technische Universität, Berlin

Leon Urbas,
Center of Human-Machine-Systems, Technische Universität, Berlin

Abstract

This chapter is about the use of metaphors and adaptable navigation in the context of the technological standard SCORM. Our theoretical focus is on hypertext navigation in SCORM compliant learning modules and the potential of adaptable navigation metaphors within this standard. In the empirical section, we present a case study about navigation design and usability evaluation of a learning module prototype. This learning module was developed for the subject matter of steady-state modelling in process systems engineering, and features an adaptable navigation with a novel process control metaphor. We conclude with a discussion on the didactical value of navigation metaphors and adaptability in SCORM, and provide some suggestions for future research in this area.

Introduction

Standardisation is regarded as an important issue for the sustainability of hypermedia systems in education and training. The Sharable Content Object Reference Model (SCORM) is a set of technological specifications for designing Web-based learning materials, established by the Advanced Distributed Learning initiative (ADL) of the US Department of Defense (ADL, 2002). While technological standards like SCORM are often considered to be didactically neutral we will show that there is a need for research on the pedagogical implications of this standard to develop more sophisticated guidelines for the didactical designers. In this chapter, we will focus on the didactical potential of metaphors and adaptable navigation in SCORM. Our theoretical argument is completed with a case study, which presents the design of a learning module prototype and an empirical usability evaluation study. The module features an adaptable navigation with a novel process control metaphor, which was especially developed for the subject matter of process systems engineering. We assumed that metaphors support the didactical coherence of a modular SCORM course and that adaptable navigation allows the users to access the learning objects according to their individual goals and preferences. We will discuss if the findings of the evaluation study provide evidence for these assumptions and identify questions for further investigation.

Background

Navigation in SCORM

An essential characteristic of SCORM—as of other technological standards for e-learning—is modularity. A SCORM course consists of several sharable content objects (*SCOs* or *objects*). An object is the "smallest logical unit of instruction" (Learning Systems Architecture Net [LSAN], 2003) and represents a single instructional objective. It is composed of one ore more (multi)media files, called assets. Each object is conceived as a stand-alone lesson which can be integrated into different courses or learning modules without modification. Therefore, the content of an object must be independent from its context (i.e., the other objects of the learning module). In consequence, hyperlinks can only refer to assets within the sharable object in which they are set. It is not possible to set hyperlinks from a sharable object to any other sharable object—even of the same module—nor to any other reference outside the object. This strong restriction in the interlinking has been discussed by Clark (2003):

"A course built from such learning objects consists of a set of completely isolated sets of activities or information with no cross-referencing, much like a book written under the rule that nothing written on any one page can refer to anything written on any other page. There clearly are enormous pedagogic assumptions built into any learning platform that embodies such a structure. It would seem to be fair to say that in this instance the technological imperatives have driven the pedagogic stance of the product." (p. 4)

Clark (2003) points out that the strict segmentation of the learning content into separated pieces is problematic for many disciplines. From a didactical point of view, it is clear that the interchangeability of single isolated learning objects is limited—especially in complex domains like engineering, which build on several basic disciplines. Some learning atoms will only make sense within larger molecules. Another problem concerning the shareability of learning objects is that there is no general consensus about the granularity of learning goals (Wiley, 2003), which determines the size of the objects (each meant to represent a single goal, see above). As a result, it is technologically easy to create a course of various SCORM compliant objects while it still might be difficult to integrate sharable objects from different sources into a didactically coherent learning module.

We propose to distinguish three different levels of didactical design in the context of SCORM:

1.   **Micro level:** didactical design of single sharable objects.
2.   **Meso level:** didactical design of a learning module composed of several objects.
3.   **Macro level:** didactical design of the curriculum which can include a broad variety of instructional settings, methods and media.

In this chapter, we concentrate on the meso level, on which the task of the didactical designer consists in organising the structure for the content objects of a module in an xml file, the manifest. ADL (2002) has developed guidelines for SCORM offering different structuring methods, for example, linear, grid, hierarchical, or Web. In addition to the overall structure, the designer has also the possibility to define a logical sequence of the objects.

Consistent with the levels of didactical design, we can also distinguish different levels of navigation for the learners in a SCORM course (see Figure 1): (i)

Figure 1. Levels of navigation in a SCORM module

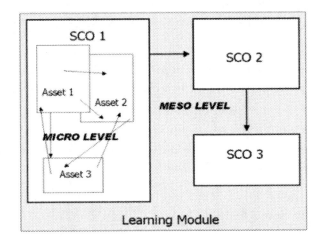

navigation within an object (micro navigation) and (ii) navigation between the objects (meso navigation). These two navigation levels can be seen as an adaptation of Kuhlen's (1991) general distinction between internal and external hypertext navigation to the SCORM world.

After this classification, the macro level would concern the navigation between courses and beyond. This is not the scope of the SCORM standard.

Metaphors in SCORM

Meyer (2002) proposes to distinguish four categories of metaphors in learning environments:

1. **Design metaphors:** metaphors used during the design process of the learning environment by the designers in order to think about the system.

2. **Interface metaphors:** metaphors at the user interface level which are perceptible by the learner.

3. **Scenario metaphors:** metaphors used in the instructional scenario creating a unifying context able to link the various elements of a domain knowledge.

4.   **Content (or instructional) metaphors:** metaphors used to explain topics of the subject matter.

According to this classification the "classical" hypertext navigation metaphors belong to the group of interface metaphors. Navigation metaphors generally provide spatial and temporal orientation in a hypermedia system (Schulmeister, 1996). Oliveira (1992, p. 6, cited from Schulmeister, 1996) also assumes that "analogies between the real world of a hyperdocument and the real world or a scientific theory which is to be studied, facilitate for the users, as long as a good metaphor is chosen, the construction of a mental model" (however, we should avoid drawing simplistic analogies from the structure of a hypertext to the structure of internal representations, cf. Dillon, McKnight & Richardson, 1993; Shapiro & Niederhauser, 2004).

Given the segmentation of the learning content in SCORM into single sharable objects without cross-referencing we assume that metaphors could play a crucial role for the didactical coherence within a course. In particular, we suppose that navigation and scenario metaphors on the meso level can create a meaningful framework supporting the learners to integrate the separated pieces of learning content from the single objects into a coherent internal representation of the learning content of the whole module.

Adaptable Navigation Metaphors

Meyer (2002) raises the question whether the didactical designer should implement several possible metaphors of the same category into a learning environment. For content metaphors, she assumes that the users' free choice among several metaphors is important. What about interface metaphors for navigation?

First of all, as it is common in this area of research, we will not distinguish between the abstract concept of navigation metaphor and its materialisation, the navigation tool. There is some empirical evidence that the effectiveness of a specific navigation tool depends on the characteristics of the task (MacDonald & Stevenson, 1999, 1998). Also from a theoretical view, we regard this argument as conclusive. For the task of hypertext navigation, there are various categorisations of goals (Cove & Welsh, 1988; O'Connor, 1985; Salomon, 1990; all cited from Unz, 2000). In her review on navigation research, Unz (2000) proposes the distinction into (1) goal-directed searching (the user is looking for certain information) and (2) explorative browsing (the user has no clearly defined target of navigation). It seems obvious that there can not be the one best navigation tool which is adequate for all the various goals in navigation tasks.

Instead, the specific tasks probably require specific support by different navigation tools.

In addition to the task, also individual differences of the learners are known to influence the effectiveness of navigation tools. Especially the prior domain knowledge of the learners has shown to be an important factor. Moeller and Mueller-Kalthoff (2000) compared an educational hypertext with versus without navigational overview. Learners with low domain knowledge benefited from the structural information provided by the overview while there was no difference for learners with high prior knowledge. Also, general findings in research on hypertext and learning (Unz, 2000) suggest that learning performance is influenced to a greater extent by navigation metaphors for novice learners than for domain experts. The stronger influence of navigation design on novice learners has to be taken into account for the design of adaptable navigation. The task to choose out of several navigation metaphors the one that fits best to their level of knowledge could particularly affect the learning performance of learners with low prior topic knowledge. Altogether, while the variety of goals in navigation and learning tasks suggests that the implementation of adaptable navigation metaphors should be favourable, the impact of individual differences in topic knowledge on learning reminds us that we have to consider carefully the effect of adaptable navigation metaphors, especially on learners with low prior knowledge. Meyer (2002) points out that there is the possibility that the learners could be confused by the use of different metaphors in the same learning module. The results of Tripp and Roby (1990) suggest that the combination of different orientation metaphors could activate conflicting mental models.

Case Study

After the theoretical considerations in the previous section, we present a case study on the design and evaluation of a learning module prototype in the following. The module features an adaptable meso level navigation with a novel process control metaphor.

The Learning Module

The Process Control Metaphor

For the meso level navigation in learning modules for the subject matter of process systems engineering, which is part of the study course of chemical engineering, we introduced a novel process control metaphor. Modern chemical plants are controlled by computer-based process control systems (PCS, e.g., *ABB Freelance2000*). The graphical user interface of a PCS displays a structural picture (the "flowsheet") of the plant and its process units (e.g., reactor, distillation column, reboiler). The operators who control the plant navigate through the PCS by clicking on the graphical components of the user interface to display trend diagrams of measurands or to operate actuators.

With the process control metaphor in the learning module, the learners navigate between the learning objects in a similar way like operators in the chemical industry navigate through the PCS user interface. Correspondingly, the design of the process control navigation display complies with the guidelines for graphical interfaces of process control systems for chemical plants as promoted by the Association of Engineers and the Association for Electrical, Electronic & Information Technologies (VDI/VDE 3699-3, 1999). We expect that this navigation metaphor from the engineering practice supports the students who are learning in this domain to relate the theoretical knowledge of the learning module to real world engineering problems. In our prototypical module, the process control navigation display (PCND) is placed in a frame in the left third of the screen while in the bigger right frame the content objects are displayed (see Figure 2).

Figure 2. The module with process control navigation and a learning object

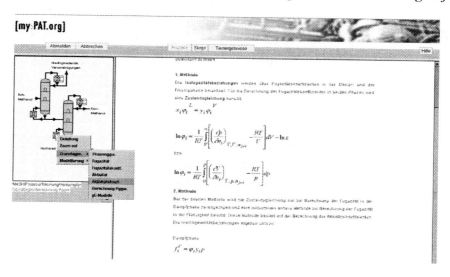

The plant we chose for the process control display in our prototypical module comprises an industrial process for Methanol-Water-Distillation, a typical example for learning about chemical plants. The process control display shows a zoomable flowsheet of this plant, which is structured into four hierarchical levels. On the first and global level, only the input and the output of the process are displayed while the process itself is shown as a black box. On the fourth and most detailed level, single components of process units are presented. Each sharable content object of the module is assigned to the appropriate level of detail of the chemical process and to the appropriate process unit. The learners have access to the content objects of a level via a context menu, which is opened by clicking on the graphical components of the navigation display.

To further support the linkage of the theoretical learning content to the engineering practice, we developed some additional learning objects for the module prototype. These "story objects" provide a description of the chemical process and the plant on the four different levels of detail of the process control navigation display. When the learners enter a level of the process first the story object of that level is displayed before they can proceed to the proper content objects.

Adaptable Navigation

Taking into account the mentioned classification of navigation tasks (see above) the process control navigation display seems to be most appropriate for brows-

Figure 3. The module with tree navigation and a learning object

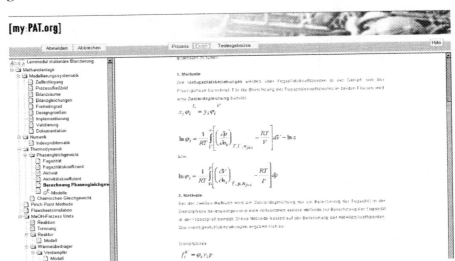

ing, providing an offer to explore the different levels of the chemical plant. On the other hand, directed search could be delayed because the process navigation does not provide a complete overview of the structure of the module's content.

In view of these supposed characteristics of the process control navigation, we decided to implement a second navigation tool which should better support goal-directed search. This was realised with a common "tree", which presents an overview of the hierarchical structure of the objects of the module (see Figure 3).

Navigation display choice was made adaptable, that is, the learners have the possibility to switch between the two alternative displays—process control and tree—whenever they want.

Evaluation

The module prototype was developed in an iterative user-centred process with two cycles of heuristic evaluations (Mayhew, 1999). The heuristic evaluations of early versions of the system were conducted with qualitative methods (interviews, think aloud protocols), small sample size (n=4 per cycle), and different types of experts (students, teaching staff, software engineers). At the end of each cycle, the module prototype was revised according to the results of a qualitative analysis of the data. After the heuristic evaluations, the usability of a highly developed version of the prototype was evaluated in a controlled field study, which is presented in the following.

Objectives

The aim of the study was the evaluation of the adaptable navigation with free choice between the novel process control metaphor and the common tree navigation display. The following questions were addressed:

1.   Is the implemented adaptable navigation usable and does it provide enough orientation for the learners?

2.   How do the students make use of the two alternative navigation metaphors?

3.   Do individual differences in learner characteristics influence navigation metaphor usage and learning outcome?

Method

Facing the complexity of learning and navigation in hypermedia, we assessed the usability of our prototypical module with a multi-method approach combining subjective ratings with performance and behavioural measures. In doing so, we expected to achieve a more valid usability assessment than with subjective ratings alone—since there is some evidence that learners tend to overestimate their learning performance in hypermedia systems (Gerdes, 1997).

Besides domain knowledge (see above), interest and motivation of the learners are seen as critical elements of computer based learning processes (Lepper, 1985; Shapiro & Niederhauser, 2004; Unz, 2000). Following the distinction between personal and situational interest (Alexander, Kulikowich, & Jetton, 1994), we distinguish between longer-term motivational orientations and current motivational states of the learners. Furthermore, we suspected individual differences in navigation to be affected by experience with computers, and usability ratings to be influenced by general attitudes toward computer-based learning (CBL). Figure 4 shows the set of variables we considered in the evaluation study on the levels of input, processes, and outcomes of the learning process (referring to the heuristic framework for research on e-learning provided by Friedrich, Hron, & Hesse, 2001).

Beyond the inspection of usability and acceptance, the purpose of the study was explorative regarding the relations between input, processes and outcome variables. There was no variation controlled by the experimenters. All participants learned with the same version of the module and had the possibility to switch between the two navigation tools whenever they wanted.

Materials

- **Learning content.** The module prototype was developed as an additional offer for self directed learning accompanying the face-to-face lecture of Process Systems Dynamics, held by Prof. G. Wozny at the Technische

Figure 4. Variables considered in the evaluation study

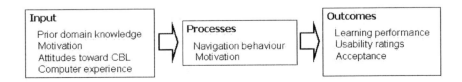

Universität Berlin. The learning content of the module prototype, steady-state modelling, is a complex topic, for which the students have to integrate knowledge from several domains like chemistry, mathematics, thermodynamics and engineering. In the lecture, the teaching of the chapter realised in the module lasts about four sessions of 90 minutes. From this content, 43 sharable content objects were generated, composed of about 250 assets. The assets consisted of text, formulas, diagrams, figures, and also a short video. The size of the objects varied from a paragraph of text up to three html pages. Additionally to the objects that referred directly to the content of the lecture, the module contained five new "story objects", in which the plant displayed in the process control navigation was explained.

- **Learner characteristics.** We developed a learner characteristics questionnaire (LCQ) with 17 items about computer experience, attitudes toward computer based learning, and motivational orientation of the learners. Computer experience was measured by a rating of how often the students used different computer applications for studying (e.g., "*I use my computer for application sharing with other students*"). Attitudes were measured with three items adapted from the INCOBI questionnaire (Richter, Naumann, & Groeben, 2001; e.g., "*Computer-based learning is superior to classical lectures or courses*"). To assess longer-term interest (motivational orientation), subjects were asked about intrinsic motives for participating in the lecture and in the study (e.g., "*I'm attending to the lecture because the topic is interesting*"). Prior knowledge of steady-state modelling was assessed with a computer based topic knowledge test (TKT) with 15 multiple choice questions (e.g., "*What do you have to do to determine a model's degree of freedom?*"), for which the students had to chose the correct answer(s) out of 5 to 10 options, but were not told how many of the possible answers were correct.

- **Processes.** Log files of the interaction with the module were tracked for each subject for meso level navigation (between objects) while micro level navigation (within objects) was not considered in this study. Navigation was analysed in terms of retrieved objects and use of navigation tools. The current motivation of the subjects was measured with five items adapted from the QCM questionnaire (Rheinberg, Vollmeyer & Burns, 2001; e.g., "*I'm having fun learning with the module,*" "*I would rather stop learning with the module*"). The current motivation questionnaire was applied five times during the study in online and paper-and-pencil versions.

- **Outcomes.** A detailed questionnaire for usability and acceptance (QUA) with 54 items was constructed (e.g., "*Orientation in the module was easy,*" "*I would like to use the module again*"). The QUA comprised the sections didactical structure, system design (ease of use, orientation, joy of use), learning experience, and acceptance. In addition to rating questions, the QUA contained also open questions about how the module could be improved. To assess learning outcome, the students completed the topic knowledge test (TKT) a second time directly after the interaction with the module. At the beginning of the following lecture session, three days after the study, the TKT was applied once again in a paper-and-pencil version without prior notice.

Participants

The participants, 17 men and one woman (age range 22 to 41), were students of the lecture Process System Dynamics, for which the module had been developed. All participants were advanced Process Systems Engineering MSc students.

Procedure

The evaluation was carried out as a controlled field study during the time of their regular lecture session. The content of the learning module had already been taught a few weeks before. So, this was a realistic scenario for the intended use of the module as an offer for self-directed in-depth learning of topics which had been introduced in the lecture. During the study, each student worked on a personal computer. Subjects completed the learner characteristics questionnaire before they logged in into the learning management system and tested their prior knowledge. After a short introduction to the navigation tools by the experimenters, the subjects had around 40 minutes time to learn with the module. During this period, each student had access to a list of the topics (but not the questions in detail) in which they had made mistakes in the prior knowledge test. Students were told that they would complete this test a second time after the interaction with the module. After the learning period, students filled out the usability and acceptance questionnaire. Finally, the post knowledge test was administered. The whole session lasted about 100 minutes.

Results

If not otherwise noted, all items of the questionnaires were rated on a 5-point scale from 0 = "very negative" / "strongly disagree" to 4 = "very positive" / "strongly agree". For the variables which were assessed with several items, means of sum scores were calculated.

- **Learner Characteristics.** Most participants were experienced internet users, but did not have much experience with learning software. For their studies, they were using the computer mainly for communication via email and for the exchange of files with others, or for searching literature in the internet. Attitudes toward computer based learning were neutral (M=2.0, SD=0.7), interest in the topic was moderate (M=2.3, SD=0.8). In the prior knowledge test, results were quite poor (48-points-scale, range 5 to 20, M=11.0, SD=4.4).

- **Processes.** Overall, the students navigated about half of the time with the process display (range 5 to 100%, M=50%, SD=34). Most subjects either switched only one time from the default process display to the tree display, or did not switch at all. One third of the subjects switched more than two times between the displays. In the 40 minutes of interaction with the module, each student retrieved on average about two-thirds of the sharable content objects contained in the module (range 42 to 91%, M=67%, SD=17.5). Initial current motivation of the students was moderate, and barely changed during the session, with a general positive but not significant trend (initial current motivation: M=2.3, SD=0.5; final current motivation: M=2.6, SD=0.5).

- **Outcomes.** Altogether, acceptance and usability of the module were rated positive (QUA score: M=2.5, SD=0.4). In particular, the navigation in the system obtained good ratings (M=2.8, SD=0.5) and the students did not report any orientation problems. Since the data of the second knowledge test directly after the learning period was lost for 11 subjects (due to problems with the database), we conducted a paper-and-pencil retest three days after the evaluation. In this test, the students achieved better results than in the pre-test (TKT post score range from 8 to 36, M=19.0, SD=6.5). This increase in learning performance was statistically significant (Wilcoxon test, Z=-3.2, $p<.01$) with a very strong effect size (d'=2.0).

- **Exploration of relations between variables.** Table 1 shows a set of bivariate correlations between learner characteristics, navigation tool measures and learning outcome. Navigation display usage—measured as number of switches between the process control and tree display (NDS), and the percentage of time with the process control display (TPN)—neither was significantly related to any of the outcome variables nor to learner characteristics.

Learner characteristics—interest, attitudes toward computer based learning (ATT) and computer experience (CEX)—were significantly interrelated. There were no significant correlations between prior topic knowledge (PTK) and any

*Table 1. Correlations (Spearman-Rho, *p<.05, **p<.01)*

	Interest	ATT	CEX	PTK	NDS	TPN
Attitudes towards CBL (ATT)	.57**					
Computer experience (CEX)	.52*	.51*				
Prior topic knowledge (PTK)	-.02	.18	-.16			
Navigation display switches (NDS)	.01	-.03	-.23	.24		
Time with process navigation (TPN)	-.08	.03	-.11	.11	-.35	
Learning outcome	.56*	.15	.53*	-.18	-.04	.09

other of the variables. Learning outcome was positively related to interest and computer experience.

Discussion

Concerning the use of the adaptable navigation metaphors there was a wide range between subjects though the learning time was quite short and the sample was small. This suggests that the learners in our evaluation study accepted the adaptable meso level navigation and made use of the choice it offered. They gave positive ratings for the usability of the module in general and the navigation in particular. These ratings are consistent with the positive effect of the interaction with the module on learning outcome. We found no evidence that the adaptable navigation with the free choice between process control metaphor and hierarchical tree caused any disorientation problems. Since there was no influence of navigation tool usage on learning outcome, we assume that the learners found their individual best ways of taking advantage of the adaptable navigation.

The findings of Moeller and Mueller-Kalthoff (2000, see above) can be interpreted that notably for learners with low topic knowledge a well designed hypertext navigation with helpful metaphors is essential. The fact that we did not find any substantial correlations between pre knowledge and learning performance indicates that the adaptable navigation did at least not impair learners with low topic knowledge. However, from the present evaluation study we can not draw the conclusion that adaptable meso level navigation with the novel process control metaphor has any advantages compared to a simpler design with only one navigation display, for example a hierarchical tree, which is an already existing navigation tool for SCORM modules and very common for hypertext in general.

The lack of influence of topic knowledge on learning outcome could also be caused by a lack of variation within the sample. Possibly there would have been an influence if we had compared our MSc students with lower grade high-school students. For studies on hypermedia learning systems, it is essential to define the target group for which the system is designed. Also, it has to be noted that learning outcome was measured with a multiple choice test. In future studies, deeper levels of knowledge like problem solving ability and transfer should be investigated.

Regarding the system design, the significant correlation between interest and learning outcome is an important finding. It remains a challenge to develop systems that enhance the learners' interest in the topic through motivational design (Keller, 1983). Metaphors are assumed to have a big potential to enhance motivation (Meyer, 2002). Future research should investigate the potential of different metaphors for motivation in detail. In our study, we could not demonstrate any positive influence of our meso level navigation metaphors on motivation since current motivation did not strongly increase during the session and was not related to navigation tool usage patterns. Generally, navigation measures derived from log files like the mentioned usage patterns are often difficult to interpret without additional qualitative data. For a better insight into navigation and learning processes, log file analysis should be combined with methods like retrospective video confrontation or think aloud protocols.

Altogether, our study has two major methodological limitations which restrict the generalisability of the results: (i) we had only a small sample and could not realise a control-group design, and (ii) we did not control the learning task (i.e., we did not explicitly ask the students to "search" or "browse"). Both limitations are due to the fact that the primary purpose of our study was to test the usability of the adaptable navigation design within a development project. The main focus of this project is on the development of e-learning solutions with a high usability, not on experimental research about navigation metaphors. Therefore the purpose of the study was rather formative, that is, we were looking for information how to improve the prototype, and we decided to keep the learning task for the evaluation as "natural" as possible. In comparison to the learning tasks in experimental studies which are often quite artificial, we regard the ecological validity of the present study as higher since the learners were more personally involved and learning was self-directed. So, our evaluation study is merely explorative and the findings should be confirmed by comparing it with experimental studies.

Future Trends

The potential of metaphors in SCORM for the integration of learning objects should be further investigated to overcome the limitations of the study we presented. It also should be noted that the sharable content objects of our prototypical module were not put together from different sources but derived from a single coherent lecture script. Therefore the integration on the meso level of didactical design probably was not as essential as it might be in more "eclectic" modules. Referring to the categorisation of Meyer (2002), we suppose that interface metaphors—especially for meso level navigation—and scenario metaphors are powerful tools for the didactical designer to create coherency in a SCORM module. Further research is needed, ranging from exploratory case studies to controlled experiments, to clarify the benefits of specific metaphors on specific levels. Concerning the use of several metaphors of the same level in the same module, our results suggest that an adaptable meso level navigation with two different tools does at least not cause any problems of confusion, disorientation or "conflicting mental models" in terms of Tripp and Roby (1990, see above)—provided that the single navigation tools do not disturb the learners by bad design.

Meyer (2002) also raises the question about the relations between metaphors of different categories. The current prototype is only a first basic application of the process control metaphor in modules for the subject matter of Process Systems Engineering. Beyond navigation, the process control metaphor could also be extended to a broader scenario metaphor, in which the learners play the role of on-plant process optimisation engineers in the chemical industry and use the process control display also for the control of interactive simulations. As a general guideline we propose to consider scenario metaphors as higher ordered metaphors which can be supported by adequate interface metaphors.

The didactical compatibility of navigation metaphors could cause a SCORM specific problem which—as far as we know—has not yet been addressed in research. A single sharable content object "can consist of several html pages with navigation between each page …[and] could have numerous interactions, simulations, or tests within it, with all of the navigation occurring as intra-SCO branching" (i.e., micro level navigation) (LSAN, 2003, p. 33). Given this great variety in micro level navigation within a single object, we see the risk that different micro level navigation metaphors in content objects from different sources as well as different micro and meso level navigation metaphors could interfere. It would be very interesting to study whether this theoretical apprehension of conflicting navigation metaphors can be empirically confirmed. The question is if and under which conditions interfering navigation metaphors (micro vs. micro level as well as micro vs. meso level) can cause problems for the learners and how such problems can be avoided. For the moment, we would suggest conventional, "neutral" metaphors—like a hierarchical tree—for micro level navigation to smooth the interchangeability of objects from different sources. Creative, unusual metaphors should preferably be used on the meso level.

However, the power of special navigation metaphors in SCORM could also be scrutinised in general. We were not able to provide an empirical argument against Chen and Rada (1996, cited from Shapiro & Niederhauser, 2004), who concluded in their review that the organisational structure of information in hypertext systems is the key factor affecting user performance, while navigation tools like "indices, tables of contents, and graphical maps may have a relatively weaker influence" (p.145).

Another interesting topic for which systematic research is needed is the potential role of adaptive support in SCORM. Brusilovsky (2003) points out that regarding adaptive systems in general, "we have too many developed techniques and too few studies" (p. 496). Transferring the two main classes of adaptive systems (Brusilovsky, 1996) to the SCORM world, we propose that adaptive presentation could be used on the micro level (within SCOs) while adaptive navigation support could rather play a role on the meso level (between SCOs). On the meso level, the extant technology already enables the didactical designer to restrict the access to a SCO or to determine the sequencing of SCOs, for example as a function of the performance in a knowledge test. However, we would suggest always to be careful with restrictions. If we attempt to design a system which—in a certain way—shall be smarter than the user, we should found our efforts on a solid empirical basis. For the two alternative navigation tools in our prototype we had taken into consideration to design the navigation display choice adaptive instead of adaptable. But since there was neither an influence of learner characteristics on the use of navigation tools nor of tool usage on learning outcome we concluded that the navigation display choice should be controlled by the learners. From a pedagogical point of view, to support an active, self-directed way of learning, we generally recommend to give the learners as much control as possible over their own learning process, and to use adaptation only if we can expect a clear didactical benefit from adaptive support.

We conclude this section with another general remark on adaptive support in hypermedia learning systems. An adaptive system builds the model of a user, and adapts to that individual user according to this model. Various variables have been proposed to be included in user models because they have shown to affect learning processes. As a rule of thumb we suggest to preferably build the model with variables which can be assessed embedded in the learning task. For example, a test of prior topic knowledge can have several functions within a learning setting: (i) give feedback to the learners about their current level of knowledge, (ii) motivate the learners, and (iii) provide data for the adaptation model. In contrast, hypothetical constructs like field dependence are assessed with methods which have, at least from a learner's point of view, nothing to do with the proper learning task. We should always keep in mind the holistic learning task if we design an adaptive support system to ensure acceptance.

Conclusions

In this chapter, we discussed the role of adaptable navigation and navigation metaphors in web based learning modules complying with the SCORM standard. To systematise analysis and discussion, we introduced the distinction between different levels of navigation and didactical design in SCORM, focussing on the meso level. On this level, where the single learning objects are put together (possibly from various different sources), the didactical designer has to create a pedagogically meaningful framework for the module. We concluded from the discussion on the role of metaphors in SCORM that we expect a great potential of interface and scenario metaphors on the meso level, which should be further investigated in the future. In the empirical section, we presented the didactical design and the evaluation study of a prototype for learning modules for the subject matter of Process Systems Engineering. The prototype featured an adaptable meso level navigation which allowed the learners to choose between a novel process control metaphor and a hierarchical tree. In the evaluation, which was carried out as a controlled field study, interaction with the module had a strong positive effect on learning performance. A detailed analysis of the results showed that the adaptable navigation was usable and did not cause any problems like disorientation or confusion. Due to the limitations of the study, we could not provide evidence whether the adaptable navigation is superior to a simpler design with only one navigation tool and without process control metaphor. We identified some questions for further research and made some general comments about adaptive support for web based learning modules. Concluding, the current debate about didactical issues of SCORM focuses on the unsolved question of how to describe learning objects by didactical metadata (e.g., Brenstein & Wendt, 2003). Beyond this rather technological question, there remain serious concerns that SCORM compliant systems are no "true" hypermedia because of the restriction in the interlinking of objects. This restriction can be considered as at odds with the fundamental nature of hypermedia, which is flexible and non-linear linking between nodes of information. Therefore, we see an urgent need for a thorough analysis of the didactical implications of standards like SCORM, which goes beyond the metadata question.

Acknowledgments

The work presented in this chapter was carried out in the [my:PAT.org] project, financed by the German Ministry of Education and Research within the "New Media in Education" programme. The module prototype was developed at the Department of Process Dynamics and Operation, Technische Universität Berlin, by Rodolphe Zerry and Christopher Hausmanns. Our work was kindly supported by Prof Guenter Wozny, Joerg Huss, Thomas Zachar, and the ZMMS User Modelling Group, financed by VolkswagenStiftung. We also want to thank the reviewers for their very helpful comments.

References

Advanced Distributed Learning Initiative (2002). SCORM overview. Retrieved August 30, 2003, from http://www.adlnet.org.

Alexander, P. A., Kulikowich, J. M., & Jetton, T. L. (1994). The role of subject-matter knowledge and interest in the processing of linear and nonlinear texts. *Review of Educational Research, 64*(2), 201-252.

Brenstein, E., & Wendt, A. (2003, June 15-18). Didactic modelling of learning objects: Evolving standards and methods of evaluations in metadata-based course development. In A. Szücs, E. Wagner, & C. Tsolakidis (Eds.), *The quality dialogue – Integrating quality cultures in flexible, distance and elearning. Proceedings of the 2003 EDEN Annual Conference*, Rhodes, Greece (pp. 53-59). Budapest: EDEN.

Brusilovsky, P. (1996). Methods and techniques of adaptive hypermedia. *User Modelling and User Adapted Interaction, 6*(2-3), 87-129.

Brusilovsky, P. (2003). Adaptive navigation support in educational hypermedia: The role of student knowledge level and the case for meta adaptation. *British Journal of Educational Technology, 34*(4), 487-498.

Chen, C., & Rada, R. (1996). Interacting with hypertext: A meta-analysis of experimental studies. *Human-Computer Interaction, 11*, 125-156.

Clark, P. M. (2003). Quality in the digital age. In A. Szücs, E. Wagner, & C. Tsolakidis (Eds.), *The quality dialogue – Integrating quality cultures in flexible, distance and e-learning. Proceedings of the 2003 EDEN Annual Conference*, Rhodes, Greece (June 15-18, pp. 1-5). Budapest: EDEN.

Cove, J. F., & Welsh, B. C. (1988). Online text retrieval via browsing. *Information Processing & Management, 24*(10), 31-37.

Dillon, A., McKnight, C., & Richardson, J. (1993). Space – The final chapter or why physical representations are not semantic intentions. In A. Dillon, C. McKnight & J. Richardson (Eds.), *Hypertext – A psychological perspective* (pp. 169-188). Chichester, UK: Ellis Horwood.

Friedrich, H. F., Hron, A., & Hesse, F. W. (2001). A framework for designing and evaluating virtual seminars. *European Journal of Education, 36*(2), 157-174.

Gerdes, H. (1997). *Lernen mit text und hypertext.* Lengerich: Pabst.

Keller, J. M. (1983). Motivational design of instruction. In C. M. Reigeluth (Ed.), *Instructional design theories and models: An overview of their current status* (pp. 383-434). Hillsdale: Lawrence Erlbaum.

Kuhlen, R. (1991). *Hypertext. Ein Nicht-lineares Medium Zwischen Buch und Wissenschaft.* Berlin: Springer.

Learning Systems Architecture Net (2003). SCORM Best Practices Guide for Content Developers. Carnegie Mellon University, USA. Retrieved September 9, 2003, from http://www.lsal.cmu.edu/lsal/expertise/projects/developersguide/developersguide/guide-v1p0-20030228.pdf

Lepper, M. R. (1985). Microcomputers in education: Motivational and social issues. *American Psychologist, 40*(1), 1-18.

MacDonald, S., & Stevenson, R. J. (1998). Effects of text structure and prior knowledge of the learner on navigation in hypertext. *Human Factors, 40*(1), 18-27.

MacDonald, S., & Stevenson, R. J. (1999). Spatial versus conceptual maps as learning tools in hypertext. *Journal of Educational Multimedia and Hypermedia, 8*(1), 43-64.

Mayhew, D. A. (1999). *The usability engineering lifecycle.* San Francisco: Morgan Kaufmann.

Meyer, C. (2002, September). Metaphors in learning environments: Towards a taxonomy. *Proceedings of ICALT 2002, IEEE International Conference on Advanced Learning Technologies,* Kazan, Russia (pp. 448-452).

Moeller, J., & Mueller-Kalthoff, T. (2000). Lernen mit Hypertext: Effekte von Navigationshilfen und Vorwissen. *Zeitschrift für Pädagogische Psychologie, 14*(2-3), 116-123.

O'Connor, B. C. (1985). Access to moving image documents: Background concepts and proposals for surrogates for film and video works. *Journal of Documentation, 41,* 209-220.

Oliveira, A. (1992). Hypermedia and multimedia. In A. Oliveira (Ed.), *Hypermedia courseware: Structures of communication and intelligent help* (pp. 3-10). Berlin: Springer.

Rheinberg, F., Vollmeyer, R., & Burns, B. D. (2001). QCM: A questionnaire to assess current motivation in learning situations. *Diagnostica, 47*, 57-66.

Richter, T., Naumann, J., & Groeben, N. (2001). Das Inventar zur Computerbildung (INCOBI): Ein Instrument zur Erfassung von Computer Literacy und computerbezogenen Einstellungen bei Studierenden der Geistes- und Sozialwissenschaften. *Psychologie in Erziehung und Unterricht, 48*, 1-13.

Salomon, G.B. (1990). Designing casual-use hypertext – The CHI 89 information booth. *Proceedings of CHI 90: Computer-Human Interface* (p. 451).

Schulmeister, R. (1996). *Grundlagen hypermedialer lernsysteme. Theorie – didaktik – design*. Bonn: Addison-Wesley.

Shapiro, A., & Niederhauser, D. (2004). Learning from hypertext: Research issues and findings. In D. H. Jonassen (Ed.), *Handbook of research for education communications and technology,* (2nd Edition, pp. 605-620). Mahwah: Erlbaum.

Tripp, S. D., & Roby, W. (1990). Orientation and disorientation in a hypertext lexicon. *Journal of Computer-Based Instruction, 17*, 120-124.

Unz, D. (2000). *Lernen mit hypertext: Informationssuche und navigation*. Münster: Waxmann.

VDI/VDE 3699-3 (1999). *Process control using display screens. Mimics*. Berlin: Beuth.

Wiley, D. (2003). *Learning objects: Difficulties and opportunities*. Ogden, UT: Utah State University. Retrieved January 30, 2004 from http://wiley.ed.usu.edu/docs/lo_do.pdf

Section III

Authoring and Exploring Content

Chapter X

Authoring of Adaptive Hypermedia

A. Cristea, Eindhoven University of Technology, The Netherlands

Craig Stewart, University of Nottingham, Jubilee Campus, UK

Abstract

This chapter focuses on the aspect of Authoring *in* Adaptive Hypermedia *from some of its different perspectives. It starts by showing the necessity of research in this area, then describes a new framework model for authoring of Adaptive Hypermedia, LAOS. Within LAOS, the adaptation model, which is the main aspect of adaptive hypermedia, is detailed into a separate model, LAG. The flexibility offered by the LAOS framework is analyzed and estimated. To illustrate the theory, the chapter describes an implementation of this framework, MOT, and test results. The chapter ends with conclusions and discussion on future trends.*

Introduction

Adaptive Hypermedia (AH) (Brusilovsky 2002) is here, and researchers in the field (Bajraktarevic et al., 2003; Brailsford et al., 2002) hope that it is here to stay. Although a relatively new field (dating back only to the early 1990s), it has taken on board the advantages, while avoiding the pitfalls of its parent disciplines, Intelligent Tutoring Systems and User Modelling. An advantage it shares is offering a *personalized environment* (adaptive or adaptable[1]). Moreover, AH moves this environment to the Web. The main pitfall that it managed to avoid is complexity: traditional AH systems are simple, built on sketchy user models, mostly featuring a knowledge attribute overlaid on a simple domain model. This *simplicity* gives it the power of fast response and wide usage range.

From an authoring perspective, however, it turns out that efficient AH is not simple to design. Even with basic domain and user models, creating a powerful adaptive environment requires many alternatives of contents, linking, etc. Furthermore, granularity of information chunks, alternative display modes, etc., have to be taken into consideration.

Therefore, our main aim is to create a framework for powerful, flexible authoring tools for authors of adaptive hypermedia. This chapter translates the main aim into requirements of this framework: *data storage* with sufficient metadata labelling for reuse (both for collaborative authoring and adaptive presentation), *data clustering* depending on the intended level of reuse, and '*automatic authoring*', i.e., automatic generation of some default content structure, labelling and behaviour. We shall see how the products of this research also lead to patterns that could be used to extend existent standards (e.g., LOM, simple sequencing standard, SCORM) or even to generate new standards for AH.

The remainder of this chapter is structured as follows. First, we will give more background information on the driving forces behind the research on authoring of adaptive hypermedia systems, as well as a very short glimpse into the state of the art. Next, we present LAOS, a theoretical framework for authoring of AH, that we claim allows enough flexibility to embrace not only the existing adaptive hypermedia systems, but also to establish a solid basis for structured, pattern-based authoring of adaptive hypermedia. The latter is enabled by LAG, the three-layers model of adaptation granularity. We will also show some automatic transformations allowed by LAOS that give it its flexibility. Following that, we describe MOT (My Online Teacher) (Cristea & De Mooij, 2003a), a system that is gradually implementing the LAOS framework, and sketch the first tests done with MOT. Finally, we try to extract future trends for this line of research, and conclude.

Background

Adaptive hypermedia systems were traditionally custom-designed applications for single use implementing hypermedia-based user models (Brusilovsky, 2002).

Only recently, their authoring aspect started being taken into consideration, partly because initial AHs were of small size (Brusilovsky et al., 1996). In such systems, reuse was not an issue. The interest in authoring shows the field's first steps toward maturity, as authoring first requires widely accepted common characteristics.

There are many other reasons why the time is now ripe to concentrate on authoring in adaptive hypermedia instead of on new adaptive hypermedia techniques. Some reasons include (i) the fact that the field is advanced enough; (ii) that we cannot expect any major break-through theoretical advances[2]; and (iii) that there are a number of common features we see repeated in almost all adaptive hypermedia, such as *user model* (Brusilovsky, 2002), *knowledge level* (De Bra & Calvi, 1998), *goals* (Grigoriadou et al., 2001), etc. A framework covering these features could, in principle, cover any type of AH system.

However, the main impetus for authoring research and development in AH comes from outside of the field: from *distance learning* and *Web-based educational systems*, but also from *e-commerce*—all driven by pressure from the fastest growing hypermedia system—the *Web*. The Web is a huge information resource, not just for research laboratories, but for everybody. The 'lost-in-hyperspace' syndrome, which adaptive hypermedia set out to fight, is becoming more of an everyday reality. Personalization is urgently required, in the sense of *adaptability* and *adaptivity* to the end-user. The many successful (educational) hypermedia authoring tools (WebCT, Blackboard, etc.) do not offer enough personalization. Adaptive hypermedia has the answers, but not yet the tools. This fact is gradually being perceived by the AH community, which is now investing more effort now into the authoring issue (Brusilovsky, 2003).

When this research started, authoring research was almost non-existent within adaptive hypermedia. AH taxonomies (Brusilovsky, 2002) and frameworks (AHAM) (Wu, 2001; The Munich model, Koch & Wirsing, 2001) that were developed were primarily aimed at describing and classifying extant AH systems. The authoring benefits of a common framework were merely a side-effect.

Recently, AH authoring has started developing along "two main axes" (Brusilovsky, 2003): *mark-up* (Interbook; AHA!; WHURLE; Brailsford et al., 2002) and *form (or GUI)-based AH authoring* (the newer AHA! 3.0, emerged from discussions on benefits of concept-based visualization; De Bra et al., 2002; MetaLinks, Murray 2002) linking form-based concepts in a hyperspace; SIGUE, Carmona et al,. 2002, an open corpus AH authoring approach, with external documents only; complex interface approaches, e.g., NetCoach, Weber et al., 2001—"the only commercial AH authoring system," according to Brusilovsky 2003—and ALE, Specht et al., 2002). The form-based approach is considered more beneficial for inexperienced authors (Brusilovsky, 2003).

Our implementation approach is, according to the above classification, form based. The theoretical framework, however, enables both types of approaches. Next we describe this theoretical framework.

Theoretical Framework

This research has two major parts:

- **Theory:** gradual creation of a new framework for AH authoring, LAOS (and LAG).
- **Implementation:** integration of the framework's concepts and ideas into an AH authoring environment, MOT, the platform for analysis and testing.

Testing in this context has two directions:

- **Testing with designers and authors:** authoring environment testing, with all necessary criteria (expressivity, adaptive flexibility, collaboration issues, author satisfaction, etc.) and methodologies (questionnaires analysis, tracing author's work, etc.),
- **Testing with adaptive hypermedia users:** testing of the created AH environment with AH users.

LAOS

LAOS (Layered WWW AHS Authoring Model and their corresponding Algebraic Operators) (Cristea & De Mooij, 2003a) is a general framework of data storage and manipulation model for authoring of adaptive hypermedia, composed of five components (Figure 1):

- *domain model* (DM),
- *goal and constraints model* (GM),
- *user model* (UM),
- *adaptation model* (AM), and
- *presentation model* (PM).

Figure 1. Five levels AHS authoring model

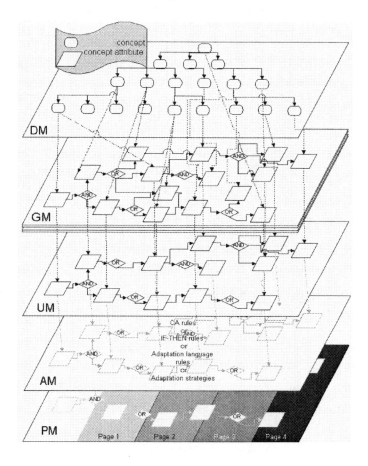

LAOS builds on AHAM (Wu, 2001), one of the first, well-known adaptive hypermedia architecture models. The major differences are:

- The clear separation of *information* (or knowledge) and *presentation-goal related connectivity* (e.g., pedagogical methodology in educational hypermedia). This is done to facilitate information reuse, by separating information chunks from specific context.

- The above separation generated two different models instead of one: a domain model (DM) and a goal and constraints model (GM). This separation can be understood easily if we use the encyclopaedia metaphor: the DM represents the encyclopaedia(s) on which the presentation (e.g., with PowerPoint™ and represented by the GM) is built. From one encyclopaedia (or DM) we can construct several presentations (here, GMs), depending on our *goal*. These presentations don't contain everything in the encyclopaedia, just some (*constrained*) part of it, which we consider relevant. Moreover, a presentation can contain information from several encyclopaedias. This separation therefore gives a high degree of flexibility, as shown later.

- Another important difference is given by the notion of 'concept' that we use in the domain model. Our concepts have different representations given by their attributes, which can also represent resources (as in RDF). The only restriction is that concepts should have a *semantic unity* (unlike in AHAM).

- The adaptation engine has to actually implement not only *selectors*, but also *constructors* (Wu, 2001), as presentations can contain any type of combination of (ordered and weighted) concept attributes (which is different to AHAM).

Next we look at the LAOS composing models in more detail.

Domain Model (DM)

The domain model is composed of concept maps, containing linked concepts. These concepts are further comprised of attributes. This model represents the learning resources and their characteristics.

Goal and Constraints Model (GM)

This model filters, regroups and restructures the previous (DM) model, with respect to an instructional goal. It allows ordering and AND-OR relations between these attributes, as well as weights for the OR relations. The actual interpretation of this structure is done by the adaptation model.

User Model (UM)

UM and AM have been described relatively well by AHAM. Another way of representing the UM (Cristea & Kinshuk, 2003) is to view it also as a concept map. In this way, relations between the variables within the user model can be explicitly expressed as relations in the UM, and do not have to be "hidden" within adaptive rules.

Figure 2. LAG: The three layers of adaptation

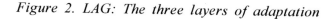
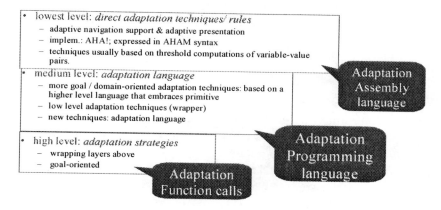

Adaptive Model (AM): Layered Adaptation Granulation (LAG)

The AH adaptation model traditionally consists of a set of IF-THEN rules that are triggered when some event occurs (e.g., accessing of a page or a concept). However, this type of structure has proven to be quite cumbersome for authoring. To overcome the limitations of the inexperienced author, but also to allow enough flexibility for the advanced author, we have introduced (Cristea & Calvi, 2002, 2003) a new three-layer adaptation model (by adding, over the typical low level *assembly*-like *adaptive language*, a medium level *programming adaptive language* and *adaptive strategies* language) called LAG (Figure 2).

This model allows different difficulty levels for different authors, being a "frame-based model" (Brusilovsky, 2003) with added semantics. Moreover, as the higher levels of authoring imply grouping of low level adaptation constructs, reuse can occur. In this way it is possible to reuse not only the AH content, but also adaptive techniques, moving towards discovery of adaptive patterns.

In the following, these layers are described in more detail, by the type of rules they allow.

Direct Adaptive Techniques: Adaptive Assembly Language

Low-level adaptive techniques are techniques traditionally used in adaptive hypermedia applications ((i) *content adaptation*—adaptive presentation: inserting/removing of fragments, altering fragments, stretchtext, sorting fragments, dimming fragments; and (ii) *link adaptive* techniques: adaptive guidance—

adaptive navigation support: direct guidance, link sorting, link hiding/ removal/ disabling, link annotation, link generation, map adaptation), summarized by Brusilovsky (2002). They are usually determined by a mixture of fine-grained elements of the domain, user, adaptation, goal (GM) (Calvi & Cristea, 2002) and presentation model (PM).

Adaptive Language

This level is determined by grouping the elements of the previous layer into typical adaptation mechanisms and constructs (low-level rules into *higher-level adaptive rules*; operators or language constructs and variables into *adaptive language interface variables*). The result is a 'programming language' for adaptive strategies (Cristea & Calvi, 2003), called *adaptive language*. The instantiation of this language is the basis for elaborating adaptation patterns in the Minerva ADAPT project. Constructs now in use are: *while-do, for-do, generalize* and *specialize*, but we are looking at extending this basic set. These constructs have the purpose of allowing (semantic) grouping and labelling of typical adaptive behaviour.

Example: To illustrate the compression power with a simple example, and to show how they translate into if-then rules (so into regular adaptation rules), let's consider we want to show all seven sub-concepts of the 'NN Introduction' concept in the goal and constraints map derived from the 'NN – intro' course in Figure 3.

In regular adaptation rule syntax, we would write seven lines:

IF NN Introduction.access == 'yes' THEN NN Introduction.Title.available = 'yes';

IF NN Introduction.access == 'yes' THEN NN Introduction.Keywords.available = 'yes';

IF NN Introduction.access == 'yes' THEN NN Introduction.text.available = 'yes';

IF NN Introduction.access == 'yes' THEN NN Introduction.How Neural ....available = 'yes';

IF NN Introduction.access == 'yes' THEN NN Introduction.The biological neural....available = 'yes';

IF NN Introduction.access == 'yes' THEN NN Introduction.The von Neuman....available = 'yes';

IF NN Introduction.access == 'yes' THEN NN Introduction.The biological neuron.available = 'yes';

Figure 3. GM concepts

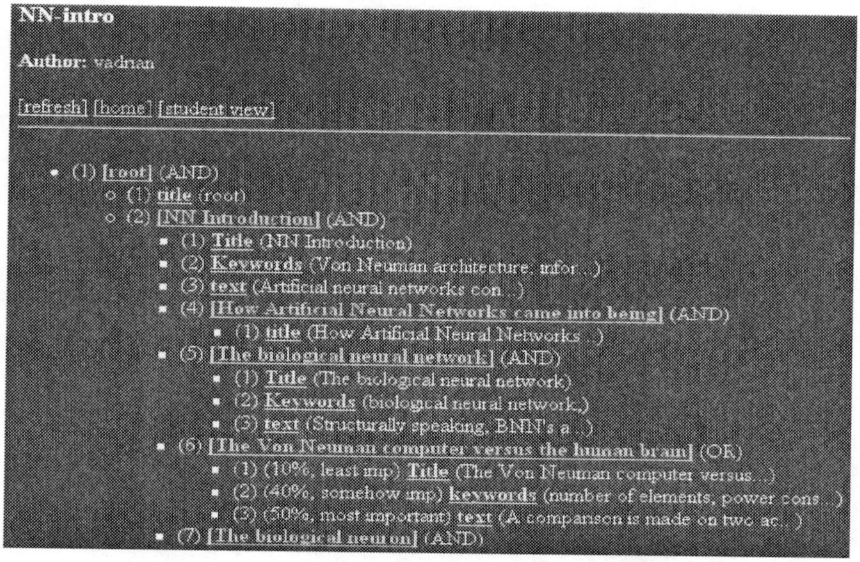

In adaptation language constructs this would transform into:

IF NN Introduction.access == 'yes' THEN

(NN Introduction.i = 1;

FOR 7 DO (NN Introduction[i].available = 'yes'; UM.NN Introduction.i +=1))

The latter form, as can be seen, is much shorter. In MOT, this looks like in Figure 4.

These language constructs represent the first level of *adaptive pattern reuse*.

Adaptive Strategies

What we have done is to use the above building blocks (*adaptive language* or direct *adaptive techniques*), to build higher level programs. The four-line program above can itself be saved as a higher level compound, called *adaptive procedure* or *adaptive strategy*. Actually, more complex adaptive strategies than the one created in Figure 4 can be created, e.g., instructional strategies based on learning styles (Bajraktarevic et al., 2003; Cristea & De Bra, 2002), or tours, knowledge-related strategies, taste-oriented strategies (especially for commercial purposes), etc.

Figure 4. AM in MOT

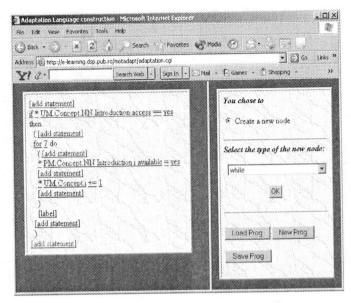

Presentation Model (PM)

The PM takes into consideration the physical properties and environment of the presentation and provides the bridge to the actual code generation for different platforms (e.g., HTML, SMIL). The presentation model in LAOS is similar to the user model, as it is a combination of an overlay model of both the domain model and the goal and constraints model, as well as of independent variables and their respective values. This structure allows attaching to each specific concept a certain representation type on screen, while at the same time retaining independent representation types, which depend on the current values of the user model.

Authoring Steps in LAOS

The authoring steps[3] in LAOS are shown in Table 1.

With the LAOS structure, flexible (adaptive) presentation generation becomes possible, as follows. The actual presentation seen by the user can contain both elements of the goal and constraints model as well as domain model. (E.g., clarification of a text-attribute from the GM, the system can leave the prescribed GM path to show other attributes of the respective DM parent concept, or other concepts related to this parent concept. This is similar to a pointer back to the

Table 1. Adaptive authoring steps in LAOS

STEP 1	write concepts + hierarchy (in *DM*)
STEP 2	define concept attributes (main and extra attributes) (in *DM*)
STEP 3	fill concept attributes (write contents) (in *DM*)
STEP 4	perform selection and redesign hierarchy given the GM goal (design alternatives – AND, OR, weights, add extra narrative smoothening attributes, etc.) (in *GM*)
STEP 5	add UM related features (simplest way, tables, with attribute-value pairs for user-related entities; UM can be represented as a concept map) (in *UM*)
STEP 6	decide among adaptive strategies, write in adaptive language medium-level adaptive rules (such as defined by LAG) or give the complete set of low level rules (such as condition-action, or IF-THEN rules) to decide interpretation of GM (or DM). (in *AM*)
STEP 7	define format (presentation means-related; define chapters) (in *PM*)
STEP 8	add (if necessary) adaptive features regarding presentation means (define variable page lengths, variables for figure display, formats, synchronizations points, etc.) (in *AM*)

encyclopaedia from which the presentation as generated.) This increases flexibility and expressivity of the adaptive presentation creation process. This flexibility can be estimated, as we shall see, looking at automatic transformations in LAOS.

Automatic Transformations in LAOS

The flexibility of an authoring system determines the capacity of performing 'automatic authoring'. Here we present some examples of automatic transformations between the models in LAOS which can be performed directly by the authoring system.

In regular AH design and authoring, the equivalent of these processes are done by hand, which is time-consuming. We have identified *patterns* based on the structure of LAOS that allow generalizing and automatically performing these transformations, leading to possible reuse; the reuse range can be estimated as a flexibility degree.

Definition 1. The *flexibility index, flex,* is defined as the combinatorial index enumerating all the possible results that can be generated by a specific (set of) automatic transformation(s).

From Domain Model to Domain Model (DM→DM)

Implicit DM information can become explicit, via some information retrieval technique.

DM→DM According to Concept Attribute Type

The easiest way to enrich the domain model is by automatically finding new links between existing concepts[4]. In Cristea and De Mooij (2003b) we have developed formulas for the *relatedness calculations* between the different concepts, to find potential links between concepts sharing a common topic. These were computed at concept attribute level, using the name of the attribute as a type. Concepts C1, C2 can be linked in MOT if:

$$link(C1,C2,label,weight) = link(C1,C2,attribute\text{-}name,weight\text{-}formula)$$

Here, the link detection flexibility index, *flex(*, *)*, enumerates all possible links of unequivocal type[5]. If types can be mixed, we obtain the *mixflex(*, *)* index. Next, we show how we estimate these indexes.

Theorem 1. The *flexibility link index* for link generation based on concept attribute type for concept map C is can be estimated as:

$$flex(*,*) \geq \sum_{i=1}^{C} \sum_{j=i+1}^{C} A_{min} = \frac{C(C-1)}{2} A_{min}$$

where: A_{min} - minimum number of attributes per concept; $C = card(C)$.
The *mixed link flexibility index* of concept map C is:

$$mixflex(*,*) \geq \frac{C(C-1)}{2} A_{min}^{2}.$$

Proof: The *mixed link flexibility index* of the links that can be generated between concepts C_1 (current concept) and C_2 is:

$$mixflex(1,2) = A_1 A_2 \geq A_{min}{}^2 ;$$

where: A_i the actual number of attributes of concept C_i.
For links that having unequivocal type, we obtain:

$$flex(1,2) = card(\mathcal{A}_{c1} \cap \mathcal{A}_{c2}) \geq card(\mathcal{A}_{min}) = A_{min} .$$

where $\mathcal{A}_{ci}$ is the set of attributes of concept C_i

The *flexibility index* of linking concept C_1 with the rest of the concepts in C is:

$$flex(1,*) = \sum_{j=2}^{C} card(\mathcal{A}_{c1} \cap \mathcal{A}_{cj}) \geq (C-1)A_{min} .$$

The *mixed flexibility index* for concept C_1 is:

$$mixflex(1,*) = A_1 \sum_{j=2}^{C} A_j \geq (C-1)A_{min}{}^2 .$$

Therefore, the (concept attribute type based) link generation *flexibility index* for concept map C is:

$$flex(*,*) = \sum_{i=1}^{C} \sum_{j=i+1}^{C} card(\mathcal{A}_{ci} \cap \mathcal{A}_{cj}) \geq$$
$$\geq \sum_{i=1}^{C} \sum_{j=i+1}^{C} A_{min} = \frac{C(C-1)}{2} A_{min} .$$

Similarly, the *mixed link flexibility index* of concept map C is:

$$mixflex(*,*) = \sum_{i=1}^{C} A_i \sum_{j=i+1}^{C} A_j \geq \frac{C(C-1)}{2} A_{min}{}^2 . \text{q.e.d.}$$

Example: concretely, in MOT, A_{min} ={title, keywords, introduction, text, explanation, pattern, conclusion}, so A_{min}=7. In the concept map called 'Neural Networks I' (Figure 5) C=card(**C**)=145, so: flex(*,*)³10440*7= 73080 and mixflex(*,*)³10440*49= 511560. Please note that these are connections implied by only one concept map. MOT already allows inter-linking of concept maps, increasing this number.

Therefore, it results that many (annotated, semantic) links can be generated automatically, making the adaptive hypermedia process easier.

DM→DM According to Link Type

It is also possible to create new links via a link-type check algorithm. The most common links (hierarchical) are already exploited in the adaptive language, via constructs such as *specialize* and *generalize* (Cristea & Calvi, 2003).

However, the most important contribution of link analysis would be comparing similar concepts[6] and finding missing attributes (or even sub-concepts) (*verification*).

Example: The concept (Figure 5: concepts in left frame, attributes in right) called 'Discrete Neuron Perceptrons' from a Neural Networks course has an 'Example' attribute, whereas the concept 'Continuous Neuron Perceptrons' doesn't, although they are linked via their 'Title' attribute (weight: 67%). Here, the system could look for possible examples via other links to this concept, or just signal the missing content item.

For a concept map **C**, the extra attribute *flexibility index* can be shown to be:

$$flex(*,*) = \sum_{i=1}^{C} \sum_{j=i+1}^{C} card(A_{cj} - A_{ci}) \geq 0 .$$

Please note that an extended version of the content search could look *outside* the space defined by the LAOS model.

DM→DM Combination of Concept Attribute - and Link Type

We have seen above some computations for concept attribute type and link type only. Combining the above automatic transformations would require a tree-type

Table 2. Combination of concept attribute — and link type automatic transformations

```
FOR ALL Ci DO # Ci in set of concept maps
{ # Compute possible automatic links from current concept Ci
  FOR ALL Cj, j?I DO
  { IF accepted(Ci,Cj,link,label,weight) THEN
      {
        link(Ci,Cj,label,weight); # Or just notify user about it
      }
    # Compare attributes of Cj;
    IF EXISTS(link(Ci,Cj,*,*))AND NOT(EXISTS(Ci.attr[k]))
      AND EXISTS(Cj.attr[k])
      {# Notify user about missing attr[k]
      Alert('missing attribute',Ci,attr[k]);
      }
    # Compare links of Cj with Cj.link.type=label=1;
    IF EXISTS(link(Cj,Ck,label, weight))
      AND NOT(EXISTS(link(Ci,Ck,label,*))
      {# Notify user about missing link[k];
      Alert('missing link',Ci,link[k],label, weight);
      }
  }
}
```

check of the whole space. Table 2 gives the pseudo-code algorithm for this combination.

Example: The concept called 'Discrete Neuron Perceptrons' from a Neural Networks course (Figure 5) has a link via the label='Title' attribute to the concept called 'Continuous Neuron Perceptrons' (with some weight). The latter has a different link via the 'Title' label to the concept 'The artificial neuron'. The system can notice this link and prompt the user to consider connecting the first concept to the last (with, e.g., the same label, 'Title', and 33% weight).

The computation of the flexibility index for the combined version is gained by combining the flexibility degree for the separate versions.

There are many more possible transformations from the domain model to the others, but in the following we limit ourselves to essential ones from the point of view of adaptivity and LAOS design originality.

From Domain Model to Adaptation Model (DM→AM)

Adaptive rules, by definition, are what make a hypermedia system adaptive; and should therefore be independent from the domain representation. However, a good domain representation can be the basis of smart adaptive behaviour. Moreover, domain model features can be interpreted to automatically generate adaptive rules. This can happen at the *direct adaptive technique* level, or at a higher level of *adaptive language* or *adaptive strategies* (LAG; section 3.1.4). Therefore, instead of assigning a specific transformation for a given link type (or concept type), the same link (or concept) could be transformed differently, according to a different (e.g., pedagogically or financially rooted) adaptive strategy.

DM→AM According to Concept Attribute Type:

Attribute Type Related Rules

Attribute types can be used to create rules that determine which specific attributes are shown in some specific conditions. These conditions can be automatically deduced by the system (as in adaptivity) or triggered by the AHS user (adaptability).

Example: A specific automatic adaptive low-level rule can determine showing the 'text' attribute of concept C1 only after the 'title' and 'introduction' were read:

IF (C1.title.access='yes' AND C1. introduction.access='yes')
THEN C1. text.available='yes';

Note that we have written the condition in this form for the purposes of simplification, but that attribute variables such as 'access' and 'available' are part of the user model[7]. For this to be a *generic automatic transformation rule*, for any concept C in the domain model, all concepts in the overlay user model reflecting the DM should have attributes 'access' and 'available'.

Example: Instead of the rule above, the following generic rule can be used:

IF (C.title.access='yes' AND C. introduction.access='yes')
THEN C. text.available='yes';

The number of possible rules to generate is potentially infinite, because it is dependent on newly added UM variables (besides of *access* and *available*, referring to the state of some concepts with respect to the user, we can add general user variables such as *motivation, interest*, etc.). Even in the case with *s=2* variables, as above, and with the restriction that the 'access' variable can only be found on the left side of the rule, we obtain for the rule generation *flexibility degree*:

$$ flex(1) = \left(\sum\nolimits_{i=1}^{A_{min}} C(A_{min}, i) \right)^3 = \left(\sum\nolimits_{i=1}^{A_{min}} \frac{A_{min}!}{(A_{min} - i)! \, i!} \right)^3. $$

DM→AM According to Link Type

The links between concepts can be also interpreted in an adaptation model, so that, e.g., only specific links are 'fired' by the adaptation engine. In Cristea and Calvi (2003) we have already used the inherent structure of the DM by defining the 'generalize' and 'specialize' adaptive language commands.

From Goal and Constraints Model to Adaptation Model (GM→AM)

This type of transformation is more natural to the design of the LAOS structure, as the GM model contains a pre-selection of the material to present to the hypermedia user, according to some (pedagogical) *goal* and delimited by some (spatial, time, pedagogical, etc.) *constraints*.

The GM also pre-orders the DM information. This structure can already be interpreted in terms of the adaptation to be performed on it. For instance, the GM allows 'AND' relations between concepts, as well as 'OR' relations with some weights.

Example: Expressing that all concepts in an 'AND' relation should be read:

IF ((C.name.access='yes' OR C.contents.access='yes') AND link(C,C2,'AND',*))
  THEN { C2.name.accessible='yes'; C2.contents.accessible='yes';}

Similarly, an 'OR' relationship can be interpreted as inhibiting reading of other related concepts [8]:

IF ((C.name.access='yes' OR C.contents.access ='yes') AND link(C,C2,'OR',*))
  THEN { C2.name.accessible='no'; C2.contents.accessible='no';}

In such a way, various constructs can be automatically added to the generic adaptive rules, directly by interpreting the *goal and constraints model*.

Practical Implementation

This section describes the practical implementation and its testing.

MOT

MOT (My Online Teacher) instantiates the LAOS theoretical framework in the context of adaptive educational hypermedia. MOT is an AHS Web-authoring environment, based on MyET (Cristea et al., 2000). MOT implements at present a first version of three of the LAOS models: domain model (DM), lesson model (GM) and adaptation model (AM).

MOT has been tested for authoring purposes in a classroom setting, using a first version which implemented the DM and GM; and then as a version with three models (DM, GM, AM). Further work is underway which will allow MOT to interface with AHA! (version 3.0) system (De Bra et al., 2002).

MOT Testing

At the time of the first tests, MOT could demonstrate the ideas of separating domain model and goal and constraints model, as well as some of the ideas on automatic authoring and transformations (specifically, automatic generation of links within the concept domain model and automatic generation of an instance of the goal and constraints model from an instance of the domain model). The adaptation model interface based on LAG (Figure 4) was not yet present. Since then, more tests have been performed using the extended version of the system, and the results will soon be processed and reported.

MOT was designed and implemented to illustrate the ideas of the theoretical framework, and makes no great claims to a good user interface or information display facility. Therefore, as described in the experimental settings section, our main testing goal was mainly to *validate the theoretical ideas* and their implementation. However, we also allowed as a secondary goal *feedback on user-system interaction*, as this was the main expertise of the students involved. This testing experiment belongs to the first category of tests mentioned in section 3: testing of design and authoring.

Figure 5. The authoring interface for the domain model.

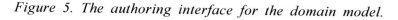

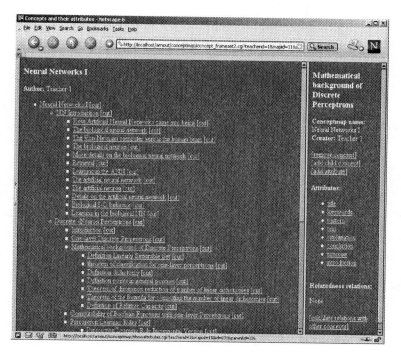

MOT is currently being further developed according to the flexible LAOS five-layer adaptation model for AH and adaptive Web-material, towards reflecting all the separate models (domain, goal, user, adaptation and presentation models).

Testing Goal

With the first tests of MOT within a classroom environment, we wanted to get feedback on:

1. the extent to which our goals were realized with this system from an outsiders' perspective (LAOS representation, separation of domain and goal and constraints model, automatic authoring and automatic linking) and
2. the usability of the system.

In particular, we wanted to find answers to questions as listed in Table 3.

Table 3. Goal point of view evaluation

Collaboration more authors collaborating at a course;	-	What are the problems? Suggestions for solving them? How did you try and solve them? What are the good points?
	-	Comparison - with collaboration (two or more working at one course together: experimental group) and without collaboration (one person only, with a smaller task: control group); the satisfaction degree should be measured, as well as the result evaluated.
Completeness looking at given goal (LAOS)	-	What is the perceived percentage of completeness? What is the expressivity? What is the (perceived) connectivity degree? Should there be more connections, or less? What would these extra connections be? What should be deleted (e.g., is superfluous)?
Adaptivity	-	How much flexibility is perceived?
Design range	-	How much more can be achieved in this way as compared to the linear model?

The Class

The group consisted of about 20 students following a post-graduate two-year study of user interfaces and user-system interaction (USI). Students came from different backgrounds (art to mathematics), and had different nationalities, genders and previous degrees. They were exposed to an intensive two-week course with the following teaching and testing procedure:

1. Background knowledge on adaptive systems, user modelling, focusing on AH

2. Exercises with building concept maps on paper

3. Theoretical framework of the MOT system (LAOS, LAG)

4. Exercises with writing LAOS-based rules on paper

5. Course evaluation: questionnaire (anonymous, individual)

6. Installing, experimenting and finally creating a presentation using MOT (domain and goal and constraints model) and on paper (adaptation, user and presentation model) in groups of 2-4.

7. Project evaluation: questionnaire (anonymous, individual)

8. MOT system evaluation: questionnaire (anonymous, individual) and free evaluation around the points listed in Table 4 (not anonymous, in groups).

9. Evaluation of assignments and staff grading

The questions on the questionnaires were mapped using a Likert scale (0:min to 5:max). Issues that students wanted to point at were included in free evaluations.

The students were told from the beginning that a negative evaluation of the system would not affect their grades, but that thoroughness and constructiveness of their answers would.

Evaluation

The students' numerical evaluation results for the MOT system were analysed for:

- the mean,
- standard deviation, and
- correlation.

The analysis was made using online statistical software.

The student course creation results themselves were analysed, in order to reflect on the:

- time necessary to familiarize oneself with MOT,
- perceived flexibility of MOT,
- perceived freedom of expression in MOT, and
- time necessary to create some courseware with MOT, etc.

Students were asked to make a MOT presentation on any theme they wanted within adaptive systems. Selected themes were 'concept maps for adaptive systems', 'complex adaptive systems', 'intelligent tutoring systems', and 'introduction to artificial intelligence'. Their concept maps and respective lessons are on the online Unix version of MOT.

From the performed evaluations, we present here those of interest to the research and development of the MOT (Figure 6, third questionnaire). However, these results are not completely independent from others; e.g., students missing theoretical background or unhappy with the course structure might have had difficulty in understanding the MOT system functionality. To ameliorate this problem, the first question concerns their understanding of how MOT works. The response is slightly positive (over 2.5), but must be taken as a prior probability influencing the precision of the further responses. Another question

Figure 6. MOT evaluation

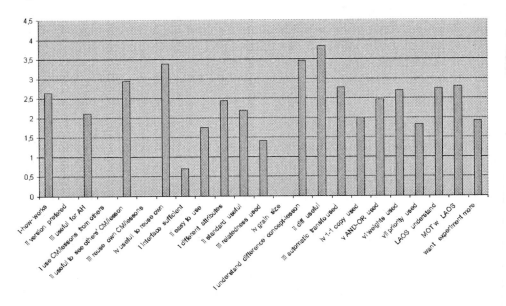

refers to their understanding of LAOS, the theoretical model behind MOT. The students' response is similar (over 2.5). This understanding is again another prior probability influencing the certainty of the given responses.

With this premises we can look at the results.

Results

In Figure 6, alpha-numeric results are not represented; e.g., the preferred MOT version was the online version. Students declared they used concept maps of others as well as their lessons and link structures. On the issue of reuse of their own material, responses were varied. The granularity of stored concepts also varied.

Among numeric results, it is interesting to note that students claimed they understood (Mean = 3.46; Standard Deviation = 1.20) the difference between domain model and lesson (i.e., goal and constraints) model, and that they find this difference very useful (Mean = 3.83; Standard Deviation = 0.389). This result is extremely important because this difference has been introduced as one of the originalities of the LAOS framework, intending to separate pure content related issues (e.g., concepts, their hierarchies and their relations) from presentation relation issues (such as how different aspects of concepts should be presented together, in what order, etc). Until recently the necessity of this separation has been a controversial issue in AH academic and research circles, but the students accepted it without any hesitation as being intuitive, and were able to work well with it.

Reuse of personal material (domain model, lessons) was considered useful, as well as the reuse of other teachers' makeshift material. One response involves pure reuse whereas the other response involves collaboration. Nevertheless, a comparison 'useful to see other's CM/lessons' with 'useful to reuse ones own' shows a 60.6% correlation between the two variables, pointing to the fact that these responses are related.

Another interesting and important result was that the students used automatic translations from the domain model to the lesson (goal and constraints) model. This is important because MOT was trying to illustrate that, although adaptive educational hypermedia authoring requires a complex process and the population of many models in order to achieve the best performance, simplifications and automatic transformations (as in section 3.2) are possible and can help the beginner author. Therefore, as the students were indeed beginner authors, their option for automatic translations confirms this hypothesis.

The special features of the goal and constraints model, such as weights (importance or difficulty of items to be presented), priority ordering of the items to be presented and grouping into AND or OR relations were used, but moderately. Therefore, the appropriateness of the components of this model has to be tested further.

A very low usage score was given to the relatedness relations between concepts, which can be computed automatically by the system. It seems that some students haven't even discovered this feature of MOT. The problem seems to be that the present implementation doesn't allow any direct application of these relations (except for informing the author about the existence of these relations).

The current domain model provides a set of predefined attributes for each concept. Students have used those moderately, but also have defined their own (which is allowed in MOT). The predefined attributes can be used to semantically label the concept and allow automatic machine processing (such as automatic concept linking). Different attributes were used with a mean of 2.19 and a standard deviation of 1.33 (actual responses varying from 0 – no other attributes used — to 4 — almost only other attributes used). The added attributes are more difficult to interpret, but nevertheless seem to be necessary for allowing full expression of the intentions of the author.

Conclusions and Future Trends

In this chapter we described a framework for authoring of adaptive hypermedia, LAOS, with its detailed adaptation model, LAG. This structure is in conformity with the requirements of W3C towards the third generation Web, called the Semantic Web.

Validation of this proposal was first based on existing background research and on an existing well-known framework, AHAM, which is not refined enough to allow flexible automatic authoring. The flexibility of LAOS was estimated theoretically, and some examples were given. Moreover, tests with real students were performed in MOT.

The research and development of AH authoring are new and will be developed in the future. We have pointed in this chapter to many possible future trends and developments within this area, which are briefly reviewed here. The main two axes of developments that we shall see in the future in this field are *theory* and *praxis*.

Theory developments will reflect improved organization of AH contents, as well as improved representations of the manipulation techniques. Especially, we shall see more collaborations between the semantic Web community and the AH community towards better meta-data representations. For manipulations in AH, we shall see new, emerging patterns of adaptive behaviour, leading to new standards for the Web. This means, patterns that can be used to extend existent standards (such as learning object metadata LOM, simple sequencing standard or SCORM) or even generate new standards for adaptive hypermedia. These patterns will allow various automatic transformations and data generation for adaptive hypermedia, towards the AH that writes itself. Especially in the educational domain, high granularity patterns can emerge from embedding learning styles and cognitive styles research into AH.

Moreover, it is interesting to note that products of this research match with findings from research on open (adaptive) hypermedia systems (see Henze & Nejdl, 2003). There, the necessity of creating patterns emerges not from authoring needs, but for needs of better interfaces between the objects of the open hyperspace. However, the solutions are similar and will eventually merge.

This is actually a time where benefits can come from cross-field developments, such as connections to ontological research, open hypermedia, Web standards, etc.

From a praxis point of view, we will need research related to implementing these frameworks, but also, a lot of consideration will have to be given to visualization techniques for the great bulk of information contained in AH systems. The author will have to benefit of fish-eye, bird-eye, and other views, slices through the information, etc.

Acknowledgment

This research is supported by the Minerva project ADAPT. MOT can be downloaded at: http://wwwis.win.tue.nl/~acristea/HTML/USI/MOT/. MOT can be tried out at:

- http://e-learning.dsp.pub.ro/mot/ (or http://wwwis.win.tue.nl/MOT03/ TeachersSite-html/enter.html) and
- http://e-learning.dsp.pub.ro/motadapt/

LAOS discussion and MOT testing has been performed within two courses:

- April-May 2003, TU/e, Netherlands: http://wwwis.win.tue.nl/acristea/ HTML/USI/index.html/
- January 2004, UPB, Romania: http://wwwis.win.tue.nl:/~acristea/HTML/ PUB04/

Thanks to organizations involved in the process of *refining of adaptation patterns*: IFETS discussion group, (LTSC)(Kinshuk), CEDEFOP, University of Pittsburgh (Peter Brusilovsky).

References

ADAPT project. (n.d.). Adaptivity and adaptability in ODL based on ICT. (European Community Socrates Minerva 101144-CP-1-2002-NL-MINERVA-MPP). Retrieved from http://wwwis.win.tue.nl/~alex/HTML/ Minerva/

Bajraktarevic, N., Hall, W., & Fullick, P. (2003). *Incorporating learning styles in hypermedia environment: Empirical evaluation.* AH 2003 Workshop Session at HT'03 Conference, Nottingham, UK. Retrieved from online at http://wwwis.win.tue.nl/ah2003/schedule-ht.html

Brailsford, T. J., Stewart, C. D., Zakaria, M. R., & Moore, A. (2002, May). Autonavigation, links, and narrative in an adaptive Web-based integrated learning environment. *Proceedings of World Wide Web 2002 Conference*, Honolulu, HI.

Brusilovsky, P. (2003) Developing adaptive educational hypermedia systems: From design models to authoring tools. In T. Murray, S. Blessing & S. Ainsworth (Eds.), *Authoring tools for advanced technology learning environment*. Dordrecht: Kluwer Academic Publishers.

Brusilovsky, P. (2002) Adaptive hypermedia, *User Modeling and User Adapted Interaction, Ten Year Anniversary Issue, 11*(1/2), 87-110.

Brusilovsky, P., Schwarz, E., & Weber, G. (1996, October). A tool for developing adaptive electronic textbooks on WWW. In H. Maurer (Eds.), *Proceedings of WebNet'96*, October, San Francisco (pp. 64-69). AACE.

Calvi, L., & Cristea, A. (2002). Towards generic adaptive systems: Analysis of a case study. *AH 2002, Adaptive Hypermedia and Adaptive Web-Based Systems,* LNCS 2347 (pp. 79-89). Springer.

Carmona, C., Bueno, D., Guzman, E., & Conejo, R. (2002, May). SIGUE: Making Web courses Adaaptive. In P. De Bra, P. Brusilovsky & R. Conejo (Eds.), *Proceedings of Second International Conference on Adaptive Hypermedia and Adaptive Web-Based Systems (AH 2002)*, Málaga, Spain (pp. 376-379).

Cristea, A.I., & Calvi, L. (2003) The three layers of adaptation granularity. *Proceedings of UM'03,* LNAI 2702 (pp. 4-14). Springer.

Cristea, A., & De Mooij, A. (2003, May) LAOS: Layered WWW AHS authoring model and its corresponding algebraic operators. *Proceedings of WWW'03, Alternate Education track*, Budapest, Hungary. ACM Press.

Cristea, A.I., and Kinshuk. (2003) Considerations on LAOS, LAG and their Integration in MOT. *Proceedings of ED-MEDIA'03*, Honolulu, Hawaii, AACE.

Cristea, A., & De Mooij, A. (2003a, February / March). Adaptive course authoring: MOT, my online teacher. *Proceedings of ICT-2003, "Telecommunications + Education" Workshop*, Tahiti Island in Papetee - French Polynesia. IEEE LTTF IASTED.

Cristea, A., & De Mooij, A. (2003b, April). Designer adaptation in adaptive hypermedia. *Proceedings of ITCC'03*. Las Vegas, NV. IEEE Computer Society.

Cristea, A. I., & De Bra, P. (2002, October). Towards adaptable and adaptive ODL environments. *Proceedings of AACE E-Learn'02*. Montreal, Canada (pp. 232-239).

Cristea, A. I., & Aroyo, L. (2002). Adaptive authoring of adaptive educational hypermedia. *Proceedings of AH 2002, Adaptive Hypermedia and Adaptive Web-Based Systems*, LNCS 2347 (pp. 122-132). Springer.

Cristea, A., Okamoto, T., & Cristea, P. (2000, July). MyEnglishTeacher - An evolutionary, Web-based, multi-agent environment for academic English teaching, *Proceedings of CEC 2000*, San Diego, CA. Published on CD.

De Bra, P., & Calvi, L. (1998) AHA! An open adaptive hypermedia architecture. *The NewReview of Hypermedia and Multimedia, 4,* 115-139.

De Bra, P., Aerts, A., Smits, D., & Stash, N. (2002, October). AHA! Version 2.0, More adaptation flexibility for authors. *Proceedings of ELearn 2002* (pp. 240-246). AACE.

Grigoriadou, M., Papanikolaou, K., Kornilakis, H., & Magoulas, G. (2001, July). INSPIRE: An INtelligent System for Personalized Instruction in a Remote Environment. In P. D. Bra, P. Brusilovsky, & A. Kobsa (Eds.), *Proceedings of Third workshop on Adaptive Hypertext and Hypermedia*, Sonthofen, Germany, Technical University Eindhoven (pp. 13-24).

Henze, N., & Nejdl, W. (2003). Logically characterizing adaptive educational hypermedia systems. *Proceedings of AH 2003 Workshop Session at WWW'03 Conference*, Budapest, Hungary. Retrieved from http://wwwis.win.tue.nl/ah2003/proceedings/www-2/

IMS simple sequencing protocol (2003). Retrieved from http://www.imsglobal.org/simplesequencing/index.cfm

Koch, N., & Wirsing, M. (2001, July). Developing adaptive educational hypermedia systems: From design models to authoring models. In P. D. Bra, P. Brusilovsky, & A. Kobsa (Eds.), *Proceedings of Third workshop on Adaptive Hypertext and Hypermedia.*

LOM: Draft Standard for Learning Object Metadata. (n.d.). Retreived from http://ltsc.ieee.org/wg12/doc.html

Murray, T. (2002). MetaLinks: Authoring and affordances for conceptual and narrative flow in adaptive hyperbooks. *International Journal of Artificial Intelligence in Education, 13*(1).

SCORM: The sharable content object reference model (2001). Retrieved from http://www.adlnet.org/Scorm/scorm.cfm

Statistical tools online (n.d.). Retrieved from http://home.clara.net/sisa/

Specht, M., Kravcik, M., Klemke, R., Pesin, L., & Hüttenhain, R. (2002). Adaptive learning environment (ALE) for teaching and learning in WINDS. *Proceedings of Second International Conference on Adaptive Hypermedia and Adaptive Web-Based Systems (AH 2002)*, LNCS 2347 (pp. 572-581). Springer.

W3C, RDF (Resource Description Framework). Retrieved from http://www.w3.org/RDF/

W3C (n.d.). Semantic Web. Retrieved from http://www.w3.org/2001/sw/

W3C (n.d.). SMIL, Synchronized Multimedia Language. Retrieved from http://www.w3.org/AudioVideo/

Weber, G., Kuhl, H.-C., & Weibelzahl, S. (2001, July). Developing adaptive Internet based courses with the authoring system NetCoach. In P. D. Bra, P. Brusilovsky, & A. Kobsa (Eds.), *Proceedings of Third workshop on Adaptive Hypertext and Hypermedia*, Sonthofen, Germany (pp. 35-48). Retrieved from http://wwwis.win.tue.nl/ah2001/papers/GWeber-UM01.pdf

Wu, H. (2001). *A reference architecture for adaptive hypermedia applications*. Doctoral dissertation, Eindhoven University of Technology, The Netherlands.

Endnotes

1   Adaptivity implies the system making inferences about possible choices, and then executing them. In adaptability, the inferences about possible choices, as well as the selections are made by the user.

2   Benefits can come from cross-field developments, e.g., connections to ontological research, open hypermedia, Web standards, etc.

3   Some steps can be done in parallel, or in different order, and even by different, collaborating authors.

4   New links can be between concepts of current content (concept map: e.g., course), between current content and some other content created by the same author, or created by a different author.

5   Meaning that attributes determining the link are of same type in both concepts.

6   Concepts sharing the father-concept, or at the same level of the hierarchy, or related with each other via some special link (of a given type), etc.

7   More precisely, part of the overlay part of the UM, as the UM can contain also other attributes such as user's prior knowledge, user's interest, etc., that are not an overlay model of the DM (or GM).

8   In such a case, an 'OR' relationship acts actually as a 'XOR'.

Chapter XI

Authoring of Adaptive Hypermedia Courseware Using *AHyCO* System

Natasa Hoic-Bozic, University of Rijeka, Croatia

Vedran Mornar, University of Zagreb, Croatia

Abstract

This chapter describes an approach to the development of an adaptive hypermedia Web-based educational system and presents the model of an AHyCo (adaptive hypermedia courseware) system. An adaptive educational system should contain not only the learning environment for students, but also the authoring environment for teachers. A user friendly authoring module should be the integral part of such a system. The authoring of adaptive hypermedia consists of the development of actual hypermedia content (lessons, tests, etc.) together with the definition of the rules for adaptation. The authoring component of an AHyCo system, described in this chapter, includes both. By utilizing intuitive form-based user interface, it enables teachers from areas other than IT to produce and interconnect complex hypermedia content.

Introduction

Traditional computer-aided teaching techniques have been greatly enhanced recently by utilizing the hypermedia paradigm. Hypermedia learning programs demand more activity from students, who advance through learning materials in their individual manner. Diverse non-textual media improve student's motivation, resulting in easier learning.

Despite the advantages introduced by hypermedia and WWW, some problems related to the usage of such systems become apparent as well. Traditional organization of courseware inherited the disadvantages of node-link data model, which does not separate the structure of hypermedia database from its content (Maurer & Scherbakov, 1996). Users can get disoriented, and predefined links do not permit the courseware to be adapted to the users of different backgrounds, qualities and interests.

Adaptive hypermedia (AH) is contemporary area of research within the field of hypermedia. An adaptive hypermedia system (AHS) adapts the presentation of hypermedia content, based on the user model (Brusilovsky, 1999).

An adaptive hypermedia educational system (AHES) should contain not only the learning environment for students, but also the authoring environment for teachers. Easy to use authoring module should be the integral part of such a system.

Here we describe our approach to the development of an AHES and present the model of AHyCo—the system for development and distribution of the adaptive Web-based courseware. Our goal is to develop a complete courseware management system offering learning environment with adaptive navigation, testing, course management and computer-mediated communication, all backed up with corresponding authoring tools. In contrast to the majority of available systems, for example WebCT and TopClass (Robson, 1999), AHyCo system is adaptive. The online tests are used not only for grading of student's knowledge, but also for the guidance in navigation. Only synchronous and asynchronous collaboration facilities have not been implemented yet, but the development of these facilities is in progress.

Particular attention is given to the design of the authoring component, which enables the specification of prerequisites for each lesson, and simplifies the creation of test questions.

Background

According to Brusilovsky (1996), under the term adaptive hypermedia systems we denote all hypertext and hypermedia systems that reflect some features of the user in the user model and apply this model to adapt various visible aspects of the system to the user. An adaptive hypermedia system (AHS) adapts the presentation of content or links, based on the user model. We distinguish the two major technologies in adaptive hypermedia: adaptive presentation and adaptive navigation support. Adaptive presentation adapts either the content of a document or the style of the text. Adaptive navigation support concentrates on changing the presentation of links.

The most popular area for adaptive hypermedia research is the educational hypermedia, where the goal of a student is to learn the material on a particular subject (Brusilovsky, 1996). The most important element in educational hypermedia is the user knowledge of the subject that is being taught. Certain students may know almost nothing about the same lesson that may be trivial and boring for another. In both cases the students need navigational help to find their way through the knowledge because they can "get lost in hyperspace" (Maurer & Scherbakov, 1996).

A number of first-generation adaptive hypermedia systems (Carver, Hill, & Pooch, 1999) were built between 1985 and 1993. They were generally standalone PC or Macintosh-based systems with limited adaptability through stereotype-based user models and limited adaptation techniques. ISIS-Tutor is a good example of a first generation adaptive system (Brusilovsky & Pesin, 1994).

Since 1993, the Web has become the primary platform for developing AHES (Brusilovsky, 1999). These second-generation AHS were generally platform independent. They introduced new features such as adaptive multimedia. Some examples are ELM-ART (Brusilovsky, Schwarz, & Weber, 1996), InterBook (Eklund & Brusilovsky, 1998), DCG (Vassileva, 1997), AHM (Da Silva, 1998), CALAT (Nakabayashi, 1997), KBS Hyperbook (Henze & Nejdl, 2000), ALICE (Kavcic, 2001), AHA (De Bra & Ruiter, 2001), and AHA! (De Bra, Aerts, Berden, De Lange, Rousseau, Santic, Smits, & Stash, 2003), NetCoach (Weber, Kuhl, & Weibelzahl, 2001), ALE (Specht, Kravcik, Pesin, & Klemke, 2001).

The second-generation AHS mostly use link annotation. A variant of the overlay model for representing the student's knowledge is used, sometimes in combination with stereotypes. The educational state of the concepts from the domain model is updated if user visits the page that presents the concept's content. Some of the AHS (CALAT, InterBook, ELM-ART, KBS Hyperbook, ALICE, NetCoach) use the tests as additional and more reliable criteria.

The most important shortcoming of an AHS is its authoring. The process of authoring should include the development of the actual hypermedia content (lessons, tests, etc.) and the definition of the rules for adaptation. According to Brusilovsky (2003), there are two major approaches used by the authoring tools: the markup approach and form-based GUI (graphic user interface) approach.

Some AHS (ELM-ART, ALICE) do not have the authoring component at all. The others (AHA, InterBook) use complicated markup approach where the content and the rules for adaptation are interleaved. For example, in Interbook the author must write structured, annotated MS-Word files. In AHA, the author must create annotated HTML files. The combination of content, links and adaptation rules makes it difficult for course authors to maintain a clear picture of how the concepts relate to each other. This leads to the lack of courseware usability. The before-mentioned approach does not allow the authors to use the hypermedia lessons from a certain domain to build diverse courseware by simply redefining adaptation rules or prerequisite relationships.

Another problem of today's AHS authoring components is that insufficient attention is paid to the generation of tests. Furthermore, to motivate more authors to use the adaptive hypermedia, the authoring process should be made much simpler than in some existing GUI-based authoring tools (NetCoach, ALE). The authoring component should enable the straightforward creation of concepts, the linkage of concepts by prerequisite relationships, and easy generation of the test questions. It should be user-friendly enough to enable a person who is not a computer expert to design the courseware. That includes the development of a graphic editor for concept networks, which will enable the authors to define the prerequisite relationships with a drag-and-drop interface.

In our AHS AHyCo, particular attention is given to the authoring component of the system. AHyCo user interface is form-based, as in AHA!, NetCoach, or ALE. We strictly separate the learning dependencies (prerequisite relationships) from the actual content (multimedia fragments). This separation allows the authors to use the same set of fragments from a domain to build diverse courseware by simply defining new prerequisite relationships and the values for adaptation rules (Hoic-Bozic & Mornar, 2003).

AHyCo, like ALE, attempts to provide a complete courseware management system for practical courses. AHyCo is delivered as Open Source software (AHyCo, 2003), like AHA!. It uses an easy to use graphical drag-and-drop interface for the definition of the prerequisite relations between the learning objects. Like NetCoach, AHyCo is designed to enable the authors to develop adaptive learning courses without the knowledge of programming. Both systems implement knowledge assessment with tests, but the creation and usage of questions and tests in NetCoach is rather simplified.

Particularly, the support for the creation and usage of questions and tests is where AHyCo distinguishes most from other AHS.

The Models of an Adaptive Educational Hypermedia System

The theoretical model of AHyCo, with some extensions and adjustments, is similar to the models of other AHS. The goal was not to develop a new model, but to design and implement a user interface that would facilitate a trouble-free preparation of course materials.

Our model is comparable to an existing model for adaptive hypermedia, AHAM (Wu, Houben, & De Bra, 1998). It consists of the domain model, the student model and the adaptive model. The domain model describes the structure of the learning domain as a set of reusable concepts (lessons and tests), linked together with prerequisite relationships. The student model encompasses the student's knowledge of the lessons. The adaptive model contains the rules for adaptation. The rules define how the domain model and the student model are combined to perform adaptive navigation support. The system is composed of two environments: the authoring environment and the learning environment (Hoic-Bozic, 2002).

The main distinction of AHyCo compared to existing theoretical models in other AHS is the proposal that tests are the special cases of concepts. Exceptional attention was paid to the authoring of questions and tests, which are fundamental for updating of the student model and for the implementation of adaptive navigation (Hoic-Bozic, Mornar, & Pukljak Zokovic, 2003).

The Domain Model

The domain model of AHyCo has a two-level structure and consists of concepts. A concept is an elementary piece of knowledge for the given learning domain (Figure 1).

The first domain level is a graph (C_k, LC_k), where C_k is the set of concepts and LC_k is the set of arcs, $LC_k \subseteq C_k \times C_k$. The links represent the prerequisite relationships, $\prec$. These relationships denote the pedagogical constraints. $K_i \prec K_j$, for example, means that "concept K_i should be learned before concept K_j". In contrast to AHAM model, for example, this is the only pedagogical strategy used in our model, because we intended to make the linkage of concepts as simple as possible.

Figure 1. An example of a domain model

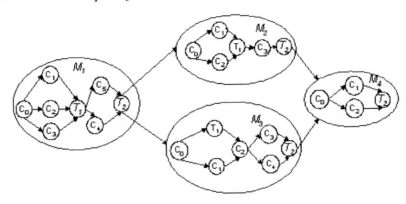

To split the domain into more manageable units, concepts are grouped into modules M_k. The second level of the domain model is a directed graph $\mathcal{D}=(\mathcal{M}, \mathcal{LM})$, where M is the set of modules and $\mathcal{LM}$ is the set of arcs, $\mathcal{LM} \subseteq \mathcal{M} \times \mathcal{M}$. The arc connecting modules M_k and M_l exists if $M_k \prec M_l$. The prerequisite relationship p for a module pair means that a certain minimum acceptable knowledge level for module M_k should be reached before the student can start to learn the lessons from M_l. The entire directed graph $\mathcal{D}$ *(the domain) is equivalent to one* course the student has enrolled.

The majority of concepts in the graph are lessons C_i. Some of the concepts in the graph are tests T_j that contain the questions about the lessons.

A concept-lesson C_i is defined as ($\mathcal{FC}_i$, $\mathcal{PC}_i$, Q_i, R_i, wc_i, lMy_i) where:

- $\mathcal{FC}_i$ is a set of multimedia fragments (small building blocks, e.g. a piece of text, graphics, sound, video clip…).

- $\mathcal{PC}_i$ is a set of prerequisite lessons, which are essential for the student to understand the lesson C_i.

- Q_i is a set of questions related to lesson C_i. The questions are multiple-choice/single answer.

- R_i is the rank of the lesson C_i calculated as

  - $R_0 = 0$ (for lessons with no prerequisites, $\mathcal{PC}_i = \varnothing$)
  - $R_k = \max R_j + 1,$
    $$j \mid C_j \in \mathcal{PC}_k$$

- wc_i is the weight of the lesson C_i with respect to the containing module M_k, determined by the author. $wc_i \in (0, 1)$ and $\sum wc_i = 1$.
- lMy_i is a *predefined* minimum acceptable knowledge level *of the lesson* C_i, calculated by MYCIN formula (Anjaneyulu, 1997, Ng & Abramson, 1990), $lMy_i \in (-1,1)$.

Each question from Q_i is defined as ($\mathcal{FQ}, q, \mathcal{A}, \mathcal{H}, \mathcal{B}$) where:

- $\mathcal{FQ}$ is the set of hypermedia fragments that form the question (stem). The stem of the parameterized questions contains the parameters.
- q is the confidence level of the fact that student either knows the lesson if he/she answers the question correctly, or does not know the lesson if he/she answers incorrectly, $q \in (0, 1)$. It is predefined by the author. Easier questions have smaller q.
- $\mathcal{A}$ is the set of the offered answers. Each offered answer A_j is a set of hypermedia fragments. Answer A_j of the parameterized questions is a function $f_j (p_1, p_2, ..., p_n)$ that evaluates a candidate answer on the basis of parameters $p_1, p_2, .., p_n$. Function f_j is defined in a scripting language and is evaluated after the parameters have been randomly generated.
- $\mathcal{H}$ is the set of indices of correct answers or functions.
- $\mathcal{B}$ is the set of lower and upper bounds for parameters $p_1, p_2, ..., p_n$.

A concept-test T_j is defined as a ($\mathcal{PT}_j, n_j, \mathcal{N}_j, \mathcal{R}_j$) where:

- $\mathcal{PT}_j$ is a set of prerequisite concepts-lessons, $\mathcal{PT}_j = \{ C_i \mid C_i \prec T_j \}$. T_j will contain the questions related to lessons from $\mathcal{PT}_j$.
- n_j is the total number of questions in T_j.
- $\mathcal{N}_j$ is the set of configuration rules that specify how many questions for each lesson C_i should be placed into the test T_j.
- R_j is the rank of the test T_j.

A module M_k is defined as a ($C_k, \mathcal{PM}_k, lm_k, R_k$) where:

- C_k is a set of concepts that create the module.
- $\mathcal{PM}_k$ is a set of prerequisite modules for module M_k.
- lm_k is *the* minimum acceptable knowledge for module, $lm_k \in (-1,1)$.
- R_k is the rank of the module M_k.

The main purpose of the tests T_k from the domain model is to govern the navigation within the module and the navigation between modules by updating of the student model.

This representation of the domain structure is suitable for representation of the learning materials from different areas (computer science, mathematics, medicine, art, etc.). The structure of the knowledge is not hierarchical (chapters, subchapters, pages) but rather concept-oriented (Hoic-Bozic, 2001). The pedagogical constraints between the lessons depend on the subject area. For example, for the math lessons, $C_i \prec C_j$ usually means that it is impossible for student to start learning C_j if he/she has not gained the knowledge of C_i. For some other subject areas, the prerequisite relationships simply denote the sequence of learning, proposed by the author. For the same set of lessons, another teacher may choose a completely different learning sequence, that is, prerequisite relationships.

Student Model

The two-level student model, a variant of the overlay model for representation of the student's knowledge (Brusilovsky, 1996), is proposed for the AHyCo system.

The first level represents the estimate of students' knowledge about the lessons C_i, denoted by r_i and k_i.

r_i is the estimate of the fact that the student has read the lesson C_i or not. Initially, $r_i = 0$ for every C_i. To set r_i to 1, the student must not only retrieve the page containing the lesson, but also navigate to one of the suggested continuation concepts proposed by the system, which are enumerated at the bottom of the page.

k_i is the estimate about the student's knowledge of the lesson C_i. It is calculated by a variant of the MYCIN model, a widely used expert systems' model (Anjaneyulu, 1997; Ng & Abramson, 1990). The estimation of the student's knowledge is an uncertainty problem. A possible approach to solve such a problem is the certainty factors utilization, implemented in the MYCIN expert system. This approach has been chosen in AHyCo, because it simple to implement and understand. The fact that the student has answered the question correctly contributes to the hypothesis "the student knows the concept C_i". The opposite fact contributes to the negation of the same hypothesis.

The knowledge level of a lesson is set by testing and can range from -1 (student does not know the lesson) to 1 (student knows the lesson). Before the student takes any of the tests, all lessons in the student model have an initial level of $k_i = 0$.

After answering to a question related to the lesson C_i, the new knowledge level k_i' for the lesson C_i is calculated according to (1). The new level k_i' is based on the previous knowledge level k_i and the factor q, the confidence level of the fact that the student knows or does not know the lesson if he/she knows that question. If the student answers the question correctly, $f = q$, otherwise $f = -q$.

$$k_i' = \begin{cases} k_i + (1 - k_i) \times f, & k_i > 0, \ f > 0 \\ k_i + (1 + k_i) \times f, & k_i < 0, \ f < 0 \quad (1) \\ (k_i + f) / (1 - \min(|k_i|, |f|)) & \text{otherwise} \end{cases} \qquad \textbf{(1)}$$

The model asymptotically increases/decreases the knowledge level for a concept with each correct/incorrect answer, according to the previous knowledge level k_i and the question weight q from the domain model.

The second level represents the knowledge about the modules. For every M_k the AHS is recorded the knowledge level about module km_k. The knowledge level km_k of the module M_k is calculated according to the formula: $km_k = \sum k_j \times wc_j$ for each C_j from the module M_k, where wc_j is the weight of the lesson C_j (Hoic-Bozic, 2002). According to the formula, the more important lessons for the module (with higher weight wc_j) influence more when calculating the knowledge level km_k.

Adaptation Model

In our system, we employed the adaptive navigation, which is a combination of free and guided navigation. A student can freely follow any hyperlink within a single module, but a list of suitable hyperlinks is offered, according to the navigation plan generated on the basis of the student model. AHyCo uses a combination of link sorting and link annotation adaptive techniques.

The presentation component of the system displays hyperlinks to various concept types in different colors. All the hyperlinks within the module are functional, so the student can follow any hyperlink. Nevertheless, as aimless searching through the concepts is not advisable, the navigation within a graph $(\mathcal{M}, \mathcal{LM})$ is restricted and depends on the student's knowledge level km_k. The freedom of navigation is thus somewhat reduced. The aforementioned adaptive navigation support is based on the adaptation model, which consists of adaptation rules. The adaptation rules define how the domain model and the student model are combined to perform the adaptation.

According to the student model, the concepts from the module M_k are classified into several subsets: learned concepts, recommended concepts where all prerequisite concepts have been read, and not recommended concepts.

Navigation within the module M_k is actually the traversal of a directed graph (C_k, LC_k), following the hyperlinks suggested by the system on the bottom of the page. The model uses tests or quizzes T_j to check the students' knowledge and to update the student model while he/she navigates within the module. This navigation goes on until the student reaches the marginal knowledge level km_k. When this happens, hyperlinks to other modules become active.

Implementation of the Model

In the development of AHyCo system we rely on the Microsoft .NET technology (Hoic-Bozic, 2002).

AHyCo network application is based on the relational database management system. The system components are: Microsoft SQL Server 2000 database, Microsoft Access forms as an interface for authors, middle-tier component for communication between the Web application and database, and Microsoft ASP.NET C# Web application as AHyCo learning environment. The students use the Web browser based interface to access AHyCo hypermedia courseware (Figure 2).

All the information about the subject matter and the students are stored in a SQL database. The database stores the domain model, the student model and the adaptation model, which are defined and updated through Microsoft Access forms as an interface for authors.

The midle-tier component is responsible for communication between Web application and the database. It applyes the rules for adaptation. To generate the pages, the system consults the middle-tier component. This component determines which content will be shown next, according to the adaptation rules and information from the domain model and the student model. Based on the information returned from the middle-tier component, appropriate HTML fragments are composed together by the Web application that is responsible for displaying the lesson or test's question, simultaneously with the rest of the page (hyperlinks and buttons for navigation).

AHyCo learning environment is a Microsoft ASP.NET C# Web application. This is the only part of the system visible to the students

Figure 2. The components of AHyCo system

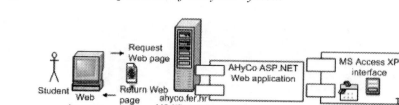

The Web application needs to perform the following tasks: authenticate the student, display the list of courses related to the student, display lessons' content and navigational elements, display tests' questions and submit the students' answers, and display test results.

The Web pages presented to the student are generated adaptively (on the fly) when student requests them, based on the contents extracted from the database. There are three kinds of pages: lessons, questions, and special pages (e.g., login page, help, and test results page).

The Learning Environment

The student has to be authenticated in order to use the AHyCo learning environment. After the process of authorization, the student has to choose the course for learning. For the selected course, the Web page containing the lesson C_i is generated. This lesson is chosen in accordance to the adaptation rules and the data stored in the student model, corresponding with the students' previous knowledge. The upper part of the page is static and contains the navigational bar with buttons for accessing the standard application pages, for example, help, students' results, and logout page.

On the bottom of the page, the hyperlinks to the continuation lessons or tests proposed by the system are enumerated. The suggested hyperlinks are automati-

Figure 3. The question's WWW page

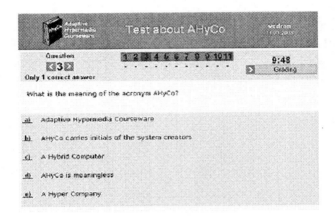

cally generated before the page is shown and are annotated with various colors which correspond to the concept's recommendation.

The concepts are listed in the following order:

- Completely recommended or main concepts: green color annotates the concepts where all prerequisite concepts have been read. These concepts are the best continuation for C_i according to the directed graph (C_k, LC_k).

- Recommended concepts: orange color annotates all other concepts where all prerequisite concepts have been read.

- Not recommended concepts: red color annotates the concepts where some of the prerequisite concepts have not been read or the knowledge level of some prerequisite $k_i < lMy_i$.

- Read concepts: blue color annotates the lessons with $r_i \neq 0$.

Some of the concepts in the graph of a module are tests. The test questions and the sequence of the offered answers are generated randomly (Figure 3).

The transition to another module is possible when the student reaches the marginal knowledge level lm_k, providing that there exists no lessons C_i with $k_i \leq lMy_i$. Such lessons, if they exist, are offered for repetition.

The Authoring Process

The process of authoring hypermedia courseware in AHyCo includes the development of both the learning materials and the adaptation rules. When preparing for the courseware creation, the author should divide the subject matter into lessons or concepts. The lessons should be connected by prerequisite relations and grouped into modules (Hoic-Bozic & Mornar, 2003).

During the authoring phase, the author sets the rules for adaptation by defining the prerequisite graphs of concepts (C, LC) and modules (M, LM). The graphs are created and connected with a drag-drop user interface. When defining the lessons in a module, the author determines the weight wc_i of the lesson for the particular module, as well as the minimum acceptable knowledge level for each lesson in the module lMy_i. When defining the test questions, the author defines the weight q of the questions for the associated lesson. For each module in a domain, the minimum knowledge level lm_k is set. Hence non-technical educators are able to use the adaptive features in a simple manner. The authors do not need to take in account any other adaptation rules, nor do they need to use any other tool. The authoring process is thus concentrated on the definition of prerequisites and the establishment of the difficulty level for lessons and tests. The responsibility for the adaptive navigation remains on the AHyCo system.

Microsoft Access XP forms are used as an authoring interface. This tool was chosen for its rapid application development capabilities, as well as for its integration with other Microsoft Office products used for the preparation of the learning content (Word, PowerPoint and Excel). In the interface design, the care has been taken to enable authors to perform the necessary steps in courseware preparation as simple as possible. The authors should be familiar only with fundamentals of working in MS Office. In addition, the forms for administration of static student and organizational data have been prepared.

In the remainder of this chapter we will present the main steps in the authoring process of the hypermedia courseware using AHyCo.

Creation of Hypermedia Lessons

The first step includes the creation of the set of hypermedia fragments FC_i (text, image, etc.) that represent the content of the lesson C_i (Figure 4). The lessons are stored in the database as Word, Excel, or PowerPoint objects, so the author could use the familiar Microsoft Office applications for preparation and updating. It is common that teachers already have some teaching materials in digital

Figure 4. MS Access form with Word OLE object containing the text of a lesson

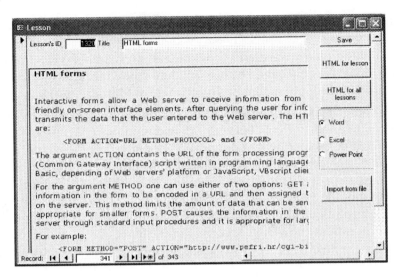

form, usually written in Microsoft Word or PowerPoint. The authoring interface enables them to import these materials and to prepare the courseware without knowing HTML.

The objects may contain hypertext, formulas, and smaller multimedia elements. Larger multimedia objects, such as video or audio clips, are stored separately and are connected to the lessons by hyperlinks. To enhance the performance of the system and to ensure better scalability, the lessons are also stored on the Web server as sets of HTML documents during this courseware preparation phase.

Creation of the Questions

A set Q_t of multiple-choice/single answer questions related to the lesson C_i is created during this phase. AHyCo distinguishes two types of questions: hypermedia questions and parameterized questions. A question may be associated to several lessons, with different difficulty levels q (Figure 5).

For simplicity for the authors, the sets $\mathcal{FQ}$ *(stem)* and $\mathcal{A}$ (the set of the offered answers) are grouped together as a specially structured Word object and stored in the database. Fragments $\mathcal{FQ}$ and $A_j \in \mathcal{A}$, are separated with bookmarks in the Word document.

Figure 5.   The form containing the hypermedia question

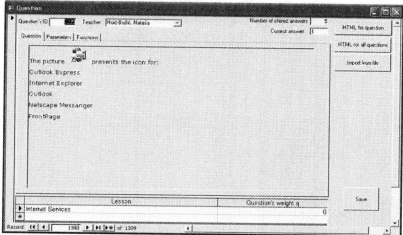

To enhance the performance of the system and ensure better scalability, the Word object is automatically partitioned in HTML fragments for $\mathcal{F}Q$ and A_j and stored on the Web server. The order of the fragments for answers A_j is created randomly, so the correct answer will not always be at the same position during the learning phase.

The parameterized questions allow the author to create an unlimited number of tests from the same set of questions and can help to eliminate cheating.

The stem $\mathcal{F}Q$ of the parameterized questions contains the parameters. Each answer A_j of the parameterized questions is a function f_j $(p_1, p_2, ..., p_n)$ that evaluates a candidate answer (Figure 6). Function f_j is defined in a scripting

Figure 6.   Stem and distracters of parameterized question

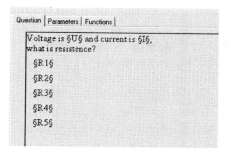

Figure 7. Evaluation of parameterized question's functions

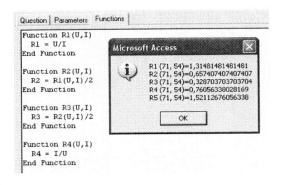

Figure 8. Test definition form

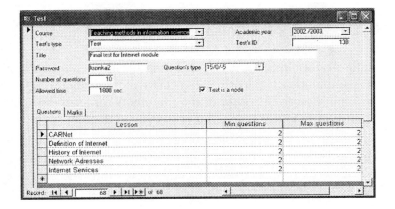

language and will be evaluated after the random generation of the parameters (Figure 7).

Design of the Tests

A test T_j is defined with: a set $\mathcal{PT}_j$ of prerequisite lessons, the total number n_j of questions in T_j, a set $\mathcal{N}_j$ of configuration rules that specify how many questions for each lesson $C_i \in \mathcal{PT}_j$ are placed into the test T_j (Figure 8). During the process of learning, tests will be created randomly, so explicit enumeration of questions is not necessary, only the structure of the test should be specified. The same test will consist of different set of questions for each student.

Figure 9. Module definition form

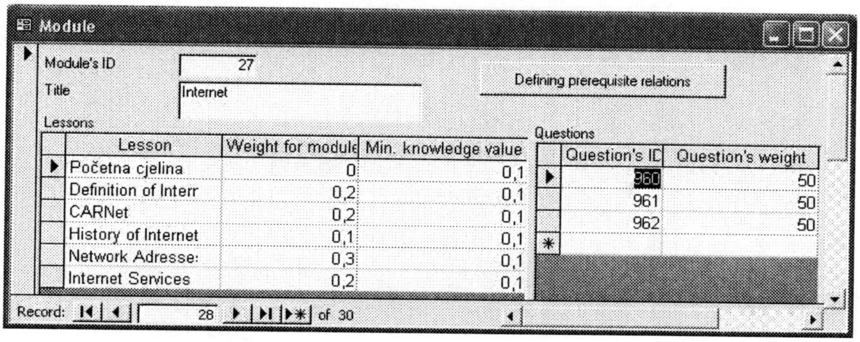

Creation of the Module

During this phase the author should define the set C_k of concepts that create the module M_k. For each lesson C_i, the weight $wc_i \in (0,1)$ as well as *the* minimum acceptable knowledge level for MYCIN model lMy_i are defined (Figure 9). If the courseware is created for the first time, the author usually sets the $lMy_i=0$. The lower or higher value can be introduced according to the students' results in gathering the knowledge.

Creation of the Concept Graph

The author creates the graph (C, LC) based on prerequisite relationships between the concepts (Figure 10). The author arbitrarily adds, deletes, or connects the nodes in the graph. For every concept $K_i \in C_k$ the rank R_i is calculated.

Creation of the Course

In this phase the course, i.e., the graph of modules (M, LM) is created, based on the prerequisite relationships between the modules. The minimum acceptable knowledge lm_k for each module is defined and the ranks for modules are calculated.

Figure 10. Creating the graph of concepts

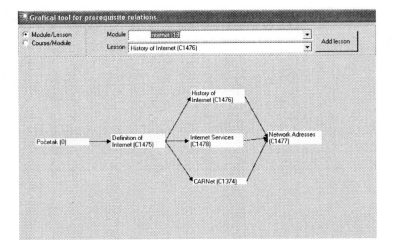

Definition of the Static Part of the Student Model

The author needs to create only the static part of the student model (e.g., student's name, login, and password) by using a separate Access form. The initialization of the dynamic part of student model (values r_i, k_l, km_k) is accomplished automatically so the author needs not to do it by himself.

Before the students start to learn, the author should join the group of students to the created course.

Results of *AHyCo* System Evaluation and Future Plans

The AHyCo system is currently being used in education of the students at the Faculty of Philosophy, University of Rijeka. The research has been conducted at the Department of Information Science on 19 senior students of information science in the context of the class "Teaching Methods in Information Science". A part of the class's subject matter has been presented as an AHyC's course. The course has been written in Croatian and consists of six modules.

The main goal of the system evaluation was to find out how the adaptation rules could be corrected according to the students' results in gathering the knowledge. According to the students' knowledge results, the teacher finds out possible shortcomings in the prepared learning materials. The teacher should also correct the adaptation rules. In that way the teachers/authors learn how to create and structure the learning material to use the system in a better way (Hoic-Bozic, 2002).

The purpose of the research was also to find out the students' attitude concerning AHyCo usage. The questionnaire about the effectiveness and quality of AHyCo and the level of students' acceptance of AHyCo as a teaching resource was prepared. The students were supposed to express their opinions on the 1-5 agreement scale, checking 5 if they strongly agree, 4 if they agree, 3 if they neither agree nor disagree, 2 if they disagree and 1 if they strongly disagree with the statement. According to the questionnaire results, the students accepted the new way of learning with AHyCo quite well. The results have shown that student consider tests as the most usable component of the system. The most interesting opinions are presented in the Table 1.

After the students had finished the learning with AHyCo, the evaluation of the system has been performed according to the students' knowledge levels about the concepts (k_i) and modules (km_k). The aim was to find out how to adjust the

Table 1. Questionnaire results

	Avg	StDev
AHyCo is easy to use	3.93	0.27
I like the *AHyCo* design	3.07	1.07
The text is readable and clear	4.14	0.53
Buttons and hyperlinks are obviously marked	3.50	1.09
Hyperlink offering is usable	3.71	0.73
I mostly followed the navigation guidance	4.07	1.00
I tried to solve all test	4.64	0.63
I am satisfied with work conditions (equipment, available time)	3.36	0.84
I am satisfied with new presentation methods	3.79	0.80
New presentation methods helps learning more efficiently	3.71	0.83
Compared to traditional teaching, *AHyCo* helps to learn more	2.93	0.92
Compared to traditional teaching, *AHyCo* requires more time to learn	2.21	0.70

variable part of the adaptation rules (the question weight q, the lesson weight wc_i, the MYCIN level lMy_i, the module level lm_k) and to verify if the prerequisite relationships were correctly defined.

By the basic statistical analysis (mean, median, standard deviation, and quartile values), the correlation coefficients for k_i and km_k, as well as by cluster analysis, recommendations for the authors have been proposed about the corrections of the adaptation rules.

As an example, we present some recommendations for adjustment of the prerequisite graph of concepts.

The first step is to compute correlation coefficients $r(k_i, k_j)$ and $r(k_i, km_k)$ and to perform cluster analysis for lessons of the module M_k. According to cluster analysis the author could:

- Remove or reformulate the isolated lessons that do not belong to any cluster
- Include the lessons that belong to less significant clusters into more significant clusters (significance is defined according to the author's opinion about the lessons content)
- Change the prerequisite relation for lessons in important clusters according to the following rules:

    1. For statistically significant ($p < 0.05$) and positive $r(ki, kj)$ if:

        $C_i \prec C_j$ - the prerequisite relation is correctly defined

        $C_i \nprec C_j$ - the author has to add the prerequisite relation according to rank

    2. For statistically significant ($p < 0.05$) and negative $r(ki, kj)$ if:

        $C_i \prec C_j$ - the author has to remove the relation

        $C_i \nprec C_j$ - the author has to analyze the lessons and possibly remove them from module.

- Redefine tests Tj so that the number of tests corresponds to the number of clusters

A similar approach is taken when proposing the adjustment of other adaptation rules (Hoic-Bozic, 2002).

The next step in our research will be to verify the proposed recommendations for the authors about the adjustment of the adaptation rules. We plan to change the developed courseware and to present it to the next generation of our students.

Conclusion and Future Trends

A lot of exploration has been done in the area of adaptive hypermedia during the recent years. This trend is expected to continue into the future. Many AHS have been developed, particularly for the educational purposes.

Until now, more attention has been devoted to the theoretical model than to the practical implementation. Especially, one could easily find out the shortage of the authoring tools for straightforward courseware preparation. Because of that, the AHS have not been widely accepted, in contrast to the courseware management systems with no adaptation features, like TopClass or WebCT (Robson, 1999).

In our opinion, the main trends in the AHS development will lead to the systems that would offer all the features of non-adaptive courseware management systems (preparation and delivery of the course materials, tests and quizzes, synchronous and asynchronous communication, student administration), in addition to the adaptive navigation and presentation. The tests in such systems are used not only for the knowledge level assessment, but also for the implementation of adaptive navigation.

The authoring component is crucial for an AHS. It should facilitate the courseware and test preparation, as well as the definition of the adaptation rules. A graphical editor for the concept networks should be an integral part of the system. This tool should enable the creation of relations among the concepts by a simple drag-and-drop interface. Only a user-friendly authoring component will attract sufficient number of users in schools and universities, making the system usable not only by specialized personnel.

In this chapter we have presented the AHyCo (adaptive hypermedia courseware) system for development and distribution of the adaptive Web-based courseware, with accent on the implementation of adaptation, as well as on the authoring component. A new approach to the process of authoring is described, which includes the development of both the learning materials and the rules for adaptation. We consider the proposed implementation is simple enough to attract even the teachers who are not IT specialists.

The authoring component is based on forms. It allows the definition of relatively independent and reusable knowledge concepts, which are arranged into a graph. The links between nodes in the graph denote the pedagogical constraints, i.e., prerequisite relationships. Prerequisite relationships enable the system to offer the best learning path for the students, taking into consideration the fact that reading of some concepts requires the understanding of one or more previous concepts. All of the information about the subject matter and the students is stored in a database.

The system includes a graphical editor of concept networks, so the authors are able to define connections between the concepts simply by placing concepts onto a working window and connecting them with a drag-and-drop interface.

Particular attention was committed to the definition of questions and tests. Together with a concept, a set of test questions is defined. Multiple-choice/single answer questions are associated to the appropriate lessons. The question text and the offered answers can be composed of multimedia fragments. To enlarge the diversity of the questions, it is possible to define a set of functions that will evaluate the candidate answers at runtime, upon the randomly generated parameters. Tests are created dynamically, according to the rules preset by the author, who defines how many questions that examine the knowledge of each lesson should be generated.

In order to verify the results, the sample courseware has been generated at Faculty of Philosophy, Rijeka. The main purpose of the evaluation was to find out how the adaptation rules could be adjusted according to the students' knowledge levels about the concepts and modules. According to the results of statistical analysis, recommendations for authors have been proposed about the corrections of the adaptation rules and improvements of the prerequisite graphs.

The students who had used the system have evaluated it favorably. The engagement of other teachers at Faculty of Philosophy who would prepare the courseware from diverse areas (math, physics, pedagogy, psychology, art, etc.) is planned. Based on their suggestions, the work on the authoring component will continue.

Acknowledgment

The research and development of the AHyCo system has been conducted under the projects "Adaptive Hypermedia Courseware" (reference number 2002-085) and "Computing support to education" (reference number 0036041), supported by Croatian Ministry of Science and Technology.

References

AHyCo Home Page (2003). Retrieved from http://ahyco.fer.hr/ (in Croatian).

Anjaneyulu, K. (1997). Concept level modeling on the WWW. *Proceedings of AI-ED 97 8th World Conference on Artificial Intelligence in Education, Knowledge and Media in Learning Systems*, Kobe, Japan.

Brusilovsky, P. (1996). Methods and techniques of adaptive hypermedia. *User Modeling and User-Adapted Interaction, 6,* 87-129.

Brusilovsky, P. (1999). Adaptive and intelligent technologies for Web-based education. *Künstliche Intelligenz, Special issue on intelligent systems and teleteaching, 4,* 19-25.

Brusilovsky, P. (2003) Developing adaptive educational hypermedia systems: From design models to authoring tools. In T. Murray, S. Blessing, & S. Ainsworth (Eds.), *Authoring tools for advanced technology learning environment.* Dordrecht: Kluwer Academic Publishers.

Brusilovsky, P. & Pesin, L. (1994). ISIS-Tutor: An intelligent learning environment for CDS/ISIS users. *Proceedings of the interdisciplinary workshop on complex learning in computer environments (CLCE'94),* Joensuu, Finland.

Brusilovsky, P., Schwarz, E., & Weber, G. (1996). ELM-ART: An intelligent tutoring system on World Wide Web. *Proceedings of the Third International Conference on Intelligent Tutoring Systems ITS'96,* Montreal, Canada.

Carver, A.C., Hill, J.M.D., & Pooch, U.W. (1999). Third generation adaptive hypermedia systems. *Proceedings of WebNet 99, World Conference on the WWW and Internet,* Honolulu, Hawaii.

Da Silva, D. P. (1998). Concepts and documents for adaptive educational hypermedia: A model and a prototype. *Proceedings of the 2nd Workshop on Adaptive Hypertext and Hypermedia HYPERTEXT'98,* Pittsburgh, PA.

De Bra, P. (1999, June). Design issues in adaptive Web-site development. *Proceedings of the 2nd Workshop on Adaptive Systems and User Modeling on the WWW,* Banff, Canada.

De Bra, P., & Ruiter, J. P. (2001). AHA! Adaptive hypermedia for all. *Proceedings of the WebNet Conference,* Orlando, FL.

De Bra, P., Aerts, A., Berden, B., De Lange, B., Rousseau, B., Santic, T., Smits, D., & Stash, N. (2003). AHA! The adaptive hypermedia architecture. *Proceedings of the ACM Hypertext Conference,* Nottingham, UK.

Eklund, J., & Brusilovsky, P. (1998). Individualising interaction in Web-based instructional systems in higher education. *Presented at The Apple University Consortium's Academic Conference,* Melbourne, Australia.

Henze, N., & Nejdl, W. (2000). Extendible adaptive hypermedia courseware: Integrating different courses and Web material. *Proceedings of Adaptive Hypermedia and Adaptive Web-Based Systems AH 2000,* Trento, Italy.

Hoic-Bozic, N. (2002). *Adaptive hypermedia courseware.* Ph.D. thesis, in Croatian, Zagreb: Faculty of Electrical Engineering and Computing, University of Zagreb.

Hoic-Bozic, N., & Mornar, V. (2003). An approach to adaptive hypermedia courseware authoring. *Proceedings of Hypermedia and Grid Systems, MIPRO 2003*, Opatija, Croatia.

Hoic-Bozic, N., Mornar, V., & Pukljak Zokovic, D. (2003). The model for testing in adaptive hypermedia courseware. *Proceedings of ITI 2003*, Cavtat, Croatia.

Kavcic, A. (2001). *Adaptation in Web-based educational hypermedia with regard to the uncertainty of user knowledge.* Ph.D. thesis, in Slovenian, Ljubljana, Slovenia: Faculty of Computer and Information Science, University of Ljubljana.

Maurer, H., & Scherbakov, N. (1996). *Multimedia authoring for presentation and education: The official guide to HM-Card.* Bon: Addison-Wesley.

Nakabayashi, K. (1997). Architecture of an intelligent tutoring system on the WWW. *Proceedings of the 8th World Conference of the AIED Society*, Kobe, Japan.

Ng, K., & Abramson, B. (1990). Uncertainty management in expert systems. *IEEE Expert, 2*(5), 29-47.

Robson, R. (1999). WWW-based course-support systems: The first generation. *International Journal of Educational Telecommunications, 5*(4), 267-269.

Specht, M., Kravcik, M., Pesin, L., & Klemke, R. (2001). Authoring adaptive educational hypermedia in WINDS. *Proceedings of ABIS 2001*, Dortmund, Germany.

Vassileva, J. (1997). Dynamic course generation on the WWW. *Proceedings of AI-ED 97 - 8th World Conference on Artificial Intelligence in Education*, Kobe, Japan.

Weber, G., Kuhl, H. C., & Weibelzahl, S. (2001). Developing adaptive Internet-based courses with the authoring system NetCoach. *Proceedings of Third workshop on Adaptive Hypertext and Hypermedia*, Sonthofen, Germany.

Wu, H., Houben, G., & De Bra, P. (1998). AHAM: A reference model to support adaptive hypermedia authoring. *Proceedings of the Conference on Information Science*, Antwerpen.

Chapter XII

Text-Col:
A Tool for
Active Reading

Anders Broberg, Umeå University, Sweden

Abstract

Traditionally, much of the efforts to develop computer-based tools has been concentrated on developing production or authoring tools, such as word processors, drawing programs, and so on, and not so many consumption or reading tools have been developed except Web browsers and different kinds of media players. Authoring plays an important role in the learning process, and good tools are needed, but reading—especially active reading— and exploring are is at least as important. Traditionally, computer-mediated texts have little support for an active way of reading. This means that reading computer-mediated texts, as on the WWW, tends to be a very passive form of reading. The development of Text-Col addresses this problem. Text-Col is a tool designed to support readers in deep processing of texts by letting the readers change appearance of the text based on different strategies for categorizing words. Text-Col is a reading tool and exploring tool aimed to make the reading process more active.

Introduction

The work that this chapter presents is founded in a view on learners as persons who continuously alter their conceptions and ideas by working with data, information and knowledge, i.e., to see the learners as knowledge workers. This view encourages the development of new tools aimed to support in a broad sense the learning process (Broberg, 2000). Text-Col is a reading tool aimed to make the reading process more active (see Figure 1). As a reading tool and exploring tool, it is designed to work together with standard WWW-browsers.

This chapter introduces and discusses Text-Col in order to give a sense of how one can support the readers to be more active in their readings. The first section discusses the pedagogical basis for the development of Text-Col. The second section presents the basic ideas and concepts for the Text-Col tool. The next section presents the application and the interface. After that is a section that discusses how the tool can be used. The last two sections present a study of some of the basic ideas of Text-Col and summarize the discussion about Text-Col.

Figure 1. The user interface of the Text-Col

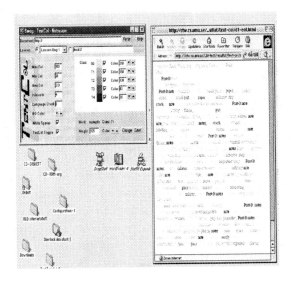

Phenomenological Approach to Learning

Learning as a phenomenon has always fascinated people in many different disciplines, and there are many theories and thoughts about what learning is. One can go as far back as to Plato (428 - 347 BC) to find theories of learning and knowledge (Phillips & Soltis, 1991). Greg Kearsley has built a database (Theory Into Practice) containing 50 theories relevant to learning and instruction (Kearsley, 1994); the theories in this database are all from the 20th century. The TIP-database gives a very broad view of learning theories. Hveem (1992) discusses learning and learning theories as widely different as Skinner, Piaget, cognitive science, and neural nets. Each single theory often focuses on a very particular concept, age, or topic to learn and are not so general. The purpose with this section is to discuss the phenomenological perspective learning, which is the theoretical basis for the design of *Text-Col*.

The area of pedagogy traditionally takes a positivistic and quantitative view on knowledge and learning, and much of the research in this area has been focused on the teacher side of the learning situation. The positivistic idea of knowledge implies that there always exists one right answer and all the others are wrong, and the quantitative view of knowledge implies that one measures knowledge in the amount of right answers. The phenomenological approach has quite a different view. From their point of view, knowledge is the understanding of phenomena, and learning is viewed as a process where these understandings are changed; this is a central principle. According to the phenomenological approach, it is possible to identify qualitative differences in understandings of phenomena. Consequently knowledge can be judged by its quality (Marton, 1974; Marton, Hounsell, & Entwistle, 1984).

Moreover, if one accepts the qualitative attitude to knowledge and learning, many interesting results from the phenomenological research on learning can be utilised in a model for a computer system that supports learning. Where active reading is one of the most salient characteristics that Marton et al. (1984) found when they made a study of the characteristics of depth directed studying.

A Phenomenological Approach on Active Reading

In the phenomenological approach knowledge is described in qualitative terms focusing on the message or the point in the text. In this context "text" has a very broad sense—it could be a written text, a talk, a video, or some other sort of presentation of information. They see knowledge as a comprehension or attitude to a phenomenon and they see learning as a change of comprehension and attitude to the phenomenon in question. But is it not the case that either one

Figure 2. The functional relations in the results from the TIPS-*project*

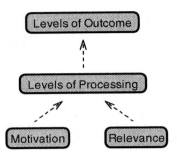

grasps the point of the text or not? And then we would still be stuck in the positivistic view. The answer is no, because it is possible to describe the understanding of the text in qualitative terms. The phenomenological research shows that it is possible to find clusters of subjects with same level of understanding of the text and these clusters form a hierarchy of *levels of outcome*. The number of levels of outcome depends on the character of the text and the phenomenon that is described in the text. The level of outcome depends on the learner's level of processing. The kind of motivation and the kind of relevance of the topic are two important factors that affect the level of processing, (see Figure 2).

The functional relationship between the level of outcome from the learning process and the strategy or the level of processing that the learners use, is the result from the phenomenological research which is the strongest and also one of the corners stones in the concept of active reading. Active reading in this perspective has at least four components:

- **Explore:** The ability to study the topic partly in the course material and partly by searching for material that is relevant in the learner's personal context (on one's own).

- **Form:** The ability to form and process the text: by adding notes, making references to other relevant material, by changing the structure of the texts, change the text to fit the learner's understanding and previous knowledge, and more.

- **Analyse:** The ability to analyse the topic and/or the intended meaning of the text, ask oneself processing questions, working with the structure of the text, or by analysing how oneself and other learners have worked or processed the material.

- **Administrate:** The ability keep track of the exploring, forming and analysing activities by administrating source references, recording how one have worked with the text, which questions one has asked oneself, and so on.

Text-Col: The Basic Concept

Reading documents from computer screens can be a very frustrating experience, and many prefer to print out a paper copy and read this version instead of reading directly from the monitor. There are several reasons for this behaviour. One common explanation is the difference in legibility between the two mediums: the paper version is more comfortable to read. Another explanation has more to do with the possibility or support the medium has for an active way of reading. Traditionally, computer-mediated texts have little support for an active way of reading. This means that reading computer-mediated texts, as on the WWW, tends to be a very passive form of reading, where the reading has more the characteristics of a scanning process (Broberg, 1999, 2000). The design process of the *Text-Col* tool addresses this issue. The focus for this work has been on the form and analyse components of active reading. The XLibris application from FX Palo Alto Laboratory is a computer artefact developed also with active reading in focus (Price, Schilit, & Golovchinsky, 1998). The main difference between XLibris and *Text-Col* is the focus that XLibris has on annotation and *Text-Col* has its focus on expressing and working with information value. Kosara, Miksch, and Hauser (2002) have developed a similar tool as *Text-Col,* but instead of using a grey scale to put word in the foreground/background, they use sharpness/blurriness.

To Support Active Reading

With computers and the Internet, totally new conditions for texts as medium for communication are set up. The Internet is an infrastructure that bridges various kinds of distances between authors and between readers, but also between authors and readers. It is very easy to make changes in computer-based texts both for readers and for authors, and the distribution of a new or different version of a text is quite easy. Hypertext exemplifies another feature that computers can add to the texts, the interaction. Hence, computer-mediated texts need not be as static as paper mediated texts. Our hypothesis is that it is good for the outcome from the reading process if this old, static view of text changes so that texts are viewed as entities that are more dynamic.

Metaphorically, to read solid black texts compared to grey-coded texts is like the difference in experience between driving a car on a superhighway at the same speed mile after mile and driving on a local curvy road. The driving culture or atmosphere differs. The superhighways are just a way to get from point A to B as fast and easy as possible, it is forbidden to stop at interesting sites, turn around, and so on. Therefore, if one is interesting to see and explore interesting sites, local roads are preferred. In the case of reading, instead of reading the text at almost constant speed (the highway style), to read texts where the saturation varying the reading speed follows these variations (the local road style), that is, with high reading speeds at lighter parts, lower reading speeds at darker parts.

Our hypothesis is that variation in saturation can be utilised in order to raise the level of activation in the reading process. We believe that readers of a grey-coded text both unconsciously and consciously react to the words' degree of saturation in relation to the way they comprehend the text. This will cause a deeper processing of the text than with a standard way of reading. The idea is that to react on the way a word is presented in a text it is necessary that the readers match the proposed way of interpreting the word with their own mental model or conception of the text. *Text-Col* offers the readers a more sophisticated and deliberate way of raising the level of activation of the reading process. Users of *Text-Col* can:

- Set or change a word to a category, and thereby they have performed an action that is related to the way they comprehend the text or a collection of texts.
- Select which of the categories of words that will be visible, and thereby actively explore texts.
- Select or change which kind of categorisation a text should be grey-coded with, thereby actively exploring texts from multiple perspectives.

To Express Differences in Information Value of Words

There are many systems for categorising words: general categorisations like parts of speech and more contextual categorisations like keywords for a topic, but also very personal categorisations or valuations of words exist. In other words, the information values of words differ between individuals, with the time, with the context, and so on. There are techniques to express differences in information value of words in a text, both techniques used by authors and techniques used by readers. There are typographic variations, such as **bold face**, *italic*, and <u>underlining</u> used by authors' to signal personal values of words or concepts. This gives the authors a nominal scale by which they can express eight categories of words, but without any form of order between the eight categories. It is almost the same situation for the readers. Readers utilise colour mark-up pens or underlining to record their personal values of words and concepts, and some readers use different colours to express their categorisations of words. The main difference compared to the author's situation, is the factor that limits the number of possible categories. For the readers it is the number of colours of their pens that sets the limit and for the authors it is the number of widely accepted typographical variations.

Norman (1991) argued for the importance of minimising the cognitive gap between a representation and the represented in order to get a natural interaction with artefacts. None of the methods, the readers' or the authors', offer the user a natural way to keep track of any kind of ordering between the categories of words. Hence, there is a risk for a mismatch or gap between the encoding and the interpretation. There are situations where it would be desirable if one as author or as reader had access to a natural way to express some kind of order between categories of words in texts—in other words, an ordinal scale to express or record categorisations of words—especially in learning situations where the text is viewed as a means to active learning.

Figure 3. Browser window with a Text-Col parsed document

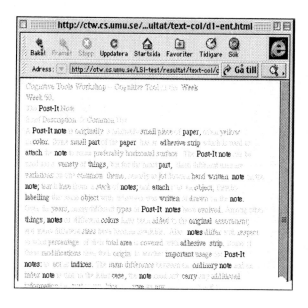

Text-Col utilises differences in contrast between the background and the words in a text. For texts on light backgrounds, words printed with higher degree of saturation is normally taken as words more worth or highly rated than words printed with a lower degree of saturation (see Figure 3). This creates an ordinal scale that can be used by *Text-Col* users to express categorisations of words and keep track of the order between them. The subjective part of the study of *Text-Col* verifies this idea.

Information Value Lexicon

Text-Col bases the grey coding of documents on information value files (IV-lexicon). An IV-lexicon is a data file containing information about a set of words. Each row in an IV-lexicon has three fields: <concept>, <code>, and <value>. The concept-field holds the entry word. The code-field is a parser-specific field (e.g., it can be used to hold part of speech information). The value field holds a numerical value used by *Text-Col* to place the word into a specific category.

One of the strengths of the Text-Col tool is the high degree of control that the user has over the behaviour. For example, it is very much up to the user to select the strategy by which the words are categorised. Some examples of strategies for categorisation of words are: key words for an area, the origin of words, the length, random, and so on. It is possible for a user of *Text-Col* to have a collection IV-lexicons. These IV-lexicons can model different areas of interest, different perspectives of an area of interest, and it is also possible to use shared IV-lexicons such as IV-lexicons authorised by an organisation, a colleague, friend, and so on. This feature gives the readers the possibility to easily walk between different readers' and persons' valuation of words or to set the text into different contexts.

There are several ways of constructing and editing an IV-lexicon. First, the simplicity of the format makes it possible to manually create and edit lexicons with the help of a simple text editor. Second, an IV-lexicon tool has been developed which lets the user construct IV-lexicons based on different strategies mostly derived from the areas of information theory and computational linguistics. IDF, information weight (Church & Gale, 1995), and entropy (Shannon, 1948) are some examples of strategies to base an IV-lexicon on. The motivation for this lexicon tool is the idea of modelling areas of interest or focus with the help of collections of documents. Modelling of knowledge is a comprehensive area of research within computing science, especially in the AI field. Broberg (1997) discusses different perspectives on knowledge and learning and some of the more traditional techniques for modelling knowledge such as rule-based systems and semantic networks. Generally, we are interested in ways of

Figure 4. The application window of Text-Col

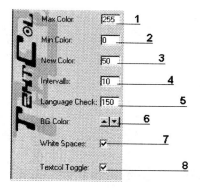

Figure 5. The parser control panel

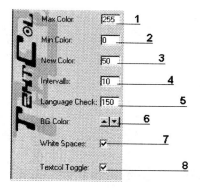

modelling personal interests or focus. Broberg (2000, 2001) discusses the character of focus as a complex entity, which is vague, personal, dynamic, and possible to describe in various levels. Third, *Text-Col* supports interactive editing of IV-lexicons, for example, one can change the weight of a word, delete a word from an IV-lexicon, and add a word to an IV-lexicon.

With this in mind, *Text-Col* is a tool designed to support the users with active reading (exploring collections of documents) by letting them work with different categorisations of words based on different foci and strategies.

Figure 6. The IV-lexicon control panel

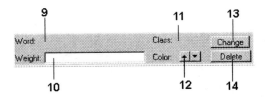

The Application

The purpose with this section is to discuss the functionality and user interface of the *Text-Col* tool. The *Text-Col* application window (see Figure 4) is divided into four distinct areas: an address field, a parser control, a colour control, and IV-lexicon control. The functionality of each of these areas is discussed below.

- **The Parser control panel:** In this part of the application window, the user can control some of the basic characteristics of the grey coding of a document. For example, set the colour for the highest/lowest ranked word category, and for words not in the current IV-lexicon; number of categories, and so on.

- **The IV-lexicon control panel:** In this part of the application window (see Figure 6), the user controls the current IV-lexicon with which the documents should be parsed. When the user clicks on a word in the browser window, information about the word is presented in this area: information about which category it belongs to and what colour (weight) it has. It is also possible to change which category a word belongs to. This can be done in two ways. First, by selecting one of the current categories—this means that the numerical value changes to the middle point for the new category. Second, it is possible to directly adjust the value in the <value-field>, which does not necessarily mean that the word moves to another category. These changes can be temporary or permanent, permanent meaning that one saves the changes to the current IV-lexicon. It is also possible to add/delete a word from the current IV-lexicon.

- **The colour control panel:** In this part of the application window, the user can adjust the grey levels for each of the categories of words (see Figure

Figure 7. The colour control panel

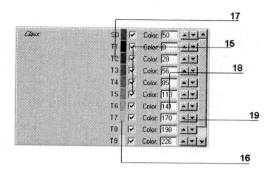

Figure 8. A document with only the two highest ranked categories visible and the white space flag set to off

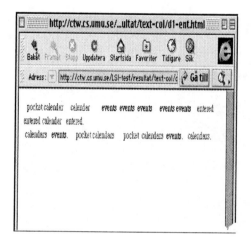

7), and also turn on and off the visibility of each of the categories in order to hide or show categories of words (see Figure 8 and Figure 9).

- **The address field:** In this part of the application window the user selects which document to parse and load and save IV-lexicon, and so on (see Figure 10).

Figure 9. A document with only the two highest ranked categories visible and the white space flag set to on

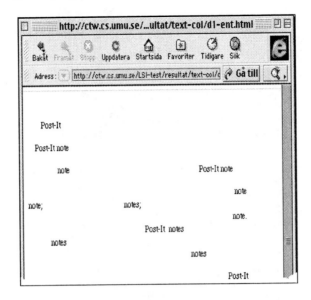

Figure 10. The address field

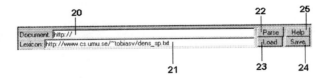

How to Use *Text-Col*

One of the basic characteristics of a tool is that its users develop their own ways of use and develop their skill in using the tool, by using it. For a new tool like *Text-Col* for which no rules, praxis, or community have been established, this is particularly true. Even if *Text-Col* is aimed to support readers/users to take a more active role in their readings of computer mediated texts, it is for these reasons very hard to predict how it will be used. From the very beginning ideas have existed about hypothetical uses and through the development of *Text-Col* new ideas of hypothetical uses of the tool have emerged. The purpose with this section is to give a broader picture of the *Text-Col* tool and the possibilities it has to support the reader by briefly discussing some of the ideas of alternative uses.

Virtual Mark-Up Pen

One of the major drawbacks with computer-mediated documents and especially WWW-based documents is the lack of possibilities to mark words or pieces of texts as interesting. *Text-Col* has the possibility to work as a kind of virtual mark-up pen by constructing an IV-lexicon consisting of those words that the reader picks out as being of particular interest. There are some major differences between the virtual version and its physical counterpart. First, the virtual pen offers the user an ordinal scale to be used for the classification of words and the physical only offers a nominal scale. Second, with *Text-Col* it is very easy to change to another IV-lexicon, that is, to change the strategy by which words in a document should be categorised. With a physical version, this is hard and time consuming. Third, once a word is marked or adjusted every occurrence of it is affected, where the particular IV-lexicon is used.

Exploring Tool for Meta-Information

We believe that meta-information and tools for processing meta-information play an important role in a learning situation—for the way a reader adjusts the conception or the understanding of a text or a collection of texts. For example, a document that has been conceived as very central can drop in ranking when one discovers that very few persons refer to that document. The way *Text-Col* works gives the users a possibility to work with meta-information. Working with IV-lexicons based on: the length of words, the origin of words, part of speech, and the age or date of introduction of words give information about the character or the genre of documents.

Text-Col gives the user/reader the ability to make meta-information-based visualisation of texts. The tool also offers the user/reader possibilities to actively explore meta-information in documents. For example, users have the possibility to visualise the same document with different kinds of IV-lexicons but also the other way around: keeping the IV-lexicon fixed and changing the document. This could be used to explore a set of documents and to see, for instance how different authors tend to use foreign words, extremely long words, and so on. *Text-Col* allows the user to interact with the document, for instance hide/show categories (see Figure 11), get information for a particular word, adjust a word's weight, and so on.

Figure 11. IV-lexicon based on word length parsed using itself as IV-lexicon, with only the longest words visible

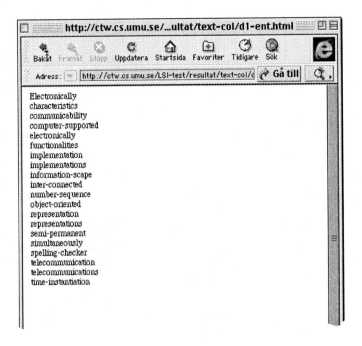

Indexing Documents

Very much of a knowledge worker's daily work is to find suitable information. Search engines play an important role in this process of seeking information. Even if a search engines has found documents that matches one's intentions it can be very tough to find where in a document the interesting parts are, and to extract the information that one has a special interest in (a focus). *Text-Col* can make it easier find where in a document the interesting parts are, visually the interesting parts stand out when words of interest are darker than other words. It is also possible to get a picture of how dense documents are by the intensity and the distribution—based on this one gets support to decide whether it is worth to read the document or not.

Looking for New Concepts

Documents with more than one author are common, and collaborative authoring demands a great deal of cognitive efforts from all involved. For example, to keep track of changes between revisions which new ideas, which new concepts are introduced and by whom concept is introduced. By utilising the fact that concepts that are not found in the current IV-lexicon are marked as a special category (S0), Text-Col can be used to find new concepts between different versions of a document. The feature that makes it possible to easily switch between different revisions of IV-lexicons makes it possible trace of the history concepts in a document.

A Legibility Study of Saturation Coding

The previous section introduced the *Text-Col* tool. This section presents an empirical study of one of the very basic ideas with *Text-Col*. The overall design criterion for the study was to evaluate how the grey coding of text affects the reading process. The primary target for the study was to get some preliminary answers to the question of how the fluctuations in saturation and the strategy behind the grey coding affect the readability/legibility. Of course, questions concerning learning effects are also important to study, and a secondary target for the study was to get some preliminary indications whether this way of coding text has any effects on the quality of the outcome from the reading process.

The Subjects

The study involved 90 subjects divided into three groups with 30 subjects in each group. There was one control group (group C), and two test groups (group A and group B). The subjects were randomly placed into the three groups. The subjects were mainly students and employees at Umeå University. There were 64 males, 24 females and two persons who did not state their sex. The majority judged their reading capability to be normal or good, and most of the subjects judged themselves as very experienced or experienced users of computers.

The Texts

Each subject read four texts. With regard to the content and the basic layout all 90 subjects read the same four texts. The variations between the groups was in the first and third text, where group A's texts were coded with information weights (Church & Gale, 1995), group B's texts were randomly coded, and the texts for the control group were all solid black. The second and the fourth text were both solid black texts for all groups. All four texts were in Swedish and taken from editorial and debate pages in Swedish daily and evening papers. The motive for this choice of texts was simple: the texts should have a clear message and a language that every subject should be familiar with. The mean length of the texts was 524 words, hence with a normal reading speed, the reading times for each of the texts should be in the range of one to four minutes.

The Procedure

The procedure was almost the same for all the subjects: they were invited to take part in a study of readability/legibility of texts from computer screens. All the subjects were informed about the procedure in the same way, that they would read four texts, and the way of measuring readability/legibility. They also knew that the reading time would be measured and that they would answer a questionnaire with questions about the content of one of the texts. There was one major difference in the procedure between the control group C and groups A and B. All the subjects in group A and B were interviewed about how it was to read the grey coded texts compared to solid black texts. This phase of the study was the last. The purpose of this interview was to collect ideas on how to utilise this kind of variation in saturation in the text. From an experimental point of view, this study was a between-subjects design with one independent variable to study.

The Objective Measure of Legibility

One common way of measuring changes in legibility is to study how the reading speed changes, that is, changes in number of words per minute. The ranking between the groups is the same for all texts, that is, on average group C reads faster than group A that reads faster than group B.

The question is: is any of the variance in means of reading speed between the groups significant? In order to evaluate this, four one-way ANOVA tests were performed (one for each text). The result from this is that the only text for which one can show any significance between variations in means is text 1, where

Table 1. A summary of one-way ANOVA-test for text 1. F(2.87)=2.78, p<0.1, Fcv= 2.37

Source	df	SS	MS	F
Between groups	2	36274	18138	
Within groups	87	566890	6516	2.78
Total	89	603164		

$F(2.87)=2.78$, $p<0.1$ $F_{cv}=2.37$. For all of the other texts $F(2.87)<F_{cv}$. and for text 2 and 3 $F(2.87)<1$. The results of the ANOVA suggest a significant difference among the means of reading speed of the three groups. Tukey's Honestly Significant Difference (HSD) is used to make pair wise comparisons among the means.

Tukey's HSD:

Equation 1 $$HSD_{.05} = Q_{.05}(3.87)\sqrt{\frac{MS_w}{n}}$$

Equation 2 $$HSD_{.05} = 2.8135\sqrt{\frac{6516}{30}} \Rightarrow$$

Equation 3 $$HSD_{.05} \approx 41$$

From equations 1 to 3 the smallest difference between any two means in the study that still is significant with a=.05 is 41.

Table 2. Differences between each pair of means in the legibility study of text 1

	C	A	B
C	–	28	49
A		–	20
B			–

It is only the difference between group B and C (the control group) that is significant, that is, greater than $HSD_{05} \approx 41$, (see Table 2).

The Subjective Measure of Legibility

In order to evaluate what influence the grey coding of texts has on the subjective experience of reading, the subjects answered questions related to how it was to read the grey coded text compared to solid black texts. There were questions concerning this both in the written questionnaire and in the interview. The first question in the interview was: concerning the layout, how was it to read the grey-coded texts compared to traditional texts? Figure 12 and Figure 13 show a difference between group A and group B. In group A, 52% of the subjects felt that it was easier to read the grey coded text than black texts, and 21% had a more neutral experience of reading the grey texts. Twenty-four percent of the subjects in group A felt that it was harder to read the grey-coded texts. For group B, the experiences of the subjects go in the opposite direction: 52% felt that it was harder or much harder to read the grey coded texts than solid black texts, and 17% had a neutral experience. Twenty-one percent of the subjects in group B had a positive experience of reading grey coded texts.

Figure 12. The subjective experience of the difference between reading grey coded texts and solid black (group A)

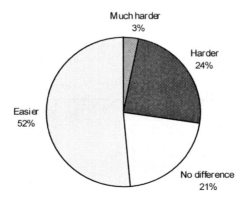

Figure 13. The subjective experience of the difference between reading grey coded texts and solid black (group B)

Group B

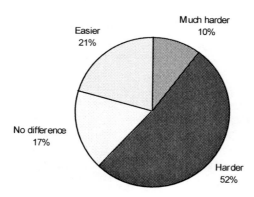

Another question in the questionnaire which also concerned the readers' subjective experience of reading grey-coded texts was: with respect to the layout of the text, do you have any comments about how it was to read it?

Almost every subject in both groups had comments about the grey coding of the texts, but there is a clear difference between the two groups. The majority of the comments from group B are negative and the majority of the subjects from group A have a positive attitude in their comments.

The negative comments from group B are stronger than those from group A, and they are unanimous: it is hard to keep the flow in the reading, and it is common that the readers are forced to jump back in the text, (see Citation 1). Even the positive comments are quite unanimous between the subjects, and many of the comments give an expression of a factor of familiarisation when reading grey coded texts. Also, it is common in this category with comments about the use of the saturation level to express some kind of information value for the words, (see Citation 2).

Citation 1. Examples of negative comments; the first four are from group B and the last is from group A (all the comments are translated from Swedish)

"Got stuck on the words with the lowest level of saturation. It was hard to get continuity in the text."

"Hard to read the words that were grey shaded in combination with solid black words."

"Horrible, it was terribly irritating with characters that disappear, consequently one was forced to read the same pieces several times when one loses the thread."

"The words that were marked with solid black disturb and get a stronger meaning than they normally should have."

"It is quite clear that it was heavier going with some of the words in a higher level of saturation than other words. In the beginning it was heavy, but after a while I became used to it."

Citation 2. Examples of positive comments; the first five are from group A and the last is from group B (all the comments are translated from Swedish)

"First, I thought it was real unpleasant, but when I got used to it, it became to feel quite good to read with different levels of saturation ..."

"It was of the difference s comfortable to read, but one felt that the black colour words were amplified, which sometimes was against one's own comprehension."

"It felt a little unfamiliar to read a text with different levels of saturation, but anyway it was quite nice to read. It was easier to keep track where one was in the text..."

"Very pleasant for the eyes, felt easier to read...."

"It does not feel so uncomfortable, but it is clear that one sometimes get stuck on words with a higher level of saturation. At the same time they make it easier to grasp the meaning of the text if the keywords are marked."

"Very readable, nicer to read with grey-levels. Good flow in the reading, it was not so compact."

The Learning Effects

Even if the primary target of the study was to test the effect on legibility, part of the study concerned learning effects—is it possible to identify any significant differences between the groups in terms of: comprehension, recall test of important words, and word recognition? Half of the subjects in each group performed the word recognition test and the other half performed a word recall test.

In the word recall test, the subjects were asked to list a number of representative words from the text. To find any significant differences between the groups in this part is hard, but some interesting indications are possible to identify. More of the subjects in group A than the other two groups tend to give words that exist in the text and are marked with a relatively high information weight. For example, *women* ("kvinnor") is a high-rated word for both group A and B, and 87% in group A had *women* among their words, but only 40% in group B and 33% in group C.

The Interview

As mentioned earlier there were mainly two purposes with the interview part of the study: to catch ideas and to get comments on the experience from reading grey-coded texts. The subjects' attitudes to a demo of a prototype implementation of *Text-Col* are mainly positive. Also, it is possible to identify a clear difference between subjects of group A and B in how they respond to a question concerning a hypothetical use of *Text-Col*.

- In group A, it was more common with comments on a hypothetical use of *Text-Col* where the subjects discuss in terms of "reading for comprehension" or "grasp the meaning of the texts".
- In group B, it was quite common to discuss a hypothetical use of *Text-Col* in terms of indexing, scanning, and browsing texts.

Discussion of the Results

The basic idea with *Text-Col* is to amplify the reading process of on-screen texts by utilising the level of saturation to express differences between information values of words. The amplifying of the reading process has not so much to do with increase of reading speed; instead it concerns the quality of the outcome from the reading process in terms of conception. Therefore, the small negative impacts of the objective legibility are not to be considered as a negative result for us, especially when the responses from the subjects were mainly positive.

When the reader read random-coded text for the first time, it was the only condition where the difference in means was significant. One possible explanation is that humans are very good at adapting to current circumstances, but in the long run we believe that no one would prefer to read randomly coded texts compared to texts with a more normal look. There is proof for that in the study.

The evaluation in subjective terms of the impact on the legibility from the variations of the level of saturation shows a big difference between group A (texts coded with information-weight) and group B (texts randomly coded) in how they perceive the reading of the coded texts. That means that the semantic content of the coding has effects on the legibility. On a direct question about how it was to read the coded texts compared to solid black texts, group A had mainly a positive attitude to the coding of the texts, group B had mainly a negative attitude. Also in a more open question about the reading experience from coded texts there was the same relation between the groups, with many positive comments from group A and few negative and vice versa from group B. A tentative conclusion from this is that although it may reduce the reading speed, many readers prefer grey-coded texts to traditional solid black texts, but they must be coded with some relevant strategy/method like keywords or information weight.

To summarise, "good" reading is more important than high reading speed.

Summary

Two relevant questions are, what is it that makes *Text-Col* a cognitive tool for learning, and how is the functionality of *Text-Col* anchored in the knowledge worker approach? Broberg (2000) discusses different kinds of cognitive tools for learning and the ideas behind. From this, it is possible to relate the underlying mechanisms for learning in the cognitive tools for learning approach to the theoretical suppositions of the knowledge worker approach (Broberg, 1997).

First, in the phenomenographic view of learning and knowledge the level of activation in the learning process and the factors of relevance and motivation are important for the level of outcome from the learning process (Marton, 1974; Marton et al., 1984). Second, one of the common characteristics of cognitive tools for learning is that they all offer the learners the ability to create, process, and view knowledge structures, that is, learners as knowledge workers learn by working with information, data, and knowledge.

One of the basic ideas with *Text-Col* is to function as a tool for working with computer-mediated texts in a structural way, which in some sense anchors it in the knowledge worker approach. In addition, texts and corpora can be viewed as a kind of micro-world, with words, paragraphs, and other linguistic constructions as building blocks. This qualifies *Text-Col* as a cognitive tool for learning in the same manner as hypertext, micro-worlds, and so on are classified as cognitive tools for learning. The grey coding of texts and the possibility to manipulate with these are stressed as important elements serving to raise the activity level of the reading process, and thereby important for how the tool supports changes in readers' conceptions (the texts in the study were static and there was no way for the subjects to change the appearance of the texts).

The data in the study that supports *Text-Col* as a cognitive tool for learning are found in the subjective part of the study. Even if the data that confirm the hypothesised underlying learning mechanisms supported by *Text-Col* and the basic ideas of the knowledge worker approach are few, there is nothing in the data that refuses the basic ideas; therefore, the results from the study encourage us to proceed with the development of *Text-Col*.

Part of this work is more studies and experiments. We are already in the next phase with experiments with new ways of coding texts, where we incorporate a more sophisticated parser, both in the creation phase of IV-lexicons and in the reading tool (Björkäng, 2000). Now when we know that the grey-coding does not have any greater impact on the reading speed and many readers have a positive attitude to variations in the level of saturation, the next step of *Text-Col* will be more focused on learning effects, and on evaluations of the hypothetical positive effects for the outcome from the reading process that we believe *Text-Col* can give.

References

Björkäng, J. (2000). *Part of speech tagging with markov models in Text-Col: A tool for extracting information values of word.* Unpublished Master Thesis, Umeå University, Umeå.

Broberg, A. (1997). *Cognitive tools for learning.* Licentiate Thesis No. UMINF 97.18. Umeå: Umeå University.

Broberg, A. (1999). *A case study on knowledge workers view of computers.* Technical report No. UMINF 99.xx. Umeå: Department of Computing Science.

Broberg, A. (2000). *Tools for learners as knowledge workers.* Unpublished Doctoral, Umeå University, Umeå.

Broberg, A. (2001). *Some thoughts on using context awareness for enhancing knowledge work environments.* Paper presented at the UM 2001.

Church, K. W., & Gale, W. A. (1995). *Inverse document frequency (IDF): A measure of deviation from poisson.* Paper presented at the Third Workshop on Very Large Corpora, Massachusetts Institute of Technology, Cambridge, USA, June 30.

Hveem, P. (1992). *Computer aided learning, simulation, and electrical motor drives.* Unpublished Doctoral Thesis, Norges Tekniska Høgskole, Trondheim.

Kearsley, G. (1994). *The Theory Into Practices (TIP) database.* Retrieved from http://gwis2.circ.gwu.edu/%7Ekearsley/

Kosara, R., Miksch, S., & Hauser, H. (2002). Focus+context taken literally. *IEEE Computer Graphics and Applications, 22*(1), 22-29.

Marton, F. (1974). Inlärning och studiefärdigheter (No. 121): Pedagogiska institutionen Göteborgs Universitet.

Marton, F., Hounsell, D., & Entwistle, N. (1984). *The experience of learning (Vol. 1).* Scottish Academic Press.

Norman, D. A. (1991). Cognitive artifacts. In J. M. Carroll (Ed.), *Design interaction, psychology at the human-computer interface* (pp. 17-38). Cambridge: Cambridge University Press.

Phillips, D. C., & Soltis, J. F. (1991). *Perspectives on learning (Vol. 1).* New York: Teachers College Press.

Price, M. N., Schilit, B. N., & Golovchinsky, G. (1998). *XLibris: The active reading machine.* Paper presented at the CHI'97.

Shannon, C. E. (1948). A mathematical theory of communication. *Bell System Technical Journal, 27*(July and October), 379-423 and 623-656.

Uljens, M. (1992). *What is learning a change of?* (No. 1992:01). Department of Education and Educational Research University of Göteborg.

Section IV

Approaches to Integration

Chapter XIII

From Non-Adaptive to Adaptive Educational Hypermedia:
Theory, Research, and Design Issues

Michael J. Jacobson, National Institute of Education,
Nanyang Technological University, Singapore

Abstract

In this chapter, it is argued that research involving adaptive educational hypermedia will be advanced by attention to two main areas: (a) the articulation of principled design features for adaptive hypermedia systems and (b) rigorous research documenting the learning efficacy of particular design approaches for different domains and learner groups. As an example of design and research in these two areas, a case study of a program of hypermedia research related to the knowledge mediator framework (KMF) is provided. First, a discussion of non-adaptive KMF hypermedia design elements and learning tasks is provided, followed by a short overview of the research findings from studies involving the use of different KMF systems. Next, current efforts are discussed to create adaptive KMF hypermedia using a learning agent module that employs semantic assessment and learner modeling in order to provide adaptive content and adaptive learner scaffolding. A general consideration of theory, research, and methodological issues related to current work in the field of adaptive educational hypermedia is also provided.

Introduction

The use of hypermedia technologies for learning in conjunction with collaboration technologies (or e-learning, as some have construed such approaches) has the potential to transform globally the infrastructures of education. Anywhere, anytime access to distributed information resources, online Web courses offering accredited degrees or subjects of personal interest and enrichment, corporate training, and professional development are but a few of the areas that employ at the core technologies involving the use of hyperlinks to interconnect digitally encoded nodes of text, multimedia, dynamic computer models, and potentially even immersive "virtual reality" simulations.

However, despite the pervasive and increasing use of hypermedia technologies for educational applications, a critical look at the research into learning with hypermedia systems raises important issues. Although there have been empirically successful examples of educational hypermedia systems, many earlier systems have been criticized for being atheoretical and for focusing on technical issues rather than those of learning and cognition (Jacobson, 1994). There has also been widespread criticism of methodological flaws in much of the hypertext and hypermedia literature (Dillon & Gabbard, 1998; Shapiro & Niederhauser, 2003; Tergan, 1997). More recently, of relevance to themes in this volume, there have been proposals to address problems with educational hypermedia through the use of "adaptive hypermedia" that employ techniques derived from work on artificial intelligence and intelligent tutoring systems (Brusilovsky, 1996, 2001). Unfortunately, as pointed out in a recent comprehensive review of the literature related to learning with hypertext and hypermedia that included a section on adaptive hypermedia work (Shapiro & Niederhauser, 2003), no studies to date have rigorously documented the educational effectiveness of adaptive hypermedia approaches (although the review authors comment further work in this area is warranted).

Given these concerns about current research related to adaptive educational hypermedia, it is argued in this chapter that future work in this area will be advanced by attention to two main areas:

- The articulation of principled design features for adaptive hypermedia.
- Careful and rigorous research documenting the learning efficacy of particular design approaches for different domains and learner groups.

Further, given much of the work on adaptive hypermedia has been developed in the information systems, computer science, and engineering communities, it will be important that these two design and research areas also be informed by theory, research, and principles from the science of learning. Research in this area, that integrates cognitive science and educational research, has been rigorously exploring various dimensions of competent human performance, cognition, learning, and teaching for nearly 50 years (National Research Council, 2000).

In order to illustrate how learning science-based design principles and research methods may be employed in educational hypermedia research and development projects, this chapter discusses as a case study a program of research related to the knowledge mediator framework (KMF) (Hynd, Jacobson, Reinking, Heron, & Holschuh, 1999; Jacobson, 2004; Jacobson & Archodidou, 2000a, 2000b; Jacobson, Maouri, Mishra, & Kolar, 1996; Jacobson & Spiro, 1991, 1995). This chapter first provides an overview of KMF hypermedia design elements and learning tasks, followed by a short overview of the research findings from three major studies involving the use of different KMF systems. Next, current efforts are discussed to create adaptive KMF hypermedia using a learning agent module that employs semantic assessment and learner modeling in order to provide adaptive content and adaptive learner scaffolding. The chapter concludes with a general consideration of theory, research, and methodological issues related to current work in the field of adaptive educational hypermedia.

KMF Hypermedia Tools for Learning

KMF hypermedia systems provide a set of hyperlinked resources that support learning activities in which a student receives special types of scaffolding in order to enhance the learning of conceptually challenging knowledge. KMF hypermedia systems are not intended to "deliver" content per se or to "cover" entire curricula. Rather, these systems are intended to be one of many tools and resources in the overall learning environment (e.g., books, papers, Web-based resources, intelligent tutoring systems, collaborative interactions with more experienced peers or experts, discussions and lectures, laboratory equipment,

Figure 1. Schematic of main the functional elements for non-adaptive Knowledge Mediator hypermedia

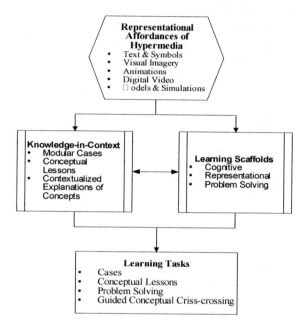

inquiry, or project-based activities) that may be used to achieve the difficult learning goal of deep and flexible knowledge building in various subject areas.

The framework is also intended to help address the need of instructional designers who must confront the often difficult challenge of bridging from general theory and research principles to specific design features for useable systems (Jacobson, 1994). The original framework, briefly described in this section, was articulated for non-adaptive hypermedia technologies, and significant conceptual change and knowledge transfer outcomes have been found in research involving the use of these KMF systems (Jacobson & Archodidou, 2000a; Jacobson et al., 1996; Jacobson & Spiro, 1995). Current R&D efforts, discussed below, are integrating an intelligent learning agent to create adaptive KMF systems that it is hoped will be even more effective tools for learning.

Non-Adaptive Knowledge Mediator Framework Functional Elements

The primary functional elements in non-adaptive KMF hypermedia systems are represented schematically in Figure 1. Three of these elements—Representational Affordances of Hypermedia, Knowledge-in-Context, and Learning Scaffolds—are design features for the link-node organization of KMF hypermedia systems. The fourth element, learning tasks, refers to specific types of learning activities that are optimized for these design features. The arrows in the figure are intended to depict the interconnected ways in which the design features reinforce each other, yet the one way directional flow of information from a non-adaptive hypermedia system to the learner and the learning activities.[2] These KMF features, which are based on a series of studies over the past several years (Hynd et al., 1999; Jacobson, 2004; Jacobson & Archodidou, 2000a, 200b; Jacobson et al., 1996; Jacobson & Spiro, 1991; Jacobson & Spiro, 1995), are discussed in turn.

Representational Affordances of Technology

The top box in Figure 1 shows the first KMF design element, Representational Affordances of Hypermedia.[3] Given the power of modern personal computers and globally networked servers, hypermedia may be viewed as a powerful "meta-technology" for learning in which links and nodes permit the flexible integration of a variety of digital representations of knowledge using text and symbols, visual images, animations, video, and computer models and simulations (Jacobson & Archodidou, 2000a). Thus the Representational Affordances of Hypermedia design element provide the digital resources that are available to the two other major functional elements of the framework, Knowledge-in-Context and Learning Scaffolds.

Knowledge-in-Context

The middle left box in Figure 1, Knowledge-in-Context, represents a fundamentally important element of KMF hypermedia systems. This emphasis on the contextual aspects of knowledge is inspired by a significant transformation in perspectives on the nature of competent human performance, expertise, cognition, and learning that has been occurring over the past quarter century (National Research Council, 2000). Rather than regarding knowledge as a "thing" in the mind of an individual, knowledge is increasingly being viewed as a constructed phenomena that emerges in specific contexts and situations (Brown, Collins, & Duguid, 1989; Clancey, 1993; Cognition and Technology Group at Vanderbilt, 1990; Lave & Wenger, 1991; Vosniadou, 1996).

One way in which knowledge is represented in contexts in KMF systems is through a library of modular cases and lessons. The KMF uses hypermedia to richly represent cases in order to provide learners with a variety of computer-

Figure 2. Screen from the Gulf of Tonkin Knowledge Mediator with menu showing the four text cases and subsections

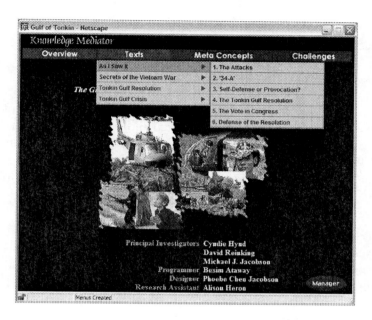

mediated contexts in which to see and to apply knowledge. For example, in the hypermedia, evolution, and conceptual change study (Jacobson & Archodidou, 2000a, 2000b; Jacobson, Sugimoto, & Archodidou, 1996), four contrasting cases of evolutionary biology were employed, while in the Gulf of Tonkin Incident study (Hynd et al., 1999), four conflicting texts with modular subsections were authored (see Figure 2). Multiple concise cases (that may be primarily text or combinations of text with multimedia, simulations, computer models, and so on) are employed as the primary type of learning anchor in KMF systems as they provide knowledge for students to learn in rich yet cognitively manageable contexts. The cases are authored to be contrasting in terms of surface features while sharing important structural conceptual components of the particular domain of study.

Note that there is an important difference in terms of how KMF cases are authored and used compared to other case-based learning (CBL) approaches (Jacobson & Archodidou, 2000a). In the KMF, multiple relatively short, modular cases are used to embed the organized conceptual knowledge to be learned. In contrast, many CBL approaches use detailed cases studied individually to illustrate particular sets of concepts or principles. However, with such approaches, there is the danger for students (even at the graduate level) that the principles or concepts learned in separate, individual cases may become "inert" knowledge and thus be difficult to apply or transfer to new situations (Thompson, Gentner, & Loewenstein, 2000).

Learning Scaffolds

The middle box on the right of Figure 1 depicts the three main types of Learning Scaffolds that have been used in KMF hypermedia systems: cognitive, representational, and problem solving.[4] An important thematic strand in recent learning science research has been perspectives on scaffolding and learning, in particular scaffolding provided by technological tools (Collins, Brown, & Newman, 1989; Guzdial, 1995; Jackson, Krajcik, & Soloway, 2000; Jacobson, Angulo, & Kozma, 2000). Yet despite recommendations that scaffolding be incorporated into hypermedia in order to foster significant learning outcomes (Tergan, 1997), there are been relatively few reports of scaffolding techniques in the hypermedia research literature (Azauedo et al., in press).

Cognitive scaffolding refers to ways that important conceptual aspects of the material being learned are made cognitively salient to the user. This type of scaffolding is provided in several ways in KMF hypermedia. KMF systems employ a "top-down" and "bottom-up" treatment of the organized conceptual structure in a particular subject. Typically, a set of concepts, themes, ideas, principles, and so on are specified by the author that reflect important perspectives in the area of study. For example, in the Gulf of Tonkin Knowledge Mediator, which had the goal of helping students learn to "think like a historian," four "meta concepts" were employed: sourcing, context, agreement, and disagreement (Hynd et al., 1999). Figure 3 shows the pull down menu list of hyperlinks to the meta concepts, with the general explanation of disagreement shown in the popup window.

To convey contextual aspects of the concepts or themes, KMF systems provide "expert-like" explanations for how abstract concepts apply in the context of various case sections using "deep structure commentaries." Figure 4 shows the deep structure commentary for the "disagreement" abstract concept on the right side of the screen in the second section of the *As I Saw It* text. In another case text, such as Phillip B. Davidson's *Secrets of the Vietnam War*, the deep structure commentary for "disagreement" is quite different, as he asserts there was virtually no evidence that the Gulf of Tonkin attack even occurred. (Texts for this program were authored or edited by Dr. Cyndie Hynd.)

Of course, it is important for learners to be able to understand important abstract concepts and ideas in a domain. However, the main rationale for the contextualized explanations of abstract concepts is based on a significant body of learning science research that has consistently shown novice and intermediate learners

Figure 3. Gulf of Tonkin Knowledge Mediator screens showing abstract concept list and node with discussion of meta concept "disagreement"

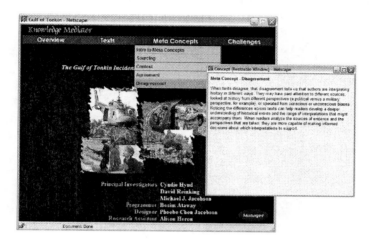

have great difficulty in applying or seeing the relevance of abstract concepts to problems or situations (Chi, Feltovich, & Glaser, 1981; Chi, Glaser, & Farr, 1988; Gentner, 1983; Gick & Holyoak, 1987; National Research Council, 2000). Thus the deep structure commentaries serve not only as important information but also provide cognitive scaffolding for the learner.

Representational scaffolding builds on the capability of KMF hypermedia to depict knowledge using various representational forms in the cases and conceptual lessons. Given research that has documented how experts exhibit representational flexibility when working in professional settings (Kozma, 2000; Kozma, Chin, Russell, & Marx, 2000), the ability to create hypermedia learning materials with a variety of representations that are appropriately linked potentially may help learners develop their understanding of and skills with the representational forms of a discipline. Helping students to develop representational flexibility thus could be an important compliment to the cognitive learning of domain knowledge with hypermedia. However, just as the atheoretical use of hypermedia based materials has not generally lead to significant learning gains compared to non-hypermedia based controls (Dillon & Gabbard, 1998; Jacobson, 1994; Neuman, Marchionini, & Morrell, 1995; Shapiro & Niederhauser, 2003; Tergan, 1997), merely providing a wide range of representations to learners is unlikely to foster representational flexibility. Rather, careful authoring and scaffolding must be provided to learners so that the linked representations are grounded in an organized conceptual framework and embedded in problem solving and knowl-

Figure 4. Example of a deep structure commentary that explains how the abstract meta concept "disagreement" applies in a text by former Secretary of State Dean Rusk

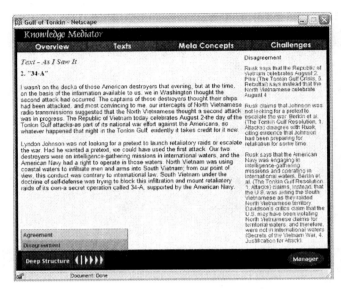

edge building learning activities requiring the use of the representations and the related conceptual knowledge (Kozma, 2000).

For example, in a new KMF hypermedia system being developed to help students learn emerging conceptual perspectives from the study of complex and dynamical systems, one of the cases deals with how ants forage for food (see Figure 5). This case includes not only text and pictures of ants, but also links to an embedded agent-based computer model of ants foraging for food with a color coded representation of varying concentrations of a chemical ants use to communicate with each other (which is, of course, invisible to the human eye when observing ants) and dynamically created graphs related to running the model (Wilensky, 1998).

Another type of representational scaffolding is the use of cognitive visualizations. A cognitive visualization (CV) provides a dynamic visual representation of a learner's or an expert's mental model about a particular problem or phenomena (Jacobson, 2004; Jacobson & Archodidou, 2000a). In contrast to concept maps that provide a schematic of the conceptual organization an individual might have about a domain, CVs provide both a representation of a particular knowledge structure (e.g., a learner's preconceptions or an expert's organized cognitive framework) and a runnable visualization of the consequences of applying a particular representation to a problem.

Figure 5. Screen examples of representational scaffolding in which texts, photos, computer modeling, and quantitative graphing are interlinked

 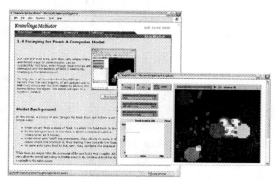

For example, Figure 6 shows a screen from a CV that was used in the evolution, hypermedia, and conceptual change study (Jacobson & Archodidou, 2000a; Jacobson et al., 1996). The subjects ran this CV of a common Lamarckian preconception about how evolution works (i.e., a species is largely homogeneous, the species "tries" to evolve to meet some environmental "need") as well as a second CV of an expert neo-Darwinian view of evolution by natural selection. After running the two CVs, the high school subjects in the study were asked which of the visualizations was closest to the way they thought about evolution. Out of eight subjects, six selected the Lamarckian preconception, which was consistent with other online, written, and verbal protocol problem solving data that indicated these students thought about evolution problems in a non-Darwinian manner. This pilot testing of a CV embedded in a hypermedia system suggests that the approach may be used to help identify a learner's "way of thinking" and thus could be used in conjunction with other techniques for assessing the learner model as part of adaptive hypermedia systems.

Scaffolded problem solving is a third type of scaffolding used in KMF hypermedia systems. This type of scaffolding is integrated into the Learning Tasks component of the framework. For example, one approach to scaffolding or supporting the learner's problem solving is the Problem Solver module,[5] which employs what may be called "non-intelligent AI" (Nathan & Resnick, 1994). The Problem Solver module is based on cognitive research into the nature of the conceptual representations that learners at different age and developmental levels commonly use when solving problems. However, no attempt is made for the system to use AI knowledge representation techniques such as production rules to construct intelligent models of the user, subject area, or pedagogy. Rather, Problem Solver employs an algorithmic approach to provide the learner with a set of possible solution statements to a given problem in which some of the statements are consistent with common preconceptions, some statements are consistent with expert understandings, and some statements are neutral. It was hypothesized that learners would select those statements consistent with the mental models they construct in their open ended problem solutions.

Figure 7 shows an example of the Problem Solver used in the evolution, conceptual change, and hypermedia study (Jacobson & Archodidou, 2000a, 2000b). The learner in this example was asked: "How did giraffes get their long necks?" From the randomly arranged, cognitively based statements on the left side of the screen, the learner would select statements she wanted to use in her response and copy them to the right side of the screen. She could then rearrange the statements to be in a preferred order, and also "unselect" a statement by moving it back to the left side of the screen. Clicking on the "Finished" button, the algorithm in Problem Solver would total up the values associated with the selected statements (coded "+1", "-1", and "0" for "expert," "naïve," and "neutral" respectively), and then a popup window would provide feedback.

A second type of scaffolded problem solving is provided as part of guided conceptual-criss crossing for the challenge questions. In this approach, the learner is given a question to answer and then provided a set of conceptually-based links to portions of the cases, conceptual lessons, concepts, and deep structure commentaries in the hypermedia system that are relevant to answering the challenge (see the section *KMF Learning Tasks* below for a fuller

Figure 6. Screen from a cognitive visualization of a common "Lamarckian" preconception of evolution

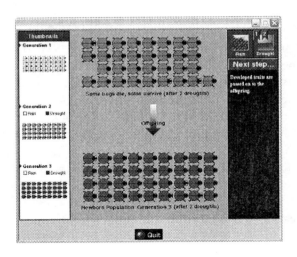

discussion). In this approach, the conceptually-based links are the scaffolds, as it is assumed novice and intermediate learners will have difficulty seeing how the conceptual structure being learned applies across contrasting cases and materials in the hypermedia library.

Selected KMF Learning Tasks[6]

The final functional element of a KMF hypermedia system is Learning Tasks, the bottom box shown in Figure 1. As noted above, KMF hypermedia are intended to help learners achieve specific learning goals, in particular, constructing solid understandings of important conceptual dimensions of a domain and the ability to apply these understandings to new problems and situations. To achieve these learning goals, a set of learning tasks have been employed in the research projects to date that involve the functional elements in KMF hypermedia systems discussed above.

There are four main types of learning activities in KMF systems: cases, conceptual lessons, problem solving, and guided conceptual criss-crossing. The first, cases, provides the learner with a set of contrasting cases that contain the abstract and case-specific explanations of concepts, figures and images, online problems, animations, digital video clips, and/or computer models and simulations. Second, conceptual lessons are carefully authored materials dealing with important concepts, themes, ideas, and/or principles in the area of study. These multimedia lessons include interactive elements such as Problem Solver and cognitive visualizations. Special conceptual lessons provide cognitive preparation by directly focusing on naïve ideas or pre-conceptions learners are likely to have in certain domains. Cognitive preparation conceptual lessons are particularly important when there is reason to believe that students may have ways of thinking about the area of study that are qualitatively different from experts, such as a Lamarckian view of evolution (Bishop & Anderson, 1990; Samarapungavan & Wiers, 1997) or an impetus mental model of the movement of physical objects (Hestenes, Wells, & Swackhamer, 1992). Cognitive preparation lessons incorporate techniques that have been found to help foster conceptual change, such as online problem solving activities to make the learner's ideas explicit, illustrate gaps or deficiencies in these ideas, and seed the new ideas and concepts that are relevant to the cases in a particular KMF unit of study (Jacobson & Archodidou, 2000a). Overall, the activities in cases and conceptual lessons allow the learner either to begin to construct or to enrich their understandings of the organized conceptual structure of the domain and the application of these ideas in multiple case contexts.

Figure 7. Scaffolded problem solving with the problem solver module

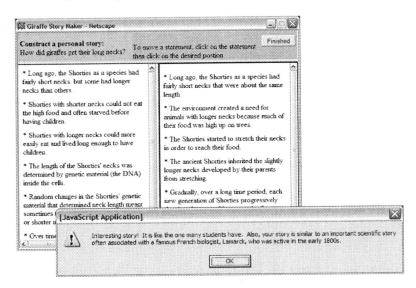

The third type of learning task in KMF hypermedia systems is problem solving. Problems for the learner may be presented using modules such as problem solver (discussed above) that cognitively scaffold the learner's solution as well as multiple choice and/or true-false items. A new technique for computer scoring of open ended problem solving responses, latent semantic analysis,[7] is also being explored in new KMF research projects (see section *Knowledge Mediator and Adaptive Hypermedia*).

The fourth learning task, guided conceptual criss-crossing, is actually a special type of problem solving with cognitive scaffolding (see section *Learning Scaffolds* above) that involves inter-case explorations of the cases and conceptual resources in the KMF library. Guided conceptual criss-crossing provides the learner with a problem or challenge question that requires the integration of knowledge distributed across multiple cases and conceptual lessons in the KMF hypermedia knowledge base. A set of conceptually-based links are provided for the challenge questions that are intended to support "expert-like" non-linear navigation through the cases, conceptual lessons, abstract concepts, and context specific concept commentaries.

An example of guided conceptual criss-crossing is shown in Figure 8 from the Gulf of Tonkin KMF system (Hynd et al., 1999). This figure shows the second challenge question dealing with Agreement and Disagreement issues in the source texts (these are two of the four meta concepts associated with how a historian thinks about history, in contrast to student thinking about history as the memorization of facts). The window lists the challenge question, relevant meta concepts, and a set of conceptually-based hyperlinks for non-linear navigation to different sections of the program relevant to the conceptual dimensions of the question. The availability of the conceptually-based hyperlinks to selected content nodes in the KMF hypermedia functions as a type of cognitive scaffolding for initial and intermediate learners in a particular subject area.

Overview of KMF Research

The design elements and learning activities of the Knowledge Mediator Framework have been the focus of three main studies investigating the learning of conceptually challenging knowledge in different domains (Jacobson & Archodidou, 2000a; Jacobson et al., 1996; Jacobson & Spiro, 1991, 1995). These studies each involved the use of the respective systems for periods ranging from five to seven hours spread over two weeks. The assessments of learning included measures of declarative knowledge acquisition (i.e., factual information in the case and conceptual lesson materials) and solving novel problems in order to document changes in conceptual understanding and the ability to transfer knowledge to new situations.

Social Impact of Technology Hypertext and Transfer Study 1

While the first Social Impact of Technology study (Jacobson & Spiro, 1991, 1995) predated the articulation of the KMF (Jacobson & Archodidou, 2000a, 2000b), it employed several of the design elements now included in the KMF (e.g., reify the deep structure of knowledge with organized abstract domain concepts and contextualized explanations of these concepts, guided conceptual criss-crossing). The study empirically tested the effects of the cognitive scaffolding associated with guided conceptual criss-crossing in the experimental condition with a computer-based drill being used by the subjects in the comparison condition. The subjects were university students who used the hypertext system that consisted of six cases dealing with the social impact of technology and six major themes or abstract concepts in this area that were identified from the literature. The subjects read a hypertext case or two per session followed by the experimental intervention during a "study period" in which the experimental group used the guided conceptual criss-crossing treatment that provided nonlinear links on conceptual connections across the case sections, while the comparison group used a computer based drill that provided practice on learning declarative knowledge in the cases. Not surprisingly, one of the study's findings revealed that the main comparison drill group scored significantly higher on the tests of factual recall. In terms of the performance on the problem solving essay transfer tasks, which dealt with social impact of technology problems not studied in the study's hypertext case materials, there was no difference between the two groups after two sessions. However, by the end of the second week of the study (four session), the experimental group scored significantly higher on the transfer task. This finding demonstrated the efficacy of guided conceptual criss-crossing and suggested that learners need time in order to construct useable understandings of challenging knowledge before being able to apply that knowledge to novel problem situations.

Social Impact of Technology Hypertext Study 2

In a follow-up study funded by the Spencer Foundation, the same content was employed as the earlier study (Jacobson et al., 1996). In a similar format as before, the subjects read a hypertext case or two per session followed by the experimental intervention during a "study period." However, the focus of this study was on issues related to the degree of scaffolding and the degree of learner control. To explore these issues, the experimental and comparison conditions consisted of three different types of linking structures: (a) open hyperlink access that provided high learner control and low cognitive scaffolding (i.e., essentially like the majority of links on the Web), (b) learner selected conceptual criss-crossing that provided moderate learner control and moderate cognitive scaffolding, and (c) guided conceptual criss-crossing that provided low learner control and high cognitive scaffolding (i.e., essentially the same treatment as in the first Social Impact of Technology Hypertext study). In the second condition, learner selected conceptual criss-crossing provided the subjects with problem questions that would require information from selected case sections that had been read, and then a search engine in which the subjects would select a concept or set of concepts they felt were related to the questions. The system then would generate a filtered list of links to those case sections that had been indexed with the specific concept or concepts.

The original hypothesis was that learner selected conceptual criss-crossing would result in higher transfer scores due to additional depth of processing associated with determining relevant concepts and moderate degree of learner control. Surprisingly, the subjects in the open hyperlink access and the learner selected conceptual criss-crossing conditions scored higher on the declarative knowledge acquisitions items, while the guided conceptual criss-crossing group scored significantly higher on the knowledge transfer problem scenario essay than either of the other two conditions. The interpretation of these findings concluded that since the subjects were novices in the domain of the social impact

Figure 8. Guided conceptual criss-crossing screen from the Gulf of Tonkin Knowledge Mediator hypermedia system

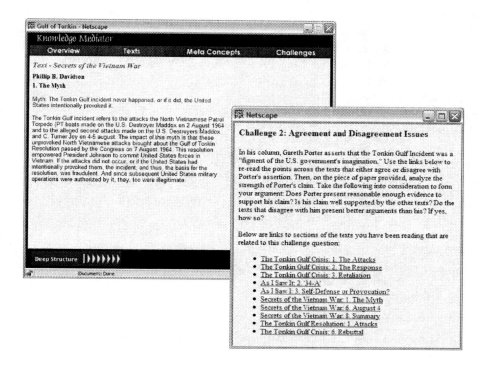

of technology, those subjects in the no and low scaffolding conditions (open hyperlink access and learner selected conceptual criss-crossing) tended to focus on the surface features of the cases during the study period (like novices in other cognitive research), hence their higher scores on the declarative knowledge tests. In contrast, the guided conceptual criss-crossing subjects were being scaffolded by the system to make non-linear connections based on conceptual dimensions of knowledge across multiple case contexts. As a result, it was proposed that these learners had constructed a deeper, more flexible, and more integrated understanding of the hypermedia content that better prepared them for knowledge transfer tasks. As in the earlier study, the significant differences between the groups did not appear until the end of the second week of using the system, a finding that again suggests there is a gestation period necessary for learners to build knowledge understandings they can transfer to new problems.

Hypermedia, Evolution, and Conceptual Change Study

This study, which was funded primarily by the Applications of Advanced Technology program at the National Science Foundation, involved a complete redesign of the experimental hypermedia system and the articulation of new design elements and learning activities such as scaffolded problem solving, cognitive visualizations, and cognitive preparation and conceptual lessons (Jacobson & Archodidou, 2000a; Jacobson & Spiro, 1997; Jacobson et al., 1996). The main study with the new system involved a within subjects design with eight students taking a high school biology class. The biology class had not yet covered evolution at the time of the study. The hypermedia system consisted of four contrasting cases of evolutionary biology and five core concepts associated with neo-Darwinism that included all of the KMF design elements discussed above. As in the earlier studies, the subjects used the system during a two week period over four sessions for a total of about five to six hours of system time. Learning was assessed in several ways, including verbal protocols while problem solving, written essays, short answer factual questions, and computer logs of online scaffolded problem solving profiles (i.e., problem solver module). An evolution mental model framework was developed and validated to code the verbal and written problem solving solutions in terms of component ideas related to novice preconceptions and expert neo-Darwinian concepts.

The data revealed that six of the eight subjects had preconceptions that were predominately "Lamarckian," that is, they believed evolution occurred, but they thought a species was homogeneous in terms of its traits (e.g., all ancient giraffes had short necks, all modern giraffes have long necks) and that evolutionary changes were purposeful and teleological. After two weeks of working with the system for approximately six hours, six of the subjects were solving difficult evolution problems that had not been previously studied with predominantly modern scientific conceptual answers, and two subjects employing "synthetic" solution models that had components of both neo-Darwinian and Lamarckian conceptions (i.e., they had integrated or learned some of the new conceptual knowledge, but they still had not undergone a complete process of conceptual change).[8]

Another important finding emerged from a follow-up evolution problem solving study a year after the initial study (and six months after the end of the biology class). This study involved six of the students who worked with the evolution hypermedia system and six students who had taken the same biology class but who had not worked with the system. Although all students in the follow-up study received "A" or "B" grades in the class, none of the control students solved any of the evolution problems using neo-Darwinian models, while all of the experimental students did (even the two who had used synthetic models at the end of the first study) (Jacobson & Archodidou, 2000a).

Knowledge Mediator and Adaptive Hypermedia

Thus far in this chapter, a discussion has been provided of a program of research into design features and studies of learning involving non-adaptive KMF hypermedia systems. This section discusses current planning efforts to create adaptive KMF hypermedia by integrating a Learning Agent module that employs semantic assessment and learner modeling in order to provide adaptive content and adaptive learner scaffolding. The schematic for the functional areas of the new adaptive KMF hypermedia is shown in Figure 9. As a comparison with Figure 1 shows, essentially an adaptive KMF hypermedia system has the same functional elements as the older non-adaptive KMF systems, but with a Learning Agent module consisting of four components integrated into the system (represented by the diamond box in Figure 9). However, integrating the learning agent into KMF hypermedia also mediates bi-directional flows of system information between the learning tasks, Knowledge-in-Context, and Learning Scaffolds elements of the system, as shown with the bi-directional arrows, rather than just a unidirectional flow of system information from Knowledge-in-Context and Learning Scaffolds to the learner involved with the activities in learning tasks.

The first component of the Learning Agent will provide semantic assessment of the learner's online problem solving activities using new types of cognitively-based assessment technologies such as latent semantic analysis (see above, footnote 7) and artificial neural networks (National Research Council, 2001). These techniques will compliment the assessment use of the non-AI based Problem Solver and cognitive visualization modules discussed above. The use of semantic assessment technologies will allow a KMF hypermedia system to obtain a principled indication of the learner's conceptual understanding to inform the learner model that goes beyond what can be inferred from the use of just multiple choice and true/false items. This enhanced learner modeling capability will be very important given the cognitively challenging subject areas for which KMF hypermedia systems may be developed (e.g., complex scientific and social systems, bio-medicine, history, economics).

Based on the learner model classification during a session, the Learning Agent will adaptively provide content nodes and types of Learning Scaffolds. For example, a learner who solved an online problem about evolution using a Lamarckian model would, in an adaptive KMF hypermedia system, be provided with an integrated set of selected evolution concepts, conceptual lessons, cases, scaffolded problems, and challenge questions for guided conceptual-criss crossing that are suited for an introductory stage learner studying evolutionary biology. In contrast, an adaptive KMF system would provide a student with an advanced stage learner model with a different set of more advanced evolution concepts and conceptual lessons (perhaps covering areas such as exaptation or punctuated equilibrium), different and/or more detailed case content, and less scaffolding during learning tasks.

Another way that the learning agent could adaptively vary the content is through the use of "conceptual and content overlays" that would add new concepts to previously studied cases and/or elaborations to the content initially presented in particular cases. For example, during the first or second session in an adaptive KMF hypermedia learning module, the student might have a core set of three to four concepts and three cases to learn with. However, during the third or fourth session, an additional set of more advanced concepts could be provided to the learner with more details added to the three initial cases as well as two new cases. In this way, an adaptive KMF hypermedia system could provide resources that support trajectories of enhanced and enriched learning as well as provide additional challenges to learners in ways that a non-adaptive system simply could not.

Adaptive Hypermedia:
General Issues and Perspectives

This chapter has discussed a program of research involving the knowledge mediator framework as a case study in which various design, research, and methodological issues related to non-adaptive and adaptive hypermedia systems and learning were considered. This section transitions from the specifics of the KMF case study to a more general discussion of research and methodology concerns in current work on adaptive educational hypermedia systems.

In reviewing a number of papers on adaptive hypermedia applied to education (e.g., Beaumont & Brusilovsky, 1995; Brusilovsky, 1996, 2001; Brusilovsky & Eklund, 1998; Brusilovsky & Pesin, 1998; Weber & Specht, 1997), it appears that the adaptive hypermedia research to date has been thoughtful and technically very sophisticated, however there are few references to important theoretical and research perspectives emerging from the cognitive and learning sciences that are transforming our understanding of how the mind learns and how to

Figure 9. Schematic of main functional elements for adaptive knowledge mediator hypermedia

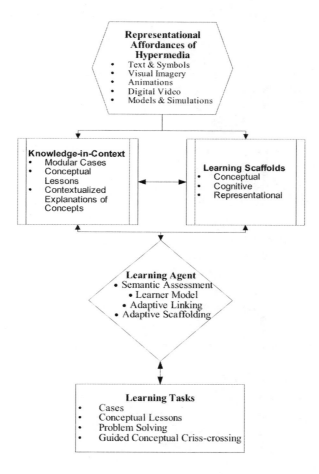

construct effective learning and teaching environments (both technological and non-technological) that foster deep understanding (National Research Council, 2000, 2001). Principles from learning science research that could enhance work on adaptive educational hypermedia include:

- Provide contextualized learning based on multiple real world problems, cases, and situations.

- Provide scaffolds and tools to enhance learning and metacognitive skills.

- Consider the preconceptions and prior knowledge of the learners engaged in learning activities.

- Support learning by doing, rather than learning by telling and showing.

- Foster thoughtful collaborations amongst local and even global communities of learners.

- Assess learning using measures of reasoning, understanding, complex problem solving, and knowledge transfer, not just in the recall of factual information.

Conceptualizing educational hypermedia from the perspective of research based principles for learning such as these could lead to the development of new classes of hypermedia—both adaptive and non-adaptive—that would have solid prospects for achieving significant learning goals.

There are also potentially exciting ways that adaptive hypermedia approaches might be integrated with computer supported collaborative learning (Koschmann, 1996). While adaptive hypermedia research has so far focused on individual cognition and learner models, there would seem to be rich research opportunities to explore how an adaptive system might model distributed cognition across multiple learners who are using adaptive hypermedia resources as part of collaborative knowledge building activities.

Given the importance of user modeling in adaptive hypermedia, researchers in this area should head the advice of Brusilovsky (2001) to explore new AI and non-AI symbolic technologies that show promise in providing an estimate of the learner's understanding, such as concept graphs, machine learning, statistical models, and adaptive natural language generation, and non-AI approaches such as case-based reasoning, Bayesian models, and neural networks. Another approach, discussed above, that should be explored for use in adaptive hypermedia is latent semantic analysis (LSA) (Landauer, Foltz, & Laham, 1998; Magliano & Millis, 2003). The possibility of using techniques such as LSA to embed open ended, machine scoreable, formative assessment items has the potential to greatly enrich the quality of the learner model the system can construct. It also has the potential to expand current adaptive modeling techniques that construct a single model of the goals, preferences, and knowledge of the user and employ it throughout the interaction with the system (Brusilovsky, 1996) to having the system determine learner models that might evolve during the course of learning (particularly learning over extended periods of weeks or months). This would be particularly important given cognitive research into conceptual change that suggests in many domains, learners go through a series of transformations in their mental models about difficult domain concepts, progressing from initial preconceptions through one or more synthetic models, and only then to more expert understandings (Vosniadou & Brewer, 1992, 1994; Wiser & Carey, 1983). Of course, for any of these potential user modeling techniques, there must be research to show their validity and reliability before being used in a particular adaptive educational hypermedia systems.

Finally, it will be important for research on adaptive educational hypermedia to attend to methodological issues. As mentioned at the start of this chapter, a recent review of the literature on hypertext and hypermedia in education concluded that there were methodological problems in the research to date involving adaptive educational hypermedia systems (Shapiro & Niederhauser, 2003). It is hoped that research methodologies used to investigate cognitively based hypermedia, such as in the KMF hypermedia systems discussed above, and other types of learning science-based technological learning systems (Jacobson & Kozma, 2000), might provide methodological models for adaptive hypermedia research involving systems for learning. The comprehensive synthesis of research on assessment by the National Research Council (2001) should also be of value in planning rigorous research into learning with adaptive hypermedia technologies. Overall, attention to theoretical, research, and methodological issues such as those discussed in this section should compliment and enhance adaptive hypermedia research coming from the engineering, information science, and computer science communities that involve systems intended for use in educational and training settings.

Conclusion

This chapter has discussed critical issues that have been raised in the literature related to design, research, and use of adaptive hypermedia systems in education. To address these issues, it was argued that attention should be paid to two centrally important areas: (a) the articulation of principled design features for adaptive hypermedia, and (b) rigorous research documenting the learning effectiveness of particular design approaches. It was also argued that adaptive educational hypermedia work should be strongly informed by theory, research, and principles from the science of learning to compliment the perspectives of researchers in this area from more technical fields. The core of the chapter discussed, as a case study, the knowledge mediator framework program of hypermedia and learning research that is based on learning science design and research perspectives, and current efforts to create adaptive KMF hypermedia systems. A general consideration of theory, research, and methodological issues related to current work in the field on adaptive educational hypermedia approaches was also provided.

In closing, this is an exciting developmental phase for research involving advanced designs for educational hypermedia systems, in particular, for designs involving intelligent and adaptive approaches. There appear to be great opportunities for cross-fertilization between engineering and computer science advances dealing with the technological functionality of globally distributed hypermedia and intelligent systems with research-based perspectives involving cognition, learning, and the design features of effective learning technologies. Given the complexities of human learning, we are still at a relatively early stage of research involving hypermedia technologies for learning, whether adaptive or non-adaptive, even as technological efforts are ongoing that are globally transforming the infrastructures of education. Nonetheless, there is a continuing need for systematic and rigorous research on learning with adaptive and non-adaptive hypermedia systems and their integrated use with other types of collaborative and learning technologies. It is hoped aspects of the research discussed in this chapter might contribute to ongoing efforts to develop robust and effective technological systems and infrastructures that empower transformative learning.

Acknowledgment

The preparation of this chapter has been supported in part by the Center for Teaching and Learning at Korea University. Research projects by the author that were discussed in this chapter have been support in part by grants from the National Science Foundation (RED-9253157 and RED 9616389), Allison Group, Spencer Foundation, The University of Georgia, and the University of Illinois at Urbana-Champaign.

References

Allen, B. S., & Otto, R. G. (1996). Media as lived environments: The ecological psychology of educational technology. In D.H. Jonassen (Ed.), *Handbook of research for educational communications and technology* (pp. 199-225). New York: Simon & Schuster Macmillan.

Azevedo, R., Cromley, J. G., & Seibert, D. (in press). Does adaptive scaffolding facilitate students' ability to regulate their learning with hypermedia? *Contemporary Educational Psychology.*

Beaumont, I., & Brusilovsky, P. (1995). Educational applications of adaptive hypermedia. In K. Nordby, P. Helmersen, D. J. Gilmore, & S. A. Arnesen (Eds.), *Human-computer interaction* (pp. 410-414). London: Chapman & Hall.

Bishop, B. A., & Anderson, C. W. (1990). Student conceptions of natural selection and its role in evolution. *Journal of Research in Science Teaching, 27*(5), 415-427.

Brown, J. S., Collins, A., & Duguid, P. (1989). Situated cognition and the culture of learning. *Educational Researcher, 18*, 32-42.

Brusilovsky, P. (1996). Methods and techniques of adaptive hypermedia. *User Modeling and User Adapted Interaction, 6*(2-3), 87-129.

Brusilovsky, P. (2001). Adaptive hypermedia. *User Modeling and User Adapted Interaction, 6*(2-3), 87-110.

Brusilovsky, P., & Eklund, J. (1998). A study of user model based link annotation in educational hypermedia. *Journal of Universal Computer Science, 4*(4), 428-448.

Brusilovsky, P., & Pesin, L. (1998). Adaptive navigation support in educational hypermedia: An evaluation of the ISIS-tutor. *Journal of computing and Information Technology, 6*(1), 27-38.

Chi, M. T. H., Feltovich, P. J., & Glaser, R. (1981). Categorization and representation of physics problems by experts and novices. *Cognitive Science, 5*, 121-152.

Chi, M. T. H., Glaser, R., & Farr, M. J. (Eds.). (1988). *The nature of expertise.* Hillsdale, NJ: Lawrence Erlbaum Associates.

Clancey, W. J. (1993). Situated action: A neuropsychological interpretation response to Vera and Simon. *Cognitive Science, 17*, 87-116.

Cognition and Technology Group at Vanderbilt. (1990). Anchored instruction and its relationship to situated cognition. *Educational Researcher, 19*(6), 2-10.

Collins, A., Brown, J., & Newman, S. (1989). Cognitive apprenticeship: Teaching the crafts of reading, writing, and mathematics. In L. Resnick (Ed.), *Knowing, learning, and instruction* (pp. 453-494). Hillsdale, NJ: Lawrence Erlbaum Associates.

Dillon, A., & Gabbard, R. (1998). Hypermedia as an educational technology: A review of the quantitative research literature on learner comprehension, control, and style. *Review of Educational Research, 68*(3), 322-349.

Gentner, D. (1983). Structure mapping: A theoretical framework for analogy. *Cognitive Science, 7*, 155-170.

Gibson, J. J. (1979). *The ecological approach to visual perception.* New York: Berkeley Publications Group.

Gick, M. L., & Holyoak, K. J. (1987). The cognitive basis of knowledge transfer. In S. M. Cormier & J. D. Hagman (Eds.), *Transfer of learning: Contemporary research and applications* (pp. 9-46). New York: Academic Press.

Guzdial, M. (1995). Software-realized scaffolding to facilitate programming for science learning. *Interactive Learning Environments, 4*(1), 1-44.

Hestenes, D., Wells, M., & Swackhamer, G. (1992). Force concept inventory. *The Physics Teacher, 30*(March), 159-166.

Hynd, C., Jacobson, M., Reinking, D., Heron, A., & Holschuh, J. (1999). *Reading like a historian: Development of cross-text intertextuality and disciplinary knowledge in a hypertext environment.* Paper presented at the 1999 annual meeting of the American Educational Research Association, Montreal, Canada.

Jackson, S., Krajcik, J., & Soloway, E. (2000). Model-It: A design retrospective. In M. J. Jacobson & R. B. Kozma (Eds.), *Innovations in science and mathematics education: Advanced designs for technologies of learning* (pp. 77-115). Mahwah, NJ: Lawrence Erlbaum Associates.

Jacobson, M. J. (1994). Issues in hypertext and hypermedia research: Toward a framework for linking theory-to-design. *Journal of Educational Multimedia and Hypermedia, 3*(2), 141-154.

Jacobson, M. J. (2004). Cognitive visualisations and the design of learning technologies. *International Journal of Learning Technologies, 1*(1), 40-62.

Jacobson, M. J., Angulo, A. J., & Kozma, R. B. (2000). Introduction: New perspectives on designing the technologies of learning. In M. J. Jacobson & R. B. Kozma (Eds.), *Innovations in science and mathematics education: Advanced designs for technologies of learning* (pp. 1-10). Mahwah, NJ: Lawrence Erlbaum Associates.

Jacobson, M. J., & Archodidou, A. (2000a). The design of hypermedia tools for learning: Fostering conceptual change and transfer of complex scientific knowledge. *The Journal of the Learning Sciences, 9*(2), 149-199.

Jacobson, M. J., & Archodidou, A. (2000b). The knowledge mediator framework: Toward the design of hypermedia tools for learning. In M. J. Jacobson & R. B. Kozma (Eds.), *Innovations in science and mathematics education: Advanced designs for technologies of learning* (pp. 117-161). Mahwah, NJ: Lawrence Erlbaum Associates.

Jacobson, M. J. & Kozma, R. B. (Eds.). (2000). *Innovations in science and mathematics education: Advanced designs for technologies of learning*. Mahwah, NJ: Lawrence Erlbaum Associates.

Jacobson, M. J., Maouri, C., Mishra, P., & Kolar, C. (1996). Learning with hypertext learning environments: Theory, design, and research. *Journal of Educational Multimedia and Hypermedia, 5*(3/4), 239-281.

Jacobson, M. J., & Spiro, R. J. (1991). Hypertext learning environments and cognitive flexibility: Characteristics promoting the transfer of complex knowledge. In L. Birnbaum (Ed.), *The International Conference on the Learning Sciences: Proceedings of the 1991 Conference* (pp. 240-248). Charlottesville, VA: Association for the Advancement of Computing in Education.

Jacobson, M. J., & Spiro, R. J. (1995). Hypertext learning environments, cognitive flexibility, and the transfer of complex knowledge: An empirical investigation. *Journal of Educational Computing Research, 12*(5), 301-333.

Jacobson, M. J., & Spiro, R. S. (1997). *Learning and applying difficult science knowledge: Research into the application of hypermedia learning environments (Final report to the National Science Foundation Applications of Advanced Technologies program)*. Athens, GA: The University of Georgia, Learning and Performance Support Laboratory.

Jacobson, M. J., Sugimoto, A., & Archodidou, A. (1996). Evolution, hypermedia learning environments, and conceptual change: A preliminary report. In D. C. Edelson & E. A. Domeshek (Eds.), *International Conference on the Learning Sciences, 1996: Proceedings of ICLS 96* (pp. 151-158). Charlottesville, VA: Association for the Advancement of Computing in Education.

Kintsch, W. (1998). *Comprehension: A paradigm for cognition*. Cambridge: Cambridge University Press.

Koschmann, T. (1996). *CSCL: Theory and practice on an emerging paradigm*. Mahwah, NJ: Lawrence Erlbaum Associates. (CSCL is an abbreviation for Computer Supported Collaborative Learning.)

Kozma, R. B. (2000). The use of multiple representations and the social construction of understanding in chemistry. In M. J. Jacobson & R. B. Kozma (Eds.), *Innovations in science and mathematics education: Advanced designs for technologies of learning* (pp. 1-46). Mahwah, NJ: Lawrence Erlbaum Associates.

Kozma, R. B., Chin, E., Russell, J., & Marx, N. (2000). The role of representations and tools in the chemistry laboratory and their implications for chemistry learning. *Journal of the Learning Sciences, 9*(3), 105-144.

Landauer, T. K., Foltz, P. W., & Laham, D. (1998). An introduction to latent semantic analysis. *Discourse Processes, 25*(2-3), 259-284.

Lave, J. & Wenger, E. (1991). *Situated learning: Legitimate peripheral participation.* Cambridge: Cambridge University Press.

Magliano, J. P., & Millis, K. K. (2003). Assessing reading skill with a think-aloud procedure and latent semantic analysis. *Cognition and Instruction, 21*(3), 251-283.

Nathan, M. J., & Resnick, L. B. (1994). Less can be more: Unintelligent tutoring based on psychological theories and experimentation. In S. Vosniadou, E. DeCorte, & H. Mandl (Eds.), *Technology-based learning environments* (pp. 183-192). Berlin: Springer-Verlag.

National Research Council. (2000). How people learn: Brain, mind, experience, and school. (Expanded Edition). In J. D. Bransford, A. L. Brown, R. R. Cocking, & S. Donovan (Eds.), *Committee on Developments in the Science of Learning and Committee on Learning Research and Educational Practice.* Washington, DC: National Academy Press.

National Research Council. (2001). Knowing what students know: The science and design of educational assessment. In J. Pellegrino, N. Chudowsky, & R. Glaser (Eds.), *Committee on the Foundations of Assessment, Board on Testing and Assessment, Center for Education, Division on Behavioral and Social Sciences and Education,* National Research Council. Washington, DC: National Academy Press.

Neuman, D., Marchionini, G., & Morrell, K. (1995). Evaluating Perseus 1.0: Methods and final results. *Journal of Educational Multimedia and Hypermedia, 4*(4), 365-382.

Samarapungavan, A., & Wiers, R.W. (1997). Children's thoughts on the origin of species: A study of explanatory coherence. *Cognitive Science, 21*(2), 147-177.

Shapiro, A., & Niederhauser, D. (2003). Learning from hypertext: Research issues and findings. In D. H. Jonassen (Ed.), *Handbook of Research for Education Communications and Technology* (2nd ed.). Mahwah, NJ: Lawrence Erlbaum Associates.

Tergan, S. O. (1997). Conceptual and methodological shortcomings in hypertext/hypermedia design and research. *Journal of Educational Computing Research, 16*(3), 209-235.

Thompson, L., Gentner, D., & Loewenstein, J. (2000). Avoiding missed opportunities in managerial life: Analogical training more powerful than individual case training. *Organizational Behavior and Human Decision Processes, 82*(1), 60-75.

Vosniadou, S. (1996). Learning environments for representational growth and cognitive flexibility. In S. Vosniadou, E. DeCorte, R. Glaser, & H. Mandl (Eds.), *International Perspectives on the Design of Technology-Supported Learning Environments* (pp. 13-24). Mahwah, NJ: Lawrence Erlbaum Associates.

Vosniadou, S., & Brewer, W. F. (1992). Mental models of the earth: A study of conceptual change in childhood. *Cognitive Psychology, 24*, 535-585.

Vosniadou, S., & Brewer, W. F. (1994). Mental models of the day/night cycle. *Cognitive Science, 18*(1), 123-183.

Weber, G., & Specht, M. (1997). User modeling and adaptive navigation support in WWW-based tutoring systems. In A. Jameson, C. Paris, & C. Tasso (Eds.), *Proceedings of the 6th International Conference on User Modeling* (pp. 289-300). New York: SpringerWien.

Wilensky, U. (1998). *NetLogo Ants model.* Evanston, IL: Center for Connected Learning and Computer-Based Modeling, Northwestern University. Retrieved from http://ccl.northwestern.edu/netlogo/models/Ants

Wiser, M., & Carey, S. (1983). When heat and temperature were one. In D. Gentner, & A.L. Stevens (Eds.), *Mental models* (pp. 267-297). Hillsdale, NJ: Lawrence Erlbaum Associates.

Endnotes

[1] This chapter presents the KMF design features in a more schematic and functional manner than in earlier papers (Jacobson & Archodidou, 2000a, 2000b) in order to illustrate the relationship between earlier non-adaptive and new adaptive KMF systems.

[2] See Figure 9 and the related discussion for how embedding the intelligent learning agent module will enable an adaptive bi-directional relationship between the learner's actions in learning tasks and the content and scaffolding in the KMF system.

[3] See Allen and Otto (1996) for an excellent discussion and extension of Gibson's (1979) notion of affordances or "opportunities for action."

[4] There are a number of different approaches to hypermedia scaffolding that other research teams have been exploring, such as meta-cognitive scaffolding (Azevedo, Cromley, & Seibert, in press), and so the three types of scaffolding listed here are not intended to be exhaustive. Rather, these three types are ones that have been implemented in KMF hypermedia to

date, and other scaffolding approaches may be employed in KMF hypermedia.

5   In earlier papers, this module was referred to as "Story Maker" to the high school users of the system (Jacobson & Archodidou, 2000a, 2000b). For this chapter, "Problem Solver" is used as it is more descriptive of the learning purpose of the module.

6   Given space considerations, this discussion of the learning activities for KMF hypermedia in this section is necessarily brief. See Jacobson and Archodidou (2000a) for a more complete discussion.

7   Latent Semantic Analysis (LSA) is a technique that creates a multidimensional semantic space for the meaning of words that is based on their co-occurrences in a large text. The units of text within this semantic space may then be compared with other texts, thus allowing a student essay to be compared to one written by an expert. Recent research indicates that LSA essay scoring has a reliability that is comparable to human scored raters (Kintsch, 1998; Landauer, Foltz, & Laham, 1998; Magliano & Millis, 2003).

8   See the work of researchers such as Vosniadou and Brewer (1992; 1994) and Wiser and Carey (1983) for research and theory dealing with the nature of conceptual change and the cognitive reasons for the formation of synthetic or intermediary mental models. This theoretical and research work suggests that synthetic models are probably a common—and perhaps necessary—part of the cognitive trajectories for learning challenging knowledge.

Chapter XIV

Contextualized Learning:
Supporting Learning in Context

Marcus Specht, Fraunhofer FIT-ICON, Denmark

Abstract

This chapter presents an overview of research work for contextualized learning, integrating the background of adaptive hypermedia, ubiquitous computing, and current research on mobile learning systems that enable support for contextualized learning. Several examples for new learning paradigms are analyzed on their potential for mobile learning and contextualization. In the second part, examples for systems that integrate mobile learning solutions in existing learning systems for schools and working context are presented. The RAFT project realizes application for computer-based field trip support and shows an integration of m-learning tools in an established teaching method of school field trips. The SMILES prototype shows the integration of e-learning services and its stakeholders with mobile learning technology.

Introduction

New technology develops fast, and the reality of information and learning delivery everywhere is changing monthly. Nearly every week new devices and gadgets appear on the market and enable new ways of mobile access to information, mobile games, and online applications. Currently, the new research field of m-learning and a community working on that topic is establishing, and a variety of research groups work on new approaches supporting mobile learning. Those approaches mainly come from the background of collaborative learning, mobile information systems, adaptive hypermedia, and context-aware computing. From our point of view, adaptive educational hypermedia plays a central role in new models for m-learning and contextualized learning support. Applications from this area include a range of examples from personalized guiding systems for cities, art exhibition guides, and adaptive learning management systems.

In the field of adaptive hypermedia, several approaches have been doing work on the adaptation of interfaces and contextualized user interaction to specific devices and interaction modalities. Adaptations mostly have been based on the constraints of the devices used (mostly small screens) or network constraints like low bandwidth for mobile devices. From our point of view, there is more to contextualized computing than delivering content to small screens or converting it to new technical formats. By the variety of devices and the new possibilities of ubiquitous computing, information access gets embedded in the environment and gets contextualized to the current context of use (Oppermann & Specht, 2000).

For educational applications, this enables new possibilities for learning in context and understanding artifacts in the real world with the help of computers that can support the learning process in the current situation by adapting to a variety of context parameters. The underlying theoretical background of situated cognition and situated learning (Wenger & Lave, 1991) clearly states the target and motivation for contextualized learning support. Furthermore, it demonstrates the benefits for learners and authors that can be achieved by having information available in context. Mobile learning seems to be one of the fields where new paradigms for mobile cooperation and the integration of mobile and stationary activities are analyzed in most detail up to date. Most of the empirical studies currently looking at the usage of mobile devices in learning come from the classroom and learning situations related to field trips. The classroom in this sense seems to be a highly adequate field to introduce tools and services that allow a new way of learning and handling digital media for contextualized experiences.

This chapter will try to connect the theoretical foundations of situated learning and cognition and how those relate to new forms of computer supported contextualized learning.

In the first part, we will describe our view on adaptive hypermedia and the variations of adaptive methods. Based on this, we will give examples of how contextualized learning extends current approaches for personalization of learning processes and content delivery by taking into account additional parameters of the current context (environment, location, time, social context). On this background, some applications realized in Fraunhofer FIT and the European project RAFT 1and the prototype SMILES will be presented and their usage of context information to adapt to users will be demonstrated. It will be shown that especially the combination of different context parameters with classical learner modeling approaches allows for information delivery tailored to the individual learner and his/her current situation in a very effective way.

Situated Learning and Adaptive Methods

In the following section, we will give the motivation and background for situated learning and describe current scenarios for contextualized learning applications and use of mobile devices in classroom learning.

Situated Learning and Blended Learning

Situated learning as introduced by Wenger and Lave (1991) states the importance of knowledge acquisition in a cultural context and the integration in a community of practice. Learning in this sense must not only be planned structured by a curriculum, but also by the tasks and learning situations and the interaction with social environment of the learner. This is often contrasted with the classroom-based learning where most knowledge is out of context and presented de-contextualized. On the one hand, the process of contextualization and de-contextualization might be important for abstraction and generalization of knowledge on the other hand in the sense of cognitive apprenticeship (Collins, Brown, & Newman, 1989) it is reasonable to guide the learner towards appropriate levels and context of knowledge coming from an authentic learning situation.

From a constructivist point of view, not only knowledge is always contextualized but also the construction of knowledge, for example, learning is always situated within its application and the community of practice (Mandl, Gruber, & Renkl, 1995). Stein (1998) defines four central elements of situated learning where the content emphasizes higher order thinking rather than acquisition of facts; the context for embedding the learning process in the social, psychological, and material environment in which the learner is situated; the community of practice that enables reflection and knowledge construction; and the participation in a process of reflecting, interpreting and negotiating meaning. From the perspective of situated learning, several requirements for new learning tools can be stated, such as: use authentic problems, allow multiple perspectives, enable learning with peers and social interaction within communities, enable active construction and reflection about knowledge. A shift towards a new tradition of online learning is described by Herrington et al. (2002).

Moreover, the idea of situated learning also is closely related to the ideas of "blended learning" and "learning on demand", especially in educational systems for adults and at the workplace. An important point that is not taken into account by a lot of new approaches for delivering learning on demand is the aspect that the need (demand) for knowledge and learning arises in a working context with the motivation for solving specific problems or understanding problem situations. This notion of "learning on demand" in the workplace exemplifies the potential of contextualized learning in the workplace. Learners who identify a problem in a certain working situation are highly motivated for learning and acquiring knowledge for problem solving. They have a complex problem situation as a demand, which can be used for delivering learning content adapted to their situation.

The contextualization of learning on demand can not only be seen from the point of view of an actual problem or learning situation, but also in a longer lasting process of learning activities that are integrated. Different learning activities are combined in blended learning approaches where the preparation for a task updates on base knowledge, and then the application in an actual working situation and the documentation of problem solutions and the reflection about one's activities evaluates that process. An example of a blended learning process with situated learning components and different activities in such phases is shown in Figure 1.

From this perspective, e-learning brought the possibility of delivering learning content quickly and easily to immense numbers of learners and enabled them to cooperate with computer-based tools. Adaptive educational hypermedia now gives the possibilities to adapt those curricula and learning process to the individual and his/her strengths and weaknesses. M-learning and new technologies will bring a closer integration in the life long learning process and the disappearing computer will allow the learners to access information and content in every day life where planned learning but also accidental learning can take place.

Figure 1. Integrating a blended learning solution with situated learning components

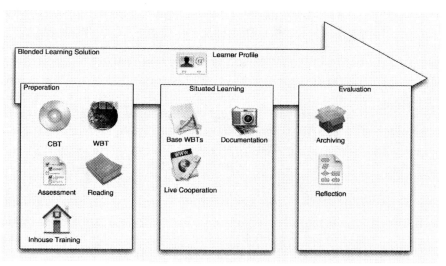

A Need for Mobile Learning Support: Scenarios

In recent years, several initiatives researched scenarios for learning and mobile information support at the workplace and in the classroom. According to Kling (2003), the classroom and research in the classroom might be one of the key drivers for a next generation of social software. The classroom gives a variety of scenarios and situations where ad hoc collaboration and the contextualization of information play an important role.

The PEP program (Tatar et al., 2002) looked especially at classroom-based learning and how mobile devices can give new possibilities for classroom based learning. In a study conducted in the PEP program, 84% of teachers strongly agreed that the quality of teaching was improved by handheld devices in the classroom. New possibilities were seen in the live interaction about data and the reflection about easily exchangeable and copied data sets. The teacher could collect feedback and get anonymous assessment for the current understanding of topics in the class. Recommendations for system designers coming out of PEP are focused application designs and a clear structure for blending of computer-based collaboration and information usage and teacher based instruction periods.

Curtis et al. (2002) identified the top five scenarios and applications on PDAs for sing the handheld in the school. These included sketching, focused simulations with curriculum integration, picture chat, concept mapping, word processing, online information research, and beaming class notes. The eSchoolbag System clusters the functionality supported in the classroom and in ad hoc learning scenarios in several functional modules like the scheduler system, a broadcasting system, voice and image transmission, text transmission, real time examination, notebook, contacts, reporting, and others (Chang & Sheu, 2002). In the context of the m-learn project user studies analyzed the different scenarios being relevant at the working context for learning (Curtis et al., 2002).

Based on a pattern approach DiGiano and colleagues (2002) are working on a systematic approach to structure and identify patterns for collaborative mobile work and learning. In that sense, most of the current research works can be clustered according to their contribution to certain patterns in collaborative learning scenarios.

Several empirical findings stress the opportunity of using mobile technologies for training and education of young adults and expect high acceptance rates for educational applications for that target group (Atewell & Savoll-Smith, 2003; Eldridge & Grinter, 2001). Usability studies about activities when interacting with mobile Web content and important findings can be seen in the Electronic GuideBook System (Hsi, 2002).

Most of the studies reported here show a high potential and acceptance for supporting new forms of mobile and contextualized learning approaches in the classroom. From our point of view, the integration of focused applications with specialized interfaces and their integration in more complex task contexts is crucial for the design of contextualized learning. The methods of adaptive hypermedia play an important role because the generation and selection of personalized views on shared data and cooperative tools is an essential aspect of the more complex cooperative applications used by individuals. In the following section, we will present some extensions for an adaptive methods classification which we perceive as important for building contextualized learning tools.

Adaptive Methods and Extensions

Adaptive educational hypermedia gives a variety of research work about questions on how to adapt curricula and learning content to individuals and groups of learners. Brusilovsky (1996) gives a comprehensive overview of adaptive methods and techniques in general. From our point of view, the application of adaptive methods to educational hypermedia applications can mainly be structured according to four main questions (Specht, 1998):

What parts or components of the learning process are adapted? This question focuses on the part of the application that is adapted by the adaptive method. Examples can be the pace of the instruction (Leutner, 1992; Tennyson & Christensen, 1988) that can be modified based on diagnostic modules embedded in the learning process or adaptation of content presentations, the sequencing of contents and others. Extensions with new forms of information delivery allow the distribution of learning materials to different learning contexts relevant to the individual user or groups of users.

What information does the system use for adaptation? In most adaptive educational hypermedia applications, a learner model is the basis for the adaptation of the previously given parameters of the learning process. Nevertheless, there are several examples where the adaptation takes place not only to the learner's knowledge, preferences, interests, and cognitive capabilities, but also to tasks and learner goals. In contextualized learning, the information used for adaptation is extended by the environmental parameters. The inference methods of the adaptive system can gain precision from the additional information of environmental sensors. A variety of sensors available from the area of ubiquitous computing can for example be seen in Schmidt (2002).

How does the system gather the information to adapt to? There are a variety of methods to collect information about learners to adapt to. Mainly implicit and explicit methods like those described in works from user modeling can be distinguished. An overview can be found in Jameson, Konstan, and Riedl (2002). Sensors play an important role in extending existing hypermedia approaches to contextualized learning. There are several works in the literature to create context sensor middleware allowing for higher-level contexts based on sensor data from different sources (Schmidt, 2002). As a simple example in learning, a tracking system in physical space can enrich the information from a user questionnaire for getting more valid assumptions about the user's preferences.

Why does the system adapt? This question mainly focuses on the pedagogical models behind the adaptation. Classical educational hypermedia system mainly adapted according for compensation of knowledge deficits, ergonomic reasons, or adaptations to learning styles for an easier introduction into a topic. Location-

Table 1. A classification schema for adaptive methods

Adaptive Educational Hypermedia		
What is adapted?	To which features?	Why?
Learning goal • Content • Teaching method • Content Teaching style • Media selection • Sequence • Time constraints • Help Presentation • Hiding • Dimming • Annotation	Learner • Preferences • Usage • Previous knowledge, professional background • Knowledge • Interests • Goals • Task • Complexity • ...	Didactical reasons • Preference model • Compensation of deficits • Reduction of deficits Ergonomic reasons • Efficiency • Effectivness • Acceptance
Extensions in Contextualized Learning		
Presentation • 3D Sound • Augmented Reality displays • Distribution to different contexts	Context Sensors • User Location • Time • Lighting, Noise • Other User's Locations	• Authenticity of Learning Situations • Situated Collaboration • Active Construction of Knowledge

based services are an example for the type of adaptation we want to discuss in the chapter situated learning and cognition. In those applications, the individual possibility for encoding and decoding information is one interesting aspect for better understanding artifacts "in context". Furthermore, the authentic collaboration on a topic is another example where co-learners can be selected according to the learning task of an individual.

Several empirical findings show that adaptation to learner models and parameters of the learning situation lead to more efficiency, effectiveness, and motivation for learning. Basically, our understanding of contextualization comes from an extension of the adaptive educational hypermedia approach. Adaptive educational hypermedia systems collect information from user assessment, feedback, the current task or user goal, and other implicit and explicit acquisition methods. Additionally, in a contextualized learning system, the current user context with a variety of environmental parameters can be taken into account. Those environmental sensors enable the application to collect much more information about the behavior of a user. Even more, by the integration of environmental sensors and user sensors, new applications can collect direct feedback from user sensors dependent on the variation of environmental parameters measured by environmental sensors like those shown in Figure 2. A good example for such an application can be a training system that monitors the users' moves while handling a complex machine and giving direct feedback for training purposes. Such systems are already used today in medical training applications like echo tutor (Grunst et al., 1995).

Figure 2. User sensors and environmental sensors for more valid inferences and validation of implicit user tracking methods

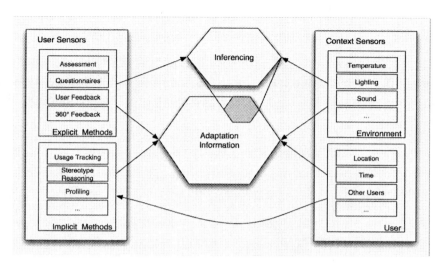

For the adaptation to individual users, the system in that sense can have shorter feedback cycles and adapt not only to the individual learner model and explicit user feedback, but also to implicit feedback loops from a variety of contextual parameters. First, simple examples for new adaptive methods in content delivery are location-based services and museum information systems like hippie (Oppermann & Specht, 2000). Besides new adaptive methods, this additionally can have an important impact on the interaction with the learning system. New forms of augmented reality training systems in this sense are not restricted to the request of information, but also enable the learner to explore the learning subject and its artifacts either in virtual reality training simulations (Rickel & Johnson, 1997) or in a tracked real training environment (Fox, 2001). From our point of view, this is not only a different way of accessing learning materials, but can be seen as support for constructivist learning approaches in combination with an adaptive intelligent system that tracks the users' learning activities and responds to them.

Another example for the extension of adaptive methods comes from the field of adaptive augmented reality systems. The LISTEN (Goßmann & Specht, 2001) system tracks the user with a resolution of 5 cm and 5 degrees, which allows to identify if a user looks onto a detail of an artwork in a gallery or just on the frame or beside the artwork. Additionally, the system can present information to the user embedded in the physical environment with 3D audio technology. So the user experiences the sound of presentations coming from the environment or from specific objects in the environment. Based on those location tracking sensors and the presentation possibilities, new adaptive methods can be realized. Some examples are:

- **Adaptation of presentation to position and object distance.** The user's position in space relative to an object in the physical space is mapped onto the direction and the volume of the sound for the presentation of the information.

- **Selection of presentation style based on position.** If a user moves in a room, s/he will get different presentation styles from the system. If the user moves into the center of a room, more general information about the room as a whole is presented and a sound collage for the single objects in the room is generated with directed sound sources coming from the objects. If a user moves close towards an objects and focuses on that object, the volume of that piece of the collage is turned up and more detailed information of the object will be selected.

- **Adaptation to movement and reception styles.** Several kinds of common behavior can be identified with people walking through the environment (e.g., clockwise in museums). By using the fine-grained tracking technology, the system can learn about preferred user movement and perception styles. The information about the time of listening to object descriptions can be combined with the movement. The selection and dynamic adaptation of tour recommendations can be adapted to the stereotypical type of movement and his/her preferred perception style.

- **Adaptation to time and lighting conditions and position of user** is a complex adaptive method taking into account environmental factors, the time, and the user position for the explanation of artworks in LISTEN. The sound presentation can be adapted to the changing lighting conditions during the day (based on sensor data) for explaining certain details that can only be visible during a certain time period or from a certain position in the room.

The contextualization of learning experiences and information is not only important on a level of presenting single contents, but is additionally important on the level of integrating and synchronizing learning activities in blended learning like those described in in the section Situated Learning and Blended Learning.

In this sense, we perceive m-learning as a natural evolution of e-learning: new technologies allow for a better support of learning than classical ways of e-learning, where the textbook often was just replaced by a computer screen. While in the current discussion about e-learning, blended learning approaches are often mentioned as a solution for the integration of e-learning in existing educational scenarios, we see m-learning and contextualized learning as a good chance to develop e-learning one step further. Often in blended learning scenarios intermixing computer-based and face-to-face learning in the learning process describe the way towards a certain educational goal. Nevertheless, this often neglects the problem of synchronization of learning steps. How should an intelligent learning environment get aware of the users' progress? How should remote peers support a user when he is in an actual learning/working context? Many of those questions can be answered when the computer disappears in the environment or gets mobile in a first step. Learners could use contextualized learning tools just like a mobile telephone where they not only could call an expert for advice but also could use a variety of other learning tools for helping in an actual situation. In this sense, we understand m-learning and the contextualization as a natural way of integrating learning technology in the learning process on demand. That this does not only work with planned instruction can be seen with examples of system that use more accidental learning like in museum environments (Oppermann & Specht, 1999).

We do not see a major question of m-learning in the conversion of learning materials into PDA formats. The idea of a mobile book in our understanding is mainly an issue of technology but not of pedagogy. Nevertheless, the use of PDAs in mobile learning scenarios can be very fruitful and get a new quality into learning. As soon as there is communication between learners new mobile devices even without a contextualization of materials and learning activities can be very helpful as seen in studies reported from the PEP program (Tatar et al., 2002).

Nevertheless, we just do the first steps towards more integrated learning tools that allow for a natural learning process with embedded intelligent learning, tutoring, and collaboration systems. From our point of view, paradigm changes can be triggered by positive experiences and integrated solutions that allow the users to use new pedagogical approaches and systems within existing infrastructures and content networks. Therefore, we want to present some examples in the following section that we think can be interesting starting points for the integration of contextualized learning into today's learning infrastructures.

Solutions and Recommendations

We want to introduce two examples of systems that are used in two different contexts at Fraunhofer FIT. The first system shows the integration of mobile learning into the school scenario of field trips that is done in the project RAFT.

The second application shows the integration of learning tools in a working scenario where different stakeholders structure and reuse information for different purposes.

Mobile Learning for Field Trips and Collaboration

In the context of the European-funded project RAFT (Remotely Accessible Field Trips), the consortium creates a learning tool for field trips in schools. The system should support a variety of learners with different tasks either in the classroom or in the field. The main objectives of the RAFT project are:

- To demonstrate the educational benefits and technical feasibility of remote field trips, with a view to promoting a market for products and to prompting best practice to support this learning activity.
- To establish extensions on current learning material standards and exchange formats for contextualization of learning material. This is combined with the embedding of learning and teaching activities in an authentic real world context.
- To establish new forms of contextualized learners' collaboration with real time video conferencing and audio communication in authentic contexts.

An additional emerging objective is to give students the opportunity to experience vocational domains for themselves before being committed to a particular course of studies for a future career.

RAFT envisions to facilitate field trips for schools and to enable international collaboration of schools. Instead of managing a trip for 30 students, small groups from the RAFT partner schools go out to the field, while the other students and classes from remote schools participate interactively from their classrooms via the Internet. The groups going to the field will be equipped with data gathering devices (photographic, video, audio, measuring), wireless communication, and a video conferencing system for direct interaction between the field and the classroom.

In the first year of the project, the different phases and functional requirements for supporting live collaboration and information access during field trips were worked out. Field trips with school kids were held in Scotland, Slovakia, Canada, and Germany in order to identify different activities in the field and in the classroom and to draw first evaluations of critical factors. Through these trials, different phases for preparing the field trip, experiencing the field trip in the classroom and in the field, and the evaluation after the field trip were identified.

In those phases a variety of stakeholders and participants contribute to the field trip and take an active role in it.

Field trips are an ideal example for an established pedagogical method that can be enhanced with computer-based tools for new ways of collaboration and individual active knowledge construction. The learners in the field can collect information and contextualize it with their own experiences and in the same time work on tasks with their peers and detect new perspectives and solutions to given problems. To foster the variety of perspectives and activities in the field trip process RAFT develops tools for the focused support of different activities in the field and in the classroom. A basic schema of some roles in the field, the used devices, and their activities can be seen in Table 2.

Table 2. Overview of field roles and their activities

User Role	Device features	Description of activity and related use cases
Scout	Gotive(WLAN), PDA-CAM(WLAN), Walkie-talkie	To look around the field trip site to identify appropriate locations to gather the data required by field trip tasks
Data Gatherer	PDA-CAM(WLAN), Gotive(WLAN), Sensors, Digital camera, Digital video camera	To gather data from the field in response to a field trip task. He/She collects raw data of type video, picture, audio and sensor data and tells sensor values to annotators for form filling.
Annotator	Tablet-PC(WLAN), PDA(WLAN) Gotive(WLAN)	To gather the raw data being generated by the Data Gatherer and to add initial meta data prior to the material being placed within a collection.
Communicator	Camcorder, Tablet-PC in Backpack with CTM2.0 Laptop PC(WLAN) Web camera	To work in partnership with a Reporter to follow the activity taking place in the field so that classroom participants can watch the activity
Reporter	PDA(WLAN)	To work in partnership with a communicator to comment on the activity taking place in the field and to interview remote experts in the field
Field Coordinator	Laptop PC(WLAN), Tablet PC (WLAN) Walkie-talkie	Overview Field Trip
Teacher	PDA(WLAN)	Overview Students. Accept/Reject task completion/deletion/creation etc
Observer	No device	Observing other field members

Figure 3. The roles in the RAFT Interactive Field trip System and the interaction flows between them

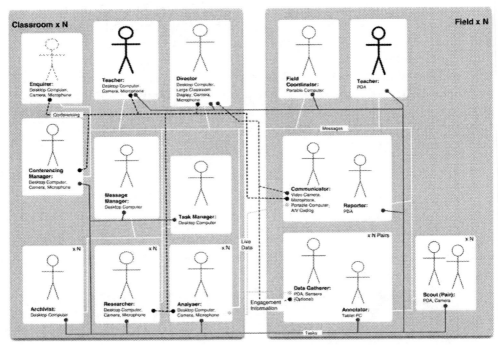

Based on these roles, the RAFT project develops focused applications that also integrate the collaboration with other team members. The interaction flow between classroom and field site on different channels can be seen in Figure 3.

The RAFT applications enable different participants in a synchronous collaborative learning situation to solve common tasks and learn with different activities about a topic. In the RAFT scenario, students should change their role either from field trip to field trip or sometimes even within one fieldtrip to learn about the different activities how to learn about a topic and also take different perspectives to the same topic. This ensures the integration of different pedagogical approaches in a "blended" learning situation, where different learning activities are distributed in a team of learners.

From the prototyping and usage of the RAFT applications by end users, we see the following main activities as new qualities of contextualized learning approaches:

- **Cooperative task work:** The distributed work on a task focuses the interaction and communication between the learners, and technology moves into the background when the curiosity about the given task and its exploration in physical and knowledge space become the main interest. The context in this sense is an enabling mean that allows the learners to immerse in the learning subject at hand.

- **Active construction of knowledge and learning materials:** Users are much more motivated when "self made" learning materials get integrated into the curriculum and they have the possibility to extend existing structures for learning.

- **Clear task structures are helpful in the school context:** In schoolwork in the field, it is highly recommendable to have structured tasks and different roles for taking of the tasks. This can be seen as giving a structured task context for individuals to contribute to a group work on a shared basis.

The RAFT applications are based on adaptive methods on different levels. The system supports the user with different tools depending on his/her current phase in the field trip process in general: preparation, field trip activity, or evaluation. During the field trip, the selection of information and collaboration tools is based on the position and current user task of a user. Based on the experiences made in the prototyping phase of the project, the implementation of different user roles and interfaces is not based on a software solution for intelligent rendering of interface components. Instead, it is developed with specialized applications for the different roles and role-specific devices for fulfilling the tasks.

Another focus was the development of contextualized learning materials in RAFT. Besides the classical learning object metadata (LOM, SCORM) attached to materials used in preparation, field trip activity and evaluation additional metadata was required for contextualized learning objects. For learners who collected materials, it is essential to be able to store information about the location where the materials where collected. For learners exploring a field trip site, it is crucial to get information that fits with the current time of the year and the position—or maybe even the weather conditions on that day. Therefore, we developed a specialized framework for collecting context sensor data in real time together with the learning materials and used the context metadata to make the collected information accessible to other participants of a field trip. As an example, a scout can collect small pictures or audio annotations and tag them with the location information (sensor metadata) from a GPS device. This tagging and the information instantly appear on the task lists of other team members and are highlighted in the user interface. Classical learning object metadata can be helpful for adaptive methods on sequencing and selecting the appropriate learning objects for a learner. Context metadata allowed for new approaches for structuring and accessing shared assets and learning objects and in RAFT. As one example, learners could browse a database of pictures in a biology field trip filtered by the location and the time of the year. Using this approach students could explore and learn about simple questions like "Which flowers grow here at what time of the year?" Additionally, metadata such as the precise time when the picture was taken and the weather conditions on that day can give interesting materials for exploring and learning about important factors of flower growth.

Situated Mobile Learning Support (SMILES)

The prototype SMILES was developed at Fraunhofer FIT for supporting the different actors in a working situation with contextualized tools that allow to record learning material and access learning materials by context parameters.

For applying contextualized learning principles to working life and learning on demand in working contexts, we have built the SMILES prototype. We have chosen a mobile maintenance scenario where a user has to work outside in the field to repair some complex machinery. Additionally, to the mobile worker there are a number of other stakeholders with different tasks, which are all integrated, in a complex training and documentation cycle.

How the different stakeholders work together with the SMILES system is shown in Figure 4.

Figure 4. The different activities and stakeholder in the SMILES scenario

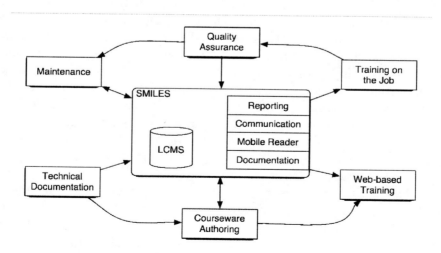

As seen in Figure 4, one main point of the SMILES prototype was the integration of heterogeneous resources that can be used for learning like technical documentation, courseware authoring, quality assurance, maintenance experts, and others. Those resources are integrated in the learning network based on SMILES and cooperate on the same database and information. Coming from the typical maintenance scenario, mobile workers in the field can request information about certain problems from the SMILES system and search in the case base for problems that are similar to their current situation. Additionally, they can document a new case if they cannot find useful information in the database, thus integrating a newly documented case in the learning environment. Technical documentation can insert content via classical authoring tools for Web-based courses and so insert live materials in the learning contexts. The courseware authoring or human resources department can use the basic documentation to integrate it with didactically structured e-learning lessons and WBT. The quality assurance takes care that the resources structured from the human resources department are technically correct and feeds back usage from maintenance people into the technical documentation. Training on the job and on demand feeds back live experiences to the quality assurance and into the system, thereby ensuring consistent learning materials. In addition, the content can of course be used for classical training and WBT.

As a base for implementation we used the ALE (Specht et al., 2002) system and extended its functionality with several frameworks. First, we needed to create specialized learning objects for collecting and structuring experiences in a different way than in learning units and learning elements and created content templates for cases, problem descriptions, and solutions similar to problem base learning approaches. Additionally, we created different applications for accessing the LCMS with a different task focus. On the one hand, we used a PDA for the maintenance person being in the field and searching for cases and problems. For extended usage and documentation in the field, we used a tablet PC that allowed the users to access the case base, search it, and contact experts for different problems via a live conferencing link. Examples for those applications can be seen in Figure 5 and Figure 6.

Based on a backend LCMS ALE and the authoring tool author42 (bureau42), the SMILES system allowed us to produce live content and synchronize it with a case base and also export the contents to different target formats that allow the usage as SCORM based courseware.

The SMILES prototype shows different examples for context adaptive methods applied in a collaborative learning and documentation application. Depending on the task and the stakeholder accessing the system, different functionalities are highlighted in the user interface. Nevertheless, all information goes into a shared repository and is instantly available to the other users. As a special need for

Figure 5. A case base searching and documentation interface

Figure 6. Tablet PC live conferencing tool

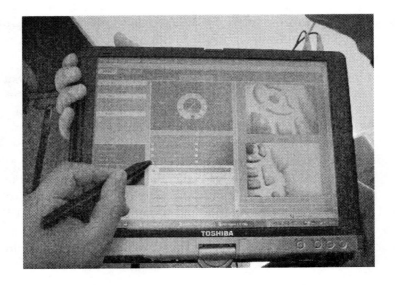

structuring the materials collected in the field, we developed an easy way of adding metadata to collected materials with the semantic concepts of the learning domain. Based on the described software backend, additional sensor data would allow for fast and implicit access to cases in the field and in cooperation with remote experts. As an essential functionality for supporting mobile workers we identified the possibility to get adaptive recommendation of experts based on their availability and their expertise focus. This information about experts connected to learning objects in the LCMS could be used for most stakeholders involved in the SMILES prototype. For learning on the job, simple extensions of the approach gave promising feedback in first user workshops. The easy access to manual and training information in the working context for example driven by barcodes was seen as a main advantage compared to classical de-contextualized e-learning in a computer room or printed manuals on the job.

Conclusion

Contextualized learning appears to be a chance to explore new paradigms for computer-based learning embedded in authentic learning situations. In the examples presented, we have looked at two target groups of current e-learning approaches and have shown how to integrate existing solutions like authoring tools and LCMS with new interfaces and tools for contextualized learning tools. In most current systems we just see that as a first step and the current drawbacks of devices often become obvious soon after starting to use a mobile tool. One of the central insights of our work is that the tools for mobile and contextualized learning must be highly focused and adaptable to the actual task and situation. On the one hand often the characteristics of the situation in which the mobile devices are used give critical constraints to the design of hardware and software. In some cases this can even lead to the conclusion that an adaptation of a tool supporting contextualized learning must be done by the hardware and software designers and not during runtime. This can lead to less flexible tools today and sometimes the adaptation can be "hardcoded" in the system. On the other hand only this procedure makes the tool usable in real mobile learning situations.

Mobile learning in that sense can also be the missing link between learning from a computer screen and the learner grasping the idea by interacting with a physical object. It offers the possibilities of interacting with virtual and physical objects and learning from the response of the objects. This is clearly linked to inquiry-based learning approaches like WISE (Slotta & Britte Cheng, 2001). Even more adaptive instructional methods can get important for learners to constrain the available information at the right time and especially on the current task at hand.

The construction of learning materials like demonstrated in the mobile collector of the RAFT project has positive effects on the learning and understanding. Moreover, this active construction of knowledge does not only have positive effects on the individual learning but also in cooperative scenarios like shown in the context of RAFT. For the application in the working context, it seems extremely important that learning can be delivered on demand in an actual working situation. In classical e-learning approaches, learners identify a problem, go back to the computer, and learn about possible solutions. This break in the learning context often has a bad impact on motivation and knowledge acquisition as such.

It should be mentioned that the chapter explicitly has taken a more pedagogically oriented viewpoint to the question of adaptive instruction and contextualization. Important technical issues like the definition and usage of metadata for storing and retrieving contextualized learning materials or the relations to semantic Web technologies have only been touched. Nevertheless, we perceive it as crucial to engineer educational systems with clear educational motivation and organizational constraints in mind.

References

Atewell, J., & Savoll-Smith, C. (2003). M-learning and social inclusion - Focusing on learner and learning. *MLEARN 2003*. London: Learning and Skills Development Agency.

Brusilovsky, P. (1996). Methods and techniques of adaptive hypermedia. *User Models and User Adapted Interaction, 6*(6), 87-129.

Chang, C. Y., & Sheu, J. P. (2002). Design and implementation of ad hoc classroom and eSchoolbag systems for ubiquitous learning. *Proceedings of the IEEE International Workshop on Wireless and Mobile Technologies in Education*. Växjö, Sweden. IEEE Computer Society.

Collins, A., Brown, J. S., & Newman, S. E. (1989). Cognitive apprenticeship: Teaching the craft of reading, writing, and mathematics. In L. B. Resnick (Ed.), *Knowing, learning and instruction* (pp. 453-494). Hillsdale, NJ: Lawrence Erlbaum Associates.

Curtis, M., et al. (2002). Handheld use in K-12: A descriptive account. *Proceedings of the IEEE International Workshop on Wireless and Mobile Technologies in Education*, Växjö, Sweden. IEEE Computer Society.

DiGiano, C., et al. (2002). Collaboration design patterns: Conceptual tools for planning for the wireless classroom. *Proceedings of the IEEE International Workshop on Wireless and Mobile Technologies in Education*, Växjö, Sweden. IEEE Computer Society.

Eldridge, M., & Grinter, R. (2001). Studying text messaging in teenagers. *Human factors in computing systems CHI*. Seattle, WA.

Fox, T. (2001). *Präsentation Neuer Interaktiver Lehrmedien in der Sonographie.* In *Dreiländertreffen DEGUM –SGUM – ÖGUM.* Nürnberg.

Goßmann, J., & Specht, M. (2001). Location models for augmented environments. *Proceedings of Ubicomp 2001, Workshop on Location Modelling for Ubiquitous Computing,* Atlanta, GA.

Grunst, G., et al. (1995). *Szenische Enablingsysteme - Trainingsumgebungen in der Echokardiographie.* In *Ulrich Glowalla/Erhard Engelmann/ Arnould de Kemp/Gerhard Rosbach/Eric Schoop (Hrsg.): Deutscher Multimedia Kongreß '95. Auffahrt zum Information Highway, S. 174 - 178.*

Herrington, J., et al. (2002). Towards a new tradition of online instruction: Using situated learning theory to design Web-based units. *Proceedings of the 17th Annual ASCILITE Conference.* Lismore: Southern Cross University Press.

Hsi, S. (2002). The electronic guidebook: A study of user experiences using mobile Web content in a museum setting. *Proceedings of the IEEE International Workshop on Wireless and Mobile Technologies in Education,.* Växjö, Sweden. IEEE Computer Society.

Jameson, A., Konstan, J, & Riedl, J. (2002). AI techniques for personalized recommendation. *Proceedings of AAAI 2002, The 18th National Conference on Artificial Intelligence,* Edmonton, Alberta, Canada.

Kling, A. (2003). *Social software.* Tech Central Station.

Leutner, D. (1992). *Adaptive Lehrsysteme; Instruktionspsychologische Grundlagen und experimentelle Analysen.* Fortschritte der psychologischen Forschung. Winheim: Beltz. 246.

Mandl, H., Gruber, H., & Renkl, A. (1995). *Situiertes lernen in multimedialen lernumgebungen.* In L.J. Issing & P. Klimsa (Ed.), *Information und lernen mit multimedia* (pp. 167-178). Weinheim: Psychologie Verlags Union.

Oppermann, R., & Specht, M. (1999). A nomadic information system for adaptive exhibition guidance. *Proceedings of ICHIM99, International Cultural Heritage Meeting,* Washington, DC.

Oppermann, R. & Specht, M. (2000). A context-sensitive nomadic exhibition guide. *HUC2K, Second Symposium on Handheld and Ubiquituous Computing.* Bristol, UK: Springer.

Rickel, J., & Johnson, L.W. (1997). Integrating paedagogical agents in a virtual environment for training. *To appear in the journal Presence.*

Schmidt, A. (2002). Ubiquitous computing Computing in context. In *Computing department*. Lancaster University, UK: Lancaster.

Slotta, J. D., & Cheng, B. (2001). *Integrating Palm technology into WISE inquiry curriculum: Two school district partnerships.*

Specht, M. (1998). Adaptive Methoden in computerbasierten Lehr/Lernsystemen. Psychology, ed. G.R. Series. Vol. 1. Trier: University of Trier. 150.

Specht, M., et al. (2002). Adaptive learning environment for teaching and learning in WINDS. *Proceedings of the 2nd International conference on Adaptive Hypermedia and Adaptive Web-based Systems.* Malaga.

Stein, D. (1998). *Situated learning in adult education.* Educational Resources Information Center.

Tatar, D., et al. (2002). *Handhelds go to school: Lessons learned.*

Tennyson, R. D., & Christensen, D. L. (1988). MAIS: An intelligent learning system. In D. H. Jonassen, (Ed.), *Instructional designs for microcomputer courseware.* Hillsdale, NJ: Erlbaum.

Wenger, E., & Lave, J. (1991). *Situated learning: Legitimate peripheral participation.* Cambridge; New York: Cambridge University Press.

Endnote

[1] The project RAFT (Remote Access to Field Trips) is funded by the European Commission under #IST-2001-34273. Information can be found on www.raft-project.net

Glossary

Active reading

A way of reading where the reader actively working with the text by adding notes and drawings, using the text for searching for relevant material, analysing the structure of the text, keeping track of the activities, and so on. The text is the mean for knowledge in active reading and not the goal.

Adaptable feedback

Allowing different learners to receive different feedback information. Different types of feedback are provided gradually or the amount of the provided feedback is gradually increasing, depending on learners' individual characteristics such as knowledge level, interaction behavior, and gender.

Adaptive educational hypermedia systems

Educational systems which reflect several features of the learner in the learner model and apply this model to personalise the content presentation and sequencing, navigation recommendations, feedback given, and problem solving support, based on specific pedagogical rules. The learner model usually represents characteristics of the learner which are relevant to learning, such as goals, knowledge of the domain, experience, preferences, and learning/cognitive style, and it is used in conjunction with a model of the target domain to enable the system adapt the interaction to suit the learning needs of the individual learner. Different levels of adaptation have been adopted, depending on who takes the initiative, the learner or the system: (i) adaptivity, that is, the system adapts its output using some data or knowledge about the learner in a system controlled way and (ii) adaptability, that is, the system supports end-user modifiability providing learners control over several functionalities.

Adaptive feedback

Allowing different learners to receive different feedback information. The adaptation of feedback is based on the structured form of the feedback supported, that is different types of feedback are provided gradually or the amount of the provided feedback is gradually increasing, and/or on learners' individual characteristics such as knowledge level, interaction behavior, and gender.

Adaptive hypermedia

Hypermedia systems that build a model of the goals, preferences, and knowledge of each individual user and use this model throughout the interaction with the user in order to adapt to the needs of that user.

Adaptive instruction

A primary principle of adaptive instruction is that no single instructional strategy is best for all learners. Consequently, in this form of instruction the pedagogical procedures are adapted or accommodated to the learners' individual differences in order to enable learners achieve learning goals more efficiently. Adaptive instruction aims to: (i) individually support learners to accomplish learning goals in a way that matches their knowledge and approach to learning and (ii) enable learners manipulate and accommodate instructional approaches to their own needs and preferences.

Adaptive methods

Methods describing what is adapted in the learning interaction, to which features of the user the learning system adapts and why (which didactical model) the system implements.

Adaptive navigation support

Adaptation at structure level, which helps users to find an appropriate path in a hypermedia system.

Adaptive platform

General-purpose adaptive systems that allow the production of courseware for more content, strategies, and interactive behaviours.

Adaptive presentation

Adaptation at content level, which is to adapt the page content to knowledge, goals and other characteristics of an individual user.

Cognitive ability level

Representing the high order thinking abilities and the underlying cognitive processes typical of the individuals classified by the Ross Test based on Bloom's Taxonomy. It is important to mention that the cognitive abilities refer to organized modes of operation in dealing with materials and problems and do not require specialized and technical information from the learner.

Cognitive tools

Mental and computational devices that support, guide, and extend the thinking processes of their users. Cognitive tools can be understood as artefacts that in some sense make the cognitive work easier—in a similar way that a hammer makes it easier to tighten two boards.

Collaborative mobile learning system

The support for a learning activity distributed in time, space, and between different people cooperating on a learning subject and tasks.

Concept drift

Changes in the target concept induced by changes in the distribution underlying the data.

Concept map

A graphical representation of knowledge to represent meaningful relationships between concepts in the form of propositions. A concept map is comprised of nodes, which represent concepts and links, annotated with labels, which represent relationships between concepts, organized in a structure (e.g., hierarchical or non-hierarchical) to reflect the central concept of the map.

Concept-relationship-concept

A proposition, which is the fundamental unit of the map. Also, a concept map may include cross-links, which are explicit relationships between or among concepts in different regions or domains within the concept map, and examples clarifying the meaning of a given concept.

Contextualized learning

Embedding learning activities in user specific situations and adapting the learning activity to the learner context.

Courseware

Computer software designed for educational or training purposes.

Design methodology

An indication of the main steps a well-shaped design process should go through in order to produce a complete and sound design for a specific type of object, along with guidelines and tools for completing each step.

Dominant meaning

The set of keywords that best fit an intended meaning of a target word.

Feedback

Guidance to (i) assist learners in identifying their false beliefs, becoming aware of their misconceptions and inadequacies, and reconstructing their knowledge; (ii) help learners to determine performance expectations, identify what they have already learned and what they are able to do, and judge their personal learning progress; and (iii) support learners towards the achievement of the underlying learning goals/outcomes.

Information filtering

The way to sort information through large volumes of dynamically generated contents and present to the user those which are likely to satisfy his or her information requirement.

Information value

Every piece of data has a value, and when data is perceived it is assigned an actual *information value* by the recipient. A common conception is that the information value is a constant attribute—a perceiver has once and for all assigned a value to a particular piece of information—but in fact, this is not really true. The information value for most information is changing all the time, in an information life cycle.

Instructional design

The process of (1) deciding what methods of instruction are best for bringing about desired changes in students knowledge and skills for specific course content and a specific student population; (ii) of developing an instructional plan that implements such a method in a viable and sustainable way. The result of instructional design is an architect's blueprint for what the instruction should be like.

Instructional strategy

A method for promoting and supporting a specific learner population to achieve desired learning outcomes. Instructional strategies are rooted into teaching and learning theories, build on the abilities of the instructor and take advantage of available learning tools.

Interface metaphors

Guiding the interaction of the users with the graphical user interface of a computer software and provide spatial, temporal, or functional orientation. To make use of an interface metaphor, users need to transfer their knowledge about Gestalt, structure, and/or interaction principles of the metaphor's domain into the application domain. A prominent metaphor is the "desktop" of current graphical user interfaces.

Knowledge worker

A knowledge worker is a person interacting principally with data, information, and knowledge as working objects, often working with these in both the physical world and the virtual world (digital information spaces), and sometimes in the borderland between them. Common work tasks are to create, search, refine, and mediate data, information, and knowledge.

Learner control

An alternative procedure for accommodating instruction to the learners' individual differences. Learners are allowed to take varying levels of initiative and direct their own learning experience. Learner control can be considered as the degree to which individuals control the path, pace, and/ or content, approach of instruction.

Learning sciences

A field that explores learning across diverse educational contexts, including both formal classrooms and informal settings like after-school programs, families, and communities. Learning sciences research is a multidisciplinary social science field that is grounded in the cognitive science. There are two main themes in learning sciences research: the influence of technological scaffolds on learners and learning environments, and the interplay of collaboration and social context on learning.

Learning styles

The different ways a person collects, processes, and organizes information.

Learning technologies

Computational media that are designed to support or scaffold learning along various cognitive, metacognitive, and collaborative dimensions in the context of an overall learning environment.

Learning trajectories

Representing the navigational behaviour of individuals belonging to a Cognitive Abilities Level class.

Machine learning

An artificial intelligence field concerned with the development of algorithms and computer programs which acquire knowledge about their operating environment and learn to automatically improve with experience.

Navigation metaphors

Interface metaphors that are used to support navigation in hypermedia systems.

Online test

Assessment tools in Web-based education. The most common use of online test is the situation where the students take a computer-based test and their answers are automatically recorded and graded. Results of online tests are frequently used to update the student model in a personalized learning environment.

Predictive modelling

A technique used to predict future behavior where some data is collected, a statistical model is formulated, predictions are made and the model is validated (or refined) as additional data becomes available.

Scrutable

The system is designed so that the user can scrutinize it when they wish, meaning that the user can determine what has been adapted, what processes caused the adaptation and what information they used for the adaptation processes.

Sharable content object reference model (SCORM)

A set of technological specifications for designing Web-based learning materials. It defines how single learning objects are combined on a technical level and sets conditions for the software needed for using the content.

Student modelling

The construction and maintenance of a student model to support personalized learning environments in adapting to specific aspect of student's behaviour.

User control

> The user can control the adaptation that the system performs in personalized systems.

Web-based learning

> Any learning, training or education that is facilitated by the use of Web technologies. Learning content is stored on a Web server and learners access the content by using widely used network technologies such as Web browsers and the TCP-IP network protocol.

About the Authors

George D. Magoulas is a reader in the School of Computer Science and Information Systems at Birkbeck College, University of London, UK. Dr. Magoulas waas educationed at the University of Patras, Greece, in electrical and computer engineering (BEng/MEng, PhD), and hold a post graduate certificate in teaching and learning in higher education from Brunel University, UK. He has secured reaserach grants from the UK Engineering and Physical Sciences Research Council, the Arts and Humanities Research Baord and the Joint Information Systems Committee, and has published more than 130 research articles in leading international journals and conferences. He co-edited the volume "Adaptable and Adaptive Hypermedia Systems" which was published by IRM Press, and guest edited two special issues in the area of personalized systems for the journal *Interacting with Computers* and the *Journal of Network and Computer Applications.* Dr. Magoulas is on the board of special reviwers of the archival journal *User Modeling and User-Adapted Interaction,* a memeber of the IEEE, the User Modeling, Inc., the Technical Camber of Greece, and the Hellenic Articial Intelligence Society. His Web page is at http://www.dcs.bbk.ac.uk/~gmagoulas.

Sherry Y. Chen is a senior lecturer in the Department of Information Systems and Computing at Brunel University. She obtained her PhD from the University of Sheffield in the UK (2000). She was the guest editor for the special issue on Individual Differences in Web-based Instruction of *The British Journal of Educational Technology.* Her major research interests focus on personalization and human-computer interaction. In recent years, she has attempted to develop personalised Web-based applications that can accommodate users' individual differences. She is the principle investigator of three research projects: [a] human factors in the design of adaptive hypermedia systems: funded by the Engineering and Physical Sciences Research Council (EPSRC); [b] cognitive approach to adaptive user interface for search engines (CAUSE): funded by Brunel Research Initiative & Enterprise Fund (BRIEF); and [c] cognitive personalised interfaces for Web-based library catalogues: funded by the Arts and Humanities Research Board (AHRB). For more information, visit her Web page at http://www.brunel.ac.uk/~csstsyc.

*   *   *

Jacopo Armani has a Masters in Computer Engineering from the Politecnico di Milano and is a PhD candidate in communication sciences at the Università della Svizzera italiana with a thesis on the authoring tools of educational adaptive hypermedia systems, Switzerland. He has been a consultant for several private companies and institutions as a Web engineer and graphic designer since 1998. His main research interests involve adaptive hypermedia systems, graphical interfaces, modelling languages for the Web, and visual communication.

Luca Botturi has a Masters in Communication Sciences and Communication Technologies and a PhD in communication sciences and instructional design. He is currently an instructional designer at the eLab—eLearning Laboratory (www.elearninglab.org)—where he works on several e-learning development projects. He is also a researcher for the NewMinE Lab—New Media in Education Laboratory (www.newmine.org)—and coordinator of the Masters program in Communication, Major in Education and Training for the ICeF—Istituto Comunicazione e Formazione (www.icef.com.unisi.ch)—at the Università della Svizzera italiana in Lugano, Switzerland. His research activity focuses on effective course design with new technologies and design team communication.

Ana M. Breda is an associate professor with the Department of Mathematics of the University of Aveiro, Portugal, and a senior researcher of the group "Algebra and Geometry" at the R&D Unit "Mathematics and Applications" of the same university. She earned her BSc in mathematics from the University of Coimbra (1982), her MSc in mathematics (1986) from the same university, and a PhD in mathematics from the University of Southampton, UK (June 1989). Breda's research interests focus on geometry, combinatorics, and didactics. She is currently engaged in the research project Geometrix whose main purpose is the conception and implementation of educational hypermedia systems to be used in schools/universities.

Anders Broberg (bopspe@cs.umu.se) has a PhD from the Department of Computing Science at Umeå University, Sweden. His research interests include computer supported learning, information visualisation, information retrieval, emergence, emergent interaction, and tools for knowledge work.

Gladys Castillo is an assistant in the Department of Mathematics of University of Aveiro, Portugal, and a researcher in the Laboratory of Artificial Intelligence and Computer Science (LIACC) of the University of Porto. She earned her master's degree in mathematics from the Faculty of Mathematics and Mechanics of St. Petersburg State University (1986). Currently she is working on her PhD, focusing on the application of machine learning and probabilistic reasoning in user modelling, incremental learning of Bayesian Networks Classifiers and adaptive methods to deal with changing environments.

A. Cristea earned her IS Dr. title and worked at the University of Electro-Communications, Tokyo, Japan. She is presently an assistant professor in the IS Group, Faculty of Mathematics & Computer Science, Eindhoven University of Technology, The Netherlands. Her research interests include AEH and adaptive hypermedia authoring, UM, Semantic Web, AI, neural networks, adaptive systems, concept mapping, ITS, and Web-based educational environments. She authored and co-authored more than 100 research papers and course booklets. She is a member of IEEE, was program committee member of Hypertext, AH, ICCE, ICAI, IKE (a.o.) and was reviewer or session chair for many conferences; she is executive peer reviewer of the *ET&S Journal*.

Marek Czarkowski is a PhD student at the School of Information Technologies, University of Sydney, Australia,. His research focus is exploring ways to provide user support for scrutinising and controlling an adaptive hypertext. He is a member of the Smart Internet Technology Research Group which conducts research in user-adapted systems, customisation, and delivery of multi-media objects.

José Palazzo M. de Oliveira is a full professor of computer science at Federal University of Rio Grande do Sul — UFRGS, Brazil. He has a doctorate degree in computer science from Institut National Politechnique — IMAG (1984), Grenoble, France; an MSc in computer science from PPGC-UFRGS (1976); and graduated in electronic engineering in 1968. His research interests include information systems, e-learning, database systems and applications, conceptual modelling and ontology, applications of database technology, and distributed systems. He has published about 160 papers and has been an advisor of 10 PhD and 45 MSc students.

Jing Ping Fan is a doctoral researcher in the School of Information Systems, Computing and Mathematics at Brunel University, UK. Her research interests focus on interface design of hypermedia learning systems. She has a background in information systems and education.

Claude Frasson is professor of computer science at the University of Montreal, Canada. Dr. Frasson specializes in the study of intelligent agents, intelligent tutoring systems, and e-commerce. He also is a director of GRITI (Inter-university Research Group in Intelligent Tutors), grouping seven universities in Quebec and about 75 researchers, and the director of the HERON at University of Montreal. He earned his PhD in computer science from the University of Nice, France (1974). He is co-founder of the international conference of Intelligent Tutoring System (ITS), as well as on the steering committee of a lot of conferences on ITS domain and e-commerce. In addition to the dozens of research papers in scientific conferences and journals, he was a co-editor of a lot of books on the intelligent tutoring system domain.

João Gama earned a PhD in computer science from theUniversity of Porto, Portugal (2000). He is currently auxiliary professor at the Faculty of Economics of University of Porto and a researcher at the Laboratory of Artificial Intelligence and Computer Science (LIACC) of the same university. His research is on machine learning, focusing in multiple learning models, incremental learning methods, and drift detection.

Boris Gauss is a researcher at the Center of Human-Machine-Systems, Berlin Technische Universität Berlin. He earned his degree in psychology in 2000, specialised in cognitive psychology and ergonomics. Since 1997, he has been doing research on human factors in different domains like aircraft evacuation, air traffic control, chemical engineering, and ship operation. He is a coordinator of the "European Network for E-Learning in Process and Chemical Engineering" (EuPaCE.net) and has gained experience in the development and evaluation of e-learning materials for engineering education. His research interest is in human-centred design and evaluation of human-machine systems.

Agoritsa Gogoulou is a PhD student in the area of didactics of informatics at the Department of Informatics and Telecommunications of the University of Athens. She earned her BA in computer science from the University of Crete and her MSc in advanced information systems from the University of Athens. Her research interests lie in the areas of didactics of Informatics, computer-based collaborative learning environments, Web-based adaptive and intelligent educational systems, learner modelling and assessment methods and tools. Her PhD research focuses on the development of Web-based adaptive tools supporting exploratory and collaborative learning in informatics.

Evangelia Gouli is a PhD student in the area of distance and open education with the Department of Informatics and Telecommunications of the University of Athens. She received her BA in mathematics from the University of Athens and her MSc in computer science from the University of Essex, UK. Her research interests lie in the areas of Web-based instruction, assessment methods and tools, Web-based adaptive and intelligent educational systems, learner modelling and computer-based collaborative learning environments. Her PhD research focuses on the development of a Web-based adaptive assessment environment providing personalised support and feedback.

Maria Grigoriadou is an associate professor of computer science at the University of Athens and director of the Educational and Language Technology Laboratory with the Department of Informatics and Telecommunications, University of Athens. Dr. Grigoriadou earned her BA in physics from the University of Athens and her MSc and PhD degrees in computer science from the University of Paris VII. Dr. Grigoriadou has worked in the fields of intelligent tutoring systems, adaptive educational hypermedia systems, student and open learner modelling, distance learning, educational software, and natural language processing. She has authored more than 100 technical papers.

Natasa Hoic-Bozic is an assistant professor with the Department of Information Science, Faculty of Philosophy, University of Rijeka, Croatia. She earned a PhD in computer science at the Faculty of Electrical Engineering and Computing, University of Zagreb, Croatia. She currently lectures on multimedia systems, seminar on hypermedia, and teaching methods in information science. Her main research interests include information and communication technology (especially hypermedia and Internet) in education. She participated in several research projects, including: innovations in computer assisted education, the quality of teaching in higher education, adaptive hypermedia courseware, and computing support to education. Currently she is a principal researcher of the project "Teaching Methods in Information Science Online".

Michael J. Jacobson is the senior associate director and an associate professor at the Korea University Center for Teaching and Learning in Seoul, Korea. Previously, Dr. Jacobson held faculty and research positions at the University of Illinois at Urbana-Champaign, Vanderbilt University, and The University of Georgia, and he has been involved with organizational and international consulting activities. His research has focused on the design of learning technologies to foster deep conceptual understanding, conceptual change, and knowledge transfer in challenging conceptual domains. Most recently, his work has explored cognitive and learning issues related to the design of learning technologies to help students understand new scientific perspectives emerging from the study of complex and dynamic systems. He will join the faculty at the Singapore National Institute of Education in the fall of 2005 where he will also serve as a senior researcher in the Learning Sciences Lab.

Marc Kaltenbach is a professor in the Williams School of Business and Economics at Bishop's University, Canada. He has a diploma from the Hautes Études Commerciales, Paris and earned his Masters of Arts at Yale, France. He earned his PhD from the University of Toronto in the Department of Electrical Engineering "Control Systems", Canada. He has co-authored papers in conferences and journals on the intelligent agent tutoring system, as well as he is in the steering committee of an ITS conference and others.

Judy Kay is an associate professor at the School of Information Technologies at the University of Sydney, Australia. She is a principal in the Smart Internet Technology Research Group, which conducts fundamental as well as applied research in user-adapted systems. The core of her work is to represent and manage personalisation that ensures the user can maintain control, being able to scrutinise and control the whole process of personalisation: the user can determine what is modelled about them, how this is managed and how it is used.

Robert D. Macredie is a professor of interactive systems and Head of the School of Information Systems, Computing and Mathematics, Brunel University, UK. Macredie's key interest lies in the way in which people and organisations use technology, and his research aims to determine how work can be more effectively undertaken by improving the way that we understand how people and technology interact in organisational settings. He has undertaken work on a range of issues associated with people, technology, and organisations and has more than 150 published research contributions in these areas.

Vedran Mornar is a professor of computer science with the Faculty of Electrical Engineering and Computing, University of Zagreb, Croatia, where he currently teaches several graduate and undergraduate computing courses. He graduated and received his PhD in computer science from the same university. As a Fulbright scholar, he studied at the University of Southern California, Los Angeles, for an academic year. His professional interest is in application of operational research in real world information systems, database design, development, and implementation. He is an editor of international journal "Computing and Information Technology".

Kyparisia A. Papanikolaou works as a research assistant with the Department of Informatics and Telecommunications, University of Athens. She is also affiliated with the Department of Technology Education and Digital Systems, University of Piraeus, Greece. She earned her BA and MSc in informatics from the University of Athens. Her PhD thesis focused on the design and development of adaptive educational hypermedia systems. Her primary research interests lie in the areas of adaptive educational hypermedia systems, instructional design for Web-based education, learner modelling, cognitive science, and artificial intelligence in education.

Mohammed A. Razek is an assistant professor of computer science at the Al-Azhar University, Cairo, Egypt. He earned his PhD in computer science from the University of Montreal, Canada. His MSc in computational mathematics was awarded from Al-zhar University, Egypt. He has co-authored papers in mainstream scientific conferences and journals on the applications of the intelligent agent on information retrieval and Web-based education. He was awarded the best student paper award at the WWW2003 conference, Hungary.

Maria Aparecida M. Souto is an associate professor of computer science at the Federal University of Rio Grande do Sul – UFRGS (Brazil). She has doctor degree in computer science (2003), and an MSc in computer science (1992) from PPGC-UFRGS, Porto Alegre, Brazil. She graduated in mathematics (1979) from UFRGS. Her research interests include learner modelling, learning environments on the Web, adaptive and hypermedia systems, knowledge acquisition.

Marcus Specht earned his diploma in psychology (1995) and a PhD from the University of Trier on adaptive learning technology (1998). Specht currently works as a post-doc researcher at the GMD German National Research Center for Information Technology. He has rich experience in intelligent tutoring systems and the integration of ITS and Web-based tutoring from former projects in the field of adaptive hypermedia and ITS (ELM-ART, InterBook, AST). His main research interests are adaptive learning and training systems, knowledge management, contextualized computing, and intelligent interfaces. He coordinated the technical development of a highly scalable e-learning platform for design and architecture in the WINDS project of the IST program of the fifth framework and was involved in the LISTEN project on audio augmented environments.

Craig Stewart is a research student in the School of Computer Science and Information Technology at the University of Nottingham, and a member of the Web Technologies Research Group. His research subjects include e-learning, adaptive hypermedia, and internationalization of educational materials and contexts. He has published 12 papers and been a reviewer for three international conferences.

Ing. Leon Urbas is spokesperson of the Center of Human-Machine-Systems, Technische Universität Berlin. After his PhD study on using simulators and the internet for operator training in chemical plants, he gained a three-year professional background on data driven process modelling, process optimization, engineering of process information systems, and management of automation projects at a leading global player in fine chemistry. Since October 2000, he has been the head of a research group that is sponsored by VolkswagenStiftung. His research interest is in user modelling and other suitable methods for the early stages of design, analysis, and evaluation of human-machine systems.

Regina Verdin is a psychologist and research assistant at Federal University of Rio Grande do Sul – UFRGS (Brazil). She has a master's degree in social psychology and personality at PUCRS – Pontifical Catholic University of Rio Grande do Sul (Brazil). She has been a researcher for the Brazilian National Research Council (CNPq) since 1994. Her research interests include distance education, computers and education, cognitive student modeling, adaptive hypermedia systems, and tutoring intelligent systems.

Index

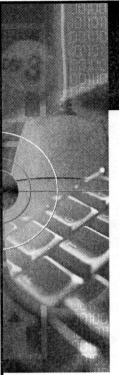